Theognis of Megara

THEOGNIS

EDITED BY THOMAS J. FIGUEIRA
AND GREGORY NAGY

OF MEGARA

POETRY AND THE **POLIS**

The Johns Hopkins University Press
Baltimore and London

This book has been brought to publication with the generous assistance of the Andrew W. Mellon Foundation.

The Johns Hopkins University Press,
701 West 40th Street,
Baltimore, Maryland 21211
The Johns Hopkins Press Ltd, London

The paper in this book is acid-free and meets the guidelines for permanence and durability of the Committee on Production Guidelines for Book Longevity of the Council on Library Resources.

Library of Congress Cataloging in Publication Data
Main entry under title:

Theognis of Megara.

  Bibliography: p.
  Includes indexes.
  1. Theognis—Criticism and interpretations—
Addresses, essays, lectures. 2. Elegiac poetry,
Greek—History and criticism—Addresses, essays,
lectures. 3. Megara (Greece)—Intellectual life—
Addresses, essays, lectures. 4. Literature and
society—Greece—Megara—Addresses, essays,
lectures. I. Figueira, Thomas J. II. Nagy, Gregory
PA4446.T48   1985   884'.01   84–21832
ISBN 0–8018–3250–0 (alk. paper)

Contents

Acknowledgments

This book, which grew out of a seminar sponsored by the National Endowment for the Humanities and held at Harvard University in the summer of 1981, owes much to a group of scholars who helped it along from the very start. The editors wish to thank in particular Carrie Cowherd and Veda Cobb-Stevens, who ought to be considered as associate editors, for their assistance was invaluable in the laborious process of putting drafts of the chapters together. Special thanks are due also to Louis Okin for his editorial support and to Lowell Edmunds for always standing ready with sound advice at every step along the way. Others too helped with timely insights, and the editors wish to single out James R. Baron and Caroline Dexter for their many generous contributions. Sarah George undertook the demanding task of organizing the Bibliography, and Holly Montague helped with the verification of references. Some of the editing was done on the text-editing system of Rutgers University, for the use of which the editors would like to thank that university. Thomas J. Figueira carried through many of his editorial tasks while a fellow at The Center for Hellenic Studies (Harvard University) in Washington, D.C. He would like to express his gratitude to that institution and to its director, Professor Bernard M. W. Knox. In addition, the editors wish to record their gratitude to Dorothy Wartenberg of the National Endowment for the Humanities and to Hugh Flick of Harvard's Committee on Degrees in Folklore and Mythology for their kind encouragement. Finally, special thanks go also to Richard P. Martin, who generously shared with the editors an advance copy of his article, "Hesiod, Odysseus, and the Instruction of Princes," *Transactions of the American Philological Association* 114 (1984):29–48. Martin's findings are an important complement to those presented in this book.

Theognis of Megara

Introduction

Veda Cobb-Stevens,
Thomas J. Figueira,
Gregory Nagy

§1. Theognis of Megara is an elusive figure. Known to us through a large collection of poems called the Theognidea, about fourteen hundred verses in all, and cited by Nietzsche as the spokesman for Hellenic nobility, he is nonetheless an opaque historical personage. Ancient tradition dated Theognis to the mid-sixth century B.C. On internal grounds, the Theognidea can be dated to the period 640–479 B.C. Thus, the poetry is situated between the heroic age, depicted by Homer, and the classical age, which attained its apex in the second half of the fifth century B.C. Specifically, verses 29–52 in the corpus (by which we mean the Theognidea) seem to portray a political situation in the **polis** 'city-state' of Megara that is analogous to the one prevailing before the rise to power of the Megarian tyrant Theagenes, dated roughly to the years 640–600 B.C., whereas verses 891–895 appear to bear witness to war in Euboea in the second quarter of the sixth century. Finally, verses 773–782 refer to the Persian invasion of the Megarid in 479 B.C. Clearly, the Theognidea are something more than the life's work—however long that life may have been—of a single poet.

§2. A line of interpretation may, in fact, be suggested by one of the reasons for the survival of the corpus itself, namely, the interest in it of fifth- and fourth-century Athenians. Plato quoted Theognis; Critias, leader of the Thirty Tyrants at Athens and an elegiac poet himself, imitated the Theognidean theme of the **sphrēgis** 'seal'. Antisthenes the Cynic philosopher and Xenophon wrote treatises on Theognis. It seems that these Athenians, troubled by the course taken by their own city's democracy, found themselves much in sympathy with an archaic proponent of aristocracy. Yet these same Athenians, as well as other ancient authorities, did not know enough about the life of Theognis to decide so basic a question as the identity of his homeland. The chief significance of the poetry of Theognis to the Athenians was that it was political poetry in its truest sense, an explication of how life is to be lived in a **polis**. The meaning of the corpus far transcended archaic Megara and its parochial factionalism.

§3. Our answer to the question of what this "something more" might be is that the figure of Theognis represents a cumulative synthesis of Megarian poetic tradition (see especially Nagy, Ch.2); an answer that, we believe, is supported by the chronological data, by ancient reactions to the Theognidea, and by the very ideological messages encapsulated in the poems themselves. Theognis is the self-representation of whoever chose to articulate the social values contained in these traditions.

§4. This understanding of the identity of Theognis is in harmony with two major insights that unite the chapters of this volume and mark a new departure in Theognidean studies. First, we shall see that the persona of the poet is traditionally based, ideologically conditioned, and generically expressed. Efforts to create a political biography of Theognis—such as correlating the warnings about the dissolution of the **polis** with a specific bout of partisan strife or the lamentations on an exile's plight with a historical banishment of the poet—yield an impoverished reading of the corpus. Such efforts fail to do justice to the persona of Theognis, one of whose salient qualities is his polyvalence: both lover/instructor and enemy/chastiser of a boy named Kyrnos; opponent of duplicity and at the same time cunning dissembler; an antagonist of hubristic monarchy while yet the sole harmonizer of the public temper.

§5. Second, the poet who speaks in the Theognidea is, as we shall see, a true and authoritative spokesman for the Megarian aristocracy. The corpus is not a mere collection of gnomic pronouncements, arbitrarily supplemented from disparate sources, but the crystallization of archaic and early classical poetic traditions emanating from Megara. The many topical continuities within the Theognidea that the following chapters attempt to explain provide substantiation for this insight. Moreover, while the corpus of the Theognidea contains passages elsewhere attributed to other poets, their presence reflects an assimilation of poetic traditions on the basis of their congruity with the indigenous social code. Such assimilation is marked by the very diction of Theognis, tapping a rich poetic heritage and laying claim to a pan-Hellenic significance.

§6. The poems of Theognis fall between two major points not only chronologically but also geographically: Nisaean, or "homeland," Megara, on the Isthmus of Corinth, was a relatively minor state situated between a potentially dominant Athens to the east and an always vexatious Corinth to the west. Thus, although the focus within the corpus itself is mainly on the dissensions arising within the **polis**, the poetry occasionally alludes to Megarian conflicts with other powers.

The scattered data on the political history of archaic Megara are collected at the end of this volume in the form of a chronological table, compiled by Thomas J. Figueira. Each of the twenty-seven dates in the table, whether absolute or relative, is argued at length in the notes accompanying it. This table is a collection of material useful for consultation where the chapters touch on historical matters.

§7. The geographical indeterminacy of the Theognidea, however, is heightened by the debate among the ancients (extended and perpetuated by modern scholars) over whether the poet derived from Nisaean Megara or from Megara Hyblaea, a Megarian colony in Sicily. Still, as a self-representation of Megarian aristocrats, Theognis need not be specifically assigned to either city, since a biographical reckoning of the content of the corpus will be shown to be unnecessary (see Figueira, Ch.5). The "Megara" of our title is neither Nisaean nor Sicilian Megara, but Theognidean Megara, a paradigmatic homeland for all archaic Greeks, and even for the dead as well as for the living (see Nagy, Ch.2).

§8. On the level of form also, Theognidean poetry appears to maintain an intermediate status. Elegy, the form of poetry represented by Theognis (and by such figures as Archilochus, Callinus, Solon, Tyrtaeus, and Xenophanes), seems to fall between two major types of archaic Greek poetic expression: the recited hexameters of epic and didactic poetry as represented by Homer and Hesiod on the one hand, and the sung stanzas of the lyric poets on the other. Even now it has not been decided with certainty whether the performance of elegy such as the Theognidea entailed recitation or singing. Nonetheless, the apparent intermediacy of elegy between the forms of epic and lyric can be seen most clearly if we consider its metrical form. The meter of elegy, known as the elegiac couplet, is composed of a dactylic hexameter

$$ -\,\overset{\smile\smile}{} \;-\,\overset{\smile\smile}{} \;-\,\overset{\smile\smile}{} \;-\,\overset{\smile\smile}{} \;-\,\smile\smile\;-\,\overset{\smile}{} $$

followed by what is conventionally called a pentameter

$$ -\,\overset{\smile\smile}{} \;-\,\overset{\smile\smile}{} \;-\,-\,\smile\smile\;-\,\smile\smile\;-. $$

The pentameter, as can be seen from this representation of its rhythmical scheme, is composed of two symmetrical halves, known as hemistichs. While hexameter is the meter of Homer and Hesiod, the hemistich of pentameter is cognate with a basic building block of such well-known lyric forms as the so-called dactylo-epitrites of Pindar.

§9. Even a broaching of the subject of the structure of the elegiac couplet inevitably calls up that most controversial question: whether elegy is formulaic. The Appendix, by Nathan A. Greenberg, is a delimited but rigorous attempt to address this question. Greenberg's finding is that the diction of the hexameters of Theognis in particular and elegy in general is related to, but different and independent from, the diction of the hexameters of Homer. It stands to reason, then, that the hexameter of elegy cannot be simply a borrowing from the earlier hexameter of Homeric and Hesiodic poetry, any more than the hemistich of the elegiac pentameter could be simply a borrowing from lyric. It is not, to be sure, generally thought that the pentameter in elegy is borrowed from lyric, but it is indeed commonly assumed that the hexameter in elegy is just a later version of the hexameter in epic. Here is where Greenberg's findings are decisive: if he is right, then not only the elegiac hexameter but also the overall form of elegy has to be considered a related but autonomous tradition.

§10. In addition to demonstrating the autonomy of Theognidean poetry, another of our major goals is to show how the program of this poetry is the restoration of a properly functioning aristocratic state. But what, then, of the Megarians who would inhabit this reconstituted polity? In order to appreciate these poems as a dynamic synthesis of poetic traditions and Megarian history, it is important at the very outset to know whether there are any sources for the history of archaic Megara that are external to the Theognidea as such. Louis A. Okin in our first chapter assesses this question. He focuses our attention on three chief sources in prose: Aristotle, Plutarch in the *Greek Questions*, and the fragments of the Megareis, Megarian local historians. The question is, do these sources depend on the internal evidence of the Theognidea, or are they independent? Okin concludes that there is little evidence for any dependence. (This lack of evidence, as we shall see, can be connected with Plato's refusal to derive Theognis from Nisaean, or "homeland," Megara.)

§11. If indeed we have ancient testimony about the history of Megara that is independent of the Theognidea, we may proceed to juxtapose a historical vision of Megara with the poet's own vision of his **polis**. In Chapter 2, Gregory Nagy examines the dialectic between the ideal function of Theognidean poetry and the discordant reality of the **polis** of its origin. Nagy argues that the poetry of Theognis is presented as a grand celebration of the ties that bind the community of the **polis** together. The ethical values upheld by the Theognidea integrate the **polis**. By contrast, ironically, the poet himself is in fact alienated from his community in general and from young Kyrnos, the focus of his affections, in particular. While being worthy of pan-Hellenic diffusion and acceptance, Theognidean poetry has "not yet" won approval from even its native **polis** (Theognis v. 24).

§12. Paradoxically, however, the very diction in which the poems are expressed indicates that they *have* attained pan-Hellenic diffusion. For they are composed not in the native Doric of Megara but in the Ionic of elegiac poetry, a diction associated with such diverse figures as Archilochus of Paros, Tyrtaeus of Sparta, and Solon of Athens.

§13. To Nagy, Theognidean poetry establishes a program for the regeneration of a debased elite, personified by Theognis' beloved, Kyrnos. The tension between Theognis and Kyrnos is analogous to the confrontation between Hesiod and Perses in the *Works and Days*, with its central contrast between **dikē** 'justice' and **hubris** 'outrage'. The key to sociopolitical reconstruction is the checking of **koros** 'satiation' or 'insatiability', the essence of which is represented as unseasonally exuberant vegetal growth. Such abnormal growth, in contrast with socially integrated husbandry, is in turn made parallel in both Hesiod and Theognis to unseasonal and acquisitively-motivated navigation. This sort of sailing is connected with the bold metaphor of the ship of state. The destruction of the **polis** by debased aristocrats can only be checked by Theognis, a **kubernētēs** 'pilot', a seasonal "sailor," and an opponent of **hubris**.

§14. The chapters that follow deal with the generic aspects of the Theognidea, with a focus on poetic forms, on the foundations of the poet's authority as a poet, and on the poet's appropriation and validation of the traditions inherited by him. At the same time, the field of vision continues to widen as comparisons accumulate with other poets and poetic traditions.

§15. The pan-Hellenic status of Theognis and his poetry is marked by a **sphrēgis** 'seal' that the poet says he places upon his words (vv. 19–20). In Chapter 3, Andrew L. Ford examines the meaning of this "seal." Ford observes that the status of poetry in the archaic period, where it circulated freely in oral performances, vitiates the thesis that the seal of Theognis is a guarantee of his status as sole author. Theognis himself insists that his utterances are not original to him but are based on what he learned as a boy (v. 28). Ford also argues that Theognis places a seal on his poetry to identify it and protect it as his property. This can be seen, Ford holds, if one recognizes the kinship of poetry and oracles in the archaic **polis**, both of which appeared in metrical form and were **epē** 'utterances', to be protected as divinely inspired, and which bestowed power on those who controlled them. The seal, akin to the public monuments of tyrants like the Peisistratid Hipparchus and the ascriptions of epigrammatists, signifies a politically oriented form of poetic authorization.

§ 16. Just as the poet appropriates and validates the content of his poetry by means of the special claim expressed by his "seal," so too, according to Lowell Edmunds in Chapter 4, does the genre of elegy plainly distinguish itself from the epic, hymnic, and didactic poetry of Homer, the Homeric Hymns, and Hesiod in two respects: (1) where it places the grounds of its authority and (2) how it construes its relation to its intended audience. The second point raises the central question of the actual function of Theognidean poetry. As Edmunds points out, the poet of elegy presents his poetry as a kind of "monument," an evocation of **mnēmosunē** 'memory', intended for the **polis**. It is the **polis** and its needs that preoccupy this poetry. The intended effect of elegiac poetry is to keep the citizens of the **polis** mindful of the normative principles that will enable them to carry out their day-to-day affairs. Hence, Theognis is preoccupied with the understanding of poetry and with creating a society of those who understand by means of a poetry which, while cryptic, may be didactic, hortatory, or laudatory. Yet, for those nominal citizens who remain outside the community of those who understand, the poet has only blame.

§ 17. In Chapter 5, our investigation shifts from a consideration of the generic aspects of the Theognidea and from the persona of its poet to a consideration of the social context of the corpus and its ideology. Here Thomas J. Figueira explores how the Theognidea functioned in the institutional setting of sixth-century Megara. The failure of both the *Constitution of the Megarians* and the Megareis (local Megarian historians) to make use of the Theognidea on the one hand, and of Theognis to give greater detail on Megarian political history on the other hand, is unparalleled and particularly perplexing. The former problem is to be explained by the virtual extinction of all archaic Megarian ideology in the course of sixth- and fifth-century civil strife. The second difficulty finds a solution in the hypothesis that the Theognidea were the repository of an aristocratic ideology current in both homeland Megara and its colonies. Still, the operation of Theognidean ideology cannot be appreciated without a recognition that a parallel populist ideology existed, the genre of which was comedy. Both oligarchic and populist ideology claim to be normative and emphasize their own particular conceptualization of a common inherited emphasis on redistribution of material goods as an integrating mechanism for the community. By a failure to adapt to the fifth-century world of monetary exchange and of hostile power blocs, archaic Megarian ideology lost its capacity to explain reality to later Megarians.

§18. With the sixth chapter, the perspective changes fundamentally: the last four chapters of our volume will focus directly on the nature of the elite of a **polis** and on how that elite can be restored to its proper estate. First, Veda Cobb-Stevens explores Theognis' portrayal of the Megarian aristocracy as it is. His less than ideal **polis** is one rife with conflicts, betrayals, duplicities, and uncertainties, all of which can be traced to a reversal that has, in Theognis' estimation, set his world in turmoil. This reversal, where the **kakoi** 'base' come to dominate the **agathoi** 'noble', can be correlated with the dissociation of economic, hereditary, and moral criteria for identification of the **agathoi**. Thus, increasingly complex semantic shifts are created in the basic social, economic, and normative terms of ordinary discourse. A poet who would quicken his community (those who are still truly **agathoi**) in circumstances such as these must forge his own ambiguities in the fragile hope that they will be properly understood by precisely those who *should* understand them.

§19. As can be seen in the contributions of Cobb-Stevens, Edmunds, Ford, and Nagy, the poetry of Theognis is based on the value system of the **agathoi** 'noble', those with whom Theognis associated as a boy, and his seal is the guarantor of the poetry's aristocratic provenience and its suitability for educating aristocratic youths who will perpetuate its precepts. Chapters 7 and 8, by Daniel B. Levine and John M. Lewis, respectively, show that the poems of Theognis, as a storehouse of advice to a **pais** 'boy' on erotic, sympotic, and civic matters, represent poetry as it informs politics through **paideiā** 'education'; for the foundation of Greek political life was the instruction of young boys in the values of their own **polis** through poetry.

§20. Levine explores an aspect of **paideiā** in Theognis, which, like **paiderastiā** 'love of boys', provides an instance of semantic fusion in the corpus: the institution of the symposium, it appears, is presented by the Theognidea as a stylized vision of the **polis**. That is to say, the primary social context of the poetry of Theognis, revealed by Levine to be the symposium, is represented in language that would be appropriate for representing the **polis** at large. Moreover, the symposium is a microcosm and a model of the larger community, for the characteristics of a well-ordered symposium are the same as those of a good polity. In this forum, where the education of future citizens takes place, two sets of messages are highlighted. First, the social dangers of excess are pointed up through demonstrations of the importance of moderation in sympotic behavior. Second, cunning and duplicity, central to the survival of an embattled aristocracy, receive their apprenticeship in the symposium.

§21. For Lewis, the erotic language of the Theognidea serves as an expression of civic behavior; in other words, the language of love in Theognis is at the same time the language of politics, and **paiderastiā** is a mechanism for the inculcation of adult citizen roles. An affective terminological system can be outlined wherein the bonds between lovers form the basis of the community of **agathoi**, and their condition yields a reading on the political and ethical health of the **polis**. As the **polis** envisaged by Theognis is degenerate, erotic relationships are filled with pain, in the face of which the lover, assimilated to the hero of epic, endures. In the properly functioning **polis**, although the onset of eros can be violent, it tames the youth, readying him for socialization. By rejecting **paiderastiā**, however, the youth leaves the boundaries of human society in a flight from his nature, as symbolized by the myth of Atalanta. So also betrayal of a lover is equated with defection from the elite to its opponents.

§22. The last chapter in the volume, Chapter 9, by Walter Donlan, attempts to assess the Theognidea in Greek sociocultural history. Donlan probes a fundamental dilemma that recapitulates our initial sense that the poetry of the Theognidea represents something "in between," something intrinsically elusive and difficult to define. We have seen in the Theognidea a form of artistic expression that affirms its links with the heroic past and its continuity as proceeding from that past. But, at the same time, we have been struck by the dramatic social changes that are revealed by contrasting Homer on the one hand and Theognis on the other. The poetry of the Theognidea is struggling to maintain values that its own **polis** cannot seem to realize. The very basis of these values, the bonds of friendship, seems in doubt, and betrayal is an ever-present fear. In Donlan's words, "The poetic tradition knows what friendship ought to be like, while at the same time it knows what friendship has become." Even in its uncertainty and ambiguity, the poetry reflects the **polis**.

1
Theognis and the Sources for the History of Archaic Megara

Louis A. Okin

§1. Our knowledge of the historical events that occurred during the late seventh and sixth centuries,[1] the events simultaneous with the evolution of the Theognidean corpus, is based on relatively few sources, mostly literary in nature. My purpose is to survey our extant sources, investigate what materials, including the Theognidean poems themselves, may ultimately lie behind these late passages, and comment where appropriate on the trustworthiness of our information on archaic Megara.

§2. The earliest source available to us on archaic Megara is Thucydides (1.126.3–11). In order to explain a curse on the influential Alcmaeonid family, he relates the story of Kylon's conspiracy. Kylon of Athens was an Olympic victor and the son-in-law of Theagenes, tyrant of Megara. Hoping to establish himself as tyrant in Athens, Kylon received a favorable, but ambiguous, oracle from Delphi, troops from his father-in-law, and support from his friends. He seized the acropolis at Athens, but the population did not support his cause, and Kylon and his followers soon found themselves besieged. Kylon and his brother managed to escape; the rest surrendered to the archons, led by the Alcmaeonid Megakles. Although Kylon's followers had made themselves suppliants to Athena and had been promised that no harm would come to them if they surrendered, they were murdered. For this sacrilege the murderers and their descendants, including the Alcmaeonid family, were considered accursed.

§3. The date of Kylon's Olympic victory is known, and for this reason Thucydides' narrative is an important source for the chronology of Theagenes' tyranny.[1] Thucydides' version includes many details not

---

§1n1. All dates are B.C. unless otherwise indicated.
§3n1. Kylon was an Olympic victor in 640. His conspiracy falls between that date and the legislation of Drakon in 621. For a full discussion, see *HCT* 1.428–430.

found in the parallel account of Herodotus (5.71), including Kylon's marital connection to Theagenes. All the new Thucydidean details, according to Mabel Lang, are either legendary or added to exculpate the Alcmaeonid family.[2] Were Lang correct, our conception of Theagenes and his date would have to undergo drastic revision. Her argument, however, that Kylon's marriage was invented in accord with the belief that one achieved power through one's wife is not convincing. Surely the daughter of a more important figure than the obscure Theagenes, perhaps Kypselos, powerful tyrant of Corinth, would have been preferred.[3] Furthermore, Thucydides seems to have had more and sounder information on the Kylonian conspiracy than Herodotus. Herodotus' statement that the "presidents of the **Naukrāroi**" then "ruled" in Athens (5.71) and were responsible for suppressing the uprising does not inspire confidence.[4]

§4. Thucydides is the only historian of the fifth century to comment directly or indirectly on Megara in the age of Theognis. The remainder of our information about this period comes from later sources. Except for one passage, this information is derived from the historical tradition about Megara proper. The exception is a passage mainly concerned with historical events on the island of Samos. It is found in the writings of Plutarch (*Greek Questions* 57 = *Moralia* 303E–304C). In this passage, Plutarch is answering the question, "For what reason is the banqueting hall on Samos called **Pedētēs** 'Fettered'?" The reason, Plutarch explains, is the result of a war between Samos and Megara. The Megarians had attacked the Samian colony of Perinthos in the Propontis. The **Geōmoroi**, the ruling group of landowners on Samos, sent a relief expedition commanded by nine generals. The Samian force was victorious, capturing six hundred Megarians as well as the fetters with which they intended to bind their prisoners. At this point, the generals decided to overthrow the regime of the **Geōmoroi**. When the Samian government sent a letter ordering the prisoners to be brought to Samos bound in their own fetters, the conspirators, by showing the letter to the captives, won them over to the plot. The Megarians were placed in rigged fetters, which looked secure but in reality were unlocked and easy to remove, and were given swords. When they were paraded before the **Geōmoroi** assembled at the Samian Council House, they suddenly threw off their

---

§3n2. Lang 1962.243–249.
§3n3. Sealey 1976.105n5 (at 106).
§3n4. Macan 1895.214, commenting on Herodotus 5.71.5; Sealey p.105n5 (at 106).

fetters and slew the astonished oligarchs. The Samians, who had apparently hated the rule of the **Geōmoroi**, granted citizenship to those Megarians who wished it and constructed a great building in which they dedicated the discarded fetters. For this reason, they named the building "Fettered."

§5. Plutarch, writing in the late first and early second century A.D., depends on earlier authors for his material. His source in this instance is uncertain. Two reasonable possibilities exist. The first is Aristotle.[1] In his *Greek Questions*, Plutarch makes considerable use of the vast collection of constitutions of various states compiled by Aristotle and his school, the Lyceum.[2] There is no doubt that Plutarch was familiar with the *Constitution of the Samians*; he cites it by title twice in his *Life of Pericles* (26 = fr. 577 Rose; 28 = fr. 578 Rose).

§6. The second possible source for Plutarch is the historian Duris of Samos. Duris studied at the Lyceum under Aristotle's successor, Theophrastus (*FGH* 76 T 1-2). Later he wrote, among other historical works, a local history of his homeland, the *Samian Chronicle*. Although Plutarch never cites this work by name, Felix Jacoby in his collection of citations (fragments) of lost Greek historians plausibly assigns four Plutarchean citations to this book (*FGH* 2A, 144-146, 152-155). One fragment (*FGH* 76 F 67 = Plutarch *Pericles* 28) is from Duris' account of the Samian-Athenian War of 441-440 and can scarcely be from any other work of this author. It also seems probable that Plutarch used the *Samian Chronicle* for other parts of his *Greek Questions*. Questions 54-57 concern Samian practices and may all come from Duris.[1] Duris seems a particularly good possibility as a source for *Question* 56 (= *Moralia* 303D-303E). This passage explains that certain ancient bones visible on Samos were the bones of elephants from the army of the god Dionysos. The elephants had been slain in a battle against the Amazons. This tale cannot come from the *Constitution of the Samians* for two reasons. First, the usual explanation for the prehistoric bones on Samos was that they were

---

§5n1. Aristotle himself is not likely to have written all the constitutional treatises on which Plutarch draws, though he probably did organize and supervise their production.

§5n2. This was convincingly demonstrated by Giessen 1901.446–471.

§6n1. Halliday 1928.203. Jacoby in *FGH* 3b *Text* 466 agrees with Halliday that *Questions* 54–57 come from a single author but prefers Menodotus, a Samian chronicler of around 200, to Duris. Since Plutarch never cites Menodotus in any of his numerous other works, but quotes Duris by name twelve times, I find Jacoby's arguments unconvincing.

the remains of fabulous beasts called Neides, not of elephants.[2] In an epitome of Aristotle's *Constitutions* by one Heracleides,[3] the Neides on Samos are mentioned (*FHG* 2.215 = fr. 611 Rose = fr. 30 Dilts). Since Heracleides, if one judges by his excerpts from the extant *Constitution of the Athenians*, followed his original text very closely,[4] it follows that the *Constitution of the Samians* accepted the common explanation, not the one given in *Question 56*, for the origin of the fossil bones.[5] Secondly, the story in *Question 56* is based on conceptions of the god Dionysos that are likely to have been developed after the career of Alexander the Great. According to these conceptions, Dionysos first conquered India; then on his return trip to Greece, he defeated the Amazons.[6] The source of the Plutarch passage would not in this case have been Aristotle.[7] The *Constitutions* were probably written too early to have been influenced by these ideas.[8] Duris, however, wrote some decades later, when stories connecting Dionysos with India and the Amazons were better known.[9] Moreover, he was interested in the fabulous adventures of Dionysos; in one fragment he tells of Dionysos' Indian campaign (*FGH* 76 F 27).[10] Duris is therefore the most logical candidate for the author Plutarch to borrow from in *Question 56*.

§7. A choice between Aristotle and Duris as the source for *Question 57* is difficult to make. The passage is an explanation for a peculiar word usage, but this fact is no help. Both authors give such explications. The *Constitution of the Samians* contains one for the phrase "the dark-

---

§6n2. Halliday p.208.

§6n3. The identity of this Heracleides is still disputed. Bloch 1940.31–33 gives a summary of the various identifications proposed by scholars. On pp. 33–39, Bloch argues that the epitomator was the second-century scholar Heracleides Lembus, a position supported by Dilts 1971.8. Bloch's arguments have not been universally accepted; Weil 1960.101n37 takes a neutral position on the identity of the epitomator.

§6n4. Sandys 1912.xxxvi. Cf. Weil p.101n37.

§6n5. Halliday 1928.203.

§6n6. Halliday pp.207–211.

§6n7. Nock 1928.21–29. Nock pp.26–27 shows that the idea of a Dionysian conquest of India began no earlier than the last decade of the fourth century.

§6n8. Halliday 1928.203; *FGH* 3b *Text* 467.

§6n9. The latest datable event in the fragments of Duris is the death of Lysimachus in 281 (*FGH* 76 F 55). This fragment is from his *Makedonika*. We do not know the relative order in which Duris wrote his works, but he is unlikely to have written anything before the last decade of the fourth century.

§6n10. *FGH* 76 F 27, from Duris' *Peri Nomōn*. The proper translation of the title of this book is uncertain; see *FGH* 2C 122 and Okin 1974.127–128 (cf. also Okin 1980).

ness around the oak" (fr. 576 Rose). In his *Samian Chronicles*, Duris gives an explanation for how the expression "dressing like a Dorian" had come to mean "not wearing a **khitōn**" (*FGH* 76 F 24), while in his *Peri Nomōn*, he explains how the word "to put on the breast-plate" (**thōrēssesthai**) had received the meaning "to make oneself drunk" (*FGH* 76 F 27). In my judgment, the evidence favors Duris as Plutarch's source. *Question* 57 occurs in a series of questions on Samian matters. It is reasonable that Plutarch placed them in a sequence because they were all drawn from a single author.[1] Aristotle is apparently not the source of *Question* 56 (see §6). No objection can be raised against Duris as the source for the whole series. Moreover, *Question* 57 has a strong dramatic quality, and so do the fragments of Duris. The Plutarch passage, with its parade through the streets, its unlocked fetters, and its sudden massacre of the **Geōmoroi** is reminiscent of Duris' dramatic description of the fate of the sole survivor of an Athenian attack on Aegina (*FGH* 76 F 24) and has the kind of color and suspense that led Plutarch in a pedantic moment to accuse Duris of "composing a tragic drama" in his narration (*FGH* 76 F 67 = *Pericles* 28).[2] Finally, there are structural similarities between *Question* 57 and Duris' account of Dionysos' Indian campaign (*FGH* 76 F 27), as a comparison of the two passages makes clear. Both passages show an interest in deceptions. They also display the same sequence of events: a description of a trick, the successful and violent outcome of the trick, and an explanation of an unusual word usage.

§8. Whatever the source, there is no reason to question the basic truthfulness of Plutarch's account. Samian local histories were written as early as the fifth century (Euagon *FGH* 535). Both Aristotle and Duris would have utilized Euagon, and Duris at least would have known local traditions about the island's oddly named building. While the principal events, the war over Perinthos and the destruction of the **Geōmoroi**, are historical, certain episodes are unclear. Why did the **Geōmoroi** appoint as generals nine men, every one of whom proved perfidious?[1] Perhaps Plutarch has compressed the episode,

---

§7n1. Halliday 1928.203 and *FGH* 3b *Text* 466.

§7n2. This accusation did not prevent Plutarch, who *au fond* enjoyed colorful accounts, from frequently using Duris. He cites him twelve times by name, and undoubtedly used him unacknowledged in several other places. For example, compare Plutarch *Pericles* 26.3–4, only a couple of paragraphs before his complaint, and *FGH* 76 F 66.

§8n1. Jeffery 1976.214 suggests that the **Geōmoroi** knew that the generals were suspect and hoped that the disaffected would settle permanently at Perinthos.

which in its present form also fails to indicate the cause of the popular hatred toward the Geōmoroi.[2]

§9. The main body of material for seventh- and sixth-century Megara is preserved in three authors: Aristotle, Plutarch, and Pausanias. Pausanias mainly contributes incidental information; the key texts are from the other two. On closer inspection, however, the two resolve into one, for Aristotle (or at least the Lyceum) is the probable source for Plutarch's version of Megarian history. It has long been argued that Plutarch's narratives about Megara in the *Greek Questions* (18 = *Moralia* 295D; 59 = *Moralia* 304E–F) derive from Aristotle's *Constitution of the Megarians*.[1] *Questions* 18 and 59 are clearly interrelated. Both mention the **Palintokiā** 'Return-Interest', and *Question* 59 adds further examples of disorder under the Megarian "Unbridled Democracy" to those already given in *Question* 18. These passages must therefore come from a single source. Since a *Constitution of the Megarians* existed (fr. 509 Rǫse = Strabo 7.7 C322) and must have contained a historical section, as does the extant *Constitution of the Athenians*, and since the *Greek Questions* draws from other *Constitutions*, the *Constitution of the Megarians* is Plutarch's logical source.[2] The only other reasonable candidate, the local Megarian historical tradition, is unlikely. In *Question* 16 (= *Moralia* 295A–B), Plutarch totally ignores Megara's version of its own early history, and this suggests that he did not consult Megarian local historians while compiling the other *Greek Questions*.[3] To these arguments can be added verbal similarities between Aristotle and Plutarch in their portrayal of the Megarian democracy. In Aristotle's *Politics* (1302b), the democracy was overthrown because of the disorder (**ataxiā**) and anarchy that prevailed there. In Plutarch (*Question* 59), the democracy is "unbridled" (**akolastos**) and unable to punish malfeasants because of "the disorder of their government" (**ataxiān tēs politeiās**).[4] All in all, the case for the *Constitution of the Megarians* as the source of Plutarch's Megarian sections is a plausible one.

---

§8n2. On the historical problems of this episode and all other historical questions concerning Megara in the time of the Theognidean corpus, see Legon 1981 and Figueira Chronological Table.

§9n1. Giessen 1901.446–471; Halliday 1928.92.

§9n2. Aristotle's name is actually mentioned in *Greek Questions* 14 = *Moralia* 294C and *Greek Questions* 19 = *Moralia* 292B.

§9n3. Halliday 1928.92.

§9n4. Legon 1981.104–105.

§10. Aristotle and the other members of his School were not, of course, contemporaries of the Megarian events described. They had to depend on a study of sources for their own conclusions. Because the problem of the Lyceum's sources is a difficult one, our conclusions must be considered tentative.

§11. Of particular interest is the question whether Aristotle and his school used the Theognidean corpus. Their usual method was to pay close attention to poetry as a historical source. In the *Constitution of the Athenians*, the poems of Solon are quoted frequently.[1] In other writings, the poetry of Tyrtaeus is used.[2] It is therefore surprising that the Theognidean corpus appears to have been used sparingly, if at all. The major incidents reported by Aristotle and Plutarch—the "Return-Interest," the attack on the envoys to Delphi, the temple robbery, and the victory of the returning exiles—cannot be paralleled in Theognis.[3]

§12. Although it does not seem likely, some think that Aristotle's statement that the nobles were exiled and their property confiscated (*Politics* 1304b) was based on the following passages:

χρήματα δ᾽ ἁρπάζουσι βίῃ
Theognis 677

They seize possessions by force

αἶσα γὰρ οὕτως ἐστί, τίσις δ᾽ οὐ φαίνεται ἡμῖν
ἀνδρῶν οἳ τἀμὰ χρήματ᾽ ἔχουσι βίῃ
συλήσαντες·
Theognis 345–347

For this is the way it was destined, and yet repayment does not appear
to me
from those men who robbed me of my possessions [khrēmata]
by force . . .

. . . καί μοι κραδίην ἐπάταξε μέλαιναν,
ὅττί μοι εὐανθεῖς ἄλλοι ἔχουσιν ἀγρούς,
οὐδέ μοι ἡμίονοι κυφὸν ἕλκουσιν ἄροτρον
τῆς ἄλλης μνηστῆς εἵνεκα ναυτιλίης.
Theognis 1199–1202

---

§11n1. Aristotle *Constitution of the Athenians* 5, 12.
§11n2. Aristotle *Politics* 1306b–1307a; Aristotle *Nicomachean Ethics* 1116a.
§11n3. For discussions of these incidents, see Figueira Chronological Table.

... and it roused my somber heart,
for other men now possess my flowery fields,
and my mules no longer pull my curved plough—
all because of that other sea voyage that is on one's mind.[1]

But Aristotle could not derive his information on the return of the exiles and their overthrow of the democracy from these verses of the Theognidean corpus (*Politics* 1302b, 1304b).[2]

§ 13. Plutarch's *Greek Questions* 18 (= *Moralia* 295D) mentions demagogues who are corrupting the people. It is a perfect situation in which to give their background, if there was anything noteworthy about it. But Plutarch does not refer to the striking portrayal of the new rulers of Megara presented in the following verses:

Κύρνε, πόλις μὲν ἔθ' ἥδε πόλις, λαοὶ δὲ δὴ ἄλλοι,
   οἳ πρόσθ' οὔτε δίκας ἤδεσαν οὔτε νόμους,
ἀλλ' ἀμφὶ πλευραῖσι δορὰς αἰγῶν κατέτριβον,
   ἔξω δ' ὥστ' ἔλαφοι τῆσδ' ἐνέμοντο πόλεος.
καὶ νῦν εἰσ' ἀγαθοὶ Πολυπαΐδη· οἱ δὲ πρὶν ἐσθλοὶ
   νῦν δειλοί.
     Theognis 53–58

Kyrnos, this city is still a city, but truly the people are different.
Those who, in the past, knew neither justice nor laws
but wore out the goatskins which covered their sides
and grazed like deer on the outskirts of this city,
now these men are the nobles [agathoi], son of Polypaos, and those who
    before were of the nobility [esthloi]
now they are inferiors [deiloi].

§ 14. Only one passage of Plutarch offers a possibility of having been based on Theognis.[1] Plutarch describes the advent of the "Unbridled Democracy" as follows:

Μεγαρεῖς Θεαγένη τὸν τύραννον ἐκβαλόντες ὀλίγον χρόνον ἐσωφρόνη-
σαν κατὰ τὴν πολιτείαν· εἶτα πολλὴν κατὰ Πλάτωνα καὶ ἄκρατον αὐτοῖς
ἐλευθερίαν τῶν δημαγωγῶν οἰνοχοούντων διαφθαρέντες παντάπασι ...
    Plutarch *Greek Questions* 18 = *Moralia* 295 C–D

---

§ 12n1. Translation after Nagy (Ch.2 § 52). Whatever the last verse may actually mean, it could have been interpreted by the Greeks of the classical period as a reference to exile.
§ 12n2. For further discussion, see Figueira Ch.5.
§ 14n1. Cf. West 1974.68.

The Megarians having expelled the tyrant Theagenes, for a short time they were moderate [verb of **sōphrōn**] with respect to government. Then, the demagogues poured out a great and unmixed draught of freedom, as Plato says [*Republic* 562D], for them. Being wholly corrupted [verb **phtheirō**], they . . .

Compare this description with the following verses:

Κύρνε, κύει πόλις ἥδε, δέδοικα δὲ μὴ τέκῃ ἄνδρα
εὐθυντῆρα κακῆς ὕβριος ἡμετέρης.
ἀστοὶ μὲν γὰρ ἔθ᾽ οἵδε σαόφρονες, ἡγεμόνες δὲ
τετράφαται πολλὴν εἰς κακότητα πεσεῖν.
οὐδεμίαν πω Κύρν᾽ ἀγαθοὶ πόλιν ὤλεσαν ἄνδρες·
ἀλλ᾽ ὅταν ὑβρίζειν τοῖσι κακοῖσιν ἅδῃ,
δῆμόν τε φθείρωσι δίκας τ᾽ ἀδίκοισι διδῶσιν
οἰκείων κερδέων εἵνεκα καὶ κράτεος
Theognis 39–46

Kyrnos, this polis is pregnant, and I fear that it shall give birth to a man who will be a straightener of our base outrage [**hubris**].
The citizens here are still moderate [**sōphrones**], but the leaders [**hēgemones**]
have veered so as to fall into debasement.
Never yet, Kyrnos, have men who are noble [**agathoi**] ruined a city,
but when base men [**kakoi**] decide to behave with outrage [**hubris**],
and when they ruin [verb **phtheirō**] the community [**dēmos**] and render
   judgments in favor of the unjust
for the sake of personal gain, and for the sake of power . . .

This passage may refer to the time before the tyranny of Theagenes.[2] Since Plato, however, believed that tyranny followed from democracy,[3] Plutarch's source may have seen the leaders (**hēgemones**) who "veered so far as to fall into debasement" as popular demagogues in a democracy.[4] With such a belief, an author may have used these verses to supplement other sources on the origins of the Megarian democracy. The notion of the "moderate" (**sōphrōn**) nature of the regime following the fall of Theagenes may conceivably be based on little more than the poet's statement that the citizens were "moderate" (**sōphrones**) until corrupted by evil leaders. The later statement that the people were "wholly corrupted" (verb **phtheirō**) may owe its

---

§14n2. West p.68; Nagy Ch.2§14, with n3.
§14n3. Plato *Republic* 562, the very passage that Plutarch himself cites.
§14n4. This is also believed by West 1974.68. For the opinion that the leaders represent degenerate members of the old aristocracy, see Nagy Ch.2§29.

formulation to the words "they [the leaders] corrupt (verb **phtheirō**) the community [**dēmos** = the common people in later Greek]."[5] But the reason for the corruption of the people, too much freedom, cannot be found in the Theognidean passage, nor can the incidents in the rest of the Plutarch passage.

§15. It is odd, given the Lyceum's usual practice, that more traces of Theognidean poetry are not to be found. It might be argued that the original corpus was larger than the extant one and that numerous references to local Megarian matters, references that underlie our received account, were lost over the course of time because they lacked pan-Hellenic appeal. Such an argument is not only unprovable but quite fanciful. Can anyone believe that verses describing the poor invading the homes of the rich (Plutarch *Greek Questions* 18 = *Moralia* 295D) or drunken rowdies rolling wagons full of women and children into a lake (Plutarch *Greek Questions* 59 = *Moralia* 304D–F) would lack wide appeal? We do not possess these verses because, I suggest, they never existed in the first place.

§16. The simplest solution to the problem of the paucity of recognizable references to Theognidean poetry is that Aristotle and his students deliberately ignored the corpus. Aristotle's teacher Plato thought that Theognis was an inhabitant of Megara Hyblaea in Sicily, and Aristotle may have followed him in this belief.[1] He and his students would therefore have considered Theognidean poetry irrelevant to Megarian questions, and they may actually have removed it as evidence from their received sources. The one possible case of borrowing (vv. 39–46 at §14) can be explained as verses already integrated into a prose narrative context in Aristotle's source and therefore undetected by him.

§17. If the historical evidence for Megara was not derived from the Theognidean corpus, what were the Lyceum's sources? This is a difficult and controversial question that can be treated only briefly here. Inscriptions and other documentary evidence, which for the earliest of these events would have been mainly on wood, cannot have been abundant. Nor, to judge by the practice employed in the extant *Constitution of the Athenians*, were oral remembrances likely to have been a major source.[1] Aristotle in his writings and the author of the *Constitution of the Megarians* (who may or may not be Aristotle)

---

§14n5. Cf. West p.68.
§16n1. Plato *Laws* 630A. See Figueira Ch.5§§17–20.
§17n1. Day and Chambers 1962.5–12, with reference to earlier literature.

in any case needed fuller sources than could be provided by chance inscriptions and memories—sources that would chronicle the whole of Megarian history and discuss specific constitutional practices and changes.[2] For this kind of data the most obvious place to look was where the author of the *Constitution of the Athenians* had looked—at the local historians of the city in question.[3]

§18. The names of four writers of *Megarika* have been preserved: Praxion, Dieuchidas, Hereas, and Heragoras.[1] The latter two (who may be the same person) cannot be dated with precision, although a fourth- or third-century B.C. date is possible.[2] Praxion and Dieuchidas, however, appear to have been father and son and to be datable to the fourth century B.C.[3] Their works, therefore, would have been available to Peripatetic authors.

---

§17n2. Aristotle, to repeat, certainly did not compose all of the 158 *Constitutions*. He is a possible author of the *Constitution of the Megarians*, since that city produced an important philosophical school in the fifth and fourth centuries (Guthrie 1969.499–507). Aristotle's disciple and successor as head of the Lyceum, Theophrastus, is another possibility; he wrote a *Megarikos* (Diogenes Laertius 5.44), apparently a philosophical tract (*FGH* 3b *Noten* 230). Still, Megara, whatever its philosophical contributions, was not a leader in political and institutional matters. It is probable that the study of this city was given to a minor member of the School. Chamaeleon from Heraclea Pontica, a Megarian colony, would have had the requisite background and interest. The evidence suggests that his life is chronologically compatible with the composition of the *Constitution of the Megarians*; see Figueira Ch.5 §37.

§17n3. For the use of local Athenian chroniclers by the author of the *Constitution of the Athenians*, see Day and Chambers 1962.5–12, with full references to earlier discussions.

§18n1. The fragments of these authors are collected by Jacoby in *FGH* 3B, nos. 484–486, and by Piccirilli 1975.

§18n2. On the difficulty of dating Hereas and Heragoras, see Piccirilli pp.56 and 75. Dover 1966.206 argues that "there is not a particle of positive evidence for the existence of any Megarian historian at any date later than the third century B.C."

§18n3. The dating of Praxion and Dieuchidas is based on the following information. Clement of Alexandria accuses Dieuchidas of plagiarizing from the *Deukalioneia* of Hellanicus of Lesbos (*FGH* 485 T 1 = T 1 Piccirilli = Clement of Alexandria *Stromateis* 6.26.8). This charge self-evidently dates Dieuchidas later than Hellanicus, who died in 395/94. More importantly, it has been demonstrated that Clement depends on a source who cited only authors earlier than c. 300 (Wilamowitz 1884.240–241; cf. *FGH* 3b *Noten* 231n4). Since Dieuchidas can be dated to the fourth century, it is logical to equate him with a Megarian temple official at Delphi named in several inscriptions for the years 338/7–330/29 and referred to as the "son of Praxion" (*Fouilles de Delphes* 3, cited and discussed by Jacoby in *FGH* 3b *Noten* 231n5). Dieuchidas presumably received his post as a reward for writing his history. Praxion, known from other evidence to have written a *Megarika* (*FGH* 484 F 1 = fr. 1 Piccirilli = Harpocration s.v. "Skiron"), obviously composed his history at an even earlier date. Cf. Prakken 1941.

§19. Only under the most unusual circumstances would these local histories have been ignored by the Lyceum. Another contributor to this volume has argued that the *Megarika*, unlike other local chronicles, were not true histories of the city. Rather, they concerned themselves only with the mythological period and the origins of Megarian institutions, and therefore the Lyceum depended on other sources for its information on Megara.[1] This position, although supported by ingenious arguments, I find unconvincing. The structure of the *Megarika* of Dieuchidas, the best-preserved writer, is, on the basis of the surviving fragments,[2] far more easily interpreted as a chronological presentation reaching well into historical times than any other way.[3] Furthermore, the Megareis are cited as the source for, in addition to many mythological data, some historical events.[4] In common Hellenistic usage, the Megareis ought to mean "Megarian local historians"; it seems unsound practice to attempt to explain away this evidence with more elaborate hypotheses.[5]

§20. The exact attitude of the Megarian local chroniclers toward the tyrant Theagenes and the Megarian democracy is unknown. Their probable views, however, can be reconstructed. Living in an oligarchic state, they would have hated tyranny, the bête noire of all oligarchs. Living in a **polis** whose greatest enemy was democratic Athens, they would have had a low opinion of democracy. Furthermore, there was present a more complex impetus to portray the archaic period in dark colors. The unequal struggle between Megara and Athens had raged during this period, resulting in losses to Megara, notably Salamis. Rather than admit to military inferiority, the Megarians preferred to attribute their defeats to factionalism; thus the loss of Salamis was blamed on the treachery of some of

---

§19n1. Figueira Ch.5§§5–18.

§19n2. In book 1, the story of Deukalion and the Flood (*FGH* 485 T 1 = T 1 Piccirilli = Clement of Alexandria *Stromateis* 6.26.8); in book 4, the date and genealogy of the Spartan lawgiver Lycurgus (*FGH* 485 F 4 = fr. 4 Piccirilli = Clement *Stromateis* 1.119); in book 5, an accusation that Solon and/or Peisistratos interpolated verses into the *Iliad* stressing the close relationship of Athens and Salamis, most plausibly in the context of the Athenian-Megarian struggle over that island during the seventh and sixth centuries (*FGH* 485 F 6 = fr. 6 Piccirilli = Diogenes Laertius 1.57).

§19n3. See the sharp comments of Jacoby in *FGH* 3b Supp. 2.279n13 replying to the attempt of Prakken 1941.351 to portray Dieuchidas' work as "a local patriotic pamphlet."

§19n4. *FGH* 487 F 12 = fr. 21A Piccirilli = Pausanias 1.40.5; *FGH* 487 F 13 = fr. 23 Piccirilli = Plutarch *Pericles* 30.2.

§19n5. For discussion of this question, see Dover 1966.204–206 and Piccirilli 1975.79–82, 138–140.

their exiles.[1] With such an outlook, the Megarian historians probably passed harsh judgment on the regimes of Theagenes and the democracy.

§21. To these distortions, associated with their sources, the Peripatetics probably added their own. The Lyceum was no friend to tyranny and also looked askance at extreme forms of democracy. For Aristotle, the fifth-century Athenian democracy must have been "the ultimate form of a degenerate kind of constitution."[1] Other Peripatetics shared this negative viewpoint.[2]

§22. Because of the prejudices that have influenced our extant sources, the reconstruction of the history of Megara at the time of the evolution of Theognidean poetry is most difficult. The sources must be carefully handled, and much reading between the lines is necessary.[1] Nevertheless, if our knowledge is to increase, it is to these accounts that we must look.

---

§20n1. *FGH* 487 F 12 = fr. 21A Piccirilli = Pausanias 1.40.5.

§21n1. Day and Chambers 1962.61.

§21n2. For example, Demetrius of Phalerum wrote a general attack on the Athenian democracy entitled *A Denunciation of the Athenians* (Diogenes Laertius 5.81).

§22n1. For attempts at reconstructions of the history of archaic Megara, see Legon 1981 and Figueira Chronological Table.

2
Theognis and Megara: A Poet's Vision of His City

Gregory Nagy

Poet and Community

§1. εἰ μὲν χρήματ᾽ ἔχοιμι, Σιμωνίδη, οἷά περ ἤδη,
    οὐκ ἂν ἀνιώμην τοῖς ἀγαθοῖσι συνών.
    νῦν δέ με γινώσκοντα παρέρχεται, εἰμὶ δ᾽ ἄφωνος
    χρημοσύνῃ, πολλῶν γνοὺς ἂν ἄμεινον ἔτι,   670
    οὕνεκα νῦν φερόμεσθα καθ᾽ ἱστία λευκὰ βαλόντες
    Μηλίου ἐκ πόντου νύκτα διὰ δνοφερήν,
    ἀντλεῖν δ᾽ οὐκ ἐθέλουσιν, ὑπερβάλλει δὲ θάλασσα
    ἀμφοτέρων τοίχων. ἦ μάλα τις χαλεπῶς
    σῴζεται, οἳ᾽ ἔρδουσι· κυβερνήτην μὲν ἔπαυσαν   675
    ἐσθλόν, ὅτις φυλακὴν εἶχεν ἐπισταμένως·
    χρήματα δ᾽ ἁρπάζουσι βίῃ, κόσμος δ᾽ ἀπόλωλεν,
    δασμὸς δ᾽ οὐκέτ᾽ ἴσος γίνεται ἐς τὸ μέσον·
    φορτηγοὶ δ᾽ ἄρχουσι, κακοὶ δ᾽ ἀγαθῶν καθύπερθεν.
    δειμαίνω μή πως ναῦν κατὰ κῦμα πίῃ.   680
    ταῦτά μοι ᾐνίχθω κεκρυμμένα τοῖς ἀγαθοῖσιν.
    γινώσκοι δ᾽ ἄν τις καὶ κακὸν ἂν σοφὸς ᾖ.
    Theognis 667–682

If I had my *possessions* [khrēmata], Simonides,[1]

The translations in this presentation are offered as exegetical tools rather than definitive renditions. Books of the *Iliad* or *Odyssey* are indicated with upper or lower case Roman numerals, respectively. Quotations from Solon and other poets of elegiac (except Theognis) follow the edition of Gentili/Prato 1979 (henceforth GP). The numbering of West 1971/1972 (henceforth W) is as a rule appended in square brackets. Quotations from Theognis follow the edition of West, unless otherwise indicated. Besides the contributors to this volume, I wish to thank the following for their kind advice: James R. Baron, Ann Bergren, David A. Campbell, Carrie Cowherd, Olga M. Davidson, Caroline E. Dexter, John D. B. Hamilton, Albert Henrichs, Leonard Muellner, William H. Race, James Redfield, Nancy Rubin, Seth Schein, and Calvert Watkins.

§1n1. There is little to be said in favor of the claim (based largely on the name "Simonides" here) that these verses should be attributed to Euenos of Paros; for an unbiased summary of the arguments in favor of this claim, see van Groningen 1966.267–269. Granted, the poet Euenos is credited with composing a verse identical

I would not be distressed as I am now[2] at being together with the noble
[agathoi].[3]
But now they [i.e., my possessions] have passed me by, even though *I
was aware*,[4] and I am speechless
because of my lack of possessions,[5] though *I would be* better *aware* than
many,[6]
[aware] that we are now being carried along, with white sails lowered,
beyond the seas of Melos, through the dark night,
and they refuse to bail, and the sea washes over
both sides of the ship. It is a difficult thing for anyone
to be saved, such things they are doing. They have deposed the *pilot*
[kubernētēs],
the noble [esthlos] one, who was standing guard with expertise.
They *seize possessions* [khrēmata] by *force* [biē], and *order* [kosmos] has
been destroyed.
There is no longer an equitable[7] division [of possessions], in the common interest,[8]
but the carriers of merchandise rule, and the *base* [kakoi] are on top of
the *noble* [agathoi].
I am afraid that perhaps a wave will swallow the ship.
Let these things *be allusive utterances* [= ainigmata] hidden by me for
the noble [agathoi].
One could be aware of even [future] misfortune, if one is *skilled* [sophos].

§2. These verses, the translation of which will be defended in what
follows, present a prime example of a familiar traditional theme in
Greek poetry: the **polis** 'city-state' is afflicted with social discord

---

to Theognis verse 472, but the phenomenon of shared doublets in the textual traditions of Theognis and other poets can generally be explained as reflecting the common
heritage of traditional poetic diction. This point is elaborated at §§33–38 below.

§1n2. For the syntax of ἤδη here at Theognis 667, see West 1974.157.

§1n3. For the syntax, see van Groningen 1966.263–264.

§1n4. The participle γινώσκοντα here at 669 is apparently an accusative singular
masculine, not nominative plural neuter; cf. Theognis 419: πολλά με καὶ συνιέντα
παρέρχεται.

§1n5. Cf. again Theognis 419–420: ἀλλ' ὑπ' ἀνάγκης/σιγῶ ...; cf. also Theognis 177–178.

§1n6. The translation here follows the interpretation offered by West 1974.157.
In another study, however, I will offer arguments in favor of emending ἄν to ἕν (which
would also affect the translation of πολλῶν) here at Theognis 670, on the basis of
parallelisms to be found in passages like Archilochus fr. 201 W.

§1n7. The word **isos** 'equitable' here refers to the *virtual* equality of the participants; cf. Detienne 1973.96.

§1n8. The expression **es to meson** is literally 'directed at the center', referring
to the communalization of possessions that are marked for orderly distribution by the
community. See Cerri 1969.103.

or—to use the Greek word for it—stasis,[1] and this affliction is here envisaged as a violent seastorm that threatens the ship of state.[2] The equation is made, as the poetry itself reveals, in a cryptic and ambiguous poetic language that is meant to be understood by the **agathoi** or 'noble' only—to the exclusion of those who are **kakoi** or 'base'.[3] The quality of ambiguity and exclusiveness, expressed by the phrase κεκρυμμένα τοῖς ἀγαθοῖσιν 'hidden for the **agathoi**' at verse 681, is also expressed by the perfect imperative ἠνίχθω of the verb **ainissomai** 'make allusive utterances' in the same verse (for the semantics, cf. the derivative noun **ainigma** 'enigma, riddle' as in Sophocles *OT* 393, 1525). This same quality of ambiguity and exclusiveness is inherent in the noun from which the verb **ainissomai** is derived: the word in question is **ainos**, designating a mode of poetic discourse that is unmistakably understandable only to its intended audience.[4] To use the terminology of Prague School linguistics: the **ainos** entails one code with at least two messages—the true one for the intended audience and the false or garbled ones for all others. There is no room here for elaboration on details that have been assembled elsewhere,[5] and it will suffice for now to cite one of the words used in the traditional language of the **ainos** to designate those who hear its true message: the word is **sophos**, which means in the context of the **ainos** not just 'skilled' but 'skilled in understanding poetry'.[6] Such **sophiē** 'skill' applies to poet and audience alike—both to the encoder and to the decoders, as it were, of the **ainos**. One aim of this study is to show that the inherent **sophiē** of the **ainos** is also at work in the ambiguous and exclusive message conveyed by the poetry of Theognis to the **agathoi**.

§3. The converse of this ideology, namely that the **kakoi** 'base' are excluded from understanding the poetry of Theognis, depends on the interpretation of the last verse in the passage under consideration (§1):

---

§2n1. Instances of the word **stasis** in Theognis: verses 51, 781, 1082.

§2n2. Another prime example is at Alcaeus fr. 208 V (= 326 LP). Note the expression ἀνέμων στάσιν 'stasis of the winds' at verse 1. On the level of diction, cf. φορήμμεθα at verse 4 of this same fragment with φερόμεσθα at Theognis 671 here. The very word for social discord, **stasis**, seems to be a metaphorical extension of a navigational concept: **stasis** is actually attested as meaning the 'lie' or 'setting' of the winds (e.g., Herodotus 2.26.2); see Silk 1974.123.

§2n3. That the **kakoi** are indeed excluded will, it is hoped, become clear as the discussion proceeds.

§2n4. The arguments are presented in Nagy 1979.238–242.

§2n5. Ibid.

§2n6. Ibid.

γινώσκοι δ' ἄν τις καὶ κακὸν ἄν σοφὸς ἦ.
Theognis 682

one *could be aware* of even [future] misfortune, if one is **sophos**.[1]

The reading offered here follows the manuscript tradition, which gives κακόν—as opposed to the emendation κακός adopted by most recent editors (but not by Douglas Young) and yielding this alternative interpretation of the same verse:

> even a base person could be aware [of what is hidden away for the noble], if he is **sophos**.

In support of the reading κακόν, there is a parallel passage where the immediate context is the mention of poets and seers as parallel types in a catalogue enumerating representatives of various social functions:

ἄλλος 'Ολυμπιάδων Μουσέων πάρα δῶρα διδαχθείς,
 ἱμερτῆς σοφίης μέτρον ἐπιστάμενος·
ἄλλον μάντιν ἔθηκεν ἄναξ ἑκάεργος 'Απόλλων,
 ἔγνω δ' ἀνδρὶ κακὸν τηλόθεν ἐρχόμενον.
Solon fr. 1.51–54 GP [= fr. 13 W]

And another man is taught the gifts of the Olympian Muses,
and such a man understands the control of desirable **sophiē**.
Far reaching Apollo makes yet another man a seer,
and such a man *is aware* of misfortune even as it is coming from afar.[2]

The next two verses go on to say that, even if one has such powers of foreseeing misfortunes, one still cannot prevent what is fated to happen (Solon fr. 1.55–56).[3]

---

§3n1. The γινώσκοι here at verse 682 can be construed as having potentially two objects: implicitly the ταῦτα ... κεκρυμμένα of verse 681 and explicitly the κακόν of verse 682. The καί of verse 682 can be interpreted as drawing attention to the explicitness of the next word κακόν, which finally uncovers what has up to now been veiled. Accordingly, it may be better to translate καί here as 'in particular' rather than 'even'. On the use of κακόν, cf. Theognis 135–136: οὐδέ τις ἀνθρώπων ἐργάζεται ἐν φρεσὶν εἰδώς, / ἐς τέλος εἴτ' ἀγαθὸν γίνεται εἴτε κακόν.

§3n2. Cf. the words of the seer Theoklymenos, directed at the evil suitors: ... ἐπεὶ νοέω κακὸν ὕμμιν / ἐρχόμενον (xx 367–368). On the traditional parallelism of **aoidos** 'poet' and **mantis** 'seer' as **dēmiourgoi**, see Nagy 1979.233–234 on *Odyssey* xvii 381–387.

§3n3. Cf. the context of **oiōnos** 'bird-omen' at Solon fr. 1.56 [= fr. 13 W] with the context of the same word at Theognis 545 (discussed at §20 below).

§4. A parallel theme is at work in the given passage from Theognis (§1): even though the poet had been aware of what was to happen, he still suffered the misfortune of losing his khrēmata 'possessions' (vv. 667–669). The verb gīnōskō 'be aware' occurs twice here, signaling not only the poet's past awareness of the misfortune that awaited him (669) but also his present awareness that the ship of state is threatened by a violent seastorm (670). The conjunction οὕνεκα 'that', dependent on the second occurrence of gīnōskō,[1] directly introduces this central image of the afflicted ship, and the parallelism of the two occurrences suggests that the poet's loss of his possessions is a theme parallel to that of a ship in a seastorm. The image of the afflicted ship is then held up for scrutiny in the coda of the passage, which contains the third and last occurrence of gīnōskō:

> ταῦτά μοι ἠνίχθω κεκρυμμένα τοῖς ἀγαθοῖσιν·
> γινώσκοι δ᾽ ἄν τις καὶ κακὸν ἂν σοφὸς ᾖ.
> Theognis 681–682

Let these things be allusive utterances made by me for the agathoi.
One *could be aware* of even [future] misfortune, if one is sophos.

The poet has experienced such misfortune, but when he is together with the agathoi (§1 v. 668) he is painfully reluctant to speak of his experience directly to them; instead, he speaks to his audience indirectly, and they are specifically named as the agathoi (681). For them the key to being aware of future misfortune is being aware of the hidden message encoded in the image of the ship in a seastorm. And to be thus aware, the audience has to be sophoi as the poet is sophos.

§5. In the inherited diction of the ainos, as mastered in the epinician poetry of Pindar and Bacchylides, one way to express the actual bond of communication between poet as sophos and audience as sophoi is to deploy the word philos and its derivatives. This subject has been treated in some detail elsewhere,[1] and it will suffice here to observe that a parallel ideology is at work in the poetry of Theognis. For an examination of Theognidean poetry in this regard, it is important to keep in mind that the mere translation of philos as 'dear' when it is an adjective and 'friend' when it is a noun is insufficient for conveying the ideology entailed by this word in the language of archaic

---

§4n1. For the construction, cf. *Hymn to Apollo* 375–376.
§5n1. Nagy 1979.241–242; also 236–238.

Greek poetry. The studies of Emile Benveniste have shown that philos conveys the state of integration, of emotional as well as strictly societal bonding;[2] moreover, the varying degrees of one's feeling philos to others amount to a measure of one's own identity.[3] In the ideology of the ainos, the community with whom the poetry communicates—and identifies—is actually conceived as an integral group of philoi. So also with the poetry of Theognis: it will become apparent that the poet is speaking to an ostensibly integral community of philoi that is the polis of Megara.

§6. The body of Theognidean poetry is inaugurated on a note of social integration: a prime theme of the multiple invocation at verses 1–18 is that of foundation—the establishment of community. But the city that is singled out at one particular moment of its foundation is not Megara but Thebes:

Μοῦσαι καὶ Χάριτες, κοῦραι Διός, αἵ ποτε Κάδμου
ἐς γάμον ἐλθοῦσαι καλὸν ἀείσατ' ἔπος·
"ὅττι καλὸν φίλον ἐστί, τὸ δ' οὐ καλὸν οὐ φίλον ἐστί"·
τοῦτ' ἔπος ἀθανάτων ἦλθε διὰ στομάτων.[1]
    Theognis 15–18

Muses and Kharites,[2] daughters of Zeus! You were the ones
who once came to the wedding of Kadmos, and you sang this beautiful
utterance [epos]:[3]

---

§5n2. Benveniste 1969 I.338–353.

§5n3. In light of a forthcoming article by Martin Schwartz on philos as derived from locative phi (cognate of English *by* in the sense of 'near'), see Nagy 1979.103–113 on the links between the semantics of philos and the concepts of ascending scales of affection and self-identification.

§6n1. Note the pre-caesura/verse-final rhyme of ... ἀτων/ ... ἀτων at verse 18, corresponding to ... φίλον ἐστί/ ... φίλον ἐστί at verse 17. Perhaps the pattern of rhyming itself conveys the concept of harmoniē (on which see below). For more on such rhyming patterns, see Nagy 1974.99–101 and 1979b.628.

§6n2. This is the pluralized personification of kharis, a word used by poetry to characterize the quality of poetry, as in *Odyssey* ix 5 (see Nagy 1979.91–92); kharis conveys simultaneously the social aspect of *reciprocity* as well as the personal aspect of *pleasure*. As Odysseus says at *Odyssey* ix 3–11, no accomplishment has more kharis than whenever the spirit of euphrosunē 'mirth' is generated for the audience by a poet's performance. On the euphrosunē of the audience as an emblem of social cohesion, see Nagy 1979.92 (and n7); on euphrosunē as the programmatic word traditionally used in the ainos to designate the occasion of the ainos, see id. p.236 (and n5).

§6n3. On the use of epos to mean not just 'utterance' but also 'poetic utterance' *as quoted by the poetry itself*, see Koller 1972.16–24; also Nagy 1979.236, 271.

"What is beautiful is **philon**, what is not beautiful is not **philon**."[4]
That is the *utterance* [**epos**][5] that came through their immortal mouths.

The song of the Muses at the wedding of Kadmos, founder of Thebes, inaugurates the **polis** just as the invocation of the Muses inaugurates the poetry of Theognis. In this way the song of the Muses at verse 17 sets the overall theme of Theognidean poetry. The song itself amounts to an equation of beauty with that which is **philon**, where the adjective **philos** in the neuter serves to convey the institutional and sentimental bonds that integrate society. In other words, the beauty of the Muses' song is equated with the social integration of Thebes and, by extension, the beauty of Theognidean poetry is equated with the social integration of Megara.

§7. Besides the word **philos**, the theme of social integration is also conveyed by the name **Harmoniē**, who is the bride of Kadmos (Hesiod *Theogony* 937, 975). As an abstract noun, **harmoniē** is actually used in the diction of archaic poetry to designate the concept of 'accord' (e.g., *Iliad* xxii 255). Moreover, the word can convey not only *social* but *esthetic* integration as well, in a musical sense roughly corresponding to "harmony" (e.g., Sophocles fr. 244 Radt). The verb root from which **harmoniē** is built, namely the **ar-** of **ar-ar-iskō** 'join, fit', can actually convey the beauty of song:

   ... οὕτω σφιν καλὴ <u>συνάρηρεν</u> ἀοιδή
   Hymn to Apollo 164

   ... so beautifully *is* their song *fitted together*[1]

In other words, the very concept of **Harmoniē** has a built-in equation of musical beauty with social integration, which is the message delivered by the song of the Muses—and by the poetry of Theognis.[2]

---

§6n4. This gnomic song of the Muses is echoed in Euripides *Bacchae* 881/901, ὅ τι καλὸν φίλον ἀεί. Ironically, the song here pertains to the death of Pentheus, grandson of Kadmos; cf. Dodds 1960.187.

§6n5. The quoted utterance of the Muses (and the Kharites) is called an **epos** both before and after the quotation (cf. Koller 1972.17 on Tyrtaeus fr. 1b.2 GP [= fr. 4 W]). Perhaps the pattern of framing itself conveys the concept of **harmoniē** (on which see below).

§7n1. For more on the traditional use of the Greek root **ar-** in referring to the craft of poetry *and of carpentry*, see Nagy 1979.297–300.

§7n2. Cf. ibid. Note the semantic parallelism of adjective **arthmios** (from root **ar-**, as in **arariskō** and **harmoniē**) with adjective **philos**, as at Theognis 326, 1312; cf. also *Odyssey* xvi 427 and *Hymn to Hermes* 524.

Thus, the invocation to the Muses reveals that the poetry of Theognis is based on an ideology that awards the highest priority to the quality of being **philos**. To repeat: like the **ainos**, the poetry of Theognis is communicating with an ostensibly integrated community of **philoi**.

§8. In the verses that follow the invocation of the Muses, the main body of Theognidean poetry commences:

> Κύρνε, σοφιζομένῳ μὲν ἐμοὶ[1] σφρηγὶς ἐπικείσθω
> τοῖσδ᾽ ἔπεσιν—λήσει δ᾽ οὔποτε κλεπτόμενα,
> οὐδέ τις ἀλλάξει κάκιον τοὐσθλοῦ παρεόντος,
> ὧδε δὲ πᾶς τις ἐρεῖ· "Θεύγνιδός ἐστιν ἔπη
> τοῦ Μεγαρέως· πάντας δὲ κατ᾽ ἀνθρώπους ὀνομαστός."
> Theognis 19–23

Kyrnos, let a seal [**sphrēgis**] be placed by me, *as I practice my poetic skill* [**sophiē**],
upon these *utterances* [**epos** plural]; that way they [i.e., the utterances]
will never be stolen without detection,
and no one will substitute something inferior for the genuine[2] thing that is there.
And everyone will say: "These are the *utterances* [**epos** plural] of Theognis
of Megara. His name is known among all men."

For an understanding of the **sphrēgis** 'seal' of Theognis, it is pertinent to review the semantics of the word **sophizomai** 'practice sophiē' in the same verse (19). To repeat: The concept of **sophiē** as 'poetic skill' embraces an ideology characteristic of the **ainos**—and of Theognidean poetry.[3] The seal placed on the poetry of Theognis through the **sophiē** of the poet himself guarantees the correct perception of the poet's message. Any use of the poet's words in an incorrect context will be exposed as theft, and any tampering with the words will implicitly garble their message and thereby produce, again, an incorrect context; in the correct context, however, the words will

---

§8n1. On the sound-pattern . . . **omenōimenemoi**, containing double . . . **men** . . . and reverse . . . **nem** . . . and double . . . **oi** . . . , see n3 below.

§8n2. On the semantics of **esthlos** as 'genuine' (and thereby 'good' or 'noble'), see Watkins 1972.

§8n3. Perhaps the artful sound-pattern in **sophizomenōimenemoi** at Theognis 19 (see n1 above) conveys the very concept of **sophiē** (cf. §6n1 and §6n5 on the sound-patterns that seem to convey the concept of **harmoniē**). In that case, the poetic artistry of Theognis *is* his **sphrēgis**.

identify and thereby glorify Theognis as the genuine poet. The occurrence of **epos** [plural] at verses 20 and 22 must refer primarily to Theognidean poetry as a whole, but the pointed use of **epos** at verses 16 and 18, in the passage immediately preceding (§6), to quote the song of the Muses colors the use of **epos** in the two occurrences now under consideration, associating what the Muses sang with all of Theognis' poetry. Moreover, since the song of the Muses is quoted in an invocation that actually inaugurates the poetry of Theognis, the theme of their song—to repeat—serves as the very foundation of Theognidean poetry. This theme glorifies the quality of being **philos**, and one is led yet again to the expectation that the audience of Theognis is an integrated community of **philoi**.

§9. In fact, the last two verses of the passage just cited (§8) make it clear that the audience of Theognis is meant to be not just local but pan-Hellenic in scope, and that the poetry of Theognis is worthy of pan-Hellenic acceptance (22–23):

> And everyone will say: "These are the utterances [**epos** plural] of Theognis
> of Megara. His name is known among all men."

The very next verse, however, which combines with the previous verse about the poet's future pan-Hellenic status to form a complete elegiac couplet, makes it just as clear that the poetry of Theognis has as yet failed to gain universal acceptance in his own **polis** of Megara:

> ἀστοῖσιν δ᾽ <u>οὔπω</u> πᾶσιν ἁδεῖν δύναμαι
> Theognis 24

> But I am *not yet* able to please all the citizens.

§10. This failure is viewed as natural even by the poet:

> οὐδὲν θαυμαστόν, Πολυπαΐδη· οὐδὲ γὰρ ὁ Ζεὺς
> οὔθ᾽ ὕων πάντεσσ᾽ ἀνδάνει οὔτ᾽ ἀνέχων.
> σοὶ δ᾽ ἐγὼ εὖ φρονέων ὑποθήσομαι, οἷάπερ αὐτὸς
> Κύρν᾽ ἀπὸ τῶν ἀγαθῶν παῖς ἔτ᾽ ἐὼν ἔμαθον.
> Theognis 25–28

> This is not surprising, son of Polypaos! For not even Zeus
> can please everyone either by raining or by letting up.
> But I, having good intentions toward you, will give you the kind of advice
> that I myself, Kyrnos, learned from the **agathoi** when I was still a boy.

By implication, the advice of Theognis to Kyrnos represents social order just as the weather as controlled by Zeus represents natural order—the cosmos itself.

§11. The attitude of Theognis toward his community is in this respect parallel to that of the generic lawgiver. Now the function of a lawgiver, as will emerge from what follows, is to create social order; paradoxically, however, the lawgiver has to become alienated from his community in the process of integrating it. With this theme of alienation in mind, it is appropriate first of all to consider the Athenian tradition about Solon, as reported by Plutarch (*Solon* 25.6). Once his laws are passed and social order is finally established in Athens, the lawgiver perceives that his presence in the community becomes instantly disruptive: the citizens keep praising or blaming this or that aspect of the laws (ἐπαινοῦντες ἢ ψέγοντες), constantly asking Solon himself to make changes in the code that he has given them (Plutarch loc.cit.). In precisely this context, Plutarch's narrative has Solon utter an actual verse from his own poetry:

> ἔργμασι ἐν μεγάλοις πᾶσιν ἁδεῖν χαλεπόν.
> Solon fr. 9 GP [= fr. 7 W]

In matters of great importance it is difficult to please all.

To cite once again the verse of Theognis (§9):

> ἀστοῖσιν δ' οὔπω πᾶσιν ἁδεῖν δύναμαι.
> Theognis 24

But I am not yet able to please all the citizens.

§12. Plutarch's account goes on to say that Solon's response to the threat of changes in his code was to leave the community altogether and to sail away on a journey of ten years' duration (*Solon* 25.6). Moreover, the laws of Solon, intended to last for a hundred years, were absolutely protected by oath for these ten years (Herodotus 1.29.2; Aristotle *Constitution of the Athenians* 7.2, 11.1; Plutarch *Solon* 25.1, 6). There is a parallel pattern in the Spartan traditions about their lawgiver Lycurgus, again as reported by Plutarch (*Lycurgus* 29.1–4): once the code of Lycurgus is adopted and the social order is finally established, he makes the Spartans swear an oath that they will not make changes in the code and that the oath will stay in effect until he comes back from a journey to Delphi. He then makes the code permanent by never returning to Sparta: Lycurgus dies abroad by starving himself to death (Plutarch *Lycurgus* 29.8, 31; Ephorus *FGH* 70 F 175 at Aelian *VH* 13.23).[1] Since the lawgiver is traditionally pictured as holding the power of changing his own laws, the threat of changing his code is removed only with the removal of the lawgiver himself from the community—whether by self-imposed exile or by death.[2]

§13. Inside the ideology of narrative traditions about a given lawgiver, his code is static, unchangeable; outside this ideology and in reality, however, the code is dynamic, subject to modifications and accretions that are occasioned by an evolving social order. For example, the traditions of Sparta in the fifth century as reported by Herodotus (1.65.2–1.66.1) ascribe the city's social order—the local word for which is **kosmos**[1] (1.65.4)—entirely to Lycurgus. And yet the events and institutions that are ascribed to him can be dated to periods so varied that they range over several centuries. According to Xenophon, Lycurgus flourished 'in the era of the Herakleidai' (κατὰ τοὺς Ἡρακλείδας: *Constitution of the Lacedaemonians* 10.8). He is identified by Herodotus (1.65.4) as the uncle and mentor of the Spartan king Labotas, the relative date for whom is around 900 B.C.[2] As the promulgator of the Great Rhetra (Plutarch *Lycurgus* 6.2), Lycurgus would have flourished somewhere in the ninth or eighth century; as the originator of the phalanx, he would presumably belong to the eighth; as an older contemporary of Tyrtaeus, he would belong to the seventh.[3] Then again, he is in effect credited with the whole set of social reforms datable to the mid-sixth century.[4] One expert sums it up this way: "In his mythical elusiveness and multivalent anonymity Lycurgus embodies the legend of Sparta."[5]

---

§12n1. Cf. Szegedy-Maszák 1978.208.

§12n2. Cf. Szegedy-Maszák p.207. In the case of Lycurgus, the lawgiver chooses both exile and death. There is a tradition that Lycurgus died in Crete and was actually buried there (Plutarch *Lycurgus* 31.7, 10); it was also in Crete that Lycurgus found laws that he could adopt for the code that he took back with him to Sparta (*Lycurgus* 4.1). Herodotus reports that, according to the native Spartan tradition, Lycurgus imported his code from Crete (1.65.4), adding that there was also another tradition according to which Lycurgus received the code from the Oracle at Delphi (ibid.).

§13n1. Cf. **to kosmion** in Plutarch *Lycurgus* 4.3 (§25 and §25n2 below).

§13n2. Tigerstedt 1965.72.

§13n3. Tigerstedt p.73.

§13n4. Ibid. Cf. Finley 1968.145: "The sixth-century revolution was therefore a complex process of some innovation and much modification and re-institutionalization of the elements which appear to have survived 'unchanged'."

§13n5. Again, Tigerstedt 1965.73.

§14. Such elusiveness is hardly surprising in view of the general tendency in Greek mythopoeic traditions to retroject each cultural institution to a primordial creation of one man.[1] And this pattern of elusiveness in figures like Lycurgus has a parallel in the figure of Theognis himself. Like the code of the lawgiver, the poetry of Theognis presents itself as static, unchangeable. In fact the **sphrēgis** 'seal' of Theognis (§8 vv. 19–23 above) is pictured as a guarantee that no one will ever tamper with the poet's words (§8 vv. 20–21). Outside this ideology and in reality, however, the poetry of Theognis is dynamic, subject to modifications and accretions that are occasioned by an evolving social order. And the poet is always there, observing it all—despite the fact that the events being observed span an era that goes well beyond a single lifetime. For now it is enough simply to cite the two chronological extremes that are most readily verifiable from the internal evidence of the poetry. On one extreme, verses 773–782 of Theognis allude to the Persian foray into the Megarid in 479 b.c. (on which see Pausanias 1.40.2);[2] on the other extreme, verses 39–52 dramatize the situation in Megara *before* the tyranny of Theagenes, which started somewhere in the third quarter of the seventh century b.c.[3] There is even a possibility, moreover, that the figure of Theognis, like Lycurgus, has links with an era as early as that of the Herakleidai: it happens that **Kurnos**, the name of the fickle youth who serves as the focus of the poet's attention, is also the name of a **hērōs** 'hero' mentioned by Herodotus (1.167.4)—a hero further identified by Servius (on Virgil *Eclogues* 9.30) as a son of Herakles! Be that as it may, the point remains that the poetry of Theognis, like the code of Lycurgus, is a dynamic institution that responds to the evolution of the community it embraces.

§15. Accordingly, it seems helpful to advance the theory that the figure of Theognis represents a cumulative synthesis of Megarian poetic traditions. The major advantage of this theory is that the poetry of Theognis may then be appreciated as a skillful and effective—maybe even beautiful—dramatization of Megara through the ages. The major disadvantage, however, is that the notion of a historical Theognis may have to be abandoned. This is not to say, how-

---

§14n1. Cf. Kleingünther 1933.

§14n2. Cf. also Theognis 757–764.

§14n3. Cf. West 1974.67–68. On the dating of Theagenes, see Oost 1973.188–189 and Legon 1981.93, 102. By the time of the Cylonian conspiracy, Theagenes was already in power (Thucydides 1.126.3–11). For more on Theognis 39–52, see further at §27 below.

ever, that the persona of Theognis does not inform the entire corpus of Theognidean poetry, which is in fact ascribed to the authorship of Theognis *by the poetry itself*. It is even true that the poetry itself actually creates the integral and lively personality of one man—an extraordinarily versatile man—whose complex identity is perhaps the only constant in the changing world of his beloved Megara. If, moreover, this theory is tantamount to calling Theognis a myth, then so be it—provided that "myth" can be understood as a given society's codification of its own traditional values in narrative and dramatized form.

§16. It is not enough to say, however, that the poetry of Theognis is simply Megarian poetry. The surviving corpus of Theognidean poetry represents Megarian traditions that have evolved into a form suitable for pan-Hellenic audiences. This poetry, as the poet himself boasts to Kyrnos, is appropriate for performance at symposia in city-states throughout Hellas (Theognis 237–254).[1] As the poet makes clear, attaining pan-Hellenic approval is the same thing as attaining permanence (vv. 251–252). But the next two verses, which round out this passage, present a striking contrast. It now becomes clear that the poet himself fails to win acceptance from the focal point of his audience, Kyrnos himself:

αὐτὰρ ἐγὼν ὀλίγης παρὰ σεῦ οὐ τυγχάνω αἰδοῦς,
ἀλλ᾽ ὥσπερ μικρὸν παῖδα λόγοις μ᾽ ἀπατᾷς.
Theognis 253–254

But I do not even get a bit of respect from you,
and you deceive me with what you say,[2] as if I were some small boy.

Similarly, the same poet who boasts of future pan-Hellenic approval at verses 22–23 (quoted at §8) declares in the very next verse that he fails to win the universal approval of his own community *in his own time*:

ἀστοῖσιν δ᾽ οὔπω πᾶσιν ἀδεῖν δύναμαι.
Theognis 24

But I am *not yet* able to please all the citizens.

---

§16n1. For more on this important passage, see Sacks 1978.
§16n2. From the parallels at Theognis 1263–1266 and 1283–1294, it is clear that the poet means, "When you *say* that you are **philos** to me, you are deceiving me." See Gentili 1977 (and Tarkow 1977).

§17. The adverb οὔπω 'not yet' here merits particular scrutiny, since it draws attention to the future tenses describing pan-Hellenic approval of Theognidean poetry at verses 19–23 (quoted at §8)[1] as well as 237–252.[2] The poetry itself is setting up a dramatic tension between its own present and the future. In his own here-and-now, the poet cannot be wholly accepted even by his own community; in the future, he will be accepted not only by all Megarians but also by all Hellenes. Yet the internal evidence of Theognidean poetry proves that this future is already a foregone conclusion. The verses of Theognis, including the very verses that foretell pan-Hellenic acceptance, are after all composed not in the native poetic diction of Doric Megara but rather in the accretive Ionic dialect of elegiac, a pan-Hellenic format suitable for transforming local traditions as diverse as those represented by Archilochus of Paros, Tyrtaeus of Sparta, and Solon of Athens. And the very fact that the poetry of Theognis has survived in its present form bears witness to its pan-Hellenic diffusion, which is, from the standpoint of the poetry, tantamount to pan-Hellenic acceptance.[3] Pan-Hellenic diffusion of such poetry seems impossible, however, without a native foundation: as the poetry itself acknowledges with the adverb οὔπω 'not yet' at verse 24 (quoted at §16), Theognis must one day win universal acceptance from his native Megara.

§18. Theognis must wait for a span of time well beyond a single lifetime before his poetry can indeed become the ideology of his city.

---

§17n1. λήσει (20), ἀλλάξει (21), ἐρεῖ (23).

§17n2. πωτήσῃ (238), παρέσσῃ (239), ἄσονται (243), ἀπολεῖς and μελήσεις (245), πέμψει (249), ἔσσῃ (252).

§17n3. On the basis of archaeological and historical evidence, A. M. Snodgrass (1971.421, 435) applies the concept of pan-Hellenism to the pattern of intensified intercommunication among the city-states of Hellas, starting in the eighth century B.C., as evidenced in particular by the following institutions: Olympic Games, Delphic Oracle, Homeric poetry. I have extended the concept as a hermeneutic model to help explain the nature of Homeric poetry, in that one can envisage as aspects of a single process the ongoing recomposition and diffusion of the *Iliad* and the *Odyssey*: see Nagy 1979.5–9. I have further extended the concept to apply to Hesiodic poetry: Nagy 1982.43–49, 52–57, 59–60; also, to Theognidean poetry: ibid., 52, 60–62. It goes without saying that pan-Hellenism must be viewed as an evolutionary trend extending into the classical period, not some fait accompli that can be accounted for solely in terms of the eighth century. Thus, various types of archaic Greek poetry, including the elegiac tradition represented by Theognis, make their bid for pan-Hellenic status considerably later than Homeric and Hesiodic poetry. Still, I see in the Theognidea a parallel pattern of ongoing recomposition, concomitant with pan-Hellenic diffusion. The most obvious reflex of this ongoing recomposition-in-diffusion is the ultimate crystallization of the Theognidea, composed not in the native Doric dialect of Megara but in an accretive Ionic dialect that is for all practical purposes the same as we see in the poetry of the other archaic poets of elegiac.

From the standpoint of the poet, this span of time is marked by strife, and the strife begins when Theagenes the tyrant comes to power in Megara (cf. Aristotle *Politics* 1305a24, *Rhetoric* 1357b33). As already noted, verses 39–52 of Theognis dramatize the poet's words to Kyrnos at a period just before this event, which must be dated to somewhere in the third quarter of the seventh century.[1] Theagenes was eventually overthrown and replaced by what is said to be a moderate oligarchy (Aristotle *Politics* 1302b30, Plutarch *Greek Questions* 295C–D), which by around 600 B.C. gave way to what is characterized as an intemperate democracy (Aristotle loc.cit., Plutarch loc.cit.).[2] It is also worth noting *en passant* that this same democracy is cited by Aristotle as the context for the origins of Megarian comedy (*Poetics* 1448a31). Then, sometime around 550 B.C., it seems that the democracy was overthrown and replaced by an oligarchical but supposedly moderate government that stayed in power through the rest of the archaic period, well into the fifth century (cf. Aristotle *Politics* 1300a17, 1302b31, 1304b34).[3] By 550 B.C., over seventy-five years of strife have elapsed since Theognis had told Kyrnos that he fears the onset of tyranny, an institution that will lead to **stasis** 'discord' (v. 51, in plural). Some seventy years still later, the poet speaks of the Persian threat to Hellas (vv. 773–788), again in terms of **stasis** 'discord' (v. 781), though here the word applies not so much to any specific situation at Megara as to the general upheaval inflicted by the Persian menace upon all Hellenes.

§19. We may conclude, then, that the poetry of Theognis, like the code of Lycurgus, is cumulative from the external standpoint of history: the poetry and the code actually embody the evolution of Megara and Sparta, respectively. From the internal standpoint of the poetry and the code, however, each is created by one man in response to the strife that afflicts his respective community.

Champions of Justice

§20. Theognis actually assumes a moral authority parallel to that of lawgivers like Lycurgus and Solon. His declaration at verse 24 (quoted at §9) that he cannot yet be approved by all the citizens of Megara is

---

§18n1. See again §14n3.

§18n2. See Oost 1973.192.

§18n3. For arguments in favor of the terminus 550 B.C., see Oost p.195n33. On the basis of Thucydides 4.66, the terminus for the overthrow of the oligarchy may possibly be set at 427 B.C. (cf. Highbarger 1927.156 and Legon 1981.236).

framed in a context of the poet's insisting on his poetry, just as Solon's corresponding declaration (quoted at §11) is preserved in the context of the lawgiver's insisting on his law code. In fact, Theognis makes such declarations of insistence more than once, in the context of stressing the impossibility of being able to please all (cf. vv. 367-370, 801-804, 1183-1184b). Like the lawgiver Lycurgus, who according to one tradition had his law code revealed to him by the Pythia of the Delphic Oracle (Herodotus 1.65.4), Theognis himself lays claim to a revelation from the same source:

> τόρνου καὶ στάθμης καὶ γνώμονος ἄνδρα θεωρὸν
> εὐθύτερον χρὴ <ἔ>μεν Κύρνε φυλασσόμενον,
> ᾧτινί κεν Πυθῶνι θεοῦ χρήσασ' ἱέρεια
> ὀμφὴν σημήνῃ πίονος ἐξ ἀδύτου·
> οὔτέ τι γὰρ προσθεὶς οὐδέν κ' ἔτι φάρμακον εὕροις
> οὐδ' ἀφελὼν πρὸς θεῶν ἀμπλακίην προφύγοις.
> Theognis 805-810

A man who is **theōros** [i.e., who consults the Oracle] must be
more straight,[1] Kyrnos, being on his guard,[2] than a carpenter's pin and
rule and square—
a man to whom the priestess [i.e., the Pythia] of the god at Delphi
makes a response, revealing a sacred utterance from the opulent shrine.
You will not find any remedy[3] left if you add anything,
nor will you escape from veering, in the eyes of the gods, if you take
anything away.

That the **theōros** must be none other than Theognis—and that his **dikē** 'judgment' itself is at stake if there is any "veering" from "straightness"—becomes clear in another passage:[4]

> χρή με παρὰ στάθμην καὶ γνώμονα τήνδε δικάσσαι
> Κύρνε δίκην, ἴσόν τ' ἀμφοτέροισι δόμεν,
> μάντεσί τ' οἰωνοῖς τε καὶ αἰθομένοις ἱεροῖσιν,
> ὄφρα μὴ ἀμπλακίης αἰσχρὸν ὄνειδος ἔχω.
> Theognis 543-546

I must render this judgment [**dikē**], Kyrnos, along [the straight line of] a
carpenter's rule and square,

---

§20n1. The image of correctness or straightness here connotes the 'straightness' of **dikē** 'justice', as in Theognis 543-546 (quoted immediately below).
§20n2. For the image of a **phulax** 'guardian' of **dikē**, see Hesiod WD 249-255.
§20n3. For another instance of such medicinal imagery in a political context, cf. Theognis 1133-1134.
§20n4. Yet another passage is Theognis 945-948.

and I must give to both sides their equitable share,
with the help of seers, portents, and burning sacrifice,[5]
so that I may not incur shameful reproach for veering.

Solon as lawgiver likewise renders **dikē** 'judgment':

θεσμοὺς δ' ὁμοίως τῷ κακῷ τε κἀγαθῷ
εὐθεῖαν εἰς ἕκαστον ἁρμόσας δίκην
ἔγραψα

Solon fr. 30.18–20 GP [= fr. 36 W]

I wrote down the laws for base and noble alike,
fitting a *straight judgment* [**dikē**] for each.

The 'straightness' of the lawgiver's **dikē** is manifested in his even-handedness, which is equated elsewhere with his refusal to add to or take away from what rightfully belongs to one of two sides (Solon fr. 7.1–2 GP [= fr. 5 W]), just as Theognis equates 'veering' with adding or subtracting (vv. 809–810, quoted above):[6] by adding to or subtracting from the words of revelation emanating from the Oracle, one would be 'veering' by taking one side or another. Solon goes on to declare that he protects 'both sides' and allows 'neither side' to win (ἀμφοτέροισι / οὐδετέρους at Solon fr. 7.5/6), just as Theognis presents himself as giving an equal share to 'both sides' (ἀμφοτέροισι at v. 544, quoted above). Elsewhere too, Theognis teaches Kyrnos to walk 'the middle road' (vv. 219–220, 331–332) and give to 'neither side' that which belongs to the other (μηδετέροισι at v. 332).[7]

§21. The stance of Theognis as one who renders **dikē** 'judgment' (§20 v. 543) is presented in a specific setting of sacrifice and ritual correctness (545; cf. §20n5 above). This thematic connection of legal and ritual correctness is a matter of Indo-European heritage, as the comparative evidence of Indic legal traditions makes clear. In the *Laws of Manu*, ritual figures as the very foundation of Indic law. Moreover,

---

§20n5. For another collocation of **mantis** 'seer', **oiōnos** 'bird-omen', and **hiera** 'sacrifice', see Solon fr. 1 verses 53, 56, and 56 bis respectively (cf. §3n3 above): in this context, it is explicit that the **mantis** relies on bird-omens and sacrifices. So also with the datives at Theognis 545 here: they are to be construed as parallel rather than antithetical. In line with this argument, these datives cannot refer to the ἀμφοτέροισι of Theognis verse 544, and the readiest interpretation is to treat them as datives of means.

§20n6. There is even a phraseological match: ἀφελών at Solon fr. 7.2 and at Theognis 810.

§20n7. See also Theognis 945–948, already cited at §20n4.

this corpus of legal and moral aphorisms is traditionally ascribed to and named after Manu, who is both ancestor of the human race and prototypical sacrificer. The root *men- of Indic *Manu-* (cognate with English *man*) conveys that he is 'mindful' of ritual, a man whose virtuosity in "the delicate art of sacrifice" confers upon him an incontestable authority.[1]

§22. Similarly in the *Works and Days*, Hesiod's warning to Perses that Zeus will in the end punish 'deeds without **dikē**' (vv. 333–334) and the poet's advice that his brother keep away from such deeds (335) is linked with the further advice that Perses should perform sacrifice in a ritually correct manner (336–341). Moreover, the expanded root *menh₂-/*mneh₂- of *men- as in *Manu-* recurs in the participle **memnēmenos** 'being mindful', used throughout the *Works and Days* in the specific context of ritual as well as moral prescriptions (vv. 298, 422, 616, 623, 641, 711, 728), and it is clear that such prescriptions are cognate with those found in the Indic legal tradition. For example, the *Laws of Manu* (4.45–50) forbid urinating on a road, while walking or standing, or into a river, or while looking at the sun; likewise in the *Works and Days*, Hesiod declares that one should be **memnēmenos** 'mindful' (v. 728) not to urinate while standing up and facing the sun (727), or on a road (729), and the prohibition extends also to rivers and springs (757–758).[1] In short, the parallelism of ritual correctness and moral rectitude in the *Works and Days* is a reflex of Indo-European legal traditions.

§23. The word that conveys such correctness and rectitude throughout the *Works and Days* is **dikē**, as in Hesiod's warning about 'deeds without **dikē**' at verses 333–334 (cited at §22).[1] In such contexts, however, **dikē** takes on the general sense of 'justice' rather than the specific one of 'judgment' as at Theognis 543 (quoted at §20). It is in fact only when Zeus himself renders a judgment (as at *WD* 9) that **dikē** assumes the sense of 'judgment' and 'justice' simultaneously. If any man renders **dikē**, however, this specific 'judgment' becomes general 'justice' only as it is validated by the gods *in the course of time*. The specificity of the **dikē** that unjust men render in *Works and Days* 39, 249, and 269 is marked by the demonstrative pronoun τήνδε in all three verses: men can make the goddess **Dikē** herself

---

§21n1. Lévi 1898.121.
§22n1. See West 1978.334–335; cf. Watkins 1979–80.
§23n1. Conversely, the opposite of **dikē**, **hubris**, conveys failure to be ritually correct: cf. Hesiod *WD* 134–139.

'not straight' (*WD* 224), but *in the end* she prevails over her opposite, **hubris** 'outrage' (δίκη ὑπὲρ ὕβριος ἴσχει/ ἐς τέλος ἐξελθοῦσα: *WD* 217–218). The *eventuality* of **dikē** as 'justice' is a cornerstone of the *Works and Days*, in that this poem dramatizes the actual passage of time in which the **dikē** 'judgment' of the unjust kings at verses 39/249/269 is transformed into the **dikē** 'justice' of Zeus by the poem as a whole.[2] Hesiod proclaims at the beginning of the *Works and Days* that the **dikē** of Zeus is indeed the realization of the poem, in that Zeus renders **dikē** while Hesiod addresses **etētuma**, 'genuine' words, to Perses (vv. 9–10).

§24. The **dikē** 'judgment' that evolves into 'justice' in the life of Hesiod as dramatized in the *Works and Days* may be contrasted with the **dikē** that Solon boasts of having rendered for the Athenians (fr. 30.18–20, quoted at §20). Whereas the frame of reference for the **dikē** of Solon is the actual law code that lies behind the lawgiver's poetry, the **dikē** of Hesiod is enacted by the poetry within which it is dramatized. This convergence of Hesiod's moral teachings with the personification of the teacher himself is clearly more archaic by virtue of being closer to the Indo-European model of legal traditions, as is evident from the comparative evidence of the *Laws of Manu*. So also with the **dikē** of Theognis as proclaimed in verses 543–546 (quoted at §20): what amounts to a personal 'judgment' inside the drama of the poet's life is really 'justice' outside it. Unlike Solon, Theognis has no separate law code that he could proclaim as **dikē** within his poetry. And yet, like Solon, Theognis boasts of rendering **dikē** as if he were some judge (χρή με ... τήνδε δικάσσαι/ ... δίκην: vv. 543–544 quoted at §20): it is as if the sum total of Theognidean poetry, dramatizing the life of Theognis himself, amounted to the rendering of a lawgiver's law code.

§25. Thus Theognis, like Hesiod, is simultaneously a poet and an exponent of law. The figure of Solon, in contrast, goes beyond such a basic Indo-European model, in that he is credited with a written law code that is distinct from his poetry. The figure of Lycurgus represents yet another step beyond this model, in that he is credited with no poetry at all. But even in the traditions about Lycurgus, there are reflexes of an earlier state of affairs. In Plutarch's *Lycurgus* (4.2–3), there is a report of a poet named Thales/Thaletas whom the lawgiver met in Crete (the very place from which his law code is said to have emanated!) and whom he sent to Sparta: the story has it that this

---

§23n2. A detailed account of this interpretation is presented in Nagy 1982.57–64.

Thales seemed like a lyric poet but that the effects of his poetry resembled the effects of the most powerful of **nomothetai** 'lawgivers' (ποιητὴν μὲν δοκοῦντα λυρικῶν μελῶν καὶ πρόσχημα τὴν τέχνην ταύτην πεποιημένον, ἔργῳ δ' ἅπερ οἱ κράτιστοι τῶν νομοθετῶν διαπραττόμενον: 4.2).[1] Specifically, the form and content of his poetry produced social as well as musical harmony (λόγοι γὰρ ἦσαν αἱ ᾠδαὶ πρὸς εὐπείθειαν καὶ ὁμόνοιαν ἀνακλητικοὶ διὰ μελῶν ἅμα καὶ ῥυθμῶν, πολὺ τὸ κόσμιον ἐχόντων καὶ καταστατικόν: 4.3).[2] Hearing his poetry, the citizens of Sparta became less disposed to internal strife (4.3), and in this sense Thales was indeed a forerunner of Lycurgus (προοδοποιεῖν: ibid.).

The Universality of a Poet's Message

§ 26. To repeat: from the internal standpoint of the Lycurgan law code and Theognidean poetry, each was created by one man in response to the strife that afflicted his particular community. In the case of Theognis, this strife in fact constitutes the central drama of the poet's words to Kyrnos in particular and his community in general. To date the strife, however, is as we have seen a difficult matter. In the case of Theognidea 39–52, for example, the historical setting does indeed seem to be that of Megara in the third quarter of the seventh century B.C., that is, before the tyranny of Theagenes.[1] The poet is saying that he fears (v. 39: δέδοικα) the coming of the tyrant. But, as we have also seen,[2] the historical setting of Theognidea 773–782 (cf. 757–764) is Megara at the time of the Persian War in 479 B.C.: the poet is saying that he fears (v. 780: δέδοικ') the heedlessness and **stasis** 'discord' of the Hellenes, occasioned by the Persian host who are pictured as threatening the city (cf. vv. 775–776). Similarly in Theognidea 51, the coming of the tyrant is correlated with the **stasis** (plural) of the Megarians. In light of such conflicting chronological indications, I have already argued that the poetry of Theognis represents a cumulative and accretive response to the evolution of Megara.[3] But I have not yet addressed the problem of how such a response could have come about.

-----

§ 25n1. Cf. also Ephorus *FGH* 70 F 149 at Strabo 10.4.19 C482.

§ 25n2. Cf. Theognis 15–18, discussed above at § 6 in connection with the word **harmoniē** (esp. § 6n1, n5; § 7n1, n2). For the expression **to kosmion** here in Plutarch's narrative, cf. Herodotus 1.65.4 on **kosmos** as the local Spartan word for social order (§ 13).

§ 26n1. Cf. § 14 (and n3) above.

§ 26n2. Again § 14.

§ 26n3. See § 15 above.

§27. The answer, I submit, is to be found in the generalized mode in which social strife is described by the poetry. For example, whereas the original reference of Theognidea 39–52 is doubtless to Theagenes the tyrant of Megara in the late seventh century, this person is not actually named in the poem, and no specifics are given. Though the poet is presented as foreseeing the emergence of a tyrant, the situation is generalized, even universalized:

Κύρνε, κύει πόλις ἥδε, δέδοικα δὲ μὴ τέκῃ ἄνδρα
    εὐθυντῆρα κακῆς ὕβριος ἡμετέρης.   40
ἀστοὶ μὲν γὰρ ἔθ᾽ οἵδε σαόφρονες, ἡγεμόνες δὲ
    τετράφαται πολλὴν εἰς κακότητα πεσεῖν.
οὐδεμίαν πω Κύρν᾽ ἀγαθοὶ πόλιν ὤλεσαν ἄνδρες·
    ἀλλ᾽ ὅταν ὑβρίζειν τοῖσι κακοῖσι ἅδῃ,
δῆμόν τε φθείρωσι δίκας τ᾽ ἀδίκοισι διδῶσιν   45
    οἰκείων κερδέων εἵνεκα καὶ κράτεος,
ἔλπεο μὴ δηρὸν κείνην πόλιν ἀτρεμίεσθαι,
    μηδ᾽ εἰ νῦν κεῖται πολλῇ ἐν ἡσυχίῃ,
εὖτ᾽ ἂν τοῖσι κακοῖσι φίλ᾽ ἀνδράσι ταῦτα γένηται,
    κέρδεα δημοσίῳ σὺν κακῷ ἐρχόμενα.   50
ἐκ τῶν γὰρ στάσιές τε καὶ ἔμφυλοι φόνοι ἀνδρῶν
    μούναρχοί τε· πόλει μήποτε τῇδε ἅδοι.
    Theognis 39–52

Kyrnos, this **polis** is pregnant, and I fear that it will give birth
    to a man
who will be a *straightener* of our base **hubris**.
The citizens here are still moderate, but the *leaders* [**hēgemones**]
have veered so much as to fall into *debasement* [**kakotēs**].
Men who are **agathoi**, Kyrnos, have never *yet* ruined any **polis**,
but when the **kakoi** decide to *behave with outrage* [**hubris**],
and when they ruin the **dēmos** and render *judgments* [**dikai**] in favor of
    the *unjust* [i.e., persons or things without **dikē**],
for the sake of private *gain* [**kerdos** plural], and for the sake of power,
do not expect that **polis** to be peaceful for long,
not even if it is now in a state of great *serenity* [**hēsukhiē**],
when the *base* [**kakoi**] decide on these things,
namely, private *gains* [**kerdos** plural] entailing *public* damage.
From these things arise *discord* [**stasis** plural], intestine *killings* [**phonoi**]
    of men,
and *tyrants* [**mounarkhoi**].[1] May this **polis** never decide to adopt these
    things!

---

§27n1. On **mounarkhos** as an attenuated synonym of **turannos** 'tyrant', see the equation in Herodotus 3.80.2/4.

So universalized is this picture that the description of the emerging tyrant is expressed in words that would be appropriate for describing the Athenian lawgiver Solon in Solon's own poetry. The tyrant of Megara will be 'a straightener of our base **hubris**', says Theognis to Kyrnos (v. 40), and the wording is parallel to the 'straight **dikē**' that Solon hands down by way of his laws (εὐθεῖαν ... δίκην: Solon fr. 30.19 GP [= fr. 36 W]). We must also compare the **eunomiē** 'good government' of Solon (fr. 3.32 GP [= fr. 4 W]), which makes everything 'cohesive' (32: ἄρτια) and 'endowed with good **kosmos**' (32: εὔκοσμα); most important, it also 'scorches **hubris**' (34: ὕβριν ἀμαυροῖ) and 'straightens crooked judgments [**dikai**]' (36: εὐθύνει δὲ δίκας σκολιάς)—themes that match those of Theognidea 40.

§ 28. Now the **hubris** condemned by Solon in the just-cited verse 34 of fragment 3 (and at verse 8 as well) is that of the rich, not of the poor: as Aristotle points out in his *Constitution of the Athenians*, the **stasis** 'conflict' that leads to the emergence of Solon as lawgiver (5.2) is consistently blamed by Solon on the rich (5.3: καὶ οὕτως αἰεὶ τὴν αἰτίαν τῆς στάσεως ἀνάπτει τοῖς πλουσίοις). This is not to say that Solon was a one-sided champion of democracy (see Aristotle *Constitution* 11.2–12.1, containing Solon fr. 7 GP [= fr. 5 W]), but the point is that **hubris** and **stasis** are in the diction of Solon catchwords for the excesses of an oligarchy (fr. 3.8/34 GP [= fr. 6 W] and fr. 3.19 GP [= fr. 4 W], respectively).

§ 29. I thus disagree with the view that **hēgemones** 'leaders', as at Solon frr. 3.7 and 8.1 GP [= frr. 4 and 6 W], means 'popular leaders', that is, champions of democracy.[1] Rather, it is a catchword for 'government' (as clearly at 8.1), even in the combination **dēmou** ... **hēgemones** (as at 3.7).[2] The word **dēmos** here bears the older and simpler meaning of 'community' (cf. **dēmosios** 'public, pertaining to the whole community' as at Solon fr. 3.26).[3] So also at Theognis 39–52: the **hēgemones** (41) represent the elite of society before the coming of the **euthuntēr** 'straightener, regulator' (40). We know from the hindsight of Aristotle that the society of Megara was oligar-

---

§29n1. See West 1974.68.
§29n2. I follow here the persuasive argumentation of Donlan 1970.388–390 on the Solonian dichotomy of **hēgemones** and **dēmos** (= the whole **polis** minus the **hēgemones**) and on Aristotle's misunderstanding of this dichotomy (as in *Constitution of the Athenians* 12). In Solonian usage, the **dēmos** includes, but is not composed of, the poorest citizens.
§29n3. See Donlan pp.392–393n26.

chical when Theagenes came to power (cf. *Politics* 1305a24; *Rhetoric* 1357b33), and we would expect the elite of this society to be the **agathoi** 'nobles', 'but the leaders [**hēgemones**] have veered so as to fall into debasement [**kakotēs**]' (43): in other words, the elite are now **kakoi** instead of **agathoi**, and the poet actually refers to them as **kakoi** (44). The reasoning is that they *must* be **kakoi**, since **agathoi** have never yet brought about the ruin of a city (43).[4] These **kakoi** are described as embracing **hubris** (44), thereby destroying the **dēmos** 'community' (45) and perverting **dikē** (45) for the sake of **kerdos** 'private gain' (46). The poet repeats that their personal gain entails the ruin of the **dēmos** (50), and he sums up by recounting the inevitable results of the decadence of the elite. These results are **stasis** (plural) 'conflicts' (51), **phonoi** 'killings' (51), and **mounarkhoi** (52)—the poet's attenuated word for tyrants.[5]

§ 30. We now see that Theognis is no one-sided champion of the elite as represented by an oligarchy, any more than Solon is a one-sided champion of democracy. Although Theognis dreads the emergence of a tyrant, such a man is still described as one who regulates the excesses of an oligarchy. And it is precisely the excesses of an oligarchy that lead to **stasis** (plural), **phonoi**, and **mounarkhoi**. Nowhere is this clearer than in the Herodotean account of the words spoken by the Persian king Darius blaming oligarchy and praising tyranny:

ἐν δὲ ὀλιγαρχίῃ πολλοῖσι ἀρετὴν ἐπασκέουσι ἐς τὸ κοινὸν ἔχθεα ἴδια ἰσχυρὰ φιλέει ἐγγίνεσθαι· αὐτὸς γὰρ ἕκαστος βουλόμενος κορυφαῖος εἶναι γνώμῃσί τε νικᾶν ἐς ἔχθεα μεγάλα ἀλλήλοισι ἀπικνέονται, ἐξ ὧν

---

§29n4. Besides the ostentatiously proleptic πω 'yet' here at verse 43, cf. also ἔτι 'still' at 41 and νῦν 'now' at 48. In the passage following verses 39–52 of Theognis, verses 53–68, the emergence of the **kakoi** is envisioned differently: instead of happening from within, it is now seen as happening from without. This time, the **kakoi** are seen as newcomers to the community, outsiders who replace the genuine **agathoi**. The **agathoi** are in turn put into the position of **kakoi**. As Gerber 1970.277 points out, the description of skin-wearing savages who used to live outside the community is parallel to the image of the Cyclopes: note the correspondence between Theognis 54 (these savages know neither **dikai** nor **nomoi** '[legislated] laws') and *Odyssey* ix 215 (the Cyclops knows neither **dikai** nor **themistes** '[divine] laws'). The **kakoi** turn the community inside out (Theognis 56–57), upside down (Theognis 679). On the fluctuating usage of **agathos** 'noble' and **kakos** 'base' in the original sociopolitical sense (upper class vs. lower class) and in the evolving ethical sense (good vs. bad), see Cerri 1968; also §30n1 and §39n2. In line with the ethical sense, the **agathoi** can become **kakoi** and embrace **hubris** simply by being exposed to **kakoi** (Theognis 305–308; cf. 317–318). On the image of the uncivilized person as clad in animal skins, see Renehan 1975.69 s.v. "**diphtheriās**."

§29n5. See §27n1.

στάσιες ἐγγίνονται, ἐκ δὲ τῶν στασίων φόνος, ἐκ δὲ τοῦ φόνου ἀπέβη ἐς
μουναρχίην, καὶ ἐν τούτῳ διέδεξε ὅσῳ ἐστὶ τοῦτο ἄριστον.
Herodotus 3.82.3

But in an oligarchy, where many men are competing for achievement
[aretē] in public life,[1] intense personal hatreds are bound to break out. For
each of them wants to be on top and to have his proposals win the day,
and so they end up having great hatreds against each other. From which
arise *conflicts* [**stasis** plural], from which arises *killing* [**phonos**], from
which in turn it all comes down to *monarchy* [**mounarkhiē**]—and in this
there is proof how superior is monarchy![2]

§31. In much the same way as Theognis, Solon dramatizes himself
within a time frame that gives him the opportunity to prophesy the
emergence of the tyrant Peisistratos: in verses 3–4 of fr. 12 GP [= fr.
9 W], the poet says that the **polis** has been debased from the status
of **andres megaloi** 'great men' into one of servitude to a **monarkhos**,
and these verses are quoted by Diodorus (9.20.2) as a **khrēsmos**
'prophecy' in which the lawgiver had anticipated the tyranny. In the
verses that immediately follow, Solon's own words make it clear that
the assertion about the city's debasement, expressed in the aorist
(ἔπεσεν, v. 4) is in fact presented as a thing of the future, something
that could still be prevented:

λίαν δ' ἐξάραντ' <οὐ> ῥᾴδιόν ἐστι κατασχεῖν
ὕστερον, ἀλλ' ἤδη χρή <τινα> πάντα νοεῖν.
Solon fr. 12.5–6 GP [= fr. 9 W]

It is a difficult thing to hold down someone who has risen too far up,
once it has happened, but now is the time for someone to take all pre-
cautions.

§32. In short, Theognis finds aristocratic values amiss within the society that we identify with the oligarchy that preceded the tyranny in

---

§30n1. Cf. Theognis 401–406: The man who is too eager for **aretē** 'achievement' (402–403: πολλάκι δ' εἰς ἀρετήν/σπεύδει), and seeks **kerdos** 'personal gain'
(403: κέρδος διζήμενος), commits a grave error (404); his divine punishment is that he
thinks that **kaka** 'base things' are **agatha** 'noble' (405) and vice versa (406). We see
here the ideological basis for an ethical characterization of upper classes debased by
greed, in terms that suit a sociopolitical characterization of lower classes debased by
poverty. On **kerdos** 'personal gain' as a correlate of **hubris**, see Theognis 835; cf. also
kerdos at Theognis 46 and 50.
 §30n2. Cf. also the speech of Otanes praising democracy and blaming tyranny
(Herodotus 3.80.2–6) and the speech of Megabuxos praising oligarchy and blaming
democracy (3.81.1–3). In each instance of blame, **hubris** is prominently mentioned:
four times in the speech of Otanes, three times in the speech of Megabuxos.

Megara. The **euthuntēr** 'regulator' of "our base **hubris**" (κακῆς ὕβριος ἡμετέρης) at Theognis 40 will be regulating the excesses perpetrated by the base men [**kakoi**] who would be constituents of such an oligarchy. Of course, the word **hubris** can implicitly apply to constituents of a democracy or to a tyrant as well.[1] In fact, there is a doublet of Theognis 39–42 where it is clearly the emerging tyrant who is the exponent of **hubris**:

Κύρνε, κύει πόλις ἥδε, δέδοικα δὲ μὴ τέκῃ ἄνδρα
  ὑβριστήν, χαλεπῆς ἡγεμόνα στάσιος·
ἀστοὶ μὲν γὰρ ἔασι[2] σαόφρονες, ἡγεμόνες δὲ
  τετράφαται πολλὴν εἰς κακότητα πεσεῖν.
  Theognis 1081–1082b

Kyrnos, this **polis** is pregnant, and I fear that it will give birth to a man who is a *perpetrator of outrage* [**hubris**], a *leader* [**hēgemōn**] of dire *discord* [**stasis**].
The citizens are moderate, but the *leaders* [**hēgemones**] have veered so much as to fall into *debasement* [**kakotēs**].

These verses seem to concern the same figure that we have seen in the doublet at verses 39–42, but the perspective is different: whereas the **hēgemones** 'leaders' of verse 1082a may again represent the exponents of an oligarchy who are themselves base and therefore implicitly marked by **hubris**, the **hēgemōn** of verse 1082, representing the single exponent of a tyranny, is also marked by **hubris**—and this time the marking is explicit. The tyrant will be a perpetrator, not a regulator, of **hubris**. Whereas verses 1081–1082b are one-sidedly negative about the emerging tyrant, verses 39–42 reveal a more even-handed—one might say "Solonian"—stance.[3]

Theognis or Theognidea?

§33. In this connection I can offer an alternative to the theories of Martin West about Theognis verses 1–1022, which contain the doublet describing the tyrant as a regulator of **hubris** (39–42), and verses 1023–1220, which contain the doublet describing the tyrant as an ex-

---

§32n1. Cf. §30n2.
§32n2. West's edition accepts the manuscript variant ἔθ᾽ οἵδε, which makes verse 1081 match 41 exactly. I see no reason, however, to reject the independent manuscript reading, ἔασι: in view of its independence from verse 41, it seems the *lectio difficilior*.
§32n3. Cf. Donlan 1970.393n27, who uses "Solonian" to describe the contents of Theognis 945–946, 947–948. On the inherited affinities of Theognidean poetry with the ideologies of lawgivers, see §§11–14, 20–25 above.

ponent of **hubris** (1081–1082b). West argues that these two stretches of the Theognidea represent selections from a larger corpus, no longer extant, in which topically similar passages tended to be arranged one after the other.[1] This argument is defended on the basis of test cases where West finds strong topical correspondences between a given string of passages taken from verses 1–1022, a stretch that he calls Excerpta Meliora, and another string of passages taken from verses 1023–1220, a stretch that he calls Excerpta Deteriora.[2] Only occasionally do the correspondences between one given stanza from the Meliora and one from the Deteriora involve actual doublets (e.g., 619–620/1114a–b), which suggests to West that the larger corpus was in fact much larger than either of the two Excerpta—so much so that it contained for most topics a generous sample of similar stanzas running one after another.[3] Thus, if both Excerpta tended to select, say, just one representative stanza from each repetitive string of topically similar passages, the chances that both Excerpta would select the same representative passage from a given string would be relatively low. Whenever the same passage is selected by both hypothetical Excerpta, however, West believes that the doublet from verses 1–1022 tends to be superior and that from verses 1023–1220, inferior: hence his terms Meliora and Deteriora.[4] And yet West himself points out that the so-called Deteriora tend to follow the apparent sequence of the larger corpus more faithfully than the so-called Meliora.[5] Moreover, West is at times forced to argue that a given version of the Deteriora is in fact superior to that of the Meliora (e.g., 1109 vs. 53–57).[6] I suggest, therefore, that we abandon the notion that the Meliora and Deteriora are superior and inferior editions stemming from the same larger corpus. Instead, I shall now argue that the so-called Meliora and Deteriora are excerpts from *different phases* of the Theognidean poetic tradition.

§34. As we address the question of different phases, we should not exclude from consideration the passages in the Theognidea that have

---

§33n1. See West 1974.40–61, esp. p.54; he further subdivides verses 1–1022 into 1–254 and 255–1022. On the subdivision 1–254, see also Gronewald 1975.

§33n2. Cf. West p.54: "The associative thread running through successive excerpts is strengthened, not weakened, when the parallel sequences [i.e., from the Meliora and Deteriora] are interwoven, which is what is to be expected if such integration takes us nearer the original, however many gaps remain."

§33n3. Cf. the repetitive string of topically similar Attic skolia preserved by Athenaeus 694C and following (= *Carmina Convivialia* frr. 884ff. Page).

§33n4. West 1974.54.

§33n5. West pp.54–55.

§33n6. West p.150.

generally been deemed to be excerpts from Solon and other masters of elegiac poetry. In West's edition of the Theognidea, the passages in question are: 153–154/Solon fr. 8.3–4 GP [= fr. 6 W]; 227–232/ Solon fr. 1.71–76 GP [= fr. 13 W]; 315–318/Solon fr. 6. (1–4) GP [= fr. 15 W]; 585–590/Solon fr. 1.65–70 GP [= fr. 13 W]; 719–728/ Solon fr. 18. (1–10) GP [= fr. 24 W]; 795–796/Mimnermus fr. 12. (1–2) GP [= fr. 7 W]; 1003–1006/Tyrtaeus fr. 9.13–16 GP [=fr. 12 W]; 1017–1022/Mimnermus fr. 12. (1–2) GP [= fr. 4.4–6 W].[1] I propose that the sharing of doublets in the textual traditions of two distinct poets, as also in that of a single elegiac poet such as Theognis, cannot be dismissed as merely a matter of textual transposition.[2] As the evidence collected by Pietro Giannini and others strongly suggests, formulaic behavior characterizes the diction of not only Theognis but also Solon, Tyrtaeus, Mimnermus, and all the other poets of archaic elegiac.[3] Moreover, the formulas of elegiac pentameter are independent from, though cognate with, those of Homeric and Hesiodic hexameter.[4] Any given sharing of doublets in Theognis, or in Theognis and another given elegiac poet—even when the match is several verses in length—can be ascribed to the workings of oral poetry, where we can expect parallel topics to be handled with parallel sequences of thematic development, which in turn will be expressed with remarkably parallel formulaic patterns. In what follows, I shall try briefly to make a case for this assertion.

§35. Wherever we come upon doublets in the corpus of extant elegiac poetry, the few formal divergences in the doublet are as revealing as the many formal convergences, since the divergent wording of each doublet in any given pair of doublets can be shown to be as much a part of a formulaic system as the convergent wording. Let us consider, for example, the following pair of doublets, with underlines indicating the divergent wording:[1]

τίκτει γὰρ κόρος ὕβριν, ὅταν πολὺς ὄλβος ἔπηται
ἀνθρώποις ὁπόσοις μὴ νόος ἄρτιος ᾖ.
    Solon fr. 8.3–4 GP [= fr. 6 W]

---

§34n1. For an articulation of the view that these passages in the Theognidea are excerpts from other poets, see, e.g., West 1974.40; cf. Legon 1981.107.

§34n2. In the case of Theognis 153–154/Solon fr. 8.3–4 GP [= fr. 6 W], we note that Clement (*Stromateis* 6.8.7) ascribes each doublet to the respective poet, even pointing out the differences in wording between the two.

§34n3. Giannini 1973; cf. also the Appendix by Greenberg in this volume.

§34n4. See again Giannini and Greenberg; also Nagy 1979b.

§35n1. For translations of the two passages that follow, see §48 below.

τίκτει τοι κόρος ὕβριν, ὅταν κακῷ ὄλβος ἕπηται
ἀνθρώπῳ καὶ ὅτῳ μὴ νόος ἄρτιος ᾖ.
Theognis 153–154

Where the Solonian ... ὄλβος ἕπηται / ἀνθρώποις ὁπόσοις ... (the sign / indicates verse-boundary) diverges from the Theognidean ... ὄλβος ἕπηται / ἀνθρώπῳ καὶ ὅτῳ ..., it converges with another Theognidean string of phraseology in the same metrical context: ... ὄλβιος οὐδεὶς / ἀνθρώπων ὁπόσους ... (Theognis 167–168). Similarly, where the Theognidean ... καὶ ὅτῳ μὴ νόος ἄρτιος ᾖ / diverges from the Solonian ... ὁπόσοις μὴ νόος ἄρτιος ᾖ /, it converges with the Theognidean ... ὅτῳ μή τις ἔνεστι δόλος / (Theognis 416 / 1164f) and ... καί σοι πιστὸς ἔνεστι νόος / (Theognis 88 / 1082d). Again, where the Solonian ... ὅταν πολὺς ὄλβος ἕπηται / diverges from the Theognidean ... ὅταν κακῷ ὄλβος ἕπηται / (note too the position of κακῷ at Theognis 151), it converges with the Solonian ... ὅτῳ πολὺς ἄργυρός ἐστι / (Solon fr. 18.1 GP [= 24 W] / Theognis 719).

§ 36. One may infer from the comparative evidence of typological parallels, to be cited below, that such patterns of phraseological convergence and divergence in parallel passages ascribed to different poets, or even in textual variants of the same poem, are a reflex of the workings of oral poetry. In oral poetry, a given "poem" is at least to some degree recomposed with every performance.[1] Of course, the degree of phraseological variation in recomposition will depend not only on the repertoire of the poet but also on the fixity or fluidity of conventions in a given poetic tradition. In situations where the conventions are fluid, however, even the factor of writing may not be sufficient to effect an immediate fixation of the text, provided that the factor of performance is still present. The given poem may become a text by way of writing, but surviving traditions of performance can leave their mark on each copy of the text: specifically, phraseological variants will reflect an ongoing process of recomposition-in-performance. Striking typological parallels are available in formulaic studies of classical Arabic and Persian poetry.[2] Closer to

§36n1. On the concept of recomposition-in-performance, see Lord 1960, esp. pp.13–29.

§36n2. Zwettler 1978, esp. ch.4, "Variation and Attribution in the Tradition of Classical Arabic Poetry"; Davidson 1983.158–200. Taking a sample passage from Firdawsī's *Shāhnāmah*, Davidson demonstrates that "every word in this given passage can be generated on the basis of parallel phraseology expressing parallel themes" in the rest of the corpus (p.181); significantly, the same goes for every major textual variant in this passage.

home, one may look to the *Chanson de Roland*, where three of the oldest manuscript versions share not a single identical verse.[3]

§37. I suggest, then, that the differences between doublets in attested Greek elegiac poetry reflect for the most part not editorial deterioration in one direction or another but formulaic versatility corresponding to different compositional needs. Moreover, the factor of ongoing recomposition in oral poetry could even account for the attestation of the "same" poem at different phases of its evolution. For example, verses 39–42 of Theognis about the tyrant as regulator of **hubris** may represent a response to the situation of Megara in the third quarter of the seventh century B.C., but such a response is more appropriate to a phase of the tradition sometime after 550 B.C., if we accept this date as the terminus for the beginning of a "moderate" oligarchy in Megara.[1] As for verses 1081–1082b of Theognis, they may represent the "same" poem in a different phase of Megarian history. Moreover, this phase may in theory be earlier rather than later. The absence of what I have called a "Solonian" stance in these verses suggests a phase of development that is more provincial, less pan-Hellenic, in orientation.[2] It is worth observing in this regard that in West's edition of Theognis, all the cited "excerpts" from Solon and other elegiac poets occur in the so-called Meliora, not the Deteriora. This convergence suggests that the stretch of Theognidean poetry called Meliora by West has topically more in common with the pan-Hellenic orientation found in Solon, Tyrtaeus, Mimnermus, and the rest. I should stress, however, that there is as yet no proof for a chronological distinction in formulaic behavior between the so-called Meliora and Deteriora of Theognis—it is just that the Deteriora have topically less in common with this pan-Hellenic orientation and perhaps reflect an orientation more idiosyncratic to Megara.

§38. Whether or not some poems in the corpus of Theognidea are more provincial than others, however, the fact remains that they all

---

§36n3. Menéndez Pidal 1960.60–63. Cf. Zwettler p.207; Davidson p.182. As for factors that make poetic conventions less fluid, Zwettler offers the following useful summary (pp.207–208): "Within a given society, factors of control over the transmission may exist, such as formal instruction; social, political, material, or religious sanctions and rewards; mnemonic devices of various sorts; or, quite significantly, the formal and internal structure of the testimony itself."

§37n1. For evidence on the terminus of 550 B.C., see Oost 1973.195n33; for a different opinion (ca. 580 instead of 550 B.C.), see Legon 1981.134.

§37n2. On pan-Hellenism as a relative rather than an absolute concept, see §17n3.

exhibit a tendency toward a pan-Hellenic perspective, in that local idiosyncrasies of the **polis** are shaded over, and the universal aspects of any given situation, such as the advent of a tyrant, are highlighted.[1] In their surviving forms, neither verses 39–52 (quoted at §27) nor 1081–1082b (quoted at §32) of Theognis need to refer specifically to Theagenes, tyrant of Megara. Either can apply to a wide variety of political situations in a wide variety of city-states.

Decadence in a City, Debasement of Mankind

§39. The exponent of **hubris** may shift from oligarch to tyrant to democrat, but one thing remains constant in the poetry of Theognis: the poet himself is always an exponent of **dikē**.[1] And he is thereby always an opponent of **hubris**. For example, the verses in which Theognis declares that he must render **dikē** evenhandedly to both sides (543–546, quoted at §20) are immediately preceded by verses warning against **hubris**—verses that may well have been linked with those following to form one passage:

δειμαίνω μὴ τήνδε πόλιν Πολυπαΐδη ὕβρις
ἥ περ Κενταύρους ὠμοφάγους ὀλέσῃ.
Theognis 541–542

I fear, son of Polypaos, that *outrage* [**hubris**] will destroy this city
—the same outrage that destroyed the Centaurs, eaters of raw flesh.[2]

---

§38n1. A historical reason for the eventual pan-Hellenization of Megarian poetic traditions may well be found in the patterns of archaic Megarian colonization as described by Figueira Ch.5 §21. Cf. also Svenbro 1982.958: His description of navigating Megarian colonists as "cette polis à la recherche d'une terre" can be compared with the image of the ship of state in Theognis 667–682 (§1 above).

§39n1. By the same token, even a tyrant may in theory be an exponent of **dikē**. See Ford Ch.3 for a discussion of the gnomic poetry of the Peisistratid Hipparchus, tyrant of Athens. (Compare too the verse associated with Hipparchus in Herodotus 5.56.1, which is parallel to [e.g.] Theognis 1029.) In this light, we may consider the parallel meanings of **Theognis** and **Theāgenēs**: 'he whose **genos** [breeding] is from the god(s)' (cf. §§43–44 below). It is as if the words of Theognis could have been, in one phase of the poetic tradition, the words of Theagenes the tyrant. Verses 39–42 of Theognis would represent a later phase, of course, in that the poet and the tyrant are here distinct. Still, although the poet deplores the emergence of tyranny in these verses, the social corrections undertaken by the tyrant are described in words that could just as well have described the social corrections undertaken by Solon (see §27 above).

§39n2. Cf. Apollodorus 2.5.4: the Centaur Pholos offers roast meat to his guest Herakles, while he himself eats his own portions of meat raw (αὐτὸς δὲ ὠμοῖς ἐχρῆτο). Cf. the description that could apply to debased aristocrats in language that suits the Cyclopes at Theognis 53–58 (discussed at §29n4).

Likewise in the doublets 39–42 (§27) and 1081–1082b (§32): the **hēgemones** 'leaders' of Megara are blamed for their explicit and implicit **hubris** respectively, which in turn signals the degeneration of the **agathoi** into **kakoi**.[3] The focus of blame is on the tyrant rather than the oligarchy in 1081–1082b, but even in this variant the **hubris** of the tyrant was implicitly made possible by the **hubris** of the debased elite who were **hēgemones** 'leaders' before him.

§40. In the traditions of other Greek city-states as well, the prime manifestation of **hubris** is consistently to be found among the rich and powerful elite. The most striking example is the following description of the Colophonians by the poet Mimnermus, who includes himself among them:

> ἐς δ᾽ ἐρατὴν Κολοφῶνα βίην ὑπέροπλον ἔχοντες
> ἑζόμεθ᾽, ἀργαλέης ὕβριος ἡγεμόνες.
> Mimnermus fr. 3.3–4 GP [= fr. 9 W]

... and we, men of overweening violence [**biē**], settled lovely Colophon, we *leaders* [**hēgemones**] of baneful *outrage* [**hubris**].

The expression Κολοφωνία ὕβρις 'Colophonian **hubris**' is in fact proverbial (*CPG* I p. 266.6–7). There is further testimony about the **hubris** of this city in Athenaeus (526C), who reports that it resulted in **turannis** 'tyranny' and **stasis** [plural] 'discord'. This theme recalls Theognis 51–52 (quoted at §27), where the **hubris** of Megara leads to **stasis** [plural] and **mounarkhoi**. In the case of the Colophonians, the prime manifestation of their **hubris** was the **truphē** 'luxuriance' of excessive wealth, in the words of Athenaeus (526A),[1] who quotes in this context Xenophanes fr. 3 GP [and W]: in the poet's sensual description, the decadent Colophonians are said to have learned **habrosunē** [plural] 'luxuriance' from the quintessentially decadent Lydians (v. 1), while the city was still free from **turanniē** 'tyranny' (v. 2).[2] What ultimately destroyed Colophon was of course **hubris**, and herein lies the lesson for Megara:

---

§39n3. Cf. §§29, 32.

§40n1. Cf. also Aristotle *Politics* 1290b14, who says that the actual majority of Colophonians had great wealth.

§40n2. For Sappho, her love of (**h**)**abrosunā** 'luxuriance' is equated with her 'lust for the sun' (ἔρος τὠελίω: fr. 58.25–26 V/LP). On the relevance of this theme to the figure of Adonis, who is himself (**h**)**abros** 'luxuriant' (fr. 140 V/LP), cf. §50 below; also Nagy 1973.172–177.

ὕβρις καὶ Μάγνητας ἀπώλεσε καὶ Κολοφῶνα
καὶ Σμύρνην· πάντως Κύρνε καὶ ὕμμ' ἀπολεῖ.
Theognis 1103–1104

Outrage [hubris] has destroyed the Magnesians[3] and Colophon
and Smyrna; and it will completely destroy you [plural] too,
Kyrnos!

Just as Mimnermus includes himself among the Colophonians when
he calls them 'men of overweening violence [biē]' and 'leaders [hē-
gemones] of hubris' (above), so also Theognis here includes Kyrnos among the Megarians who will be destroyed by hubris. The
destruction of Megara, the poet warns, will be caused by its own
elite:

πάντα τάδ' ἐν κοράκεσσι καὶ ἐν φθόρῳ· οὐδέ τις ἥμιν
αἴτιος ἀθανάτων Κύρνε θεῶν μακάρων,
ἀλλ' ἀνδρῶν τε βίη καὶ κέρδεα δειλὰ καὶ ὕβρις
πολλῶν ἐξ ἀγαθῶν ἐς κακότητ' ἔβαλεν.
Theognis 833–836

Everything here has gone to the ravens and perdition. And
not one of the immortal and blessed gods is responsible to us for this,
Kyrnos,
but the violence [biē] of men and their baneful private interests [kerdos
plural][4] and their outrage [hubris]
have plummeted them from much nobility [polla agatha] into debasement [kakotēs].[5]

§41. The kakotēs 'baseness, debasement' of the elite literally shipwrecks the ship of state:

πολλάκις ἡ πόλις ἥδε δι' ἡγεμόνων κακότητα
ὥσπερ κεκλιμένη ναῦς παρὰ γῆν ἔδραμεν.
Theognis 855–856

Often has this polis, because of the baseness [kakotēs] of the leaders
[hēgemones],
run aground like a veering[1] ship.

---

§40n3. Cf. also Theognis 603–604.
§40n4. Cf. kerdos 'private interest' at Theognis 46/50 (quoted at §27); for
more on kerdos, see §30n1.
§40n5. Cf. Theognis 42 and 1082b, as discussed at §39.
§41n1. On klīnomai in the sense of 'veer', cf. Theognis 946; see also §58.

The wording here once more recalls Theognis verses 41–42 (quoted at §27) and 1082a–1082b (quoted at §32), where the **hēgemones** 'leaders' are described as falling into **kakotēs** 'debasement' at a time when the citizens-at-large are still **saophrones** 'moderate'.

§42. From this survey of the word **hubris** in Theognis, it is now evident that Kyrnos himself is typical of the debased elite who 'often' bring the ship of state to ruin. The word πολλάκις 'often' at Theognis 855 (§41) even suggests that these **hēgemones** 'leaders' as well as the figure of Kyrnos himself are generic, much as is the figure of Theognis himself. Whereas Theognis is an exponent of **dikē** (§§20, 39), the fickle young Kyrnos is included, at Theognis verse 1104 (quoted at §40), among the elite who are exponents of **hubris**.[1]

§43. Kyrnos is not only typical of the debased elite: his very name tells the tale. In Hesychius, the word **kurnos** in the plural is glossed as meaning 'bastard' (κύρνοι· νόθοι).[1] In order to understand the semantics, it is helpful to adduce the words **agathos** and **kakos**, which originally had the genetic connotation of high-born and low-born, respectively—but which are used in the diction of Theognis to designate one who is intrinsically noble or base, regardless of birth (e.g., vv. 53–58).[2] Just as the **kakotēs** 'baseness' of the **hēgemones** 'leaders' belies their birthright as **agathoi**, so also with **Kurnos**: he may be noble by birth, but his name still proclaims that he is 'base' and a 'bastard'. And the cause of his decadence and reduction to baseness is built into his father's name: the man who made Kyrnos a bastard is a man of excessive wealth. The patronymic Πολυπαΐδης means 'son of **Polu-pāos**'.[3] This form **Polu-pāos** 'he who has acquired much' is composed of the same formal elements—**polu-** 'much' and **pā-omai** 'acquire'—that are used in the diction of Theognis to designate the generic rich man:

---

§42n1. Moreover, since Theognis considers himself **philos** toward Kyrnos (cf. §44 below), he includes even himself at verse 40 (quoted at §27) when he calls the **hubris** of the Megarians 'ours' (ὕβριος ἡμετέρης).

§43n1. The word may be non-Indo-European in origin: cf. Solmsen 1909.104. But see Forssman 1980.

§43n2. On which cf. §29n4 above. Note especially Theognis 305–308: being **kakos** is contagious!

§43n3. On the use of patronymics to designate the primary characteristic of a generic figure: Nagy 1979.146n2. For an extensive collection of forms, see Sulzberger 1926 (some of the article's basic assumptions, however, are questionable). Of course, the name **Polu-pāos** may simply be an epithet—one that may be appropriate to Herakles himself (cf. §14).

... ὃς μάλα πολλὰ πέπαται
Theognis 663
... he who has acquired much.

Now excessive wealth, to repeat, is a prime manifestation of **hubris**. As it turns out, it also makes men bastards. Theognis shows the decadence of Megara by telling how **ploutos** 'wealth' has made bastards out of everyone:

κριοὺς μὲν καὶ ὄνους διζήμεθα Κύρνε καὶ ἵππους
   εὐγενέας, καί τις βούλεται ἐξ ἀγαθῶν
βήσεσθαι· γῆμαι δὲ κακὴν κακοῦ οὐ μελεδαίνει   185
   ἐσθλὸς ἀνήρ, ἤν οἱ χρήματα πολλὰ διδῷ,
οὐδὲ γυνὴ κακοῦ ἀνδρὸς ἀναίνεται εἶναι ἄκοιτις
   πλουσίου, ἀλλ᾽ ἀφνεὸν βούλεται ἀντ᾽ ἀγαθοῦ.
χρήματα μὲν τιμῶσι· καὶ ἐκ κακοῦ ἐσθλὸς ἔγημε
   καὶ κακὸς ἐξ ἀγαθοῦ· πλοῦτος ἔμειξε γένος.   190
οὕτω μὴ θαύμαζε γένος Πολυπαΐδη ἀστῶν
   μαυροῦσθαι· σὺν γὰρ μίσγεται ἐσθλὰ κακοῖς.
Theognis 183–192

We seek to have, Kyrnos, rams, asses, and horses
that are *purebred* [with good **genos**], and everyone wants to breed them
   from stock that are noble [**agathoi**],
but a noble [**esthlos**] man does not worry about marrying a base [**kakē**]
   woman born of a base [**kakos**] man,
so long as the base [**kakos**] man gives him many *possessions* [**khrēmata**],
nor does a woman refuse to be the wife of a base [**kakos**] man
who has wealth, but she wants a rich husband instead of one who is
   noble [**agathos**].
Men give honor to *possessions* [**khrēmata**]. And one who is noble [**esthlos**] marries the daughter of one who is base [**kakos**],
while one who is base [**kakos**] marries the daughter of one who is noble
   [**agathos**]. Wealth [**ploutos**] has mixed up the *breeding* [**genos**].
So do not be surprised, son of Polypaos, that the *breeding* [**genos**] of the
   citizens is being blackened.
For whatever is noble [**esthla**] is mixed up with whatever is base [**kaka**].[4]

The mixing up of good breeding [**genos**] by **ploutos** 'wealth' corresponds to the fathering of a youth named **Kurnos** 'bastard' by **Polupāos**, the one 'who has acquired much'.[5]

---

§43n4. It is clear in this passage that **esthlos** (cf. §8n2) is throughout synonymous with **agathos**.

§43n5. Cf. the patronymic Ὕρραος assigned at Alcaeus fr. 129.13 V/LP to Pittakos. The variant Ὕρράδιος, as attested in Callimachus *Epigram* 1.2, is glossed in

§44. Perhaps one may find a way to think it touching that **Theo-gn-is**, a man whose name proclaims that his **genos** is from the gods, is also a man who loves this Kyrnos—thereby also showing his love for Megara through the ages, however debased it may become. This love, however, is not properly reciprocated: Kyrnos loves Theognis only in word, not in deed (vv. 253–254, quoted at §16), and this theme moves the poet to issue a challenge:

> μή μ᾽ ἔπεσιν μὲν στέργε, νόον δ᾽ ἔχε καὶ φρένας ἄλλας.
> εἰ με φιλεῖς καί σοι πιστὸς ἔνεστι νόος,
> ἀλλὰ φίλει καθαρὸν θέμενος νόον, ἤ μ᾽ ἀποειπὼν
> ἔχθαιρ᾽ ἐμφανέως νεῖκος ἀειράμενος.
> οὕτω χρὴ τόν γ᾽ ἐσθλὸν ἐπιστρέψαντα νόημα
> ἔμπεδον αἰὲν ἔχειν ἐς τέλος ἀνδρὶ φίλῳ.
> Theognis 1082c–1084[1]

Do not love me merely in word while you have a different intent [noos] and feelings.
If *you are a friend* [**philos**][2] *to me* and have a trustworthy intent [noos] within,
then *be a friend* [**philos**], having an intent [noos] that is pure. Otherwise, deny me
and be my enemy [**ekhthros**], overtly taking on a *quarrel* [neikos].
This is the way a man who is noble [**esthlos**] must direct his intention [**noēma**][3]
and keep it steadfast and consequential always for the man who is a *friend* [**philos**] to him.

The challenge, of course, is never answered, and the **neikos** 'quarrel' between Theognis and Kyrnos never becomes overt. The bond of being **philoi** that exists between Theognis and Kyrnos—as well as all Megara by extension—is never completely severed.

§45. Of course, a poet may give well-intended advice even to those who have indeed severed the bond of being **philoi** to him. The poet Hesiod, for example, formally declares that there is a **neikos** 'quarrel' between himself and his brother Perses (*WD* 35)—a **neikos** that

---

Hesychius as ἀπό τινος τῶν προγόνων ἄδοξος ἤ εἰκαῖος—i.e., a man of dubious paternity. In Alcaeus fr. 348.1 V/LP, Pittakos is called **kakopatridās** 'having base paternity'; cf. also fr. 72.11–13 V/LP, where someone is ridiculed for being the son of a seemingly low-born woman.
§44n1. Cf. also the doublet of 1082c–1082f at Theognis 87–90.
§44n2. On the semantics of **philos/philoi** 'friend(s)', see again §5.
§44n3. Cf. Theognis 213.

must be settled ἰθείῃσι δίκης 'with straight **dikai**' (*WD* 36).[1] Like Kyrnos—but much more overtly so—Perses is an exponent of **hubris**, and Hesiod's programmatic intent is to teach him the superiority of its opposite, **dikē**:

ὦ Πέρση, σὺ δ' ἄκουε Δίκης, μηδ' ὕβριν ὄφελλε
Hesiod *WD* 213

Perses! Listen to **Dikē**, and do not promote **hubris**!

This **hubris** is manifested in the striving of Perses for excessive wealth, as opposed to the moderate wealth won by the hard work that is espoused by Hesiod (cf. *WD* 315–316). Excessive wealth, however, is not a lasting thing:

χρήματα δ' οὐχ ἁρπακτά· θεόσδοτα πολλὸν ἀμείνω.   320
εἰ γάρ τις καὶ χερσὶ βίῃ μέγαν ὄλβον ἕληται,
ἢ ὅ γ' ἀπὸ γλώσσης ληίσσεται, οἷά τε πολλὰ
γίνεται, εὖτ' ἂν δὴ κέρδος νόον ἐξαπατήσει
ἀνθρώπων, Αἰδῶ δέ τ' Ἀναιδείη κατοπάζῃ,
ῥεῖα δέ μιν μαυροῦσι θεοί, μινύθουσι δὲ οἶκον   325
ἀνέρι τῷ, παῦρον δέ τ' ἐπὶ χρόνον ὄλβος ὀπηδεῖ.
Hesiod *WD* 320–326

Possessions [**khrēmata**] *should* not *be taken forcibly*;[2] what is given by the gods is much better.
For if a man takes great wealth by force and *violence* [**biē**]
or if he plunders wealth by way of his tongue, as often happens
when *private gain* [**kerdos**][3] leads the intent [**noos**] of men astray and
    Shamelessness drives away Shame,
the gods soon blacken[4] such a man and diminish his household.
And wealth stays with him only for a short time.

The same sentiment is echoed in Theognis: 'he who has acquired much' (ὃς μάλα πολλὰ πέπαται: v. 663, quoted at §43) can lose it all in one night (664). To repeat, this expression 'he who has acquired much' contains the same elements as in the name **Polu-pāos**, father of **Kurnos** (again, §43 above). Moreover, the meaning of **Kurnos**, 'bastard', has a parallel in Hesiod, again in the context of wealth:

§45n1. Still, Hesiod's intentions toward Perses are good: see *WD* 286 (for the diction, cf. Theognis 27–28, quoted at §10).
§45n2. Cf. χρήματα ἁρπάζουσι βίῃ 'they seize possessions [**khrēmata**] by force [**biē**]' at Theognis 677, as quoted at §1.
§45n3. Cf. §30n1, §40n4.
§45n4. Cf. *WD* 284 (n5) and Solon fr. 3.34 [= fr. 4 W], discussed at §49.

... εἰ γάρ τίς κ᾿ ἐθέλῃ τὰ δίκαι᾿ ἀγορεῦσαι 280
γινώσκων, τῷ μέν τ᾿ ὄλβον διδοῖ εὐρύοπα Ζεύς·
ὅς δέ κε μαρτυρίῃσιν ἑκὼν ἐπίορκον ὀμόσσας
ψεύσεται, ἐν δὲ Δίκην βλάψας νήκεστον ἀάσθη,
τοῦ δέ τ᾿ ἀμαυροτέρη γενεὴ μετόπισθε λέλειπται·
ἀνδρὸς δ᾿ εὐόρκου γενεὴ μετόπισθεν ἀμείνων. 285
Hesiod *WD* 280–285

For if anyone wishes to proclaim the *just things* [i.e., the things of **dikē**]
of which he *is aware*, Zeus gives wealth to such a man.
But whoever as witness knowingly swears a false oath
and lies, thus hurting **Dikē** and committing an error without remedy,
the future descendants of such a man are blackened,[5]
while the future descendants of the man who swears truly are by contrast
noble.

§46. This scheme corresponds to the Hesiodic Myth of the Five Generations of Mankind (*WD* 106–201), which operates on the central theme of contrasting **dikē** with **hubris**, the same contrast that defines the **neikos** 'quarrel' of Hesiod with Perses. This contrast of **dikē** and **hubris** has been cogently analyzed by Jean-Pierre Vernant, who has also shown that the superiority and inferiority of Generations 1 and 2 respectively are marked by their **dikē** and **hubris**, while the inferiority and superiority of Generations 3 and 4 respectively are marked by their **hubris** and **dikē**.[1] It is now also apparent, on the basis of *Works and Days* verses 280–285 (quoted at §45), that the progression from Generation 1 to Generation 2 is a matter of genetic debasement, while the progression from Generation 3 to Generation 4 is a matter of genetic improvement.[2] The key to improvement is **dikē**, while the key to debasement is **hubris**.

§47. The decadence of Megara is in fact parallel to the debasement of mankind from Generation 1 to Generation 2—from the Golden Age to the Silver Age. To repeat, what makes the Silver Men different from and inferior to the Gold Men is their **hubris** (*WD* 134), which is parallel to the **hubris** that marks the debased elite of Megara (Theognis 40/44, quoted at §27)—at a time when the citizens-at-large are still **saophrones** 'moderate' (41). At this time, the strife has not yet

---

§45n5. Cf. *WD* 325 (n4).
§46n1. Vernant 1974 I.20, 24–26; cf. also Nagy 1979.151–173.
§46n2. The reversal from debasement to improvement may help account for the absence of any metallic emblem for Generation 4. The progression Gold/Silver/Bronze of Generations 1/2/3 connotes debasement of value, which is interrupted by Generation 4.

broken out, but the **hubris** will soon be manifested in the form of **stasis** [plural] 'discord' and all the other horrors of civic disintegration (Theognis vv. 51–52, quoted at §27). For now, however, the city is still calm, but this will not last very long:

ἔλπεο μὴ δηρὸν κείνην πόλιν ἀτρεμίεσθαι,
μηδ' εἰ νῦν κεῖται πολλῆ ἐν ἡσυχίῃ.
Theognis 47–48

Do not expect that city to be peaceful for long,
not even if it is now in the position of much *serenity* [**hēsukhiē**].

The noun **hēsukhiē** 'serenity' here corresponds to the adjective characterizing the Gold Men themselves; they are **hēsukhoi** 'serene' (*WD* 119).[1] When Theognis is presented in the moral stance of a lawgiver, an exponent of **dikē**, he actually describes himself as **hēsukhos** 'serene' (Theognis 331).[2] Likewise in the diction of Solon, **hēsukhiē** 'serenity' is associated with **dikē** and contrasted with **hubris**:

δήμου θ' ἡγεμόνων ἄδικος νόος, οἷσιν ἑτοῖμον
ὕβριος ἐκ μεγάλης ἄλγεα πολλὰ παθεῖν·
οὐ γὰρ ἐπίστανται κατέχειν κόρον οὐδὲ παρούσας
εὐφροσύνας κοσμεῖν δαιτὸς ἐν ἡσυχίῃ.... 10
πλουτοῦσιν δ' ἀδίκοις ἔργμασι πειθόμενοι....
οὔθ' ἱερῶν κτεάνων οὔτε τι δημοσίων
φειδόμενοι κλέπτουσιν ἀφαρπαγῆ ἄλλοθεν ἄλλος,
οὐδὲ φυλάσσονται σεμνὰ Δίκης θέμεθλα,
ἢ σιγῶσα σύνοιδε τὰ γιγνόμενα πρό τ' ἐόντα,
τῷ δὲ χρόνῳ πάντως ἦλθ' ἀποτεισομένη.
Solon fr. 3.7–16 GP [= fr. 4 W]

But the intent [**noos**] of the *leaders* [**hēgemones**] of the community is *without justice* [**dikē**].[3] What awaits them
is the suffering of many pains because of a great *outrage* [**hubris**].
For they do not understand how to check *insatiability* [**koros**], nor can they
make order [**kosmos**][4] for their present merriment [**euphrosunē** plural] in

---

§47n1. The Gold Men are also **ethelēmoi** 'placid' (*WD* 118); cf. Apollonius of Rhodes *Argonautica* 2.656, where Dipsakos is described in a pastoral setting as **ethelēmos**, with the further detail that 'hubris did not please him' (οὐδέ οἱ ὕβρις/ ἥνδανεν: 2.655–656).
§47n2. On this and related passages, cf. §20.
§47n3. On **hēgemones** and **dēmos**, see §29.
§47n4. For **kosmeō** 'make order', cf. **kosmos** 'order' as discussed at §13n1, §25n2.

the *serenity* [hēsukhiē] of a feast [dais].[5] ...
They acquire wealth, swayed by deeds *without justice* [dikē], ...
and, not caring at all about sacred or public property,
they steal from one another by forcible seizure,
and they do not uphold the holy institutions of Dikē,
who silently[6] observes the present and the past,
and who will in the future come to exact complete retribution.

The Fruits of Insatiability

§48. The word **koros** 'insatiability' in the last passage (v. 9) is a key to understanding the difference between bad wealth as won by **hubris** and good wealth as won by **dikē**.[1] The **hubris** that brings on the debasement of men can itself be visualized as something brought on by **koros** 'insatiability' of wealth:

τίκτει τοι κόρος ὕβριν, ὅταν κακῷ ὄλβος ἕπηται
ἀνθρώπῳ καὶ ὅτῳ μὴ νόος ἄρτιος ᾖ.
Theognis 153-154

Insatiability [**koros**] gives birth to *outrage* [**hubris**] when wealth is attracted
to a man who is base [**kakos**] and whose intent [**noos**] is not fit.

τίκτει γὰρ κόρος ὕβριν, ὅταν πολὺς ὄλβος ἕπηται
ἀνθρώποις ὁπόσοις μὴ νόος ἄρτιος ᾖ.
Solon fr. 8.2-4 GP [= fr. 6 W]

For *insatiability* [**koros**] gives birth to *outrage* [**hubris**] when wealth is attracted
to men whose intent [**noos**] is not fit.

§49. There are still further implications to be found in the conceptual association of **koros** with **hubris**, as the poetry of Solon makes clear. Whereas **hubris** literally conquers **dikē** when Megara is debased (e.g., Theognis 291-292), the situation is reversed in Athens when the

---

§47n5. On **euphrosunē** as a programmatic word for the social harmony of an audience listening to poetry, cf. §6n2.

§47n6. Cf. the silence of Theognis in response to the seizure of his possessions at verse 669, quoted at §1; also at verse 420.

§48n1. Note that **koros** here at Solon fr. 3.9 is contrasted with **hēsukhiē** 'serenity' in the context of a **dais** 'feast' (verse 10). At Solon fr. 5.3 GP [= fr. 4c.2 W], the context of **koros** is still negative, but there it is only a temptation, as it were, rather than an evil that is afflicting the elite, who are described as **hēsukhasantes** 'being serene' (ibid.). The context of this fragment, as Aristotle reports (*Constitution of the Athenians* 5.3), is that Solon is addressing the **plousioi** 'wealthy', telling them not to be insatiable.

Eunomiē 'good legislation' of Solon the lawgiver rescues the city by bringing good government: as Solon proclaims in fr. 3 GP [= fr. 4 W], **Eunomiē** shackles those who are without **dikē** (33), it checks **koros** (34), it blackens **hubris** (34: ὕβριν ἀμαυροῖ), it 'withers the sprouting blossoms of derangement' (35: αὐαίνει δ' ἄτης ἄνθεα φυόμενα), and it 'makes crooked judgments [**dikai**] straight' (36: εὐθύνει δὲ δίκας σκολιάς). The vegetal imagery here is a traditional feature connected with the concepts of **koros** and **hubris**.[1] The word **hubris** is traditionally applied to excessive growth and exuberance in plants;[2] in botanical lore, an excess of nurturing (πλῆθος τροφῆς),[3] which can be equated with the poetic concept of **koros** 'insatiability', leads to a decrease in bearing fruit and a corresponding increase in wasteful leaf- or wood-production.[4] Greek botanical lore recognizes that plants are capable of indefinite expansion, and thus the growth of plants is for the Greeks appropriate for visualizing **hubris**: like some exuberant plant, **hubris** too keeps advancing until it is checked by an external force. Thus, when the tyrant of Megara emerges, he will be 'the regulator [**euthuntēr**] of our **hubris**', as the poet says (Theognis 40, quoted at §27). Significantly, the verb **euthunō** 'straighten, regulate' is even attested with the special meaning of 'control the growth of a plant' in the dialect of Arcadia (Theophrastus *Historia plantarum* 2.7.7).[5]

§50. In Greek botanical lore, the regulating of plant life by way of techniques such as pruning has the beneficial effect of promoting the fruitfulness of the plant; left unregulated, the **hubris** of the plant is manifested not only in excessive leaf- or wood-production but also in **akarpiā**, that is, failure to bear **karpos** 'fruit'.[1] In this connection, it is pertinent to cite the proverb

ἀκαρπότερος ᾿Αδώνιδος κήπων
CPG I p. 19.6–11

---

§49n1. See Michelini 1978.
§49n2. Michelini p.37 cites Aristotle *De generatione animalium* 725b35; Theophrastus *Historia plantarum* 2.7.6; *De causis plantarum* 2.16.8, 3.1.5, 3.6.8, 3.15.4.
§49n3. E.g., Theophrastus *De causis plantarum* 3.6.8.
§49n4. Michelini 1978.37–38.
§49n5. The plant in question here is the sorb apple. For this and other examples of such vocabulary, see Michelini p.43, esp. n25. Cf. the anecdote in Herodotus 5.92ζ about Periander's lesson in how to be a tyrant: Thrasyboulos goes through the field and keeps docking the tallest of the grain.
§50n1. Cf. again Theophrastus *De causis plantarum* 2.16.8 (ἐξυβρίσασαι διὰ τὴν εὐτροφίαν ἀκαρποῦσι) and 3.1.5 (ἄκαρπος γίνεται καθάπερ ὑλομανῶν καὶ ἐξυβρίζων).

more barren [a-karpos] than the Gardens of Adonis[2]

The rituals surrounding the Gardens of Adonis, as Marcel Detienne has argued,[3] are a negative dramatization of fertility. For the details, the reader should consult Detienne's intuitive analysis. Suffice it here to observe that the Gardens of Adonis are planted in the most unseasonal of times, the Dog Days of summer: the plants grow with excessive speed and vigor, only to be scorched to death by the sun's excessive heat, and this death then provides the occasion for the mourning of Adonis, protégé of Aphrodite. In opposition to the normal cycle of seasonal agriculture, which lasts for eight months, the abnormal cycle of the unseasonal Gardens of Adonis lasts but eight days (cf. Plato *Phaedrus* 276B). Like his suddenly and violently growing plants, Adonis himself dies **proēbēs** 'before maturity [hēbē]' (*CPG* I p. 183.3–8, II p. 3.10–13; cf. II p. 93.13). Adonis is thus directly parallel to the debased second generation of mankind, the Silver Men:

ἀλλ' ὅτ' ἄρ' ἡβῆσαι τε καὶ ἥβης μέτρον ἵκοιτο,
παυρίδιον ζώεσκον ἐπὶ χρόνον, ἄλγε' ἔχοντες
ἀφραδίης· ὕβριν γὰρ ἀτάσθαλον οὐκ ἐδύναντο
ἀλλήλων ἀπέχειν . . .
    Hesiod *WD* 132–135

But when the time of *maturing* and the full measure of *maturity* [hēbē] arrived,[4]
they lived only for a very short time,[5] suffering pains
for their heedlessness, for they could not keep overweening *outrage* [hubris] away from each other . . . [6]

§51. As for the unspoiled first generation of mankind, the figure of Adonis is directly antithetical to them: these men of the Golden Age live in a setting of permanent fertility (Hesiod *WD* 115–120) as expressed directly by the word **karpos** 'fruit' (*WD* 117).[1] The Golden

---

§50n2. The *Corpus Paroemiographorum Graecorum* contains this proverb more than once (cf. below).
§50n3. Detienne 1972.187–226.
§50n4. Cf. *Odyssey* xi 305–320, esp. verse 317.
§50n5. Cf. xi 307, 319–320. Note the epithet **pan-a-ōrios** 'most unseasonal of them all' as applied to Achilles; cf. the discussion of Sinos 1980.13–28 (see also Slatkin 1979).
§50n6. On the **hubris** of the Silver Men as described at *WD* 135–142, see Nagy 1979.151–153. Cf. also §§46–47 above.
§51n1. So also on the Isles of the Blessed (*WD* 171–173): the Earth bears **karpos** three times a year (*WD* 172). The Fourth Generation, whose destiny it is to attain the Isles of the Blessed, are also exponents of **dikē** (*WD* 158). Cf. Nagy 1979.155.

Age presents an idealized picture of wealth that is won by **dikē**: true and lasting, it is antithetical to the sudden and violent wealth that is won by **hubris** and that is destined not to last (*WD* 320–326, quoted at §45). Elsewhere as well, Hesiod presents the **polis** of those who have **dikē** as a picture of fertility (*WD* 225–237). By contrast, the **polis** of those who have **hubris** is a picture of sterility (*WD* 238–247): Zeus punishes them with hunger (243), with the barrenness of their women (244), and with the diminution of their household possessions (244). Moreover, the stylized city of **hubris** is afflicted with shipwrecks in seastorms brought on by Zeus himself (247), whereas the fortunate citizens of the stylized city of **dikē** do not have to sail at all (*WD* 236–237), since the earth bears for them plentiful **karpos** 'fruit' (237). This theme of shipwrecks is paralleled at Theognis verses 855–856 (quoted at §41), where the **polis** of Megara is described as running aground 'often' because of the **kakotēs** 'baseness' of the **hēgemones** 'leaders'. For Megara, its maritime eminence is not just a source of pride.[2] It is also an expression of the human condition: in the Golden Age, there would be no need to sail ships.

----

§51n2. See Hanell 1934.95–97 on Theognis 11–14, where Artemis is invoked as a protecting deity in whose honor Agamemnon himself had founded a sacred precinct before he sailed off to Troy with his fellow Achaeans. The precinct must surely correspond to the temple of Artemis at Megara (on which see Pausanias 1.43.1/3; Hanell, ibid., effectively counters the theory that the precinct in question is the temple of Artemis at Amarynthos, Euboea, on which see Callimachus *Iambi* fr. 200b Pfeiffer). Megara's link with the heroic past is implicitly but proudly affirmed by these Theognidean verses: in the local tradition, as Hanell argues, it seems that the Trojan Expedition was launched not from Aulis but from Megara itself—a fitting heroic precedent for the historical launching by the mother state of so many important daughter colonies in the Propontis and beyond in the Pontus (e.g., Kalkhedon and Byzantium). On the relationship between the pan-Hellenic poetic traditions about the Trojan Expedition and the various local poetic traditions about the **ktisis** 'foundation' of various colonies, see Nagy 1979.139–141. In the local tradition of Megara, Agamemnon had come to the city in order to persuade an illustrious resident, none other than Calchas the seer, to join the Trojan Expedition (Pausanias 1.43.1); moreover, Iphigeneia herself supposedly died and was buried at Megara, to be worshiped ever after as a cult-hero in her own precinct (**hērōion**: Pausanias, ibid.). In view of Megara's navigational preeminence in the seventh century, this local variant about the death of Iphigeneia may once have been eligible for pan-Hellenic acceptance—in competition with other variants about Iphigeneia. Granted, the reference in *Iliad* II 303–304 suggests that Aulis was ultimately acknowledged by pan-Hellenic Epos as the final place of assembly for the Achaean ships; still, in view of the *Iliad*'s silence about Agamemnon's sacrifice of Iphigeneia (in fact, "Iphianassa" is mentioned *en passant* as alive and eligible to marry Achilles at IX 145, 287), it is clear that Homeric poetry acknowledges the existence of rival versions of the assembly of ships (for a version according to which Iphigeneia was sacrificed at Brauron in Attica, see the scholia to Aristophanes *Lysistrata* 645, *Etymologicum Magnum* 747.57, Phanodemus *FGH* 325 F 1, Euphorion fr. 91 Powell).

To Plough or to Sail?

§52. There is more to this parallelism between the visions of navigation in Hesiodic and Theognidean poetry. The contrast that we see in the *Works and Days* between agriculture and navigation as opposite extremes of the human condition is itself a theme that recurs in some particularly difficult verses of Theognis. The entire passage in question will have to be examined carefully:

> ὄρνιθος φωνὴν Πολυπαΐδη ὀξὺ βοώσης
> ἤκουσ', ἥ τε βροτοῖς ἄγγελος ἦλθ' ἀρότου
> ὡραίου· καί μοι κραδίην ἐπάταξε μέλαιναν,
> ὅττι μοι εὐανθεῖς ἄλλοι ἔχουσιν ἀγρούς,   1200
> οὐδέ μοι ἡμίονοι κυφὸν ἕλκουσιν ἄροτρον
> τῆς ἄλλης μνηστῆς εἵνεκα ναυτιλίης.
>   Theognis 1197–1202

I heard, son of Polypaos, the sound of a bird making its resonant
call, the bird that comes as a messenger of *ploughing* for men,
ploughing *in season*. And it roused my somber heart,
for other men now possess my flowery fields,
and my mules no longer pull my curved plough—
all because of that *other sea-voyage* that is *on one's mind*.

The last verse of this passage has defied the understanding of editors, who have generally deemed it corrupt. It is possible, however, to justify the text as it stands through a closer examination of other passages that seem to be drawing from poetic traditions parallel to those of Theognis.[1] The adjective qualifying **nautiliē** 'sea-voyage' at verse 1202, namely **mnē-s-tē**, has been translated above as 'on one's mind' in view of parallel diction in a passage from Hesiod:

> τύνη δ' ὦ Πέρση ἔργων μεμνημένος εἶναι
> ὡραίων πάντων, περὶ ναυτιλίης δὲ μάλιστα.
>   Hesiod *WD* 641–642

Perses, you must *have on* your *mind* all things that are
in season, especially with regard to *sea-voyaging*.

Here, the expression **me-mnē-menos** 'having on one's mind' or 'being mindful' is specifically correlated with the concept of **nau-**

---

§52n1. It would be well to emphasize strongly at this point that the passages about to be adduced as parallels are not to be regarded as the "source" for the Theognidean verses in question. It is not a matter of references from one text to another but rather of parallel manifestations of common poetic traditions. See Nagy 1979.42–43.

tiliē 'sea-voyage' or '-voyaging' in the context of seasonal activities.

§53. As it turns out, however, there are two kinds of **nautiliē** 'sea-voyage': one that is in season and one that is not. Sailing is unseasonal at the very time when ploughing is seasonal. The celestial sign is the setting of the Pleiades (*WD* 614–616, 619–620): at this time, Hesiod says, the seas are stormy (621), and it is better not to sail at all (622, 624–629). At this time, one should instead be **memnēmenos** 'mindful' (623) to work the land (623). At this time, even more specifically, one should be **memnēmenos** of seasonal ploughing:

> ... τότ᾽ ἔπειτ᾽ ἀρότου <u>μεμνημένος</u> εἶναι
> <u>ὡραίου</u>· ...
> Hesiod *WD* 616–617
>
> Then you should *be mindful* of ploughing
> *in season.*

Instead of sailing when it is not in season, Hesiod teaches that one should wait:

> αὐτὸς δ᾽ <u>ὡραῖον</u> μίμνειν <u>πλόον</u>, εἰς ὅ κεν ἔλθῃ.
> Hesiod *WD* 630
>
> And you yourself should wait for *sea-voyaging in season*, until it comes.

The words **ploos** and **hōraios** in this verse recur at verse 665, where Hesiod teaches that **ploos** 'sea-voyaging' is indeed **hōraios** 'in season' when summer comes. Another good time is the spring (*WD* 678, 682), and again the word for 'sea-voyaging' is **ploos** (ibid.).

§54. To express the notion of this other season for sailing, the noun **ploos** is combined with the adjective **allos** 'other, another':

> <u>ἄλλος</u> δ᾽ εἰαρινὸς πέλεται <u>πλόος</u> ἀνθρώποισιν.
> Hesiod *WD* 678
>
> There is *another sea-voyage* for man in the spring.

The diction here is comparable to that of the last verse in the Theognidean passage (§42):

> τῆς <u>ἄλλης</u> μνηστῆς εἵνεκα <u>ναυτιλίης</u>.
> Theognis 1202
>
> ... all because of that *other sea-voyage* that is on one's mind.

To repeat: this 'other voyage' is correlated with the time for ploughing (§52 vv. 1198–1199), which is signaled by the resonant call of 'a bird' (§52 v. 1197). Similarly, in the *Works and Days* (448–451), the two messages "do plough" and "do not sail" are both conveyed by a single sign, the call of the cranes as they migrate yearly to milder climates.

§55. For some reason, Theognis is blaming the loss of his lands on a sea-voyage that is clearly unseasonal—and that is contrasted, by way of the adjective **allē** 'other' (§52 v. 1202), with one that would be seasonal. The parallel with Hesiodic usage is in this instance not exact, since the adjective **allos** at *Works and Days* 678 must be taken in the sense of differentiating one kind of seasonal voyage (spring) from another (summer). Still, the essential parallel between the Hesiodic and Theognidean passages is that the adjective **allos/allē** differentiates one time for sailing from another. The point remains that **allē** at Theognis 1202 (§52) distinguishes the time of sailing that is unseasonal—and thereby dangerous. In fact, it is a general principle in Greek that the adjective **allos** can be used euphemistically to distinguish a negative from a corresponding positive alternative (cf. **khrēm'** ... **allo** at Hesiod *WD* 344).[1]

§56. Why, then, should Theognis of Megara blame the loss of his lands on a sea-voyage undertaken out of season? The question leads back to the very first passage to be considered in this lengthy presentation (§1). A rereading of that passage at this stage helps provide an answer. Its basic theme, to repeat, is that the ship of state is afflicted by a seastorm (673–674) that threatens to engulf it (680), and this theme is concurrent with such other nautical themes as a mutiny on board (673) and the deposing of the **kubernētēs** 'pilot' (675–676). It is also concurrent with such general civic themes as the seizing of **khrēmata** 'possessions' by **biē** 'force' (677), the destruction of **kosmos** 'order' (ibid.), and the cessation of an equitable distribution of possessions **es to meson** 'in the common interest' (678).

§57. The loss of **khrēmata** is dramatized in the framework of a timeless misfortune—a ship is caught in a violent seastorm (again, §1 v. 677). But there is also a link to a past misfortune—the poet had lost his own **khrēmata** (667–669). This link is established by the verb

---

§55n1. See West 1978.243. As Lowell Edmunds points out to me, it is also possible that the **allē** at Theognis 1202 simply distinguishes the alternative of sailing from the alternative of ploughing. In view of the Hesiodic parallels, however, I prefer the more complex interpretation that has just been offered.

gīnōskō 'be aware', which occurs three times in the passage. At verse 682 (γινώσκοι), it signals the poet's present awareness of a future misfortune that is about to befall the citizens of his city. At verse 669 (γινώσκοντα), it signals the poet's past awareness of a future misfortune that has already happened and that the poet himself could not prevent—he lost his khrēmata (again, 667–669). Finally, an identification is established between the past misfortune of the poet and the future misfortune of the whole city by way of the third occurrence of gīnōskō: at verse 670 (γνούς), it signals the poet's awareness of a timeless misfortune—to repeat, a ship is caught in a violent seastorm (673–674), the kubernētēs 'pilot' is deposed (675–676), and khrēmata 'possessions' are being taken by force (677). Similarly, the verb memnēmai 'have in mind, be mindful of' in Theognis 1202 (§52) signals the poet's painful awareness of a dangerous sea-voyage that he actually blames for the loss of his possessions—those flowery fields waiting to be ploughed when the resonant call of the migrating cranes is heard throughout the land.

§58. In the ship beset by a seastorm, the loss of the ship's kubernētēs 'pilot' is linked with the loss of equity in civic affairs:

δασμὸς οὐκέτ' ἴσος γίνεται ἐς τὸ μέσον.
Theognis 678

There is no longer an equitable distribution, in the common interest.

Indeed, the kakoi 'base' now have the upper hand over the agathoi 'noble' (§1 v. 679). Moreover, the kubernētēs can be identified with none other than Theognis himself:

οἵ με φίλοι προδιδοῦσιν, ἐπεὶ τόν γ' ἐχθρὸν ἀλεῦμαι
ὥστε κυβερνήτης χοιράδας εἰναλίας.
Theognis 575–576

My friends [= philoi] betray me, since I steer clear of the enemy, much as a pilot [kubernētēs] steers clear of the reefs in the sea.

The nuances of this passage have been paraphrased by Hudson-Williams: "It is my friends who betray me; for I can easily keep off my declared enemies, as a pilot can keep his ship clear of the reefs that stand out above the surface of the sea" (a false friend is like a hidden reef).[1] These philoi 'friends' betray a man whose prime

___

§58n1. Hudson-Williams 1910.214; on khoiras as a visible reef, see the scholia to Euripides Andromache 1265.

theme is the celebration of being a **philos** (§§6–7), and they turn out to be none other than the elite of Megara: like a ship that has veered off course, the city has often run aground because of the **kakotēs** 'debasement' of its **hēgemones** 'leaders' (Theognis 855–856, quoted at §41).

A Poet's Two Kinds of Justice

§59. In a parallel stance of equity, the Athenian lawgiver Solon is likewise identified with a **kubernētēs** 'pilot'. There is a tradition reported by Plutarch (*Solon* 14.6) that the Delphic Oracle made the following revelation to the lawgiver:

> ἧσο μέσην κατὰ νῆα, κυβερνητήριον ἔργον
> εὐθύνων· πολλοί τοι Ἀθηναίων ἐπίκουροι.
> > Oracle no. 15 Parke-Wormell

Sit in the middle of the ship, *steering like a pilot* [**kubernētēs**].
Many of the Athenians are your helpers.

§60. The convergences already surveyed between Theognis and law-givers like Solon and Lycurgus as exponents of **dikē** suggest a consistent pattern reflecting a common ideological heritage. The survey could be extended much further, but the time has come to consider also a significant divergence between the figures of Theognis and the lawgivers. The passage in question is here quoted in its entirety:

> Ζεύς μοι τῶν τε φίλων δοίη τίσιν, οἵ με φιλεῦσιν,
> τῶν τ' ἐχθρῶν μεῖζον Κύρνε δυνησόμενον.
> χοὔτως ἂν δοκέοιμι μετ' ἀνθρώπων θεὸς εἶναι,
> εἴ μ' ἀποτεισάμενον μοῖρα κίχῃ θανάτου.   340
> ἀλλὰ Ζεῦ τέλεσόν μοι Ὀλύμπιε καίριον εὐχήν·
> δὸς δέ μοι ἀντὶ κακῶν καί τι παθεῖν ἀγαθόν·
> τεθναίην δ', εἰ μή τι κακῶν ἄμπαυμα μεριμνέων
> εὑροίμην. δοίην δ' ἀντ' ἀνιῶν ἀνίας·
> αἶσα γὰρ οὕτως ἐστί, τίσις δ' οὐ φαίνεται ἡμῖν   345
> ἀνδρῶν οἳ τἀμὰ χρήματ' ἔχουσι βίῃ
> συλήσαντες· ἐγὼ δὲ κύων ἐπέρησα χαράδρην
> χειμάρρῳ ποταμῷ, πάντ' ἀποτεισόμενος.[1]

---

§60n1. The manuscripts have ἀποσεισάμενος. Arguing in favor of this reading, West 1974.153 remarks, "Commentators are curiously slow to recognize a dog's invariable action on emerging from water." He translates ἐγὼ δὲ ... ἀποσεισάμενος as follows: "I was the (familiar) dog who crossed the beck in winter flood, I shook it all off." This interpretation may be appealing to some, but clear parallels seem to be

τῶν εἴη μέλαν αἷμα πιεῖν· ἐπί τ᾽ ἐσθλὸς ὄροιτο
δαίμων ὅς κατ᾽ ἐμὸν νοῦν τελέσειε τάδε.   350
Theognis 337–350

May Zeus grant me *retribution* on behalf of the friends who love me,
and that I may have more power than my enemies.
Thus would I have the reputation of a god among men,
if my destined death overtakes me *when I have exacted retribution*.
O Zeus, Olympian, *bring* my timely prayer *to fulfillment*!
Grant that I have something good happen in place of misfortunes.
But may I die if I find no respite from cares brought on by misfortunes.
And may I give harm in return for harm.
For this is the way it is destined, and yet I see no *retribution* on the
    horizon
against the men who have robbed me of my *possessions* [**khrēmata**] by
    force [**biē**].
But I am a dog and I cross the stream
with its wintry torrent, *about to exact retribution* for everything.
May I drink their black blood! And may an **esthlos** *spirit* [**daimon**] over-
    see [all this],
who *may bring* these things *to fulfillment*, in accordance with my *intent*
    [**noos**].

§61. Theognis prays to Zeus for the power to help his own friends and
hurt his enemies (337–338), so that he may thus 'have the reputation' (verb **dokeō**: δοκέοιμι 339) of being a god among men (339) by
exacting retribution before he dies (340). So far, these themes are
still convergent with those of the lawgivers. For example, Solon prays
to the Muses (fr. 1.1–2 GP [= fr. 13 W]) that they give him wealth
(1.3) and reputation (noun **doxa**, corresponding to verb **dokeō**: δόξαν
1.4) and that they enable him to help his friends and hurt his enemies (1.5–6). Also, the Pythia of the Delphic Oracle reveals to Lycurgus that he is more like a god than a man (Herodotus 1.65.3), and
the people of Sparta do indeed set up a cult of Lycurgus after he dies
(1.65.5). But now the themes diverge. Theognis as **kubernētēs** 'pilot'
is betrayed by his friends (§58 vv. 575–576)—the very ones he had
wished to help while all along hurting his enemies (§60 vv. 337–
338). Theognis (§60) goes on to wish that he may die if he finds no
relief from contemplating the hurt that he has suffered (341–344).
He yearns to hurt those who have hurt him (344), since this is the

---

lacking. At least, West cannot find any. In such situations where no parallel is to be
found, I find it an unsatisfactory solution to assume that the passage in question is
untraditional. In this particular case I prefer to accept the emendation ἀποτεισόμενος,
on the basis of parallels that are about to be discussed.

way things should be (345), but he sees no opportunity for vengeance (345) against men who took his **khrēmata** 'possessions' by
way of **biē** 'force' (346). The diction is parallel in the Theognidean
passage about the ship beset by a storm at sea (§1): when men
depose the **kubernētēs** 'pilot' (675–676), they seize **khrēmata** by way
of **biē** (677), just as Theognis himself had lost his **khrēmata** (667,
669). Solon, by contrast, who prays for wealth (fr. 1.3) and overtly
expresses the desire to own **khrēmata** (1.7), renounces any thought
of forcibly taking the possessions of others, which would be 'without
dikē' (1.7–8): sooner or later, the goddess **Dikē** as 'justice' would
exact retribution (1.8). The punishment that **Dikē** visits upon those
who seize the possessions of others is eventual (**khronōi**: fr. 3.16 GP
[= fr. 4 W])—and complete (ibid.).

§62. By manifesting himself as a paradigm of proper behavior, Solon
here expresses a personal involvement in the process of **dikē** 'justice', wherein retribution eventually overtakes those who have forcibly taken the possessions of others, but he himself is not the one
who suffers material loss. Moreover, the primary frame of reference
for **dikē** in the poetry of Solon is not his poetry itself but rather his
law code, and in fact the poet refers to this law code as **dikē** (fr.
30.18–20, quoted at §20). In the poetry of Theognis, by contrast, the
only frame of reference for **dikē** is the actual poetry. The process
that is **dikē** must emerge from his own life as dramatized in his
words addressed to young Kyrnos in particular and to other citizens
of Megara in general. The role of poetry itself as the primary frame
of reference for **dikē** is in fact the more archaic pattern. Likewise
in the *Works and Days* of Hesiod, **dikē** as 'justice' emerges from
the poet's own life as dramatized in his words addressed to his
brother Perses, who had forcibly taken Hesiod's **khrēmata** 'possessions' (v. 37 in conjunction with 320). But the fulfillment of **dikē**
is eventual, as Hesiod himself proclaims (*WD* 217–218, 220–224,
256–269), and the initial injustice perpetrated by Perses is corrected
only with the passage of time as enacted by the progression of the
poem itself. In the end, the **dikē** of Zeus as initially proclaimed by
the poet (*WD* 9) emerges triumphant—though not without moments
of pessimism or even despair (e.g., 190–194)—and Hesiod finds himself totally vindicated as Perses is ultimately reduced to utter penury
(396).

§63. So also in the poetry of Solon: **dikē** arrives eventually but absolutely (fr. 1.8 GP [= fr. 13 W]: πάντως ὕστερον ἦλθε δίκη) in the
form of **tisis** 'retribution' from Zeus (1.25), which in the end is

manifested absolutely (1.28: πάντως δ' ἐς τέλος ἐξεφάνη). For Solon, to repeat, the basis for this **dikē** of Zeus is his own law code. For Theognis, however, there is no such independent basis for **dikē** as he prays to Zeus for **tisis** 'retribution' (§60 v. 337)—that is, the power to help one's friends and hurt one's enemies (337–338). Like Hesiod, Theognis must wait for the **dikē** of Zeus to emerge from his own life as dramatized in his own poetry. Unlike Hesiod, however, Theognis is left in despair (§60): the **tisis** from Zeus is for Theognis not manifested (345: τίσις δ' οὐ φαίνεται ἡμῖν), as the men who seized his **khrēmata** 'possessions' by **biē** 'force' (346) seem to go unpunished. These men, to repeat, turn out to be the **philoi** 'friends' who have betrayed him as he was navigating like a **kubernētēs** 'pilot' (§58 vv. 575–576): they are the men who seize **khrēmata** by **biē** (§1 v. 677) as they depose the **kubernētēs** (§1 vv. 675–676) in the ship of state afflicted by the seastorm of strife. The poet is in effect saying that he fails to achieve the **dikē** of Zeus because his own city of Megara has betrayed him. In the pan-Hellenic poetry of Hesiod, by contrast, the poet succeeds at achieving **dikē** in an idealized context: there is in the end one city of absolute **dikē** 'justice' (WD 225–237), whose citizens receive many blessings, *including a dispensation from the necessity of sailing ships in order to make a living* (236–237), as opposed to another city of absolute injustice or **hubris** 'outrage' (238–247), whose citizens are afflicted by an angry Zeus exacting retribution (247: **apoteinutai**) by way of various misfortunes—*such as storms besetting ships at sea* (ibid.). In the case of a real city such as Megara, however, the ship of state threatened by a seastorm may yet be swallowed up by a gigantic wave (§1 v. 680), since the final victory of **dikē** over **hubris** is painfully in doubt. As Theognis himself says, the **tisis** 'retribution' of Zeus is for him not manifested (§60 v. 345).

§64. The poet despairs of achieving the **dikē** of Zeus—but only in the framework of his original prayer to the god. Theognis had prayed to have the power of helping friends and hurting enemies (§60 vv. 337–338, 344–345), adding that he would have the reputation of a god among men if he were to achieve this goal *within his own lifetime* (339–340). But there are other ways to exact retribution. The poet also prays (again, §60) that he may die if he finds no relief from contemplating the painful reality of his predicament (343–344), that is, the seizure of his possessions (346–347). The very next image, expressed with a timeless gnomic aorist indicative, is that of the poet as an infernal hound crossing a wintry torrent (§60 vv. 347–348) and 'about to exact retribution for everything' (348: πάντ' ἀποτεισόμενος).[1] The poet had prayed to have revenge while he was still alive (§60 v. 340), but now vengeance comes after death (348). His self-representation as a hideous dog that will drink the blood of wrong-doers corresponds to the traditional theme of the Erīnues 'Furies', self-proclaimed correlates of Dikē herself (Aeschylus *Eum.* 511–512), who are pictured as avenging dogs (*Cho.* 924, 1054; *Eum.* 132, 246) ready to drink the blood of their human victims (*Cho.* 577; cf. *Eum.* 264–266). Robert D. Murray has noticed this correspondence,[2] and he infers that the icy torrent that the hound crosses must in turn correspond to the Styx: it too is ice-cold (Hesiod *Th.* 785–787), "and the natural stream commonly identified with it was a torrent in Arca-dia fed by melting snows [Pausanias 8.17–19]."[3] In any case, what makes the image of crossing the stream seem especially frightening is that the spirits of the dead, in the folklore of a broad spectrum of cultures, ordinarily cannot or will not cross a running stream.[4]

§65. Theognis conjures up a **daimōn** 'spirit' to oversee his gruesome vengeance (§60 vv. 349–350; cf. Aeschylus *Ag.* 1476–1477: a blood-sucking **daimōn** takes vengeance against the House of Atreus). This **daimōn** is to 'bring these things to fulfillment' (350: **teleseie tade**) just as Zeus was implored to 'bring my timely prayer to fulfillment' (341: **teleson moi ... kairion eukhēn**).[1] Such a **daimōn**, acting in place of Zeus, corresponds to the countless invisible **phulakes** 'guardians' of **Dikē** who stand ready to punish wrongdoers in *Works and Days* 249–

---

§64n1. I follow Murray 1965.278–279 in emending the manuscript reading at verse 348 from aorist ἀποσεισάμενος (cf. §60n1) to future ἀποτεισόμενος. Besides the arguments adduced by Murray, I would add that the aorist ἐπέρησα and the proposed future ἀποτεισόμενος at verses 347 and 348 (see again the text as quoted at §60) are parallel to the aorist ἦλθ' and the future ἀποτεισομένη at Solon fr. 3.16 GP [= fr. 4 W] referring to the vengeance of Dikē 'Justice' incarnate against wrongdoers. Compare also the context of ἦλθε δίκη at Solon fr. 1.8, quoted at §63. Note the hesitation in the manuscript tradition between future ἀποτεισομένη and aorist ἀποτεισαμένη at Solon fr. 3.16. The former reading is clearly the preferable one.

§64n2. Murray p.279.

§64n3. Ibid. See Frame 1978 and Nagy 1979.194–197 for a discussion of Greek poetic themes involving cosmic streams that separate the realms of the living and the dead, of consciousness and unconsciousness. To cross such streams in one direction or another is to fall asleep or to awaken, to die or to come back to life. The Indo-Euro-pean root *nes-, as in Greek **noos** and **nostos**, conveys such themes of awakening and coming back to life: see §68 below.

§64n4. See Haavio 1959; also Bremmer 1983.133.

§65n1. Compare the use of the verb **teleō** in these two instances with that of the noun **telos** at Solon fr. 1.28 as cited in §63: the **tisis** 'retribution' of Zeus is *in the end* manifested absolutely — πάντως δ' ἐς τέλος ἐξεφάνη.

255 and who are identical to the **daimones** 'spirits' of stylized cult heroes at verses 122–126 of the same poem.² The punitive action of these **phulakes** is made parallel in the *Works and Days* to that of Zeus himself (256–262), just as the vengeance of the **daimōn** in verses 349–350 of Theognis (§60) is parallel to the vengeance that the poet had implored Zeus himself to exact in verses 341–342 and 337–338 (§60).

§66. That the punitive **daimōn** is actually the spirit of the dead Theognis himself is suggested by the word **noos** 'mind, intent' at verse 350 (§60): it is the **noos** of Theognis that unleashes this **daimōn**. After death, the goddess Persephone takes away the **noos** of mortals (Theognis 704–705), but she makes an exception in the case of a **mantis** 'seer' like Teiresias (*Odyssey* x 493), who retains his **phrenes** — the plural of **phrēn** and roughly translatable as 'consciousness' — even in Hades (x 493), precisely because Persephone grants him **noos** (x 494–495).¹ Like Teiresias, Theognis is exceptional: even in death, he seems to have a **noos**.² And this exception is parallel to another: in defiance of what might be expected of ghosts, this infernal hound can actually ford a running stream!

§67. Similarly, the restless spirit of the murdered Agamemnon can hear the call for revenge with his somber **phrēn** (Aeschylus *Cho.* 157–158: κλύ᾽ ὦ δέσποτ᾽ ἐξ ἀμαυρᾶς φρενός; cf. Pindar *P.* 5.101). The 'consciousness' or **phronēma** (derived from **phrēn/phrenes**) of the dead Agamemnon is indeed capable of revenge:

> φρόνημα τοῦ θανόντος οὐ δαμά-
> ζει πυρὸς μαλερὰ γνάθος,
> φαίνει δ᾽ ὕστερον ὀργάς.
> Aeschylus *Cho.* 324–326

The **phronēma** of the dead is not overcome
by the ravenous jaws of [cremation-] fire,
but it manifests its anger later.

---

§65n2. On these **phulakes/daimones**, see Vernant 1974 I.21–22; also Nagy 1979.151–155. Note the context of the derivative of **phulax**, the verb **phulassomai**, at Theognis 806 (as quoted at §20); cf. also the expression ὅτις φυλακὴν εἶχεν 'who was standing guard' at Theognis 676 (as quoted at §1).

§66n1. For further discussion, see Nagy 1980.161–166.

§66n2. To the extent that the consciousness of the dead is activated by drinking blood (e.g., *Odyssey* xi 153), the **noos** of Theognis (v. 350) seems predicated on the vengeful drinking of blood by the infernal hound (v. 349), and yet it is the **noos** of Theognis that seems to unleash this vengeance. For a parallel to this kind of "chicken-and-egg" pattern in mythopoeic thinking, see Nagy 1974b.77.

The murder of Agamemnon calls for an **Erīnūs** 'Fury' (*Cho.* 403), who is later pictured as standing ready to drink the blood of his murderer (577–578). In short, the self-representation of Theognis as an infernal hound longing to drink the blood of those who had wronged him conjures up the vision of a hero as an avenging revenant. Theognis is thus the exponent of **Dikē** 'justice' not only in life but also in death— much like those **phulakes** 'guardians' of **Dikē** in the *Works and Days* (again, 249–255). But unlike the pan-Hellenic model of Hesiodic poetry, where myriad invisible **phulakes** range all over the earth (*WD* 255), this solitary spirit presides only over his native city of Megara.

Theognis and Odysseus

§68. The **noos** of Theognis is a theme of many further ramifications: it also links this figure with the figure of Odysseus, a hero whose **noos** is the key to his **nostos** 'return' not only to his homeland of Ithaca in general but also in particular to the world of the living after his sojourn in the world of the dead.[1] This thematic connection of **noos** and **nostos**, which recapitulates the formal connection of **noos** and **nostos** as bifurcating derivatives of the verb **neomai** 'return', recurs in the poetry of Theognis (vv. 699–718):[2] the intelligence of the hero Sisyphos (vv. 703 and 712) is the key to his exceptional return to the world of the living from the world of the dead (703, 706–712). Sisyphos had swayed Persephone (704), whose function it is to take away the **noos** of the dead (705). This exceptional return of Sisyphos is also conveyed by the theme of his crossing the stream of Acheron one time more than is allotted for mortals (Alcaeus fr. 38A.1–8 V/LP; note the expression ἀνδρῶν πλεῖστα νοησάμενος 'superior to all men in **noos**' at v. 6). Comparable exceptions are the **noos** of Teiresias in Hades and the **noos** of Theognis, which makes possible his ghostly crossing of a running stream.

§69. Theognis actually likens himself to Odysseus precisely in connection with the hero's return from the world of the dead:

μή με κακῶν μίμνησκε· πέπονθά τοι οἷά τ' Ὀδυσσεύς,
ὅς τ' Ἀίδεω μέγα δῶμ' ἤλυθεν ἐξαναδύς.
ὃς δὴ καὶ μνηστῆρας ἀνείλετο νηλέι θυμῷ ...
    Theognis 1123–1125

---

§68n1. That the word **nostos** in the *Odyssey* designates the 'homecoming' of Odysseus both from Troy and from the world of the dead is demonstrated by Frame 1978.

§68n2. The passage is quoted in full by Cobb-Stevens Ch.6§22; for a commentary, see Frame pp.36–37.

Do not *remind* me of my misfortunes! The kinds of things that happened
to Odysseus have happened to me too.
Odysseus, who returned,[1] emerging from the great palace of Hades,
and who then killed the suitors with a pitiless spirit [= **thūmos**] . . .[2]

The emergence of Odysseus from Hades is here directly connected
with vengeance, much like the emergence of the infernal hound that
will drink the blood of those who had wronged Theognis. As for
Odysseus in the *Odyssey*, his heart literally 'barks' (xx 12/16: ὑλά-
κτει) as he contemplates vengeance in his **thūmos** (xx 5/9/10)
against the handmaidens who slept with the suitors, and this image
actually frames a simile in which an enraged bitch attacks a man in
order to protect her young (xx 14–15; on the Homeric image of dogs
drinking human blood, cf. *Iliad* xxii 70).

§70. Of course, the vengeance of Odysseus in the *Odyssey* is preceded
by a lengthy series of tests for the suitors. In both appearance and
mannerisms, Odysseus assumes the extrinsic baseness of a beggar,
using his verbal skills to expose the intrinsic baseness of the suitors—
men who should have been noble by birth; and in this way the hero
vindicates his own intrinsic nobility.[1] Similarly with Theognis, whose
loss of possessions has led to poverty:

ἆ δειλὴ Πενίη, τί ἐμοῖς ἐπικειμένη ὤμοις
σῶμα καταισχύνεις καὶ νόον ἡμέτερον;
αἰσχρὰ δέ μ' οὐκ ἐθέλοντα βίῃ καὶ πολλὰ διδάσκεις
ἐσθλὰ μετ' ἀνθρώπων καὶ κάλ' ἐπιστάμενον.
Theognis 649–652

Ah miserable poverty! Why do you weigh upon my shoulders
and debase both my body and my **noos**?
Forcibly and against my will, you teach me many base things,
though I am one among men who understands what is noble and
        beautiful.

Like Odysseus, Theognis espouses adaptability to each new situation:

πουλύπου ὀργὴν ἴσχε πολυπλόκου, ὃς ποτὶ πέτρῃ
τῇ προσομιλήσῃ, τοῖος ἰδεῖν ἐφάνη.

---

§69n1. For the semantics of ἤλυθεν here, cf. ἀνῆλθεν and ἤλυθε at Theognis
703 and 711.
§69n2. On the semantics of **thūmos**, see Nagy 1980.161–166.
§70n1. For a survey of these themes in the *Odyssey*, see Nagy 1979.231–237.

νῦν μὲν τῇδ' ἐφέπου, τοτὲ δ' ἀλλοῖος χρόα γίνου.
κρέσσων τοι σοφίη γίνεται ἀτροπίης.
Theognis 215–218

Have the temperament of a complex octopus, who
looks like whatever rock he has clung to.
Now be like this; then, at another time, become someone else in your
    coloring.
I tell you: **sophiē** is better than being *not versatile* [**atropos**].

To be **atropos** 'not versatile' is the opposite of **polutropos** 'versatile
in many ways', epithet of Odysseus (*Odyssey* i 1), a hero who is
actually compared to an octopus when he is about to drown at sea
(v 432–433). As for **sophiē** 'skill', this word recalls the epithet **sophos** 'skilled' applied to the man who can foresee impending misfortune like some **mantis** 'seer' (§1: Theognis 682)—a man who speaks
in the mode of an **ainigma** 'riddle' (681) about the ship beset by a
storm at sea. This man had himself lost his possessions and finds
himself in distress as he associates with the **agathoi** 'noble' (667–
670). By implication, the undying **noos** of Theognis the poet is ever
testing, by way of a timeless poetry that keeps adapting itself through
the ages, the intrinsic worth of the citizens of Megara—ever ready to
unleash a punitive **daimōn** against those **agathoi** who have failed to
live up to their heritage of nobility.

The Starving Revenant

§71. Like some seer whose vision transcends time, the poet even
seems to be alluding to a place of rest for his own corpse:

Αἴθων μὲν γένος εἰμί, πόλιν δ' εὐτειχέα Θήβην
οἰκῶ, πατρῴας γῆς ἀπερυκόμενος.
Theognis 1209–1210

I am **Aithōn** by birth, and *I have an abode* in well-walled Thebes,
since I have been exiled from my native land.

The language here and in the verses that follow seems intentionally
opaque, but at least some aspects of the message are translucent. The
word **oikeō** 'I have an abode' is a reference appropriate to a hero as a
cult figure.[1] There is a comparable use of the word in Sophocles
Oedipus at Colonus (27, 28, 92, 627, 637), in the context of the exiled
and destitute hero's intent to establish himself after death within the

---

§71n1. On the sacral uses of **oikos/oikeō**, cf. Henrichs 1976.278.

precinct of the **Erīnues** 'Furies' (for whom cf. the context of **oikeō** at *OC* 39). Hidden within the foreign earth of his final place of rest, Oedipus will have vengeance against his fellow Thebans: he predicts that his cold corpse will be drinking their warm blood as they fall fighting over Athenian territory (*OC* 621–622)—that is, 'if Zeus is still Zeus and if Phoebus the son of Zeus is accurate' (*OC* 623). This seerlike prognostication is strikingly parallel to the wish expressed by Theognis (§60) to drink the blood of those who had wronged him (349), uttered in the context of a prayer imploring the justice of Zeus (341–345; also 337–340).

§72. A few verses after the poet's naming Thebes as his abode, Theognis implies that he is in fact already dead by way of another theme: now he belongs to a city situated on the edge of the Plain of Lethe (1215–1216)—clearly, the realm of the dead (cf. Aristophanes *Frogs* 186).[1]

§73. As for the poet's assuming the name of **Aithōn** (1209), this name is also assumed by Odysseus in disguise (*Odyssey* xix 183; for the combination Αἴθων . . . γένος in Theognis 1209, cf. xix 116, 162, 166; also xvii 523). The adjective **aithōn** can mean 'burning [with hunger]' (cf. Hesiod *WD* 363, etc.)[1] and as such is an epithet suitable to characters primarily known for their ravenous hunger, such as Erysikhthon (Hesiod fr. 43 MW). Ravenous hunger also happens to be a traditional characterization of poets who use ambiguous discourse in order to ingratiate themselves with their audience—and thus get a meal.[2] Odysseus himself assumes the stance of such a poet (*Odyssey* xix 203, in conjunction with xiv 124–125 and vii 215–221), and it is in this context that he also assumes the name **Aithōn** (xix 183). Like the **Aithōn** of Theognis (§71), the **Aithōn** of the *Odyssey* is an exile (xix 167–170), a destitute wanderer who speaks with the skill of a poet (xvii 514–521). He is a master of an ambiguous form of poetic discourse known as the **ainos** (xiv 508), and the word **ainigma**

---

§72n1. On the convergence of names for mythical places (like Elysium) and names for cult places where heroes are buried and worshiped, see Nagy 1979.189–190. On the equation of the "espace politique" with the "espace sacré" where Megarian heroes are buried, see Bohringer 1980.6–7 (especially with reference to Pausanias 1.43.3). As for verses 1211–1216 of Theognis, they of course require much further study. Suffice it to note here that verses 1211–1212 reveal a theme for which there is a converse at Alcaeus fr. 72.11–13 V/LP.

§73n1. For this specialized meaning of **aithōn** and for the reading αἴθονα λιμόν at Hesiod *WD* 363, see McKay 1959.

§73n2. See Svenbro 1976.50–59; cf. Nagy 1979.261n4.

'riddle', referring to the poetic skill of Theognis himself (§1 v. 681), is actually derived from this noun **ainos**.[3]

§74. The theme of hunger as conveyed by the name **Aithōn** reflects yet another striking parallelism between Theognis and the lawgivers. Whereas Theognis as **Aithōn** is buried in Thebes as an exile from Megara (§71 vv. 1209–1210), Lycurgus the lawgiver starves himself to death in self-imposed exile from Sparta (Plutarch *Lycurgus* 29.8; 31; Ephorus *FGH* 70 F 175 at Aelian *VH* 13.23).[1] Moreover, there is a tradition that Lycurgus died and was buried in Crete (*Lycurgus* 31.7, 10)—which is where he had found the laws that he had taken back with him to Sparta (*Lycurgus* 4.1; Herodotus 1.65.4). Similarly, Theognis pictures himself as buried in Thebes (§71 vv. 1209–1210)—which is the setting of the primordial song sung by the Muses celebrating the establishment of community, a theme that inaugurates Theognidean poetry (§6 vv. 15–18). Moreover, it seems that the traditions of Thebes are not only related to but also the actual source of most pre-Doric Megarian traditions.[2]

§75. There are indications, however, that there will yet come a day when Theognis will finally be called back to his native city of Megara. In verses that rival in opacity those other verses about **Aithōn** (§71), the persona of Theognis declares:

ἤδη γάρ με κέκληκε θαλάσσιος οἴκαδε νεκρός,
τεθνηκὼς ζωῷ φθεγγόμενος στόματι.
Theognis 1229–1230

The Corpse of the Sea is now calling me home.
It is dead, but it calls with a mouth that is alive.

This passage has been preserved by Athenaeus (457A), who interprets it as a riddle about the **kokhlos** 'conch shell' used as a makeshift trumpet (ibid.). While such an interpretation may well turn out to be at least part of a solution (cf. **kērux** 'herald', the name for a trumpet-shell: Athenaeus 349C, Aristotle *HA* 528a10, etc.), it remains to ask: what is the point of a declaration that Theognis is being called home? By now it is clear that, as master of the **ainigma** 'riddle' (cf. §1 v. 681), Theognis is sending cryptic and prophetic messages to the **agathoi**, the 'noble' citizens of Megara and beyond.

---

§73n3. Cf. Nagy 1979.234–242.
§74n1. Cf. §12 above.
§74n2. See Hanell 1934, esp. pp.54–55.

Surely, then, there is more to these verses than a mere guessing-game about mollusks: there must be another dimension latent in the image of a **nekros** 'corpse' of the sea who is calling back Theognis 'with a mouth that is alive'.

§76. There are in fact traces of such a dimension in the attested native traditions of Megara. Pausanias (1.42.7) reports that Megara alone of all the Greek city-states boasts that the **nekros** 'corpse' of Ino was washed up on its shores; moreover, the Megarians worshiped Ino as a local hero in a special precinct assigned to her (**hērōion**: ibid.). In the local traditions of other regions such as Messenia, by contrast, Ino's fatal plunge from the Molourian Rocks of Megara (Pausanias 1.44.8) is followed by an altogether different course of events: instead of being washed ashore as a corpse, she emerges from the sea—in the Messenian version it happened in the sea off Mount Mathia—as the transformed White Goddess herself, **Leukotheā** (Pausanias 4.34.4). Still, why should the **nekros** 'corpse' of a distinctly Megarian Ino call Theognis 'with a mouth that is alive'? An answer emerges from the characterization **brotos audēessa** 'mortal endowed with speech' applied to Ino in *Odyssey* v 334. This expression is in marked contrast to **theos audēessa** 'goddess endowed with speech', applied in the *Odyssey* to other goddesses whose prophetic powers enable the hero to achieve a **nostos** 'return' back to his homeland (Circe at x 136, xi 8, xii 150; Calypso at xii 499).[1] The pointed description of Ino as a mortal rather than a goddess in the *Odyssey* seems to be a veiled Homeric reference to a tradition reflected in the local Megarian version, which is then immediately offset by the prevailing pan-Hellenic tradition, presented as the status quo:

> ... ἢ πρὶν μὲν ἔην βροτὸς αὐδήεσσα
> νῦν δ' ἁλὸς ἐν πελάγεσσι θεῶν ἒξ ἔμμορε τιμῆς
> *Odyssey* v 334–335

[Ino,] who was formerly a mortal endowed with speech,
but who *now* has her share of divine honors in the depths of the sea.

In much the same way, Hesiodic poetry refers obliquely to the local Theban tradition of Semele's death at Thebes:

> ἀθάνατον θνητή· νῦν δ' ἀμφότεροι θεοί εἰσιν
> Hesiod *Theogony* 942

---

§76n1. Cf. the commentary of Nagler 1977.80.

She, a mortal, [gave birth to Dionysos,] an immortal; *but now* they are both immortal.

§77. The characterization of Ino in the *Odyssey* as **audēessa** 'endowed with speech' (v 334) is appropriate: in Laconia, for example, there was a **manteion** 'oracle' of the goddess where she would prophesy to consulting worshippers in their sleep (Pausanias 3.26.1). Her instructions to Odysseus in the *Odyssey* itself (v 339–350) explicitly help further the hero's quest for survival (note esp. the word **nostos** at v 344). She speaks to Odysseus in the form of a sea bird called **aithuia** (v 337, 353)—a feminine noun corresponding to the masculine **Aithōn**. Like the Odyssean and Theognidean name **Aithōn**, **aithuia** too seems to connote hunger: this bird is noted for its voracity (Dionysius *Ixeuticon* 2.6).[1] More important, the cult epithet **aithuia** as applied to the goddess Athena herself reflects her specific traditional role as patroness of "le pilotage dans la navigation."[2] In iconographical representations, Athena **aithuia** is instrumental in saving ships at sea.[3] At Megara there is a seaside cliff named for Athena **aithuia** on which is located the tomb of the hero Pandion (Pausanias 1.5.3/1.41.6), whose corpse had been brought to the city by the goddess in the form of an **aithuia** (Hesychius 2737 Latte, with "Kekrops" corrected to "Pandion").[4]

§78. In the *Odyssey*, Ino as **aithuia** has a parallel in ensuring the salvation of Odysseus from the sea: Athena herself redirects the storm sent against the hero by Poseidon (v 382–387), and then she saves him from immediate drowning by giving him a timely idea for swimming to safety (v 435–439). It is worthwhile to observe in this regard that Odysseus is compared to an octopus in precisely this particular context (v 432–433; see §70). The submergence and emergence of the hero from the wave that would surely have drowned him had it not been for Athena (v 435, 438) corresponds closely to the preceding emergence and submergence of Ino herself (v 337, 352–353). Such a correspondence suggests that the former "mortal" who is now

---

§77n1. As for the sound of the call, despite the claims of Dionysius ibid., see *Etymologicum Magnum* 699.10 s.v. πώυγγες.

§77n2. Detienne/Vernant 1974.208.

§77n3. Anti 1920.284–287; see esp. p.287 for a painting that apparently features the accompanying inscription **oikeiou nostou**, which could mean something like 'with reference to one's personal homecoming [nostos]'.

§77n4. For the correction, see Anti pp.288–289. For a striking iconographical representation of this theme, see the illustration in Vermeule 1979.176, to be supplemented by the comments of Anti ibid.

a "goddess" (v 334, 335) is indeed a model for a transition from death to life anew—a transition that may be conveyed by the convergence of themes in the words **noos** and **nostos** (§68 above).[1]

§79. Theognis himself, to repeat, likens himself to Odysseus precisely in connection with the hero's return from the world of the dead (§69). But while the **nostos** of pan-Hellenic Odysseus is overtly achieved through the ultimate efficacy of pan-Hellenic Athena, the **nostos** of this local Odyssean figure Theognis can only be latently prophesied by the local Ino of Megara. So long as the transformation of the Megarian **nekros** 'corpse' into the White Goddess remains in a state of suspension, how can the dispossessed pilot ever return to his veering ship of state?[1]

---

§78n1. See Nagy 1979.203n2.

§79n1. An analysis of Theognidean poetry such as the one presented here reveals much that is parallel to Alcaic poetry, especially to the so-called "stasiotic" poems. To take Alcaeus fr. 129 V/LP for an example: the poet here is represented as speaking within a sacred precinct or **temenos** (vv. 1–2), praying that the gods of this precinct deliver him from painful exile (11–12) and hear his curse (10–11); the words of the curse adjure an **Erīnūs** 'Fury' to take vengeance against Pittakos, who broke the oath that binds **hetairoi** 'companions' together (13–20; cf. Theognis 337–350 and the comments at §§61, 64, 67). At Alcaeus fr. 130 V/LP, the poet again speaks of a **temenos** (v. 28), apparently the same precinct as before, which is presented as what seems to be the actual abode of Alcaeus as a lone exile (23–25; cf. Theognis 1209–1210 and the comments at §71); the verb **oikeō** 'I have an abode' here at verses 25 (ἐοίκησα) and 31 (οἴκημμι) of Alcaeus fr. 130 is the same as at verse 1210 (οἰκῶ) of Theognis (see again the comments at §71). In this light, the nostalgia at Alcaeus fr. 130.16–20 may be compared with the sentiment expressed at Theognis 1197–1202 (§§52 and following).

3
The Seal of Theognis:
The Politics of Authorship
in Archaic Greece

Andrew L. Ford

§1. We conceive of a poet Theognis and a pristine corpus of his poetry lying somewhere behind the diverse poems now under his name chiefly because of a few verses near the beginning of the collection which are known as his **sphrēgis**, or 'seal':

Κύρνε, σοφιζομένῳ μὲν ἐμοὶ σφρηγὶς ἐπικείσθω
  τοῖσδ' ἔπεσιν—λήσει δ' οὔποτε κλεπτόμενα,
οὐδέ τις ἀλλάξει κάκιον τοὐσθλοῦ παρεόντος,
  ὧδε δὲ πᾶς τις ἐρεῖ· "Θεύγνιδός ἐστιν ἔπη
τοῦ Μεγαρέως· πάντας δὲ κατ' ἀνθρώπους ὀνομαστός·"
  ἀστοῖσιν δ' οὔπω πᾶσιν ἁδεῖν δύναμαι.
οὐδὲν θαυμαστὸν Πολυπαΐδη· οὐδὲ γὰρ ὁ Ζεὺς
  οὔθ' ὕων πάντεσσ' ἀνδάνει οὔτ' ἀνέχων·
σοὶ δ' ἐγὼ εὖ φρονέων ὑποθήσομαι, οἷάπερ αὐτὸς
  Κύρν' ἀπὸ τῶν ἀγαθῶν παῖς ἔτ' ἐὼν ἔμαθον.
πέπνυσο, μηδ' αἰσχροῖσιν ἐπ' ἔργμασι μηδ' ἀδίκοισιν
  τιμὰς μηδ' ἀρετὰς ἕλκεο μηδ' ἄφενος.
  Theognis 19–30

Kyrnos, let a seal be placed by me as I practice my **sophiē** [skill]
upon these **epē** [utterances]; that way they will never be stolen without
    detection,
and no one will substitute something inferior for the **esthlon** [genuine]
    thing that is there.
And everyone will say: "These are the **epē** of Theognis
of Megara. His name is known among all men."
But I am not able to please all the citizens.
Which is not surprising, son of Polypaos! Not even Zeus
can please everyone either by raining or holding back.
But I, having good intentions toward you, will prescribe to you such
    things
that I myself, Kyrnos, learned from the **agathoi** [noble] when I was still
    a boy.

Be aware! Do not drag the things of timē [honor] or aretē [achievement]
or wealth
in the direction of deeds that are base and shameful or without dikē
[justice].

In this passage Theognis is depicted as putting a seal upon these epē,
'utterances' or 'expressions', presumably in the way that the Greeks
of his time sealed letters or treasure boxes. This curious image is
often taken metaphorically as Theognis' assertion of authorship. The
'seal' is thought to be a conceit through which Theognis declared
himself the author of the original collection of his poetry, however
badly mangled and contaminated it has become in subsequent editions. Interpreted as an assertion of authorial pride in literary property, this passage is taken as a milestone marking the emergence of
the notion of the poem as a literary object in a presumed evolution of
literary self-consciousness in Greece from the anonymity of epic to
the proud artistry of the poet in the fifth and fourth centuries.[1]

§2. A difficulty with this interpretation is that the seal can have had
little practical value as a claim of authorship in the archaic period
when poetry was circulated freely in oral performances rather than in
books. Moreover, the 'utterances' of archaic Greek poetry, even its
personal lyrics, were traditional and shared to such a degree as to
make a modern conception of the author as the "original writer"
irrelevant.[1]

§3. Theognis' description of himself in the exercise of his sophiē 'skill'
emphasizes not originality but a rational and practical skill in various
areas, including the production of poetry.[1] At the end of the seal Theognis says, 'I . . . will prescribe to you such things that I myself, Kyrnos, learned [emathon, v. 28] from the agathoi [noble] when I was still
a boy'. What Theognis will impart to Kyrnos he has himself heard from
others. Hence, in putting his seal on these 'utterances' Theognis is not
claiming that they are original with him. This is the sophiē 'skill' of the
archaic poet; he does not seek novel or idiosyncratic self-expression
but desires to speak intelligibly and with authority. The pride of archaic
poets in their singing and their hopes for glory are always tempered

---

§1n1. E.g., Jaeger 1945.1.190. For a survey of such interpretations of the seal,
see Woodbury 1952.35n4.
§2n1. Cf. Burn 1960.160 on the situation in archaic Greece; for a critique of the
modern conception of authorship, see Foucault 1977, especially p. 123.
§3n1. Snell 1924.1–20.

by a concomitant assertion that they depend for their poetry on the Muses, whom Hesiod calls the daughters of Memory.[2]

§4. If a poetic 'utterance' in an oral tradition were to be traced to an origin, it would be best to say that it comes from the Muses, not from any author. Indeed, these goddesses appear in Theognis immediately before the seal and utter the first epos (= singular of epē):

Μοῦσαι καὶ Χάριτες, κοῦραι Διός, αἵ ποτε Κάδμου
ἐς γάμον ἐλθοῦσαι καλὸν ἀείσατ᾽ ἔπος,
"ὅττι καλὸν φίλον ἐστί, τὸ δ᾽ οὐ καλὸν οὐ φίλον ἐστί"·
τοῦτ᾽ ἔπος ἀθανάτων ἦλθε διὰ στομάτων.
Theognis 15–18

Muses and **Kharites**, Daughters of Zeus! You were the ones
who once came to the wedding of Kadmos, and you sang this beautiful
  epos,
"What is beautiful is **philon**, what is not beautiful is not **philon**."
That is the **epos** that came through their immortal mouths.

This utterance of the Muses is an old and widely circulated piece of conventional wisdom;[1] they are the voices of tradition. Hence, it is not surprising that the **epē** upon which Theognis fixes his seal include many lines and passages that are found in other ancient authors and are attributed to a variety of archaic poets living before and after Theognis.[2] Indeed, perhaps it was the communality of these expressions which made such a thing as a seal necessary in order to impose the name of an individual on these **epē**.[3]

§5. Thus, the status of literature in archaic Greece and Theognis' own depiction of his practice argue against interpreting the seal as a procla-

---

§3n2. Cf. *Theogony* 55.

§4n1. Plato calls it an "ancient proverb" (*Lysis* 216C); cf. Euripides *Bacchae* 881/901. See Nagy Ch.2§6.

§4n2. For a survey of such passages of ambiguous attribution, see Burn 1960. 260ff.

§4n3. The directness of this strategy has puzzled some critics. It has been felt that the name of Theognis could not possibly be the seal, since it is incapable of protecting any verse but the one in which it sits. Hence a theory of catch phrases sprinkled through the poem has been developed; such a phrase, most commonly supposed to be the name Kyrnos, would be a personal token marking the authentic Theognidean passages. But such a device is equally inefficient and susceptible to forgery. Such ingenious critics miss the point of the seal: its purpose was not to mark each line or group of lines by Theognis but to impose his name on this mass of material.

mation of authorship. Accordingly, Leonard Woodbury has sought an alternative explanation of this passage.[1] He points out that the usual function of seals for the Greeks was "to safeguard property, rather than to attach the name of a craftsman to the product of his craft" and thus interprets the seal as an assertion of ownership rather than authorship.[2]

§6. Woodbury has clarified the meaning of the seal by purging it of extraneous literary implications; but the nature and function of Theognis' "ownership" of his poetry remain to be explained. In what sense, we may ask, are these expressions the property of Theognis? Why, and by what right, can he lay claim to them? For Woodbury, Theognis' poetry is *his* not as material property but as "spiritual property"; his "skillful variation" of poetic conventions and his "subtlety" mark his work so that he can call it his own, relying on confidence springing from his "consciousness of his artistic powers."[1] Yet we may wonder if Woodbury has not allowed the banished notion of literary authorship to sneak back into his explanation of the seal. The spiritual pride that allows an artist to identify a unique aesthetic object as his creation is not very different from authorship, even if the literary property on which it is based is an abstraction like "poetic skill."

§7. To read a notion of literary authorship into Theognis' seal is not only inappropriate but misses the real significance of this passage in the history of Greek literature. Theognis is clearly proud of these **epē** and hopes that they bring him renown. In this, his expectations are not different from those of any other performer in archaic Greece or elsewhere.[1] Self-advertisement is natural to the competitive context of Greek poetry, and we can find Hesiod, Alcman, and other archaic poets asserting the worth of themselves and of their performances within the conventions of archaic poetry.[2] But the seal of Theognis goes beyond these self-identifications in establishing a specific range of discourse as the singer's own. The seal is significant not because it names an author or a singer but because it identifies a "text." Theognis is not simply the name of a marvelous performer but the lock and key fixing a body of poetry and guaranteeing its provenience.

---

§5n1. Woodbury 1952.22–23.
§5n2. Woodbury p.20.
§6n1. Woodbury pp.24–31.
§7n1. For a collection of seallike signatures in other archaic Greek (and cognate) poetry, see Durante 1960.244–249.
§7n2. Kranz 1924.75–76.

§8. The seal as a means of identifying and appropriating poetry is attested in Greece between the end of the seventh and the beginning of the fifth centuries. Theognis was not the only poet to fix and name his work in this time. We find the elegiac poets Hipparchus, Phocylides, and Demodocus inserting their names into their epigrams. And the fixing of poetic discourse under a particular name allows poets to quote one another by name. Solon addresses Mimnermus and proceeds to recompose a line for him (Solon fr. 20 W). Simonides quotes a line from the *Iliad* as "one very beautiful [**kalon**, cf. Theognis 16] thing which the Chian man said" (Simonides fr. 8 W). The seal of Theognis is thus a sign not of a greater poetic self-consciousness but of a tendency to fix a poet's property into a stable corpus. In this connection it is interesting to note that Solon was credited by the ancients with a law prescribing that Homeric rhapsodes should recite their Homer not randomly but "on cue" (**ex hupobolēs**), and that the Homeric corpus appears to have achieved some kind of canonical formulation for performance at the Panathenaic festivals of the sixth century.[1]

§9. The special function of the poetic seal can thus best be explained not by referring to a nascent concept of authorship or to the pride of an artist but by calling attention to the strategies and motives for "publishing" and preserving poetic discourse in the tumultuous period of the Greek tyrants. In order to clarify the function of Theognis' seal and to specify the function of the "author" in this period, I shall show how poetic and formal language might be appropriated by the **polis**. I shall examine a special use of poetry by Hipparchus, son of Peisistratos and one of the tyrants of Athens. My emphasis, then, is on the political rather than the aesthetic or spiritual implications of the seal and name of Theognis.

§10. The crucial function of the seal in fixing Theognis' **epē** inviolably is evident in the double promise of verses 20–21 that his **epē** will not be stolen without detection and that no one will substitute inferior expressions for those there. This injunction is extraordinary for its concern with the integrity of the text. But there are near-parallels. Theognis elsewhere expresses a similar insistence on the preservation of the language of an oracular response:[1]

---

§8n1. Diogenes Laertius 1.57; Isocrates *Panegyricus* 159. For the phrase "on cue" and further discussion, see Davison 1955.1–15.
§10n1. See Nagy Ch.2§20.

τόρνου καὶ στάθμης καὶ γνώμονος ἄνδρα θεωρὸν
εὐθύτερον χρὴ <ἔ>μεν Κύρνε φυλασσόμενον,
ᾧτινί κεν Πυθῶνι θεοῦ χρήσασ᾽ ἱέρεια
ὀμφὴν σημήνῃ πίονος ἐξ ἀδύτου·
οὔτέ τι γὰρ προσθεὶς οὐδέν κ᾽ ἔτι φάρμακον εὕροις,
οὐδ᾽ ἀφελὼν πρὸς θεῶν ἀμπλακίην προφύγοις.
Theognis 805–810

A man who is **theōros** [one who consults the Oracle]
must be more straight, Kyrnos, being on his guard,
than a carpenter's pin and rule and square
—a man to whom the priestess of the god at Delphi
makes a response, revealing a sacred utterance from the opulent shrine.
You will not find any remedy if you add anything,
nor will you escape from veering, in the eyes of the gods, if you take
anything away.

Theognis in his seal hoped that no verses would be inserted and
none stolen, that is, excised or removed, since quoting or reusing his
expressions would be common poetic practice. Similarly, the oracular
response is to be protected from additions or deletions. In this latter
passage the **theōros** is a man delegated to carry a prophecy from the
Oracle of Delphi to those who will use it. We have here an excellent
illustration of Theognis' poetic intent to transmit his **epē** to their
future audience. In fact, one may extend the parallel by noting that
the **theōros** gets his language from a priestess who is an intermediary
to the prophetic god Apollo and that the **epē** of Theognis, which are
to be preserved in their turn, derive from the Muses.[2]

§11. These considerations have a bearing on Theognis' poetry because
for the Greeks of the archaic period there is no clear line of demarca-
tion separating "poetic" texts from oracular texts. It is worth remembering that Greek oracles were usually in meter. In fact, the Greeks
of the sixth century had no special word for poetry but referred to
poems and oracles alike with the word **epē**.[1] The closeness of these
two realms of discourse is illustrated by a famous poem of Tyrtaeus
called **Eunomiē** or 'Good Government' (fr. 4 W). This elegiac poem
framed a Delphic oracle that seems to have embodied a basic Spartan
constitutional enactment called the "Great Rhetra." At Sparta, the

---

§10n2. This connection is made explicit in Pindar fr. 150 SM: μαντεύεο Μοῖσα,
προφατεύσω δ᾽ ἐγώ 'prophesy, Muse, and I will be your interpreter'.
§11n1. Cf., e.g., *Odyssey* xii 266–267; *Iliad* I 108; Tyrtaeus fr. 4.2 W; Alcman fr.
27 P and Solon fr. 1 W.

variable interpretation of oracles played an important role in formulating external and internal policy through the fifth century.[2]

§12. Thus, control over certain forms of poetry was tantamount to power in archaic Greece. Even the forms of poetry which we might call literary entertainments, which is to say, in Greek terms, the **epē** of the Muses rather than of Pythian Apollo, could play an important role in politics. Several ancient authorities, including Aristotle (*Rhetoric* 1375b25), report that the *Iliad* was adduced in a suit between Megara and Athens. During their protracted dispute for the possession of the island of Salamis, these cities at one point put the matter before the Spartans for arbitration. In pleading the case for Athens, Solon (or Peisistratos) is reported to have interpolated a verse into the Catalogue of Ships in the *Iliad* (Plutarch *Solon* 10); the verse (*Iliad* II 557) says that Ajax, the hero and leader of Salamis, drew up his ships next to the Athenians. To be sure, the Athenians said that this charge was "ridiculous" (Plutarch ibid.), but it is not clear on what grounds; and a countercharge was made that the Megarians inserted a line of their own favoring their own cause (ibid.).

§13. The fixing of poetic texts can thus be seen as a way of appropriating their political power. The stories that Solon or Peisistratos "edited" Homer to serve their political aims are complemented by reports that these men introduced various measures to regularize the recitation of Homer at Athens (e.g., Diogenes Laertius 1.57). Smaller bodies of poetry with more localized themes could be adapted and owned more easily. Indeed, a model for the regularization of topical poetic discourse is provided by the Delphic Oracle, which threatened the **theōros** with severe religious sanctions if he opened an oracular response before he got home.[1] The response was thus sealed to ensure its authority and to prevent tampering.[2]

---

§11n2. See Wade-Gery 1943, 1944.

§13n1. Parke and Wormell 1956.33.

§13n2. It is easy to see why the Greeks would have felt it important to keep the texts of oracles uncorrupted. Oracular responses played a major role in establishing the customs within the Greek **poleis** and in guiding relations among them. That Theognis is interested in oracular responses for their political rather than their aesthetic or religious values is suggested by lines 543–546 (see Nagy Ch.2§20), where he uses the same imagery of being 'straight as a carpenter's rule' to describe how he should act in rendering a **dikē** 'judgment'. Thus, the text of an oracle is sacred, especially for the political consequences it can have. When Onomakritos, a professional interpreter of oracles, was caught interpolating verses into the oracles of Musaeus, he was banished by the tyrant Hipparchus (Herodotus 7.6.3–5).

§14. At first glance, the poetry of Theognis may not seem sufficiently important to merit a seal for similar reasons. After all, it is mainly a storehouse of advice to a **pais**, a boy, on erotic, sympotic, and civil matters. But the instruction of young boys in traditional values through poetry—**paideiā**—was the foundation of Greek political life. Poetry, politics, and **paideiā** could not be separated in the **polis**. To gain control over one it was necessary to control the others, as Plato showed so profoundly in the *Republic*. The precepts that Theognis offers to Kyrnos are guaranteed to come from **agathoi**, 'good' or 'noble' men, and the political values of the Megarian **agathoi** are present throughout the entire range of Theognidean poetry.[1]

§15. I maintain therefore that the seal of Theognis had as its prime function the codification and authorization of a body of gnomological poetry as representing the accepted standards and values of the **agathoi**. The name of Theognis guarantees not the origin of these **epē** but their homogeneous political character and their aristocratic provenience. The assertion that the seal has preserved a work intact is an assurance that this body of precepts constitutes a comprehensive, reciprocally explanatory education for an aristocratic youth.

§16. The possibility that a political regime might be interested in appropriating and disseminating a body of gnomological poetry is supported by a sketch of the leadership of the Athenian tyrant Hipparchus in the dialogue of that name attributed to Plato. This dialogue (on the very Theognidean theme of the nature of **kerdos** 'gain') contains a brief excursus on the educational activities of Hipparchus, successor to Peisistratos (*Hipparchus* 228B–229D). Socrates calls Hipparchus the most **sophos** 'skilled, clever, wise' of the sons of Peisistratos and details the deeds by which he 'displayed' (**apedeixato**) his quality of being **sophos**, that is, his **sophiē**: he reports that Hipparchus imported the **epē** of Homer into Athens and ordered the rhapsodes to recite his poetry in sequence at the Panathenaic festival. Hipparchus also brought the poet Anacreon from Teos to Athens, having sent out a trireme to fetch him. In addition, he was a lavish patron of the poet Simonides of Ceos. The rest of Socrates' description merits quotation in full, for he uses a number of terms and concepts which are suggestive of the Theognidea:

---

§14n1. Levine (Ch.7) and Lewis (Ch.8).

ταῦτα δ᾽ ἐποίει βουλόμενος παιδεύειν τοὺς πολίτας, ἵν᾽ ὡς βελτίστων ὄν-
των αὐτῶν ἄρχοι, οὐκ οἰόμενος δεῖν οὐδενὶ σοφίας φθονεῖν, ἅτε ὢν καλός
τε κἀγαθός. ἐπειδὴ δὲ αὐτῷ οἱ περὶ τὸ ἄστυ τῶν πολιτῶν πεπαιδευμένοι
ἦσαν καὶ ἐθαύμαζον αὐτὸν ἐπὶ σοφίᾳ, ἐπιβουλεύων αὖ τοὺς ἐν τοῖς ἀγροῖς
παιδεῦσαι ἔστησεν αὐτοῖς Ἑρμᾶς κατὰ τὰς ὁδοὺς ἐν μέσῳ τοῦ ἄστεος καὶ
τῶν δήμων ἑκάστων, κἄπειτα τῆς σοφίας τῆς αὑτοῦ, ἥν τ᾽ ἔμαθεν καὶ ἣν
αὐτὸς ἐξηῦρεν, ἐκλεξάμενος ἃ ἡγεῖτο σοφώτατα εἶναι, ταῦτα αὐτὸς ἐντεί-
νας εἰς ἐλεγεῖον αὑτοῦ ποιήματα καὶ ἐπιδείγματα τῆς σοφίας ἐπέγραψεν,
ἵνα πρῶτον μὲν τὰ ἐν Δελφοῖς γράμματα τὰ σοφὰ ταῦτα μὴ θαυμάζοιεν οἱ
πολῖται αὐτοῦ, τό τε "Γνῶθι σαυτόν" καὶ τὸ "Μηδὲν ἄγαν" καὶ τἆλλα τὰ
τοιαῦτα, ἀλλὰ τὰ Ἱππάρχου ῥήματα μᾶλλον σοφὰ ἡγοῖντο, ἔπειτα παρι-
όντες ἄνω καὶ κάτω καὶ ἀναγιγνώσκοντες καὶ γεῦμα λαμβάνοντες αὐτοῦ
τῆς σοφίας φοιτῷεν ἐκ τῶν ἀγρῶν καὶ ἐπὶ τὰ λοιπὰ παιδευθησόμενοι.

"Plato" *Hipparchus* 228C–D

Hipparchus did these things intending to educate [paideuein = verb of
paideiā] the citizens, so that he might rule over the best citizens possible,
thinking that it was not necessary to be stinting [phthonein] of his own
sophiē to anybody, the fine and noble man that he was. And when the in-
town citizens had been educated by him, and began to marvel at him for
his sophiē, he determined to educate the country citizens too, and set up
statues of Hermes along the road for their benefit, halfway between every
local deme and the city. He then selected the things that he considered to
be the most sopha of his own sophiē, both what he had learned [ema-
then] and what he had discovered for himself, and personally put these
things into the elegiac couplet and inscribed these poems of his on the
statues as displays [epideigmata] of his sophiē. He did this so that the
citizens should stop marveling at those clever things inscribed on the
temple of Delphi (like "Know thyself" or "Nothing in excess" and
things of that sort) and should come to consider the sayings of Hipparchus
as sopha instead. And once they got a taste of his sophiē while walking
back and forth and reading, they would make regular trips from the country to put the finishing touches on their paideiā.

This account of Hipparchus is supported by the fact that we have the
remains of one of these statues, proclaiming "This glorious herm
between the city and the (deme of) Kephale. . . . "[1] Furthermore, the
details of this description have a vivid credibility arising from Socrates' controlled irony and mock-admiration of Hipparchus. It seems at
certain points that the Tyrant's own proclamations—maybe such as "I
am unstinting of my wisdom to no one!"—might be being revived
and used against him in a subtly incredible portrait of the wise and
benevolent gentleman-tyrant.

---

§16n1. *IG* I² 837 discussed in Friedländer and Hoffleit 1948.139–140.

§17. The poetry of Hipparchus is gnomological elegy, similar in ethos to some of the expressions of Theognis. Socrates proceeds to quote from the epigrams of Hipparchus, the first of which is:

μνῆμα τόδ' Ἱππάρχου· στεῖχε δίκαια φρονῶν.

This is a reminder of Hipparchus: keep thoughts of **dikē** [justice] as you walk by.[1]

There are also many details about Hipparchus' composition and use of poetry which appear relevant to the more extensive corpus of his Megarian neighbor. Hipparchus composes his elegiac poems by selecting bits of wisdom from what he has learned; Theognis too draws on this source for his **epē** 'utterances' (v. 28). Hipparchus is also said to have found out some things for himself, but this is not an "original" element added to traditional poetry; it is just part of the ironically full description of the broad range of Hipparchus' **sophiē**. Hipparchus, as a political leader, can also exhibit his **sophiē** by importing and appropriating the poetry of Homer and patronizing the conspicuous poets of his day. The essence of Hipparchus' and Theognis' **sophiē** is the same: a mastery of poetic discourse enabling one to express the esteemed behavior of the community.[2]

§18. The central feature common to the poetry of Hipparchus and Theognis is the use of their names. The **epos** of Hipparchus quoted above—'keep thoughts of **dikē** as you walk'—is a conventional expression of the citizen's proper behavior. The same notion can be found in Theognis (vv. 395–396) and the same expression in Ion of Chios (fr. 26.16 W). It is by now clear that the important aspect of this poem of Hipparchus is not where the phrase came from but who has been able to attach his name to it. The epigram of Hipparchus is his **mnēma** 'reminder, memorial' both in the sense that he is the one speaking to us, reminding us of his advice, and in the sense that it is a memorial to Hipparchus whenever we read it or quote it.[1] His signature, and the similar signatures of Phocylides and Demodocus, function like the seal in attaching a name ineradicably (and perhaps more successfully than Theognis) to a definite poetic text.

---

§17n1. Cf. Theognis 753–756. Hipparchus' other **epos** quoted by Plato is "Do not deceive one who is your **philos**," a central Theognidean theme. See Rösler 1980.85n133.
§17n2. Cf. the reference to Theognis and Phocylides in Isocrates *To Nicocles* (2.40–44).
§18n1. Cf. the "memorial" of Theognis, as discussed by Nagy Ch.2§§71–72, 79n1; on poetry as **sēma** in the two senses of 'sign' and 'tomb', see Nagy 1983b.54n55.

§ 19. It is also clear from the *Hipparchus* that the function of the epigrammatic signature is essentially political. Hipparchus erected these herms to educate the more distant citizens. The memorials are designed to "display" or publicize the **sophiē** of Hipparchus so that he may serve as the source of the **paideiā** of his city. This is not a move of literary vanity but a battle against the well-publicized sayings inscribed on the walls of Delphi. Hipparchus had very good reasons to engage in this competition over poems: at this time, the Delphic Oracle was partial to some of his exiled Athenian opposition, the Alcmaeonids, in return for their sumptuous rebuilding of Apollo's temple. Indeed, so great was the influence of the Alcmaeonids on Delphic poetry that the Spartans were told to "overthrow the tyrant at Athens" every time they consulted the Oracle.[1]

§ 20. In this image of Hipparchus we may find the clearest illustration of the appropriation of poetic texts and their "publication" as extensions of the politics of the party in command. Perhaps the quintessential literary act of Hipparchus is his conveying Anacreon to Athens in a trireme. Many similar stories could be told of the great tyrants of this period, from Polycrates of Samos to Dionysius of Syracuse. The relation of Theognis to his city and its rulers is less clear, but there is one difficult passage that may be interpreted as summing up and commending the strategies of the poet-tyrant on the model of Hipparchus:

χρὴ Μουσῶν θεράποντα καὶ ἄγγελον, εἴ τι περισσὸν
  εἰδείη, σοφίης μὴ φθονερὸν τελέθειν,
ἀλλὰ τὰ μὲν μῶσθαι, τὰ δὲ δεικνύναι, ἄλλα δὲ ποιεῖν·
  τί σφιν χρήσηται μοῦνος ἐπιστάμενος;
  Theognis 769–772

The attendant and messenger of the Muses must, if he has any exceptional knowledge, not be stinting [**phthoneros**] with his **sophiē**,
but he should seek out and display [**deiknunai**] some things, and make some others;
what use will it be for him if he alone understands it?

The 'attendant of the Muses' is a traditional designation for the poet.[1] Yet this poet is also given the description 'messenger', as if to

---

§ 19n1. The exact date at which the Alcmaeonid building campaign began at Delphi is not clear. It is hard to tell, for example, whether the Alcmaeonidae sought the support of Delphi before the assassination of Hipparchus in 514. See Forrest 1969.277–286. In any event, the use of the Oracle and its poetic responses for political purposes is clearly demonstrated by all the historians.

§ 20n1. Cf. "Homer" *Margites* 1; Hesiod *Th.* 99.

emphasize the public function of a poet in the **polis** by depicting him simultaneously as the Muses' spokesman and as a political envoy. This poet is like Hipparchus in that he is exceptionally **sophos** and determined not to be stinting of his **sophiē**. The interpretation of the next line, 771, is, however, far from unanimous. The first verb is a rare one, which seems to mean 'seek out'.[2] But it is hard to understand what the sequence of this and the other two verbs signifies. Most commentators have sought in this line a tripartite analysis of the poet's activity. Thus, the line would be rendered: the poet must 'seek out some model, display it, and be somewhat creative';[3] alternatively, the verbs are read as denoting the didactic, encomiastic, and narrative genres, respectively.[4] But interpretations such as these are impositions of the critic's conception of the salient features of the poetic activity and reveal themselves in their attachment to anachronistic notions such as "poetic creativity" or a tripartite *partitio poetica*. The attempt to extract a triad of poetic functions out of these verbs has not yielded satisfactory results, and it is based on too narrow a conception of the **sophiē** under discussion here.[5] **Sophiē** can certainly denote poetic skill, but it has a wide range of application, and its broader sense is evoked by the complexity of the poet-messenger figure. This passage is describing not simply a poet but the man who brings the gifts of the Muses to his community. It is the poet as teacher, or the poet in the act of publicizing his **sophiē**. In this passage, the course prescribed for the poet is precisely that taken by Hipparchus in sharing his exceptional **sophiē** with the city of Athens. First, he sought out **sophiē**, on his own and from others; then, he made a display of it, in the Panathenaia or in his own compositions; finally, he *made* memorials, that is, poems to be remembered by being inscribed on stone. This last stage goes beyond 'displaying' **sophiē** and expresses the creation of artifacts that will carry one's **sophiē** through time. The verb used to express 'making', **poiein**, is commonly used on the inscribed memorials of this period, and we even find a **mnēma** 'memorial, reminder', from around 500 B.C., which proclaims that it is a 'made thing', that is, a **poiēma** or 'poem'.[6]

---

§20n2. Hesychius s.v. At *Cratylus* 402A, Plato derives 'Muses' from this word, on the grounds that they superintend "seeking" and philosophy.

§20n3. Harrison 1902.115–116.

§20n4. Van Groningen 1966.297–298.

§20n5. The translation adopted here follows the interpretation offered by Edmunds (Ch.4) below.

§20n6. *IG* XII.5 216.

§21. Thus, the seal of Theognis and the signature of Hipparchus seem to owe their currency to a politically oriented form of poetic publication. Seals make it possible for tyrants and other such rulers to marshal support from sympathetic and ideologically inalienable factions, who by poetry would express loyalty to the person of the ruler. The innovative and dangerous power of this form of propagandizing is clearly visible in a fifth-century story of a failed attempt to employ such strategies in artistically and politically conservative Sparta. Thucydides describes the career of the Spartan king Pausanias, whose power and prestige so increased after the Persian wars that he became restless in his office and began to intrigue with the East. The behavior of Pausanias had in various ways alerted the ephors that he aspired to power beyond his constitutionally granted status or **nomos** (Thucydides 1.132.2), and they began to analyze his past career for instances when he had gone beyond the **nomos**. The ephors hit upon an interesting example in which they felt that the hubristic character of Pausanias had been foreshadowed. They recalled that after the Persian wars Pausanias had dedicated a tripod at Delphi on his own behalf (ἰδίᾳ) and not as a representative of the city; he had even had this tripod inscribed with an elegiac couplet commemorating the victory and naming himself.[1] It is clear that what struck the ephors as politically ominous about his act was not simply Pausanias' boldness in acting on his own but the self-aggrandizing inscription of his name. It was not at all unreasonable to consider a personal inscription as a political tactic. In fact, an old Lycurgan law in Sparta had forbidden the inscription of names even on funeral monuments, with very few exceptions.[2] Hence, the Spartans subsequently chiseled off the verse in which Pausanias' name had been inscribed and replaced it with verses in which the victorious Greek *cities* were named. Sparta was one of the very few Greek states to avoid tyranny in the archaic age, and they were quick to recognize the tactics by which an individual might overcome the **nomoi**.

§22. The seal of Theognis therefore has its nearest analogue in the signed epigrams of Hipparchus. These are two different forms in two different media which are designed to marshal the gnomological tradition into politically serviceable form. The sealed Theognidea may resemble a book, and the seal itself may seem at first like an author's

---

§21n1. This composition was said to be by Simonides and is quoted in Pausanias 3.8.2.

§21n2. Apparently only priests and priestesses were entitled to be memorialized, though Plutarch gives contradictory accounts; see Wallace 1970.97ff.

signature, but the device of a seal is more allied in its motivation and significance to the **mnēmeia** 'memorials' of tyrants and the format of epigrammatists. The self-naming of Theognis and his contemporaries resembles specifically those memorials set up by the Greeks in which both the artist of the monument and its dedicator are glorified. In this sense the seal transforms Theognis' poetry into a **mnēma** 'memorial'.[1] It inscribes the poetry under a name and turns it into a memorial that will provide an inexhaustible reminder of Theognis for men to come. Indeed, the seal implies that the corpus of Theognis stands to be read as a stele is read. Theognis' corpus is a **mnēma**, wrought for Kyrnos, preserving both their names, even when they will not be present: "And thus everyone will say, 'these are the **epē** of Theognis of Megara, named among all men'" (22-23).[2] The "reading" that the seal predicts for itself is very like the "reading" of a memorial—like the reading of the **sēma** 'tomb' of a vanquished foe which Hector foresees continuing his glory beyond the *Iliad*:

" ' ἀνδρὸς μὲν τόδε σῆμα πάλαι κατατεθνηῶτος,
ὅν ποτ' ἀριστεύοντα κατέκτανε φαίδιμος Ἕκτωρ.'
ὥς ποτέ τις ἐρέει· τὸ δ' ἐμὸν κλέος οὔ ποτ' ὀλεῖται."
     Iliad VII 89–91

" 'This is the **sēma** of a man who died long ago,
whom glorious Hector slew in the middle of his exploits.'
Thus someone will say sometime, and my **kleos** will never die."

---

§22n1. Cf. Theognis 1209–1210, as discussed by Nagy 1983b.54n55.

§22n2. For a subtle analysis of the language of Theognis 237–254 in relation to traditional epic expressions of the connection of death and immortality to **kleos**, see Sacks 1978.

4
The Genre of Theognidean Poetry

Lowell Edmunds

§1. The Theognidean corpus presents many well-known difficulties. Even the portions generally agreed to be the work of Theognis are various in implied settings of performance, in subject matter, and in style. The poetry of Theognis manifests the same heterogeneity as Greek elegy as a whole[1] and raises the same question: what sort of poetry is this?[2] One way to approach this question is through literary history; in particular, in terms of the relation of elegy to other genres. Another way is to canvass ancient opinion on the nature of elegy. This approach has proven unsatisfactory because the ancients connect elegy with mourning,[3] whereas the remains of elegy cannot be equated with dirges, lamentations, or the like. A third way is to examine the Theognidean corpus in itself and in relation to the rest of Greek elegy for evidence of its own self-understanding. The question then becomes, how does Greek elegy, and the Theognidean corpus in particular, characterize itself as poetry? The evidence that emerges shows that Greek elegy distinguished itself from hexametric poetry (Homer, the Homeric Hymns, and Hesiod) with respect to the grounds of its authority as poetry and with respect to its role in the life of the audience addressed or assumed. Nathan Greenberg's argument that the hexameter of elegiac differs, on the basis of formulaic analysis, from the Homeric and Hesiodic hexameter, provides concrete support for this contention.[4]

§2. The self-characterization of elegy entails a critique of the very foundation of epic poetry, a reformulation and a desacralization of the function of memory. In epic, where **Mnēmosunē** 'Memory' is the mother of the Muses, her function is to provide an ultimate source

---

§1n1. West 1974.10–18.

§1n2. Maehler 1963 does not mention Theognis. Treu 1955 mentions Theognis in five footnotes and in one parenthetical reference in the text.

§1n3. Page 1936.206–230. See Rossi 1971 for a survey of ancient notions, explicit and implicit, of genre.

§1n4. See Greenberg (Appendix), this volume.

and authority. The poet prays to the goddess, the Muse, to sing his poem (*Iliad* I 1)—the Muse sings through the poet. In this way, the realm of the heroic past, otherwise inaccessible, is opened to the poet. If the Muses did not *remind* (root **mnē-**) the poet, he could never remember all his narrative (*Iliad* II 489–492). Inspired by the Muses, the poet has a direct, visionary experience of the events he recounts. Like a seer, he has knowledge transcending the present. The poetry of hexameter uses the same formulaic diction to describe the powers of poet and of seer (*Iliad* I 70; Hesiod *Th.* 32, cf. 38).[1] In elegy, by comparison, memory has been been desacralized. The poet on his own authority can determine the application of memory. In a remarkably emphatic statement, Xenophanes gives the following instructions for a symposium:

> ἀνδρῶν δ' αἰνεῖν τοῦτον ὃς ἐσθλὰ πιὼν ἀναφαίνει,
> ὡς ᾖ μνημοσύνη καὶ τόνος ἀμφ' ἀρετῆς,
> οὔ τι μάχας διέπειν Τιτήνων οὐδὲ Γιγάντων
> οὐδὲ <   > Κενταύρων, πλάσμα<τα> τῶν προτέρων,
> ἢ στάσιας σφεδανάς· τοῖς οὐδὲν χρηστὸν ἔνεστιν.
> Xenophanes fr. 1.19–23 W=B 1.19–23 DK

Praise the man who, when he drinks, brings genuine things [**esthla**] to light,
in order that there may be **mnēmosunē** and exertion over **aretē** [achievement] —
do not treat the battles of Titans and of Giants
nor of Centaurs, fictions of earlier men,
or violent seditions. In these there is nothing useful.

The battles of Titans and of Giants belong to theogony. The Centaurs figure in several hero myths. Xenophanes thus banishes from the symposium both of the two main subjects of hexameter, theogony and the **klea** 'glorious deeds' of heroes (cf. Hesiod *Th.* 100–101). In epic poetry, **mnēmosunē** is the poetic power that renews and re-presents these subjects, while in elegy it is at the service of **aretē** 'achievement'. For Xenophanes (B 1.23 DK) as for Theognis (772), poetry must be useful, and epic seems to contain 'nothing useful'.[2]

---

§2n1. For the memory of the poet, see Vernant 1974 I.80–89 and Detienne 1973.9–27.
§2n2. See Svenbro 1976.104: "Les positions politiques opposées de Xénophane et Théognis n'excluent pas une communauté de vues quant aux lois qui doivent régler la vie dans la Cité."

§3. This principle of usefulness looks to the needs of the **polis**.[1] Xenophanes uses the adjective **khrēstos** 'useful'. Its opposite, **akhrēstos** 'useless', is Theognis' way of describing the wealthy citizen whose wealth, 'being nothing', improves neither him nor his friends. With him Theognis contrasts the aristocratic warrior, the defender of his city, the possessor not so much of wealth but, through **aretē**, of immortal fame (vv. 865–868). It is this **aretē** of the warrior that is useful to the city and that deserves commemoration by the poet.

§4. No matter what a man's achievement in other respects as measured by the standards of epic, Tyrtaeus would not commemorate (root **mnē-**) him unless he showed himself a stout defender of his city (fr. 12 W). For Tyrtaeus, as for Theognis, this form of patriotism is **aretē** (fr. 12.13–14 W). Tyrtaeus imagines either commemoration or oblivion for the citizen-soldier. Either he will be remembered as a brave soldier or he will not be remembered at all. Theognis, however, envisages a third possibility. He divides commemoration, or remembrance, into two kinds:

τοὺς ἀγαθοὺς ἄλλος μάλα μέμφεται, ἄλλος ἐπαινεῖ,
τῶν δὲ κακῶν μνήμη γίνεται οὐδεμία.
Theognis 797–798

One man vehemently blames the **agathoi** [noble], another praises them; but of the **kakoi** [base] there is no **mnēmē** [remembrance] at all.

Remembrance may take the form either of praise or of blame, both of which are acceptable, at least by contrast with the oblivion that awaits the **kakos** 'base'. Theognis' division of remembrance into two kinds points to a preservation of memory not so much by the poet as in and by the city itself.

§5. Theognis is thinking of remembrance after death,[1] which may depend upon the poet (Theognis 237–250) but may also be independent of poetry. Although praise and blame seem to be inextricably bound up with remembering (cf. Semonides fr. 7.112–113 W), it is difficult to tell if **mnēmē** 'memory' in the passage just quoted means *poetic* remembrance. The surrounding passages (795–796, 799–804) suggest that Theognis is thinking of a man's reputation in the **polis** (**politai** in

---

§3n1. See the excellent collection of passages and the survey of the principle of usefulness in Kroll 1936.296–299.
§5n1. Cf. Euripides fr. 734 N².

795; cf. Mimnermus fr. 7.1 W), which will live after him. The **polis** itself, then, that arena of praise and blame, can preserve memory. What, then, of poetic remembrance? It can even appear to be dependent upon the **polis**, as in this inscription: "O guardian mistress of our **polis**, may our citadel [**polis**] preserve this monument [**mnēma**] of the prosperity of Smikros and his sons."[2] The **polis** preserves the monument, which carries an elegiac couplet, and the monument thus preserves the memory of the prosperity of Smikros and his sons.

§6. As the **polis** preserves the couplet by way of the monument, so Theognis calls for remembrance of his verses in the conduct of Megarian life. Pursue wealth in just fashion, he says, and stay out of trouble,

αἰεὶ τῶνδ' ἐπέων μεμνημένος· εἰς δὲ τελευτὴν
αἰνήσεις μύθῳ σώφρονι πειθόμενος.
Theognis 755–756

always remembering [**memnēmenos**] these utterances [**epos** pl.]. In the end
you will praise [me] if you obey my prudent word.

In this couplet, the poet is not the one who remembers or commemorates but the one who is to be remembered (cf. vv. 99–100). Further, though he is elsewhere the one who assigns praise or blame (see §14 below), here he is the one who is to be praised. The poet and his work are to become part of the city's heritage and to have a status similar perhaps to that of a monument. The intended effect of Theognidean poetry is the opposite of the forgetfulness inspired by Homeric and Hesiodic poetry. This epic poetry transports its audience out of their present world, and they forget all their cares (Hesiod *Th.* 98–103, also 53–55; cf. *Odyssey* i 337–338).[1]

---

§5n2. Friedländer and Hoffleit 1948 no. 116 = *IG* I² 643. Translation by Friedländer and Hoffleit.
§6n1. One passage in Theognis might seem to contradict the interpretation of elegiac "memory" just presented. In his invocation to Apollo, Theognis promises, "I will never forget (root **lēth-**) you" (vv. 1–2). The verb he uses, the opposite of "to remember" (root **mnē-**), seems to imply the Homeric and Hesiodic concept of memory, since these poets typically "remember" first the god and then the rest of the song, as in those epic prooimia, the *Homeric Hymns* (e.g., 3.546, 4.580, 6.21). If he "forgets" the god, the poet cannot "remember" song (*Hymn* 1.19). But Theognis, addressing Apollo, the god of music (cf. *Hymn* 25; *Margites* fr. 1.2 W), prays, "Give me **esthla** [good things]" (v. 4). Similarly, Solon, invoking the Muses, prays, "Give me wealth and good reputation" (fr. 13.1–4 W), and goes on to speak of the anticipated effect on

§7. With respect to memory, the difference between elegy on the one hand and Homeric and Hesiodic poetry on the other prompts the expectation that they will differ just as much with respect to the Muses, and in fact they do. Theognis mentions the Muses four times. The passages are best discussed against the background of what can be taken as elegiac poetry's general declaration of its relation to the Muses. There is a report that a certain Pigres, called by the *Suda* the brother of Artemisia of Halicarnassus, went through the *Iliad* and added an elegiac pentameter after each hexameter, thus presumably converting the *Iliad* into an elegiac poem. Of Pigres' work, only the first pentameter survives:

Μοῦσα· σὺ γὰρ πάσης πείρατ᾽ ἔχεις σοφίης.
Pigres fr. 1 W

Muse. For you hold the limits[1] of all **sophiē** [skill].

By Pigres' addition to *Iliad* ɪ i, the goddess, the Muse, is invoked because she is the possessor of **sophiē**.

§8. Pigres' line is programmatic, so to speak, for elegy. In Solon's "Hymn to the Muses," when he lists the occupations of men, he describes the poet thus:

ἄλλος Ὀλυμπιάδων Μουσέων πάρα δῶρα διδαχθείς,
ἱμερτῆς σοφίης μέτρον ἐπιστάμενος·...
Solon fr. 13.51–52 W

Another man, having learned their gifts from the Olympian Muses, knowing the measure of lovely **sophiē** ...

Again, the pentameter discloses the Muses as the source of **sophiē**. Theognis is consistent with Pigres and Solon. He begins his statement of the poet's duties thus:

Χρὴ Μουσῶν θεράποντα καὶ ἄγγελον, εἴ τι περισσὸν
εἰδείη, σοφίης μὴ φθονερὸν τελέθειν ...
Theognis 769–770

---

friends and enemies (vv. 5–6), i.e. in the political setting. To return to Theognis, his prayer for **esthla** (v. 4), a word that reverberates throughout the corpus in political and ethical contexts, likewise brings the poet's function into relation with the **polis**, which is the setting for this poetry.

§7n1. See Bergren 1975.132–143 for **peirata** as an element of diction and as a concept in elegiac poetry.

The attendant and messenger of the Muses must, if he has any
exceptional knowledge, not be stinting with his sophiē . . .

The rest of this passage will be discussed below. For now, note that
Theognis conceives of the poet as 'knowing' (v. 772: epistamenos) just
as Solon does (fr. 13.52 W quoted above). The conceit, then, of the
elegaic poet is that he has sophiē from the Muses, and when Theognis
puts a seal on his poetry, he speaks of himself as one practicing sophiē
(19: sophizomenos; cf. 995). Homeric and Hesiodic poetry, by contrast, is silent about sophiē in poetry and music in general except as
cithara-playing (Hesiod fr. 306 MW; Homeric Hymn 4.483, cf. 511).

§9. Two of the remaining references to the Muses in Theognis can be
understood against this background. In verses 1055–1056, Theognis
says to a companion, Let us drop this talk; you play the reed for me;
and let us both 'remember' (root mnē-) the Muses. The reed indicates
a symposium.[1] This setting is imagined by the lines that we read as
Theognis verses 1055–1056, just as 549–554 imagine the scene of im-
minent battle and 691–692 imagine a scene of departure. The poems
addressed to Khairon (vv. 691–692) and to men going into battle
(vv. 549–554) are both, of course, genre pieces, one a propempticon,
the other an exhortation. Likewise, the setting of verses 1055–1056 is
a conventional sympotic one, and it is in this setting that the Muses are
'remembered'. In short, the poetry of the Muses is not simply the
poetry of Theognis but rather the poetry that Theognis presents as
coming forth to the sound of the reed at a symposium. Similarly, in the
passage in which Theognis promises Kyrnos immortality, Kyrnos will
be sung of at banquets by young men to the accompaniment of the
reed. In this way, through the sympotic performance of poetry about
Kyrnos, his immortality is secured by the Muses (vv. 237–250).

§10. The fourth and final reference to the Muses occurs in the invocation (vv. 15–18). The invocation begins, "Muses and Kharites,
Daughters of Zeus" (15). Both the Muses and the Kharites are
daughters of Zeus, but they are from different mothers (Hesiod Th.
53–62, 907), and the Muses usually have considerably greater importance for poetry. One traditional role of the Kharites seems to be
dancing (Odyssey xviii 194, Homeric Hymn 3.194ff., 27.15; cf. Hesiod
Th. 63–64, where the Kharites are said to have their homes near the
dancing places of the Muses). In hexameter, in fact, the Muses and

---

§9n1. Theognis 533, 975–976, 1041–1042. Cf. 939–942, 975–976, which describe kōmoi. On the symposium in Theognis, see Levine Ch.7.

the Kharites are linked in the same phrase only once, and that is apropros of dancing (*Homeric Hymn* 27.15). This traditional function of the Kharites persists in Euripides' characterization of them as **khoropoioi** 'dance-creating' (*Phoenissae* 788). But Theognis does not invoke the Muses and Kharites simultaneously because of the Kharites' association with dancing. They had also another traditional role, which is indicated by their association with **Peithō** 'Persuasion' (Hesiod *WD* 73) and with **Hīmeros** 'Longing' (Hesiod *Th.* 64), and by their adorning of women (*WD* 73; *Homeric Hymn* 5.61). The Kharites can shed grace and acceptability upon the poetry of Theognis, and that is why they are invoked along with the Muses.[1] The acceptability of his poetry is a paramount concern (e.g., vv. 24, 367–370) because of the social or political function of this normative poetry.[2] The refusal to accept the poetry is a sign of the breakdown of political order. For this reason, Theognis names the Kharites along with **Pistis** and **Sōphrosunē** as divinities who have left the earth in these unrighteous times (v. 1138; cf. Hesiod *WD* 196–200, where it is predicted that **Aidōs** 'Shame' and **Nemesis** 'Retribution' will abandon the earth).

§11. By linking the Kharites with the Muses in his invocation, Theognis in effect specializes the function of the Muses to which he appeals. He appeals to the Muses as the ones who can win favor for his poetry in his community. At the same time, the Muses and the Kharites are invoked in a particular aspect as the ones who sang a beautiful **epos** 'utterance' at the wedding of Kadmos and Harmonia at Thebes. Their **epos** was, "What is beautiful is **philon** 'near and dear', what is not beautiful is not **philon**" (v. 17).[1] Theognis thus claims the Muses and the Kharites as the source of and the authority for the principle that the beautiful is **philon**, that which is proper to and unites the community. The poet is addressing "an ostensibly integral community of **philoi** that is the **polis** of Megara."[2] The utterance of the Muses and the Kharites contains, however, some negative impli-

---

§10n1. For **kharis** as a quality of poetry, see *Odyssey* viii 538, *Homeric Hymn* 24.5; cf. Odysseus' reply to Euryalos on **kharis** in the speech at *Odyssey* viii 166–185. For the notion of acceptability, see Friedländer and Hoffleit on their no. 119 (= *IG* I² 821 = *Anthologia Palatina* 6.144 and 213).

§10n2. As Ford has argued in this volume (Ch.3§20), the poet as messenger of the Muses (v. 769) brings the gifts of the Muses specifically to the **polis**.

§11n1. The proverb seems to be paraphrased in a passage of Euripides' *Phoenissae*, in which Theban legend, including the marriage of Harmonia and Kadmos, is surveyed (vv. 814, 822). For what may be another version of the Muses' song at the wedding of Harmonia and Kadmos, see Pindar fr. 30 SM.

§11n2. See Nagy Ch.2§§5–7.

cations. "What is beautiful is **philon**" was, according to Plato, an "old proverb" (*Lysis* 216C). We find it in Euripides' *Bacchae* in a passage that well depicts a characteristic Theognidean mood:

τί τὸ σοφόν; ἢ τί τὸ κάλλιον
παρὰ θεῶν γέρας ἐν βροτοῖς
ἢ χεῖρ' ὑπὲρ κορυφᾶς
τῶν ἐχθρῶν κρείσσω κατέχειν;
ὅ τι καλὸν φίλον ἀεί.
Bacchae 877–881 = 897–901

What is the **sophon**? Or what is the more **kalon**
gift from the gods amongst mortals
than to hold a more powerful hand
above the head of one's **ekhthroi** [enemies]?
What is beautiful [**kalon**] is always **philon**.

Whereas in Plato the proverb seems to refer to pursuing one's own advantage,[3] in Euripides it clearly refers to taking vengeance on one's enemies, and the chorus who speak these lines imply that the principle of vengeance is sufficient wisdom [**sophon**] for them.[4] Theognis, for whom poetry is the practice of **sophiē** (§§7–8 above), is likewise dedicated to taking vengeance on his enemies. He prays to Zeus for the power to punish them (vv. 337–340; cf. 363–364). He would divide up their possessions amongst himself and his friends (vv. 562–563). When he mentions his enemies, as he often does, he is likely to refer to his friends in the same context.[5] This polarity implies the form of the community to which Theognis addresses himself and will therefore be found to govern the practice of **sophiē** (§§15–20, 22–23 below). The utterance of the Muses and the Kharites was simply beautiful (v. 15) when they first uttered it and presumably introduced it into the world as something new and salutary. In Theognis' times, which the Kharites find intolerable (v. 1138), the beautiful utterance has become a proverb, the ambiguous implications of which will emerge in the rest of the Theognidea.

§12. For Theognis, then, the two main aspects of the Muses are **sophiē** 'skill' and community, and these Muses differ functionally

---

§11n3. So it was interpreted by Apostolius (16.87), probably on the basis of its use in Plato *Lysis* 216C.

§11n4. See Kirk 1970.96–97; cf. Dodds 1960.186–188.

§11n5. Vv. 91–92, 337–340, 561–562, 575–576, 599–602, 811–814, 869–872, 1013–1016, 1031–1033, 1079–1080, 1107–1108, 1219–1220. In each of these passages, a word formed on the base **phil-** occurs in the same context with **ekhthros** 'enemy'.

from those of Homer and Hesiod. The elegiac concept of poetic memory was also unlike the epic, in that it was related to political ends; in particular, to praise and blame (§§2–6). It is not surprising, therefore, that Theognis conceives of praise and blame as regulated by sophiē. The connection between sophiē, on the one hand, and praise and blame, on the other, emerges in a passage on the subject of wine which expresses the polarities of the poet's society:

οἶνε, τὰ μέν σ' αἰνῶ, τὰ δὲ μέμφομαι· οὐδέ σε πάμπαν
οὔτέ ποτ' ἐχθαίρειν οὔτε φιλεῖν δύναμαι.
ἐσθλὸν καὶ κακόν ἐσσι. τίς ἄν σέ γε μωμήσαιτο,
τίς δ' ἄν ἐπαινήσαι μέτρον ἔχων σοφίης;
Theognis 873–876

Wine, I partly praise you, I partly blame you. Not at all
can I ever be an ekhthros [enemy] or a philos [friend] to you.
You are an esthlon [noble] thing and a kakon [base] thing. Who would blame you,
who would praise you who had the measure of sophiē?

Only one element needs to be added to the scheme of polarities in this passage. It is clear from the invocation to the Muses and the Kharites that the kalon 'beautiful' belongs to the range of values indicated in that invocation by the neuter singular of the adjective philos. Therefore kalon can be added to the following schematic representation of the polarities embodied in the passage:

praise	blame
to be philos to/to hold something or someone as philon	to be ekhthros to/to hold something or someone as ekhthron
esthlos/-on (agathos/-on)	kakos/-on
kalos/-on	

Theognis holds that sophiē is what orients one with respect to these polarities. Sophiē is now put on a par with aretē 'achievement' (v. 790), now said to be even better than aretē (v. 1074; cf. 217–218). In other words, it is the highest political virtue (which is once called dikē 'justice' by Theognis: v. 147), as well as the mark of the poet (§§7–11).[1] The question thus arises of the relation between the political and the poetic sophiē.

_____

§12n1. See Gladigow 1965.68–69 on v. 1074: Theognis is not talking about inner worth but about practical success in life.

§13. These two functions of **sophiē** can be understood in terms of the various sorts of discourse referred to by the words formed on the base **ain-**. So far, we have considered only **ainos** 'praise'. The noun **ainos** derives from the verb ***ainomai**, which occurs in the compound **an-ainomai** 'refuse' or 'say no'. Since this verb is built with the negative prefix **an-**, the corresponding positive verb, the assumed **ainomai**, would mean 'affirm, accept'.[1] This hypothesis finds confirmation in the fact that **ainos** can mean a legislative decision or resolution.[2] The semantic range of the verbal compounds follows naturally. The verb **par-ainein** is to advise or instruct,[3] that is, to bring someone over to **ainos** in the sense of the city's resolution concerning what is best. The verb **ep-ainein**, however, is to praise. Again, it is possible to discern a connection with **ainos** in the sense of 'resolution'. As the legislative body 'approves', he who praises 'approves' the activity or virtue of the laudandus, that is, of the one to be praised. The laudandus and the matter approved by the legislative body have in common their probity.

§14. Theognis, who adopts the stance of the lawgiver,[1] is the appropriate wielder of praise and blame, the appropriate adviser. As the possessor of **sophiē**, he is the master of **ainos**, which includes the various sorts of utterances just discussed. Furthermore, it should be recalled that, in the elegiac scheme, praise and blame are also connected with memory. In this sense of memory, to remember is really 'to be mindful', and the concept looks to ritual correctness, which can be regarded as parallel to, and cooperative with, the requirements of **ainos** in the sense of resolution, approbation, praise, or admonition.[2]

§15. But **ainos** can also mean 'riddle' (Panarkes fr. (a) 1 W = Clearchus fr. 95 Wehrli) and allusive fable (Hesiod *WD* 202; Archilochus fr. 174.1, 185.1 W). On the base **ain-** is also formed the verb **ainis-**

---

§13n1. See Chantraine 1968.36 (s.v. "**ainos**"); Nagy 1979.240–241.
§13n2. *IG* IX.1 119 (verb **aineō**), from Phocis. Dittenberger comments: "Mira breviloquentia . . . populi consensus . . . indicatur, neque tamen quicquam hic est, quod cum sermonis usu pugnet; immo simplex verbum **ainein**, quo Attici fere abstinent, apud alias gentes Graecas de eo usurpatur, qui alius sententiam suo assensu comprobat. Adde quod certe compositum **diainein** et substantivum **ainos** in litteris publicis Delphorum simili vi usurpata scimus." He refers to *SIG*³ 672.15 (**ainos**), on which he there gives a lengthy and useful footnote, and to line 19 of the same inscription (verb **diainein**). See also *IG* IV² 71.4 and 10 (**ainos** in both these lines), from Epidaurus.
§13n3. Cf. Nagy 1979.238.
§14n1. See Nagy Ch.2§§11–14.
§14n2. See Nagy 1982.61.

somai, 'to riddle'. At first sight, it is difficult to understand the relation between this range of meanings and the various senses of praise and resolution discussed above. On the one hand, we have that which is declarative, public, clear; on the other, that which is muted, private, obscure. A link between the two semantic ranges of **ainos** can be discerned, however, in the notion of community. The private, obscure **ainos** is addressed to a community just as surely as the public, open **ainos**. Theognis presents the image of the ship as a riddle (v. 681: verb **ainissomai**). It is a riddle for the **agathoi** 'noble' (v. 681). One can understand it if one is **sophos** 'discerning'.¹ Theognis' riddle is thus addressed to a community of **sophoi**.² Another link between the two semantic ranges is advice or instruction. Julian observes in his Seventh Oration that **ainos** differs from myth in that "it is written not for children but for men and contains not only entertainment but also advice (**parainesis**). For the speaker wishes to offer advice and instruction covertly whenever, through fear of his audience's hatred, he avoids speaking openly" (207A).³ In Theognis' audience, the smaller community of **sophoi** will get the message, and the hostility of the others will be averted.⁴

§ 16. The two sides of **ainos**, the two functions of the poet required by the ambiguity of **ainos**, are expressed by Theognis in other terms in verse 771.¹ In this context, Theognis says that the poet must not

---

§15n1. This interpretation follows the reading of the manuscripts as found in Young's edition. For further discussion, see Nagy Ch.2§§1–4.

§15n2. Therefore, although the means of communication is in some sense private, the reception takes place in a sphere that is ultimately public. It makes no difference whether the community addressed by Theognis is conceived of as a limited public within the general public in the actual exercise of power or as participants in the private symposia. The same persons constitute both of these communities.

§15n3. Julian goes on to observe that Hesiod composed in this way (207B), and indeed I have cited Hesiod *WD* 202 at the beginning of §15. But the fact that Theognis and Hesiod both use **ainos** hardly means that their fundamental conception of poetry is the same.

§15n4. Apparently the others simply fail to make the connection between the **ainos** and themselves, even though, as Fraenkel 1920.366–367 shows, the **ainos** typically concludes by calling upon the audience or addressee to make this connection. It is worth noting that exactly the same concluding formula pointed out by Fraenkel (**kai su/se** 'you, too') occurs in an archaic grave-epigram (Friedländer and Hoffleit 1948 no. 85). If, as is argued in §24, the elegiac grave-epigram provides a parallel to the development of elegy from mourning to the general kinds of reflection that we find in the remains of elegiac poetry, then it is significant that the archaic grave-epigram shares a formal trait with **ainos**. **Ainos** as a strategy of Theognidean elegy is thus rooted in the genre.

§16n1. For a survey of interpretations of this obscure line, see van Groningen 1966.296–299, and, for a critique of his interpretation, Lanata 1963.65–66. See also

begrudge his **sophiē** (v. 770), for what is the use if he alone has understanding (v. 772)? Theognis thus invokes the principle of usefulness, which, as I have argued (§3 above), is a political one. The poet's **sophiē** must be available to the city. In the verse in question, Theognis details three ways in which the poet should be useful. He should not begrudge his **sophiē**

> ἀλλὰ τὰ μὲν μῶσθαι, τὰ δὲ δεικνύναι, ἄλλα δὲ ποιεῖν.
> Theognis 771
>
> but he should seek out and display some things, and **poiein** others.

The most problematic word has been left untranslated. The stem of this word was to produce the words for poem, poet, and poetry in English and most of the Romance languages, but in Theognis 771 its usage is likely to be much narrower. The word is used of poetry in only two other places that may be as early as the passage under discussion.

§17. One of these is in the Theognidea (v. 713). Theognis says that, compared with money-making, no intellectual accomplishment would be valued in his society,

> οὐδ' εἰ ψεύδεα μὲν ποιοῖς ἐτύμοισιν ὁμοῖα.
> Theognis 713
>
> not even if you should make [= verb **poiein**] false things similar to true things.

The context of **poiein** here is significant. This line contains an allusion to a topic found also in the passage in Hesiod in which the Muses describe their powers:

> ἴδμεν ψεύδεα πολλὰ λέγειν ἐτύμοισιν ὁμοῖα.
> Hesiod *Theogony* 27
>
> we know how to say many false things that are similar to true things.

The Muses contrast this particular capacity with another, that is, their capacity to proclaim true things when they are willing to do so (*Theogony* 28). This contrast in Hesiod between truth and plausible fic-

---

Kroll 1936.244–245. Theognis' use of **poiein** in v. 771 is difficult to understand in terms of the formulation of Svenbro 1976.207: "the key word to designate the transformation of the material world by paid labor."

tion[1] is absent in the context of Theognis 713, quoted above. In Theognis, the capacity to produce plausible fiction would be admirable, even if it is not in fact admired in his society, and he does not invoke any higher standard of truth.

§18. Theognis' reference to Nestor (v. 714) shows that the poet has epic poetry in mind. The use of the verb **poiein** can thus be compared with Xenophanes' characterization of epic and theogonic themes as 'fictions' (§2 above). Whereas, however, Xenophanes' view is negative, Theognis treats the results produced by the activity of **poiein** as positive, perhaps because he is comparing the making of epic poetry with the acquisition of wealth. The possibility remains open that, if Theognis compared the making of epic poetry with some other sort of poetic or mental production, he would rate epic poetry as inferior. In any case, the context of **poiein** in verse 713 shows that this verb refers to epic poetry as fiction, just as, in the Hesiodic context, the "false things similar to true things" could be regarded as inferior local epic or theogonic traditions as against Hesiod's pan-Hellenic claims.[1] Theognis' use of **poiein** thus conforms to a semantic possibility inherent in the word's fundamental sense of 'fabricate'.[2] To fabricate is to *make artifacts*[3] and to *use artifice*, which may be to mislead or to deceive.

§19. The other archaic occurrence of **poiein** in reference to poetry is Solon fr. 20.3 W, where it appears in the compound **metapoiein**. Solon calls upon Mimnermus to 'remake' an assertion that Solon considers incorrect. In the compound, the prefix **meta-** could have the sense of the English 'un-'. One can compare, for example, the verb **metamanthanein** 'to unlearn'. Solon calls upon Mimnermus to 'un-fabricate' his assertion.

§20. To return to Theognis verse 771, the third infinitive, **poiein**, contrasts with the first two. So the word 'others' by itself suggests, and so the particles allow.[1] The first two infinitives indicate a mental

---

§17n1. See West 1966 ad loc.
§18n1. See Nagy 1982.48.
§18n2. See Valesio 1960 and Ford 1981.
§18n3. On which see Ford Ch.3§20.
§20n1. Compare Sappho fr. 168 B (Voigt), where it is only the final δέ that contrasts with the μέν. See the explication of this poem by Clay 1970. For ἐγὼ δέ as "un tratto personale della poesia di Saffo," see Marzullo 1958.36–37. For a parallel in prose to Theognis 771, see Herodotus 2.44.5, though it should be observed that, in this passage, the first δέ is a mannerism of Herodotus, as Stein points out in his note on Herodotus 1.114 (line 23 in Stein's edition).

effort (**mōsthai**) culminating in an open display (**deiknunai**); **poiein** indicates fabrication, artifice. It must be remembered, however, that Theognis does not take a derogatory view of the activity of **poiein**, nor does he seem to agree with Hesiod that the product of **poiein**, 'false things similar to true things', is inferior. The discussion of **ainos** has shown why artifice of a sort must be a means of conveying the truth in the setting implied by the Theognidea. In verse 771, Theognis has set out a scheme of poetic **sophiē** that corresponds to the two sides of **ainos**—on the one hand, the open and direct; on the other, the obscure and indirect.

§21. **Sophiē** has the same range of obligation when it is presented from the side of citizenship. On the one hand, citizen and poet share a traditional wisdom acquired at symposia, a custom urged upon the boy Kyrnos (vv. 564–565), a custom followed by Theognis in his own boyhood (vv. 27–28). This wisdom includes the rule of dissimulation (vv. 218, 1074),[1] which closely resembles the poet's own use of ainetic indirection. On the other hand, **sophiē** may require more direct action.[2] A notable example of the citizen's active **sophiē** occurs in Theognis 1003–1006. The particular place of this example in the Theognidean scheme of **sophiē** is best discerned by comparison with four almost identical verses of Tyrtaeus:

> ἥδ' ἀρετή, τόδ' ἄεθλον ἐν ἀνθρώποισιν ἄριστον
> κάλλιστόν τε φέρειν γίνεται ἀνδρὶ νέῳ.
> ξυνὸν δ' ἐσθλὸν τοῦτο πόληΐ τε παντί τε δήμῳ,
> ὅστις ἀνὴρ διαβὰς ἐν προμάχοισι μένῃ ...
> Tyrtaeus fr. 12.13–16 W

This is **aretē** [achievement], this prize is the best amongst men
and the fairest for a young man to carry off.
This is a common **esthlon** [good] for the city and all the community
if a man stands firm and remains amongst the fore-fighters ...

These same lines occur in Theognis, with the exception of a single word. Where Tyrtaeus says 'young' (v. 14), Theognis says '**sophos**' (v. 1004).[3] Martial valor is an aspect of the citizen's **sophiē**. Thus, a

---

§21n1. See Nagy Ch.2§70 and Svenbro 1976.178, who compares Pindar fr. 43 SM.

§21n2. Cf. Heraclitus B 112 DK: σοφίη ἀληθέα λέγειν καὶ ποιεῖν.

§21n3. For the argument for taking such a discrepancy as a meaningful difference and not as a mere textual variant, see Nagy Ch.2§§33–38.

young Argive who died in battle at the end of the sixth century B.C. was praised in his epitaph as "**sophos** for his age."[4]

§ 22. To conclude, the poetry of **sophiē**, deploying itself in the various modes of **ainos**, establishes a community of **sophoi**, the true citizens. The rest of the people are negatively related to this community. Either they receive the characteristic blame of Theognis, or they do their own blaming. Megara is a city of blame (Theognis 287). Theognis does not care: they may blame me, but they cannot imitate me. No one who is not **sophos** can imitate me (vv. 367–370; cf. 23–26, 1183–1184b). Theognis' city of **sophoi** is the true city. The others are outsiders. They have literally come from outside the city, wearing the goatskins of their previous life (v. 56), which show that they are not yet city-dwellers.[1] But where is the true city? Where can Theognis' verses be put into effect (cf. §§ 16–20)? Those who are in power are not the true citizenry, and the **polis** that Theognis would reclaim is only the remembered **polis** of his own poetry. This poetry is the charter for a once and future city. Furthermore, this city is not Megara, or not only Megara but a generalized Greek **polis**, as the use of the Ionic dialect[2] and other traits[3] show.

§ 23. Can the poetry of **sophiē**, which defines itself, in contradistinction to epic, as the poetry that can guide the **polis**, escape the irony that it lacks a **polis** to guide? The answer to this question may lie in the Theognidean generalization of the Megarian situation. In every Greek city, wherever the poetry reaches, there will be the **sophoi**, the countercity, attuned to the ainetic mode of Theognis. His poetry carries its audience with it, creates its audience anew wherever it is recited. This poetry even includes instructions for some particular means of its diffusion, namely, the symposium[1] and the pederastic relationship.[2] In this way, the poetry of **sophiē** establishes its reciprocity with the city. Each **polis** provides a place in which the poetry can be remembered, at least by the **sophoi**; in return, the poetry establishes, through that which *it* remembers, the true city in that city. Each preserves the other. Theognis' use of **esthlos/-on** 'noble' as com-

---

§ 21n4. Friedländer and Hoffleit 1948 no. 136.
§ 22n1. Cf. Arrian *Anabasis* 7.9.2 and the places cited in Nagy Ch.2.§ 29n4.
§ 22n2. Nagy Ch.2 § 17.
§ 22n3. Rösler 1980.81, 84.
§ 23n1. The symposium may even be presupposed in v. 21: Svenbro 1976.84–86. See Levine Ch.7.
§ 23n2. See Lewis Ch.8.

pared with that of Xenophanes (cf. §2), where it is contrasted with 'fiction' and thus still reflects the force of the root it shares with **einai** 'to be', broadens the concept of the **esthlon** to encompass the political.[3] For Theognis, that which is, that which is true, is so in and for the city, that is, it is the good, the noble.

§24. This Theognidean reciprocity of poetry and **polis** provides a basis for reflection on the problem, mentioned in the introduction (§1), of the ancient understanding of elegy. A. E. Harvey has suggested that, if the **thrēnos** 'dirge' could take the form of a general reflection on the human condition, it becomes possible to understand how the mournfulness imputed to elegy in ancient sources could take the general form of advice which we find in the remains of this genre.[1] In particular, the elegiac grave-epigram, in its various moods of reflection (consider the example quoted in §21 above), would represent a clear-cut case of this rationalized mourning. What can be added to Harvey's suggestion is that it was through its interaction with the **polis** that elegy acquired the form in which we find it. What the Thucydidean Pericles says in the Funeral Oration, "I do not lament so much as I shall exhort" (2.44.1), would indicate the impulse behind the civic adaptation of elegy. The implication of the inscription on the statue dedicated by Smikros (§5 above) holds good for the elegiac grave-epigram also. The **polis** preserves the epigram, and the epigram, with its monitory voice, preserves the city.[2]

---

§23n3. I owe this suggestion to Richard P. Martin.

§24n1. Harvey 1955.170–172.

§24n2. See the comments of Friedländer and Hoffleit 1948 on no. 116. Cf. also Nagy 1983b.54n55 and Ford Ch.3§18 on the poetry of Theognis as a **sēma** 'sign'/ 'tomb' or **mnēma** 'memorial'. I am grateful to Richard P. Martin and Susan Scheinberg for comments on this paper.

5
The Theognidea and Megarian Society

Thomas J. Figueira

§1. The analysis of Theognis has always been inextricably bound with the reconstruction of Megarian history, so that it is not surprising that historical observation and textual exegesis have consistently been applied together in analyses of the Theognidea.[1] In any such application, there emerges a single central problem, namely, the relationship of the political, social, and historiographical traditions of Megara to the content of the Theognidea. The standard approach has been to combine individual sections of Theognis (often chosen arbitrarily) with the few attested data on seventh- or sixth-century Megara in order to create a political-literary biography of Theognis, an individual Megarian aristocrat held to be the author of the corpus or, at least, of some original authentic core of it.[2]

§2. This line of investigation, for reasons that will become clear below, obstructs rather than clarifies the relationship between Megara and Theognis. The corpus reflects history obliquely, developing in its own ideological terms and preserving vestiges of previous social situations. The Theognidean vision of Megarian realities was at every time highly selective. Thus, the focus must be on ideology throughout, because Megara was the contest ground for two opposing understandings of how a good society is to operate. Ideological systems are

---

§1n1. Cf., e.g., Harrison 1902.268–303 (from a literary critical perspective); Oost 1973 (from the vantage point of a historian).

§1n2. One particular formulation of this idea is to hold that passages that name Kyrnos are authentic, belonging to Theognis himself, and that this interpretation is supported by the **sphrēgis** (v. 19) passage. It is unlikely that anyone would have been so naive as to believe that the affixing of a name could guarantee a body of poetry against tampering. Even had Theognis meant Kyrnos by his **sphrēgis**, it is unreasonable to assume that later poets, trying to appropriate his authority, were not sufficiently competent to work the name into their verses. If Theognis' seal was the name Kyrnos, what was the seal of Critias in fr. 5 W? Would anyone care to argue that it must be the name Alkibiades?

generated to explain, both to their adherents and to others, the lives in society of those who adopt them. In the case of Megara, exigencies created by external forces (see below §49) intervened to make local ideology, perhaps already in crisis, irrelevant for state policy (cf. the Chronological Table, Notes P, R, S). The historical existence of the Megarians diverged from their inner lives, as represented in part by the value system of the Theognidea. I shall attempt below to explore the place of the poetry of Theognis both in traditions of the Megarians about their community's past and in the social history of Megara.

Megarian Traditions about their Past

§3. In any examination of the early history of Greek **poleis**, a prominent topic for discussion is always the nature and state of preservation of local traditions. For Megara, this is especially critical, as other potential sources of information (historiographical, archaeological, numismatic, epigraphical, and topographical: see the Chronological Table for the relevant citations) are scarce. Four types of witness can be adduced in an investigation of archaic Megarian history.[1] The first class is the least controversial and need be mentioned only briefly. The Atthidographers, local historians of Attica (often standing anonymously behind later accounts), provide information about the conflicts of Megara with Athens over Salamis and the Hiera Orgas, a border area of Eleusis sacred to the goddess Demeter which adjoined Megara and was supposedly encroached upon by the Megarians (see the Chronological Table, Notes H, I). They also inform us about the involvement of Solon and Peisistratos in the vindication of Athenian claims in border disputes with Megara. The historiographical problems to be faced here are not unique: chronological confusion over the successive stages of a protracted struggle, the tendency to assign Solon the responsibility for any solid accomplishment of the Athenians before 500, and ambivalence over the proper evaluation of Peisistratos. The other three classes of evidence will call for more detailed discussion. They are Aristotle's *Constitution of the Megarians*; the Megareis, writers of Megarian local histories (*Megarika*); and the corpus of the Theognidea itself.

The Constitution of the Megarians

§4. The *Constitution of the Megarians* is attested in Strabo 7.7.2 C322 (= Aristotle fr. 550 [Rose]). By convention, it is assigned to Aris-

---

§3n1. For the historical evidence about early Megara, see Okin Ch.1 above.

totle, although it is apparent that he cannot have researched or written every "Constitution" of the collection. The citation of Strabo merely informs us that the "Constitution" existed but tells us little about its content except that a pre-Greek people, the Leleges, were mentioned (Pausanias 1.39.6 = *FGH* 487 F 3; Ovid *Metamorphoses* 7.443, 8.6). A subjective judgment of the importance of Megara might lead to the argument that a student of Aristotle (cf. below, §§36–37), not the philosopher himself, would have written the *Constitution*. One may compare the argument to the effect that Aristotle must be author of the *Constitution of the Athenians*. Still, general evidence on the attribution of the "Constitutions" is lacking. The *Constitution of the Megarians* is known primarily through the use of it made by Plutarch in the *Greek Questions* (*Moralia* 295A–D, 304E–F).[1] Questions 16, 17, 18 and 59 treat Megarian history.[2] To these may be compared the notices of Aristotle on Megara and on its tyrant Theagenes in the *Politics* (1305a24–26) and again on Theagenes in the *Rhetoric* (1357b31–35). Regarding Theagenes, Aristotle in the *Politics* and the *Rhetoric* is primarily concerned with the typology of tyranny: how tyrants achieve popularity (e.g., hostility to the rich), what they use as stepping stones (e.g., procurement of a bodyguard), and how well they maintain their power. Aristotle is also concerned in the *Politics* with the circumstances under which constitutions change. Thus, the fall of the democracy (probably that of the sixth century) at Megara was of interest to him (1300a17–19, 1302b31, 1304b35–39). These notices dovetail with Plutarch's Question 18, which concerns the Palintokia 'Back-Interest' (where the interest paid by debtors to their creditors was to be paid back). Question 18 mentions at its start the fall of Theagenes. To 18 is linked 59, which begins with a reference to the extreme democracy and to the Palintokia, treated in 18. Another reference to Megara can also be mentioned at this juncture. In the *Poetics* (1448a29–b2), Aristotle introduces a claim that the Megarians originated the genre of com-

---

§4n1. Halliday 1928.92; Giessen 1901.461–465. Halliday believes that Questions 18 and 59 are almost certainly from the *Constitution*, but is less certain about 16 and 17, with his strongest doubts about 16 because of its last sentence.

§4n2. Question 16 deals with the origin in the prehistoric period of an article of Megarian women's dress, the **aphabrōma**. In Question 17, the early Megarian pattern of **xeniā** between **doruxenoi** (see the Chronological Table, Notes A, B) is traced to warfare among the five Megarian **kōmai**. The subject of Question 18 is the extreme democracy, which led to legislation providing for the return of interest to debtors, the Palintokia (Note Q). Question 59 explains the derivation of the term "wagon-rollers" by a reference to an atrocity committed against a group of Peloponnesian ambassadors on their way to Delphi at the time of the democracy (Note P).

edy. As will be seen below, the *Megarika* have been suggested as the source for this passage. These references to Megarian history by Aristotle outside the *Constitution* must be kept in mind while the *Constitution of the Megarians* is considered. The *Constitution of the Athenians* in its historical section, chapters 1–41, is drawn from the Atthidographers, local Athenian historians; therefore the Megarian local historians are the obvious candidates for the sources of the *Constitution of the Megarians*.

Megarian Local History

§5. A consideration of the source(s) of the *Constitution of the Megarians* can only be attempted after the surviving fragments of the *Megarika* have been investigated. The names of the Megareis that have descended to us are Praxion, Dieuchidas, Hereas, and Heragoras.[1] They have been treated as pairs, with Praxion and Dieuchidas as father and son, and Heragoras (cited only in a scholion to Apollonius of Rhodes [1.211–215]) equated with Hereas (or as another father-son pair).[2] That Praxion wrote a *Megarika* has been doubted on the grounds that an original citation of Dieuchidas, son of Praxion, could have been distorted to create an attribution of a history to Praxion in the source of the *Suda* and of Harpocration.[3] A first impression, therefore, received from the fragments of the Megareis is that this was hardly a vigorous school of local history, with many representatives.[4] Praxion can lay claim to a single fragment (*FGH* 484). To Dieuchidas, Jacoby assigns one testimonium and eleven fragments (*FGH* 485). Piccirilli credits him with twelve fragments (P 2). Hereas gets four fragments in Jacoby (*FGH* 486) and three in Piccirilli (P 3). Piccirilli would give a single fragment to Heragoras, whom he sees as discrete from Hereas (P 4). To anonymous Megareis, Jacoby attributes thirteen fragments (*FGH* 487). Piccirilli has twenty-four fragments in his corresponding category (P 5). He has also collected another group, *adespota* of Megarian provenience, in which he places fifteen fragments (P 6).

---

§5n1. Piccirilli 1975; Jacoby *FGH* 484–487; *Komm.* 3b.389–400; *Noten* 3b.229–237. Cf. also the discussion in Okin Ch.1§§9–10, §§18–22.

§5n2. Piccirilli 1975.9 (for Praxion and Dieuchidas); Wilamowitz 1884.259–260n22; Jacoby *FGH Komm.* 3b 394; *Noten* 233–234 (for Hereas and Heragoras).

§5n3. Prakken 1941.348; Davison 1959.221.

§5n4. The Megareis may be contrasted with the number of entries in the *FGH* for Athens (323a–375), Sparta (580–598), Samos (534–545), and Rhodes (507–533). In number of representatives the Megarian local historical tradition is comparable with that of Corinth (451–455) or Aigina (299–300).

§6. Of the eighteen separate citations comprising the fragments of named Megarian historians, four are from Plutarch, three each from the scholia to Apollonius and from Harpocration, and two from the *Stromateis* of Clement. Six other proveniences contribute one citation each. Of the fragments from the Megareis (P 5) and of possible Megarian provenience (P 6), thirty-nine in all, twenty-nine are from Pausanias (P 5: 22; P 6: 7), though some are also known through other intermediaries. Plutarch is the intermediary for five (P 5: 3; P 6: 2). It is noteworthy that, outside of the *Greek Questions*, Plutarch cites his sources by name or by the general title Megareis. On the only occasion that he does not do so (*Solon* 10.2 = P 6, F 12b), and which has the look of being from a local Megarian historian, he cites Hereas by name a few lines below (*Solon* 10.5 = Hereas *FGH* 486 F 4 = P 3, F 3). Thus, there appear to be two patterns in which Plutarch included material about Megara in his works. Generally, he made use of Megarian historians (and Atthidographers) on Megara, using variously specific or generic attributions. In the *Greek Questions*, he used the *Constitution of the Megarians*, along with other Peripatetic *Constitutions*.

§7. Let us turn now to the content of the fragments themselves. The one fragment of Praxion is what we might call mythological. Of the fragments of Dieuchidas, six treat mythology (one aetiological), one cult, two the chronology of Lycurgus, two topography, and one the Salamis dispute. Plutarch quotes Dieuchidas on Lycurgus for chronology (*FGH* 485 F 4, F 5). It is uncertain how a Spartan legislator was incorporated into a Megarian local history. An assumption, reasonable given the mythological character of so much of the work of Dieuchidas, is that he used Lycurgus to establish a date for the arrival of the Dorians in the Peloponnesus. Dieuchidas dated Lycurgus in relation to the fall of Troy and to the Spartan king-list. Hereas' fragments concern mythology (2) and the Salamis dispute (1). The single fragment of Heragoras has to do with mythology. It is noteworthy that Dieuchidas (*FGH* 485 F 6) and Hereas (*FGH* 487 F 4) comment only on the strength of Athenian justifications for ownership of Salamis, not on the actual struggle for the island.[1]

§8. The fragments from Piccirilli's classes P 5 and P 6, mainly from Pausanias, treat mythology, cult, and topography in their interconnec-

---

§7n1. De Ste. Croix 1972.387 notes Hereas' insertion of a discussion of Peisistratid interpolations into a passage dealing with Theseus (Plutarch *Theseus* 20.1–2). At particular issue are a line said to have been deleted by Peisistratos from a Hesiodic work, *Aigimios* (fr. 298) and a line inserted into the *Nekuia* (*Odyssey* xi 631).

tions. Some, however, treat history and must now be discussed in detail. F 20 (P 5) concerns early Megarian history and deals with the Olympic victor and general Orsippos. However, Pausanias (1.44.1) marks his source merely with phāsi 'they say'. He seems to base himself on an inscription dedicated to Orsippos, a copy of which has survived (*IG* vii 52). His notice is so abbreviated that it is unlikely that he had any source save the inscription and contemporary informants (see the Chronological Table, Note D). Fragment 21 (P 5, Pausanias 1.40.5) calls attention to the spoils taken by the Megarians from the Athenians in a fight over Salamis and goes on to assert that a group of traitors, the Dorykleians, were responsible for the subsequent Athenian recapture of the island. The Athenians credited Solon with this capture. Yet, it might be noted that, before he cited the Megareis, Pausanias marked his source with the term phāsi for the information that a bronze ship's ram dedicated at Megara was taken at Salamis from the Athenians. This may suggest that the term Megareis, which follows to introduce the anecdote about the Dorykleians, is to be taken nontechnically to mean merely Megarians (contemporaries of Pausanias) rather than Megarian historians. F 22 (Pausanias 1.40.2) describes the thwarting of the Persian raid on the Megarid in 479. But once more Pausanias marks his source merely with phāsi. F 23 (Plutarch *Pericles* 30.2–4) recounts the Megarian version of the responsibility for the issuance of the Megarian Decree and, thereby, for the Peloponnesian War. The interpretation of this fragment is very vexed. It is quite possible that the Megareis mentioned by Plutarch here are once more not Megarian historians but (uncharacteristically) Megarian contemporaries who were his informants.[1] In any

---

§8n1. In his discussion of the Megarian Decree, Plutarch gives an important part to the assassination by the Megarians of the Athenian herald Anthemokritos. The Megarians denied this charge and attempted to cast the blame for the Peloponnesian War on Pericles and Aspasia by citing, according to Plutarch, Aristophanes' *Acharnians* 524–527. This narrative is difficult to reconcile with Thucydides, who is silent about the incident involving Anthemokritos. Does one conclude from Thucydides' silence that the historian has deliberately suppressed evidence or merely that Plutarch must be mistaken? The latter alternative appears preferable, and one solution along these lines is to move the Anthemokritos episode to the fourth century (Connor 1962). But it is unlikely that the Megareis, cited as a source by Plutarch, can ever have been so misinformed about fifth- and fourth-century Megarian history, if Megareis means Megarian historians here (Dover 1966.204–206). Yet Plutarch's treatment of the Anthemokritos episode seems compressed. The denial of the murder of Anthemokritos and the casting of blame onto Pericles cannot have been successive stages in the same argument. After all, Anthemokritos was dead. Any Megarian exculpation for the murder of a herald, a damning accusation in any context, ought to have been much more detailed. That the Megarians denied responsibility for the death of Anthemokritos might be a deduction

event, one would not be justified in reconstructing the *Megarika* as continuous sequential political histories on the basis of this single fragment. If the Megareis dealt with Pericles' guilt for the Peloponnesian War, it is still not necessary to see a historical narrative here. The subject of Pericles can have been treated in the context of the mythico-religious justifications for Megarian ownership of Eleusinian borderlands.

§9. To Piccirilli, F 24 (P 6) concerns a claim from the *Megarika* that the Megarians invented comedy.[1] If the scanty evidence for the dates of the Megareis is any basis, only Praxion can with certainty have been available for use by Aristotle in the *Poetics*, as he would be dated to the second quarter of the fourth century. Dieuchidas, who was active in the second half of the fourth century, might have been Aristotle's source, if the *Poetics* are to be dated after 350.[2] How-

---

from the fact that they blamed Pericles and Aspasia. In this case, the chronological error belongs to Plutarch. The most that can be attributed to the Megareis here is that they cited Aristophanes for support of their charges. Periclean responsibility for the Peloponnesian War (including the causation of the Megarian Decree[s]) was a topic treated by the Atthidographers (cf. Philochorus *FGH* 328 F 121; *FGH Komm.* 3b Suppl. 1.484–491). It is likely that on this subject the Megarian local historians were carrying on their dialogue/debate with them. Yet this interpretation is not obviously preferable to the simple but more radical solution that Megareis means only Megarians here (cf. the **doruxenoi**). Connor would have us compare *Theseus* 27.8. The general character of the Megareis and the unlikelihood that the account of Plutarch is to be preferred to that of Thucydides tells against the existence in the *Megarika* of a thorough narrative on the outbreak of the Peloponnesian War (Connor 1970; de Ste. Croix 1972.246–251, 386–388).

§9n1. For Praxion (or another one of the Megareis) as Aristotle's source: Piccirilli 1975.141–150; for Dieuchidas as source: Wilamowitz 1937.384n1; for Hereas as source (which I think improbable): Gudeman 1934.111.

§9n2. Praxion and Dieuchidas have been dated to the second quarter and the second half of the fourth century, respectively, on the basis of *SIG*[3] 241.142, which mentions a Dieuchidas, the son of Praxion, as a **naopoios** 'temple-building official' at Delphi between 338/7 and 330/29 (Piccirilli 1975.9–10, 14–15). If one denies, however, that the persons mentioned in the inscription are to be equated with the Megareis, it might be possible to date Dieuchidas at the turn from the third to the second century on internal grounds (Davison 1959.221). It is possible that Hereas can only have written as he did about Athenian burial customs after the legislation of Demetrios of Phaleron in 317/16 (Prakken 1943–1944.123). Hereas ought to have preceded Hermippos and Istros (both third century), who perhaps used him and who were the intermediaries through which Plutarch had access to his work (Piccirilli 1975.55–56). If Hereas is the same man who is known as a sacred ambassador from *IG* VII 39, he is to be dated c. 300 (Jacoby *FGH Komm.* 3b.394, *Noten* 233–234). Note also the Megarian Kallikrates, son of Hereas, a **proxenos** 'consul' or 'representative' attested at Delphi (*FdD* 3.1.189; cf. *IG* VII 141).

ever, Aristotle does not attribute his remarks to any source (*Poetics* 1448a29–b2). The derivation of **kōmōidiā** from **kōmē** and the observation that the Athenians had demes rather than **kōmai** like the Megarians could have been made at any time by almost anyone—a sophist interested in the derivation of words, for instance.[3] For inclusion of this fragment in the *Megarika*, Piccirilli argues that the Megarians must have contested with the Athenians the honor of originating comedy. Megarian comedy is closely associated with Megarian democracy by Aristotle. To assert that the Megareis insisted on the priority of Megarian comedy is to posit that the Megareis had a positive appraisal of Megarian democracy. The surviving evidence, however, does not support such an assumption.

§ 10. The surviving fragments of the *Megarika* are overwhelmingly prehistoric or mythological in character. This is hardly surprising when their proveniences are considered, that is, so much from scholia and Pausanias. Yet, Pausanias, when he chose, could cite from local historians, as he did in his treatment of Messenian history, which depends on Myron of Priene and Rhianos of Bene (*FGH* 106 T 1; cf. *FGH* 106 F 3; *FGH* 265 F 42–45). The unattributed citations from the Megareis scarcely allow for a strong case to be made about the historical content of the *Megarika*. F 20 and F 22 are attributed only by the word **phāsi**. For F 21 and F 23, the term Megareis is designated in the citations, but in each case, there is some doubt about whether it need mean anything other than Megarians.

§ 11. The anti-Athenian thrust of the *Megarika* on the Salamis dispute is consonant with the spirit of some notices on mythological and religious subjects. The *Megarika* were clearly received as a polemic against Megara's historical enemies. Philochorus may have taken pains to answer charges that the Athenians had interpolated their own versions into the text of Homer (Philochorus *FGH* 328 F 212; cf. F 11, 107, 111). A context for this intense Megarian effort to defend the honor of their community can be sought in the mid-fourth century revival of controversy with Athens over the Megarid's border with Eleusis (Demosthenes 13.32–33; Androtion *FGH* 324 F 30; Philochorus *FGH* 328 F 155; cf. Pausanias 1.36.3).

§ 12. A preliminary assessment of the historical content of the *Megarika* is in order. The Megareis were primarily concerned with antiqui-

---

§9n3. Else 1957.123 suggests Dikaiarkhos or Aristoxenos.

ties of their city, that is, Megara's earliest history and the creation of its institutions. A patriotic and antiquarian interest entailed a defense of Megara's claims to the independence of its political and religious traditions and of what the Megarians considered their rightful borders; that is, that the claim to Salamis and the Hiera Orgas was grounded in the formative period of their communal existence. In such an account, the purported misrepresentations of Solon and Peisistratos found their refutation. But this refutation was placed in the context of Megarian prehistory, not of Megarian history. Moreover, perhaps appropriately for those who had the worst of the struggle so consistently, the Megarians and their local historians did not dispute the sequence of events in the hostilities with Athens or their outcome. Rather, they turned to the distant past to redress contemporary grievances. Plutarch does not cite them for any political or military details about the Salamis conflict. Even if the unattributed historical fragments of Piccirilli's P 5 classification are truly from the *Megarika*, it is still unnecessary to hold that the *Megarika* contained a historical narrative of the sixth and fifth centuries. The *Megarika* seem to have followed a nonsequential mode of presentation. The Dorykleians, the Megarian traitors who betrayed Salamis to Athens, could have been introduced to answer an Athenian claim to Salamis on the grounds that the hero Eurysakes had given the island to them. Mardonios' dispatch of troops into the Megarid in 479 could have had a rationale for its inclusion in an explanation of the cult of Artemis Soteira (cf. *IG* VII 16[?], 112), initially justified by its **aition** set in prehistory. No one quotes anything specifically from the Megareis that could remotely be called constitutional or political history.

Plutarch and the Megareis

§13. The aforesaid interpretation sets the content of the *Megarika* at a sharp variance with the valuable information in Plutarch's *Greek Questions*, of which the origin has been sought in Aristotle's *Constitution of the Megarians*, and with the interesting material on Theagenes and on the fall of the Megarian democracy preserved in the *Politics* and the *Rhetoric*. Yet this conclusion appears on the surface perverse, vulnerable to the question of where else Megarian constitutional antiquities could have been preserved except in a Megarian local historical tradition. One might object that it is far more likely that the character of the surviving citations from the *Megarika* has been skewed by accidents of transmission. In this case, the mythological, religious, and lexicographical interests of the late ancient authors who quote from the *Megarika* go far to explain the absence of historical material.

§14. Plutarch, however, must be treated differently. He thought Megarian history to be of sufficient interest to include four Megarian "Questions" in the *Greek Questions*, but elsewhere made little use of the *Megarika*, except in terms of mythico-religious claims vis-à-vis Athens. These circumstances could be explained by assuming that Plutarch used the *Constitution of the Megarians* as his source in the *Greek Questions*, and some other intermediary drawing from the Megareis in his other works. The disparity in emphasis between the *Constitution of the Megarians* and the *Megarika* is to be attributed to differences in interests and in historical acumen between the Peripatetic author of the *Constitution* and our hypothetical intermediary. As a source for the information of Plutarch (and Diogenes Laertius) on the dispute between Athens and Megara over Salamis, Hermippos has been suggested.[1] Hermippos is cited by Plutarch as a source in the *Life of Solon* (frr. 7, 8, 10 [Wehrli]) and in the *Life of Lycurgus* (fr. 85 = *Lycurgus* 23.2; fr. 86 = *Lycurgus* 5), and is generally held as a major source for the *Solon*. However, before considering Hermippos as a source on Megara, I must first explore the relationship of the Theognidea to Megarian local tradition as represented by the *Megarika*.

The Megarika and Theognis

§15. The observation to be made first about the Theognidea and the Megarian local historical traditions is that the two come together on very few points.[1] There is no reference to Theognis in the surviving bits of Megarian local historical tradition. This is a sharp divergence from the relationship attested elsewhere between cities and their poetic traditions. Solon became the embodiment of the evolution of Athenian political institutions. The expression "Laws of Solon" became equivalent to the entire sacred and civil legal code of Athens. But it might be objected that in Solon the roles of **nomothetēs** 'lawgiver' and poetic inculcator of values were fused. In response, the

---

§14n1. See Piccirilli 1975.6, 14, 31, 70, 82 for Hermippos as a source for Dieuchidas (*FGH* 485 F 5, F 6 [= Diogenes Laertius 1.57]), and for Hereas (*FGH* 486 F 3). Piccirilli also suggests the Atthidographer Istros as a source for the lives of Solon and Lycurgus, following Jacoby (*FGH* 334 *Komm.* 3b Suppl. 635). Istros is a poor choice for the one who selected out historical data as an intermediary to the *Megarika*. The *Megarika*, if they had been continuous historical narratives, would necessarily have been filled with polemics against Athens because of the frequent conflicts between the Athenians and the Megarians. The Atthidographers would have made an effort to refute anti-Athenian material and would necessarily have transmitted much Megarian historiography to Istros.

§15n1. Cf. Okin Ch.1 §§11–16 above.

position of Tyrtaeus at Sparta may be cited. In this case, it is chiefly through the agency of poetry that the influence of Tyrtaeus was felt. The political career of Tyrtaeus is merely extrapolated from his activity as encoder of values through poetry (*Suda* s.v. "**Turtaios**"; Pausanias 4.15.6, 16.2, 18.3; scholia Plato *Laws* 629A; Strabo 8.4.10 C362). Perhaps the ideology of Theognis stood somehow at variance with that which prevailed in the Megara of the fourth century and later, that of the Megareis. Nonetheless, even a poet such as Archilochus, whose poetry might have seemed to Hellenistic Parians to adopt an adversary position relative to social conventions of his time and of his **polis**,[2] could be clasped to the bosom of local historians bent upon magnifying the reputation of their mother city.[3] Some explanation for the mutual alienation of Theognis and Megarian historical tradition should be sought.

§16. Let us consider two exceptions. Theognis mentions Alkathoos, the eponym of one of the Megarian citadels (v. 774). The story of this early king is told in Dieuchidas (*FGH* 485 F 10), and his building of Megara's walls is mentioned in an unattributed citation from the *Megarika* (*FGH* 487 F 5). Another unattributed segment of the *Megarika* (P 5 F 22) describes the discomfiture of a Persian raiding party in the Megarid in 479. The same episode may have inspired Theognis 773–782.[1] It is significant that the only two points of partial contact between the corpus and the *Megarika* should lie in the same passage and in one that is obviously one of the latest datable passages in the work. To the lack of comment by the Megareis on the Theognidea is juxtaposed the general absence in Theognis of direct historical allusions. One exception is the mention of an otherwise unknown

§15n2. Fragments 5, 101, 114, 133; cf. Pindar *P.* 2.55; Critias in Aelian *Varia Historia* 10.13; Aristotle *Rhetoric* 1398b11–12; Valerius Maximus 6.3.1, external.

§15n3. The Hellenistic Parian tradition on Archilochus (somewhat surprisingly) emphasizes his service to the **polis** as good citizen and warrior and singles out his intervention in establishing the cult of Dionysos as especially significant. Archilochus may be noted in the third-century Parian chronographic document, the *Marmor Parium*, under the year 682/1 (*FGH* 239 A 33); in a biographical inscription of Mnesiepes nearly contemporary with the *Marmor Parium* (*SEG* xv.517; cf. xvi.481; xix.557); and in the Demeas/Sosthenes inscription of c. 100, which gives as its source a lost account of Sosthenes (*IG* xii.5 445 = *FGH* 502 F 1; cf. *SEG* xv.518). Note also the Archilocheion, a cult place dedicated to the poet, and the honors awarded by the Parians to the poet as attested by Aristotle (*Rhetoric* 1398b10–11). See Mayo 1973; Kontoleon 1963.

§16n1. Van Groningen 1966.301–302. Cf. Highbarger 1937.109–111, who is not to be followed in his attempts to find references in the Theognidea to the Persian conquest of Ionia in 546 and to the Marathon campaign.

sack of Kerinthos and fighting on the Lelantine plain (vv. 891–894; see the Chronological Table, Note L). Also, verses 757–768 make reference to an invasion by the Medes, probably the invasion of Xerxes in 480. Obviously, Megarian local historians' lack of interest in Theognis is parallel to a lack of detail on Megara in the Theognidea. Though arguments from silence are notorious, one may note the absence of various types of references in the Theognidea. First, references to subdivisions of the citizen body are missing: no tribes, no **kōmai**, no **hekatostues**—all of which are known to have existed at Megara.[2] Second, there are no magistrates or offices mentioned, although one might well imagine hortatory or paraenetic literature that might give political advice in specific terms. Third, there are no toponyms of the Megarid present, except for the qualifier **Megareus** (v. 23) in the **sphrēgis** 'seal' passage, with which reference this gesture of identification and appropriation could not dispense. The thirty geographical and ethnic terms, where identifiable, refer to places outside the Megarid. Fourth, the political language is very general (e.g., **astos**, **dēmos**, **lāos**, **hēgemones**). Obviously, a conventionalizing process has taken place in Theognidean poetry to remove topical grounding in archaic Megara.

§17. Yet, our conclusion might once again be countered with the objection that the lack of connections between the Megareis and the Theognidea is a result of the preoccupations of intermediaries for the *Megarika*. But the fact remains that the biographical tradition concerning Theognis is extremely meager. In line with this fact, it is not surprising that there was even controversy in antiquity over which Megara was to receive the honor of being acknowledged as the poet's homeland. Megara Hyblaea was identified as Theognis' mother city by Plato (*Laws* 630A) and by the *Suda* (s.v. "**Theognis**"). Other authorities held that mainland Megara (Nisaean Megara) was the Megara of Theognis (Stephanus Byzantius s.v. "**Megara**"; Harpocration s.v. "**Theognis**"; Didymus at scholia Plato *Laws* 630A). Harpocration and the scholiast attest to the ancient debate between the two views and attempt to reconcile the differences by making Theognis a naturalized citizen of Megara Hyblaea. Internal arguments are of little help;[1] otherwise, the question should have been settled long ago.

---

§16n2. Magistracies and political subdivisions: Oost 1973.186n4; Hanell 1934. 137–160.

§17n1. Note Beloch 1888.729–733 for the sort of precarious reasoning required for attempts to determine the homeland of Theognis on the basis of the internal evidence of the corpus. Cf. Harrison 1902.268–281.

Clearly, Theognis verses 773–774 refer to the citadel of homeland Megara. Verses 783–788 speak of the poet's journey to Sicily along with other visits. This seems to indicate the perspective of a non-Sicilian. The verses that refer to the devastation of the Lelantine plain make best sense in the mouth of an inhabitant of Megara in mainland Greece. Thus, while one may conclude that an insufficient body of biographical evidence ever existed to make conclusions on this subject, internal evidence is slightly in support of an origin in "homeland" Megara.

§18. It is most improbable, then, that ancient biographers had included lives of Theognis in their collections. This conclusion is especially significant as we consider once again that prolific author of short biographies, Hermippos, a follower of Callimachus, as well as a researcher in the Peripatetic tradition.[1] Fragments of his are known from biographies of poets (e.g., fr. 93 [Wehrli] on Hipponax) and from a series of biographies of the "Seven Sages" (frr. 5–16). It is here that Theognis, the poet of gnōmai 'maxims', would be expected. If Hermippos was the intermediary who passed on his knowledge of the Megarian local historians to Plutarch, and Hermippos wrote no life of Theognis, then it is unlikely that there was much in the *Megarika* about the life of Theognis, and it is this deficiency in the local historical tradition that may well explain the weak biographical tradition regarding Theognis.[2]

Plato and the Theognidea

§19. The fact that Plato believed Theognis to have been a Sicilian cannot be overestimated in its importance, since Plato was well aware of the poetic traditions of Sicily through his stays at the court of the Syracusan tyrants. That he assigns Theognis to Megara Hyblaea without a hint that he is making a controversial statement suggests that he encountered Theognidean poetry in circulation there and found it

---

§18n1. Wehrli 1974.

§18n2. Consider also Xenophon's treatise on Theognis. If the surviving passage is typical (Stobaeus *Florilegium* 88.14), the treatise amounted to an exegesis of passages investigating constants of human nature. Contrast Xenophon's *Hiero* on the conduct and pleasures of tyrants, which has as interlocutors the Syracusan tyrant Hieron and the poet Simonides. The last section of the dialogue, containing Simonides' advice to Hieron, was probably based on Simonidean victory odes, which offered political admonition. Whereas Simonides' poetry could be encapsulated in a dialogue, because traditions existed about his life to dramatize his relationship with Hieron, for Theognis it seems that nothing remained but the poetry itself.

treated as though it were local. One does not have to search far for a demonstration of the existence of this poetry, since the Theognidea at one time contained a poem with a definite Sicilian context. The *Suda* reports its existence (s.v. "**Theognis**"):

ἔγραψεν ἐλεγείαν εἰς τοὺς σωθέντας τῶν Συρακουσίων ἐν τῇ πολιορκίᾳ.

He [Theognis] wrote an elegy in honor of those Syracusans who survived the siege.

The credence placed in this notice, however, has been undermined by difficulties in establishing a historical context for this "elegy." A siege has been read into the Herodotean description of Hippokrates of Gela's unsuccessful war against Syracuse (Herodotus 7.154.2), but this solution has little to recommend it, as nothing suggests that a siege actually took place. Some have suggested an occasion for the poem in the abortive Athenian siege of Syracuse during the Peloponnesian War. In this line of reasoning the poem that treated it would be a late addition to the corpus, one that was later lost.[1] Unfortunately, this hypothesis entails that the elegy's author be Theognis, a late fifth-century writer of tragedies so frigid that he had the byname "Snow" (*Suda* s.v. "**Theognis**"; cf. Aristophanes *Acharnians* 11, 140; *Thesmophoriazusae* 170). That a poem of the tragedian is behind this notice involves a series of assumptions too complex to be justified. In any case, the source of the *Suda* cannot have had an inhabitant of Megara Hyblaea writing a poem in honor of Syracuse, the archenemy and eventual destroyer of his **polis**, without an explanation, of which there is no trace in the notice. An attempt to make historical sense of this notice must assume that the *Suda* distorted or carelessly summarized its source for the episode. The phrase **tous sōthentas** 'those having been preserved' ought to refer to Megarians. One might suggest that during the sixth century the Megarians in Sicily withstood an otherwise unknown siege at the hands of Syracuse. Harrison, however, suggests a reference to the successful siege of Megara Hyblaea by Gelon c. 483 (Herodotus 7.156.2).[2] To him, **eis** in the *Suda* entry above means merely 'about', not 'in honor of', and **hupo** must be inserted before **tōn Surakousiōn**. According to this theory, the poem was about the wealthy citizens of Megara Hyblaea transferred to Syracuse by Gelon and the Syracusans, and thereby safe from enslavement. The addition of **hupo** may not be necessary. The

---

§19n1. Carrière 1948.8–9; Harrison 1902.295–297.
§19n2. Harrison 1902.296–297.

word **Surakousiōn** 'of the Syracusans' could be a subjective genitive with **poliorkiāi**, or a genitive of separation with **sōthentas** 'saved from the Syracusans'. Both genitival constructions are slightly strained from the standpoint of word order, but perhaps allowable in the title of a poem. Moreover, there is no reason to think that this poem differed essentially from the gnomic, paraenetic material of the rest of the corpus. Hence, the poem ought not to be "about" the survivors, but **eis** should mean 'for' or 'against' in the same way that the surviving Theognidea are 'for' and in other contexts 'against' Kyrnos and the **agathoi** who have defected to the **kakoi**. Whether the poem addressed the survivors of an unknown siege of the sixth century or those preserved by Gelon in c. 483, one would expect the emphasis of the elegy to have been on **stasis** 'conflict between social groups', so common in Sicily, and on its causes and tragic results. The war with Gelon, one may note, was started by the elite of Megara Hyblaea without the collaboration of the **dēmos**. Consequently, it is unreasonable to expect that the poem under discussion would have provided a narrative of the siege. Rather, it was probably of the same character as Theognidean injunctions in the surviving corpus which take as their setting the eve of the Persian invasion (vv. 757–764, 773–788). A Sicilian "elegy," for the most part admonitory and normalizing, could have pervaded the whole corpus of the Theognidea.[3] I would suggest that the ancient edition of Theognis contained material of a Sicilian extraction in addition to the parts of the surviving corpus that bear associations with mainland Megara. On the basis of the Sicilian poem(s), Plato and perhaps others made the determination that Theognis was a Sicilian (Plato *Laws* 630A).[4]

§ 20. Concomitantly, Plato may also have seen Theognis as Sicilian because he encountered no particular interest in Theognis among contemporary intellectuals native to mainland Megara. He knew these well through his association with Eukleides, the founder of the Megarian school of philosophy (Megarikoi: see, e.g., Diogenes Laertius

---

§ 19n3. For a parallel, consider the putative fragments of the *Smyrneis* of Mimnermus (frr. 9, 13, 14 W; cf. 13a W, which notes the title). Fragment 14, describing the valiant deeds of a warrior, is hortatory in character, like much of Theognis. Fragment 9, however, mentioning the foundation of Colophon and the capture of Smyrna, is more grounded in history than anything in Theognis. Yet its introduction of the theme of **hubris** suggests that a crisis (envisaged as present) is to be put in a normative framework. The Sicilian elegy may have approached its occasion, the siege, in the same manner. All colonial poetical traditions shared features of the **ktisis** 'foundation' story.

§ 19n4. See Okin Ch.1 § 16 above.

1.18–19 [fr. 35 Döring]). Plato traveled to Megara in the company of Eukleides after the death of Socrates (Diogenes Laertius 3.6 [fr. 4A Döring]; cf. frr. 4E, 5–6, 26A Döring). Our sources are emphatic about the Socratic character of the Megarian school (frr. 1–3, 10A–B, 18, 20, 26A, 34–38, 43A–B Döring). This situation seems to indicate the extinction of local ideological traditions (see below, §§63–64) and of the poetic traditions that embodied them. Plato appears more interested in Theognis, whom he viewed as a Sicilian, than were contemporary Megarians from Nisaean Megara. An exception merely certifies that the Megarikoi assimilated little of the Theognidean ideology. The Megarian philosopher Diodoros of Iasos (c. 300) had among his five philosophical daughters one Theognis, named, it seems, after that archaic exponent of pederasty (Clement *Stromateis* 4.19.121.5 [fr. 101 Döring]). One may conclude that Theognidean poetry does not appear to be a topic of interest either to Megareis, Megarian local historians, or to Megarikoi, Megarian philosophers who followed Socrates. There is no reason to think that their fellow citizens differed from them. I shall argue that the reason for this situation was ideological. Conversely, local traditions claiming Theognis existed in Sicily in the fourth century, but these were literary traditions current at the Syracusan court, since Megara Hyblaea had been destroyed long before.

A Pan-Megarian Theognis

§21. As has been seen, the corpus of the Theognidea lacks a strong historical grounding in either Megara. Our discussion of the Sicilian elegy suggests the possibility that the aristocratic social code the corpus was meant to encapsulate had to do duty for Megara, Megara Hyblaea, and other Megarian colonies as well (see the Chronological Table, Note C). The existence of the same ideological polarities in the Megarian colonies explains how Heraclea, founded when the metropolis was democratic, could overthrow the democracy and establish an oligarchy in a way similar to the succession of events that took place in the mother city, and at approximately the same time. The accretions to the corpus may have had a topical grounding in the form in which they circulated in the city of their composition, but this context was filtered out in their adaptation or assimilation to the Theognidea. This does not mean that the material of the Theognidea is useless in illuminating archaic Megara. The final fixation of the Theognidean text may have suspended the filtering out of particular passages with topical valences. The corpus evolved in content from the specific to the general. This may have happened in combination with a process of abbreviation. The longer sections, especially those addressed to named individuals (except those that name Kyrnos), may be more topical, more locally grounded (see, e.g., below, §59). The names will have had original valences because the poet's audience identified those named with actual persons or recognized in their names conventional figures decipherable by the ideological reading inherent in their names. Moreover, in institutional or ideological terms, much that can be extracted from the corpus may hold good for colonial Megarians as well as for Megara. Nevertheless, some care must be exercised, as all political allusions in Theognis are likely to be at several removes by the stage of their final crystallization.

Genre and Ideology among the Megarians

Generalization and Specificity

§22. If the corpus of the Theognidea was a common possession of all the Megarians and its ideology was similarly common, how did poetry and ideology inform partisan politics in cities with external political circumstances that were superficially so different? Moreover, on which social institutions did Megarian oligarchic or democratic ideology make its influence felt, and on what level of generalization? I shall be looking especially for a level of abstraction appropriate for all Megarians, although I cannot, of course, entirely rule out the possibility that on this same plane the corpus had a pan-Hellenic significance. The political order adopted by Megara after its **sunoikismos** and independence from Corinth must have been more attractive than was the Bacchiad polity of Corinth to those Megarians whose territory was thereafter occupied by Corinth (see the Chronological Table, Notes A, B, C). The Megarians did not "in-gather" for the sake of more of the same. Yet, in the Theognidea, one passage features a stark contrast between the **agathoi** who had once led the community and the animalistic inhabitants of the countryside who had later become **agathoi**, or members of the elite (vv. 53–57: see below, §41). Parallel to this comparison of urban **agathoi** and rural **kakoi** is the repeated use of the terms **astoi** for members of the community and **astu** for **polis** or town (vv. 24, 41, 61, 191, 283, 367, 739, 868, 937, 1082a, 1184a).[1] So too we find in the corpus an emphasis on the maintenance of genetic purity by the elite and an abhorrence of intermarriage between social groups (vv. 183–192). Had these sentiments been articulated in eighth- or early seventh-century Corinth by

---

§22n1. Note that **astoi** is used in the inscription in honor of the Megarian dead from the Persian Wars (Tod 1 no. 20).

a member of the Bacchiad clan, they would seem natural. There, access to the refuge on the acropolis of Acrocorinth may have been limited.[2] The Bacchiads were a closed oligarchy who practiced endogamy, at least in principle. However, these institutions were unlikely to have survived the separation of Megara from Corinth. Plutarch's treatment of the institution of the **doruxenoi** already suggests reciprocity between the **kōmai** before **sunoikismos** (see the Chronological Table, Note B). It is hard to visualize the motivation of the rest of the **kōmai** in breaking away from Corinth only to accept a similar narrow oligarchy directed from the town of Megara. Rather, we may posit that Corinthian political institutions were used to express stances taken by the poetry of the Theognidea. In any specific political confrontation, the ideology favoring changes in Megarian society in the direction of closure expressed itself naturally on the model of the extreme closure of Bacchiad Corinth. It is even conceivable to expect that such formulations could evolve in isolation from social reality. The contrast between countryside and town would have been expressive for colonial Megarians as well, inasmuch as the hinterland of their **poleis** would have been inhabited by non-Greeks in the first place. For example, the native population in the hinterland of the Megarian colony of Heraclea Pontica, the Mariandynoi, were reduced to serfdom by the colonists (Posidonius *FGH* 87 F 8, Euphorion fr. 78 [Powell] at Athenaeus 263D; Hesychius s.v. "**dōrophorous**"; Plato *Laws* 776C–D; Strabo 12.3.4 C542; Pollux 3.83). The emotive force of the confrontations between town and country and between endogamy and exogamy, not their verisimilitude, justifies their appearance in the Theognidea.

§23. The results for the Theognidea of this generalization, which I have just posited, stand out in higher relief if we consider the relationship between the Theognidea and the *Constitution of the Megarians* as represented by Plutarch's *Greek Questions*. Aristotle is more specific than Theognis, and there is no possibility that the *Constitution* can have derived from the corpus, even from its lost portions, unless these were radically different from what has been preserved. It has already been indicated that the *Constitution* differed in focus from the *Megarika*, and this has left us in the paradoxical position of accounting for a tradition on Megara that was not represented in local histori-

---

§22n2. Such a provision would help explain the scattered villages on the site of Corinth during the eighth and early seventh centuries and the slow development of the settlement on Acrocorinth compared with the settlement on the Temple Hill (Roebuck 1972.121–127).

ography but was apparently well-informed. If competing ideologies could have acted to appropriate or exclude different sets of data on archaic Megara, then we are left with the task of considering the principles of selection that may have operated on the material in Megarian elegiac poetry.

§24. The similarities between Aristotle/Plutarch in Question 18 of the *Greek Questions* (supplemented by *Politics* 1304b34–39) on the one hand and Theognis on the other are the following (cf. above, §4):

Aristotle	Theognis
loss of **sōphrosunē**	emphasis on maintaining **phrenes** (vv. 373–392, 429–438, 452–456, 753–756, 1007–1012, 1049–1054, 1171–1176; cf. 39–52, 1135–1150)
demagogues make citizens drunk with democracy	drunkards as lacking in **sōphrosunē** (475–496, 497–498, 503–510; cf. 413–414, 837–840, 873–876)
wanton behavior toward **plousioi**	**kakoi** prone to wanton behavior (39–52, 151–152, 153–154, 306–308, 373–392, 731–735)
dēmos invades homes of rich to feast	subhumans invade city to become **agathoi** (53–68)
dēmos uses **biē** and **hubris**	**khrēmata** taken by **biē** (341–350, 667–682; cf. 289–292)
Palintokia	**khrēmata** taken by **biē** (341–350, 667–682; cf. 289–292)
confiscations (*Politics*)	anger toward current holders of his **khrēmata** (341–350; cf. 561–562)
exile of aristocrats (*Politics*)	plight of an exile (209–210, 332a–334, 1209–1216)

In Question 59, the drunken 'wagon-rollers' make their sacrilegious attack on the pilgrims bound for Delphi. This could never have been derived from the Theognidea in the way in which the *Constitution of the Athenians* uses the poems of Solon to reconstruct his reforms. Nevertheless, all these similarities suggest that both the Theognidea and the *Constitution* go back to an appraisal of democracy or, perhaps more correctly, of democratizing—an appraisal based on similar, oligarchic ideological grounds. Besides the appropriation of proper mental activity and truly human behavior by the critics of the **dēmos**, one may remark on the stereotyping of an inferior group as drunkards. The Spartiates used to get the Helots drunk in front of Spartan youths (Plutarch *Lycurgus* 28.8–10: see below, §42). The practice of making invidious comparisons of the traditions of different ethnic groups about the consumption of alcohol may also be noted (compare the stereotypes of French Canadians in Canadian "mythology").

§25. The tone of the *Constitution* is hostile to the democracy, which is seen negatively in terms of morality, not merely in terms of expediency or of political efficiency. The *Constitution* emphasizes the social dimensions of Megarian democracy rather than its institutional order. In other words, the *Constitution of the Megarians* seems to motivate a single definite political event, the Palintokia, around which its treatment of Megarian democracy turns, by observations similar to the opinions enunciated in the Theognidea.

§26. Megarian democracy is seen most of all as a manifestation of moral degeneracy. The terminology is arresting. The popular leaders provide wine for the **dēmos**: '**dēmagōgōn oinokhoountōn**'. Plutarch refers here to the metaphorical treatment of the breakdown of a democracy in the *Republic* (562C–D) of Plato, where the **polis** is thirsting for freedom (**eleutheriās dipsēsāsa**), with the magistrates acting as **oinokhooi** 'wine-pourers' until the **polis** is drunk (**methusthēi**) with **akrāton** 'undiluted wine'. Yet it is improbable that anyone reading the *Republic* would have thought of Megara rather than of Athens. The question that is important to us is why Plutarch called to mind this particular topos on democratic extremism when he chose to paraphrase the *Constitution*. In answer, let me raise the possibility that the *Constitution* offered this equation: drunkenness = extreme democracy. In other words, the treatment of Megarian rowdiness (when the **dēmos** invaded the homes of the rich) already made something of drunkenness, which suggested to Plutarch that he dramatize the progress of democratization as one of intoxication.

§27. The same note is struck by the statement that the **dēmos**, completely corrupted (**diaphtharentes pantapāsi**), invaded the homes of the rich to feast. Complete degeneracy could have been more effectively demonstrated by some other example. Why did the members of the **dēmos** eat and drink in the homes of the rich first, instead of simply confiscating their property? In other words, compulsory entertainment and the Palintokia do not seem to belong to successive stages of a political crisis, as seen from a legalistic perspective. Surely, had the Megarians wished to eat and drink their fill, they might have come up with some confiscatory mechanism that would regularize redistributions. A prudent system would keep the conflicts that ensue in such a redistributory mechanism in a public context (i.e., taxation), and not personalized as Plutarch suggests. Below, it will be argued that this series of events did have an institutional basis in some type of redistribution, perhaps made figurative (see below, §§41, 50–52). Here let me merely raise the possibility that Aristotle's source meant to keep his focus on the moral, psychological, and social aspects of Megarian democracy rather than on the organization of its constitution or legal system. Thus, the *Constitution of the Megarians* shows how oligarchic ideology at Megara, as represented by the preoccupations of Theognis, could help to shape polemical writing about a specific situation. Nonetheless, the two levels of political commentary do not interface smoothly.

Megarian Comedy: A Counterideology

§28. Generically-based oligarchic ideology at Megara as embodied in the Theognidea can be further elucidated if one considers the presence of another ideology and its generic vehicle. Aristotle associated the origin of Megarian comedy with Megarian democracy (*Poetics* 1448a29–b3). The *Marmor Parium* (*FGH* 239 A 39) gives as a date for the Athenian invention of comedy that of 580–562/1.[1] If the Megarians were thought to have invented comedy, then a tradition that comedy was performed in Megara about this time may have existed. The date for Megarian democracy coincides with the putative date for Megarian comedy. The existence of such a tradition explains how the invention of comedy could be assigned to Susarion, who is variously described as an Athenian or a Megarian.[2] According to

---

§28n1. Jacoby 1904.167. For the dates of the Megarian democracy, see the Chronological Table, Note Q.

§28n2. Susarion is mentioned in the *Marmor Parium* as an inhabitant of the Attic deme Ikaria, where tragedy supposedly originated (Clement *Stromateis* 1.16.79 = Kaibel *CGF* 1.1 no. 15, p.77). Susarion appears most frequently in association with an epigram critical of women (Stobaeus *Florilegium* 69.2). In the epigram and elsewhere Susarion is identified as a Megarian from the town of Tripodiskos (scholia Dionysius Thrax [Kaibel *CGF* 1.1 no. 2, p.14]; J. Tzetzes, *De comoedia graeca* [Kaibel *CGF* 1.1, no. 6, pp.18, 27, 77]). Other versions do not attribute the verses to Susarion (e.g., scholia Aristophanes *Lysistrata* 1039) or do not identify Susarion as a Megarian (Diomedes Grammaticus [Kaibel *CGF* 1.1 no. 11, p.58]). For all references, see Piccirilli 1975.142–143, 149; cf. Piccirilli 1974. The identification of Susarion as a Megarian

these traditions, Susarion wrote invectives with characters introduced disjointedly and is best known for an epigram deriding women. The idea that the Megarians invented comedy is reflected by a commentator on Aristotle, who is also aware of the stories concerning Susarion (Anonymous Commentator [Aspasius?] on *Nicomachean Ethics* 1123a20). Megarian comedy was known to the Attic poets of Old Comedy: Ekphantides (first victory probably 457/4) fr. 2 (Kock); Eupolis fr. 244 (Kock); Myrtilos fr. 1 (Kock); and Aristophanes *Wasps* 54–63; cf. *CPG* 1.230.

§ 29. From these citations, the character of Megarian comedy may be discerned. Aristophanes warns his audience against expecting either anything very great or anything stolen from Megara. The latter theme is illustrated by the practice of throwing nuts into the audience (cf. *Plutus* 797–799) or by the introduction of Herakles robbed of his dinner.[1] These motifs are somehow Megarian, just as Aristophanes' further examples, parody of Euripides and satire about Cleon, are by contrast his own (unless perhaps crude abuse is somehow Megarian). Consider Maison, a stock comic character, either a servant or a cook, who was portrayed with a particular mask (Athenaeus 14.659A–C; cf. Pollux 4.148; Hesychius s.v. "**maisōna**"). Chrysippus derived the name Maison from **masasthai** 'chew' (at Athenaeus). Aristophanes ·of Byzantium, however, traced the character Maison back to a Megarian actor of that name (at Athenaeus). Perhaps we ought to take him for a generic figure associated both with cooking and with Megarian comedy. Megarian comic poets are described as **amousōn kai aphuōs skōptontōn** 'uninspired, unsophisticated ridiculers' (scholia Aristophanes *Wasps* 57b). Megarian comedy is **psukhros** 'insipid', and its performance is **aselgēs** 'wanton' and **phortikos** 'vulgar' (Eu-

---

has been seen as apocryphal, since the verses attributed to him are in the Attic dialect and are perhaps reminiscent of New Comedy (Wilamowitz 1875.337–338; Pickard-Cambridge 1962.179–187). Another Megarian, Tolynos, said to have anticipated Cratinus, invented a meter called the **Tolunion** (*Etymologicum Magnum* s.v. "Tolunion," p. 761.47). Piccirilli offers a complex stemma for the surviving accounts and insists upon a basis in sound Megarian tradition, represented by the Megareis, for the idea of Megarian invention of comedy (Piccirilli 1975.144–148; 1974.1293–1299). The notion of Susarion as a Megarian attests to the associations of archaic Megara and comedy, which must have been especially strong to support such a claim in face of the obvious prestige of Attic Old Comedy.

§ 29n1. Cf. *Peace* 741–749, where the superiority of Aristophanic humor to the use of Herakles as baking (cf. Maison), fleeing, beaten, or swindling is emphasized; or *Peace* 961–965, where a slave is urged to throw barley groats to the audience. There is, however, no direct mention of Megarian comedy.

polis; Myrtilos; Anonymous Commentator). The strong association between food sharing or food stealing and Megarian comedy should be noted. Another association, that between Megarian comedy and crude invective, should also be observed.

§30. One way to explain the evolution of comedy is to posit that comedy had its social context in lower-class mockery of the elite. Aristotle in the *Poetics* associated the term **kōmōidiā** with **kōmē** 'village'.[1] Thus, comedy can be seen as a rural/populist medium for ensuring social conformity (i.e., the restriction of choice in lifestyles for community members to a relatively limited set). The most common myth about comedy's beginnings portrays the origin of the genre in the following way.[2] At Athens, a group of farmers suffered injustice at the hands of those inhabiting the **astu** 'town'. In retaliation, the farmers, entering town at night, went around shouting out the names and the misdeeds of those mistreating them, who in their turn were held up to ridicule by their neighbors. Next, the citizens, recognizing a socially beneficial practice, compelled the rustics to reenact their ridicule of the unjust in the **agorā** 'marketplace'. The **agroikoi** 'peasants', who feared the rich, smeared their faces with mud and wine lees, creating comic personae, as it were. In the final stage of development, poets were permitted to mock with impunity.

§31. The tense boundaries between different social classes and societal roles were blurred and mediated by such confrontations between groups and individuals in a forum where winning and losing occurred only on the psychological plane. Comedy not only inculcated the skills necessary for interpersonal conflict but also diverted aggression short of full-fledged **stasis**. It lessened the sensitivity of participants and audience to interclass friction. Another story about comedy's origins points up this role as a reconciler and releaser of tensions. At Syracuse, after a period of **stasis**, reconciliation took place between the parties in the context of a ritual meal and a **kōmos**, or proto-comedy (scholia Theocritus, Prolegomena Ba [Wendel]). The rustics approached the city dressed in stags' horns, sang songs, and shared

---

§30n1. For the conventional view critical of the association of **kōmōidiā** and **kōmē**, see Else 1957.118–121. See Levine Ch.7§§36–39 below for a more conservative judgment.

§30n2. Scholia Dionysius Thrax (Kaibel *CGF* 1.1 no. 4, pp.11–14); cf. *Etymologicum Magnum* s.v. "**tragōidiā**," p.764.1; John the Deacon *Commentary on Hermogenes, Peri methodou deinotētos*: see Rabe 1908. The story concludes with a reference to the origination of comedy by Susarion (Kaibel *CGF* 1.1 no. 4, p.14).

food with the city-dwellers. The sharing of food is representative of the stripping away of the "excrescences" (for they are viewed as such from a perspective of comic deflation) of class.

§32. Accordingly, early comedy would have been opposed to claims to special prerogatives or to the assumption of differentiated behavioral patterns by a presumptive elite. Comedy at Megara may be juxtaposed with Theognidean elegy. The latter attempted to indoctrinate the young, represented by Kyrnos, with emotional and mental habits appropriate to a constitution where access to political power was limited by heredity and upbringing, and to create inhibitions against communing with those who had not internalized the Theognidean system. We have already seen, however, that the myths motivating early comedy declare that its purpose is to uphold **dikē**, just as the poet of the Theognidea affirms. It is significant that by their very names early comic performers claimed a similar moral authority to that claimed by the elegiac poet. Athenaeus informs us that these performers had a variety of names (14.621D–622D; cf. *Suda* s.v. **"phallophoroi"**). Some, like **ithuphalloi** or **phallophoroi**, show the origins of the genre in rural fertility practices and cults. Two other names, **sophistai** and **deikēlistai**, are of greater particular interest for us. First of all, were poets named **sophistai** because they claimed that they possessed **sophiā** 'wisdom', or merely for their technical skill? For Pindar, poets are **sophistai** in a context where more than technical skill is implied (*I.* 5.28). It is striking that Herodotus uses the term for the Seven Sages (1.29.1, 4.95.2) and for the seer Melampus and other exegetes who followed him (2.49.1). Pindar and Herodotus authorize a prephilosophical connotation for the word, probably in much the same spirit as the equation of comic performers with **sophistai**. Thus, just as Theognis (who could describe the creator of poetry as **sophizomenos** 'exercising **sophiā**') encoded **ainigmata** which could only be decoded by the **sophoi**, who were **agathoi** (and this was the content of an aristocratic lifestyle: cf. vv. 681–682), so too the comic performers made their claim as authoritative spokesmen in parallel language.[1]

§33. At Sparta comic performers were called **dikēlistai** (Sosibios *FGH* 595 F 7), which Athenaeus glosses as **mīmētai** 'mimes' and **skeuopoioi** 'disguisers' or 'make-up men'. The term is perhaps more correctly **deikēliktās** (Plutarch *Agesilaus* 21.8). The term is derived from

---

§32n1. Cf. Edmunds Ch.4§§7–8 above; also Nagy Ch.2§§2–5 above.

deiknumi 'show' (Hesychius glosses **dikēlon** as 'phasma' 'opsis' 'eidōlon' or 'mīmēma'). Just as the word **sophistēs** suffered attenuation in its claims to intellectual or spiritual preeminence, by the fourth century **deikilistai** at Sparta were minor performers. Nonetheless, how they appeared to sophisticated fourth-century Greeks need not prejudice us against their early significance. The term **deikēla** is used to describe initiation into Egyptian mysteries in the phrase **deikēla tōn patheōn** 'passion play' or, more literally, 'a representation of personal sufferings' (Herodotus 2.171.1). It is suggestive of the **epopteiā** 'revelation' of the Eleusinian Mysteries, where objects numinous with procreative force were revealed to the initiates. The Herodotean use of the term suggests that **deikēla** 'representations' ought to be parallel to the **sēmata** (from **sēmainō**), the encoded material encapsulated by archaic aristocratic poets in their poetry. Note Theognis 808, where **sēmainō** is used in connection with the **theōros**, a persona of the poet, who must faithfully represent the inspired message of Apollo (cf. Simonides 511 fr. 1 [Page]). Rather like characters in a fairy tale, ancient comic performers dealt in anxieties and social skills basic to human interaction.

§ 34. As has been observed, Aristophanes associated Megarian comedy with sharing food with the audience and with the themes of Herakles' procuring food or being deprived of it. At Syracuse the origin of comedy is set in a story about rustics bringing food to town-dwellers. The counterimage to sharing food with the audience is that of stealing food, which was a common motif in Laconian comedy (Sosibios *FGH* 595 F 7; Athenaeus 14.621D; Pollux 4.105). Connected with this is the portrayal of the fate of someone caught stealing food. The stealer of food was a stock figure in early comedy (Epicharmus fr. 239 [Kaibel *CGF* 1.1]; cf. Aristophanes *Knights* 417–420). At Sparta, youths in the process of assimilating adult male values were taught to steal food (Plutarch *Lycurgus* 17.5–6). Comedy at Sparta thus encapsulated the experience of stealing food, which was a part of the rites of passage or rituals of adolescence.[1] If sharing food in the terms of comedic ideology means reconciliation between groups, stealing exemplifies the situation before reconciliation or even denotes a refusal to be reconciled. Megarian comedy may well have made much of

---

§ 34n1. The adolescent Spartan was the counterpart of his father, who drew his food from his **klēros** 'allotment' and ate it at a steady, moderate rate. In passing from adolescence, the young Spartiate's thefts from the Helots reenacted his forefathers' conquest of the same Helots and reaffirmed that the Helot was the ideological mirror image of the Spartiate. Cf. Figueira 1984.

redistribution of food, feasting, and stealing, with its parallel in the redistributory ideology of the extreme democracy. When we read in Plutarch that the Megarian poor invaded the homes of the rich to eat and drink, we should perhaps think of redistributory activity. Comedy rehearsed its audience for such redistribution, or subsequently celebrated the implementation of redistributory proposals.

§35. I have suggested that the proper frame of reference for Theognidean poetry is not only Megara but also its colonies. Megarian comedy seems also to be associated with Megara Hyblaea (Aristotle *Poetics* 1448a32–34). Epicharmus was associated by Aristotle with Megarian comedy in Sicily, although it is uncertain whether Aristotle believed the poet to have been from Megara Hyblaea. Epicharmus conducted his literary career at Syracuse (in the reigns of Gelon and Hieron). Traditions conflict on his place of birth, but one body of opinion held him to have been a Sicilian Megarian (*Suda* s.v. "**Epikharmos**"; Diogenes Laertius 8.78).[1] It is noteworthy that as Epicharmus was celebrated for his **gnōmai** (Diogenes Laertius 8.78; cf. Iamblichus *Life of Pythagoras* 241; Kaibel *CGF* 1.1, T 9), he was to an extent a comic genre counterpart to Theognis, master of gnomological poetry.[2] There was also a debate about from which Megara Maison came (Polemon fr. 46 [Preller]).

Megarian Comedy, Elegy, and the Constitution of the Megarians

§36. It is not surprising that the emphasis of the writer of the *Constitution of the Megarians* was on social behavior rather than on institutional change (to be contrasted with the *Constitution of the Athenians*). This emphasis is an outgrowth of the original character of the generalized and ideological source material available. The author of the *Constitution* was, however, able to sketch the complex of behavior of which Megarian comedy (a subject of greater general interest, in any case) was a part without having to treat Megarian political legalities. The lack of interest in these traditions in Nisaean Megara itself has already been posited, so that it seems reasonable to look for a source among colonial Megarians. The democratic traditions of homeland Megara, later forgotten, ought to have been remembered in its dem-

---

§35n1. Pickard-Cambridge 1962.230–239.

§35n2. Iamblichus *Life of Pythagoras* 266 (cf. Plutarch *How a Flatterer is Distinguished from a Friend* 27 = *Moralia* 68A) reports that Epicharmus was forced from fear of Hieron's tyranny to put his philosophical ideas into verse. Here the idea of encoding political values in comedy is apparent.

ocratic colony, Heraclea Pontica.[1] The subsequent shift of Heraclea to an oligarchic constitution might explain the antidemocratic tone of the *Constitution*. As a source, Heracleides Ponticus is an obvious candidate for the one who reintroduced archaic Megarian evidence to Aristotle and his contemporaries.[2] Aristotle might then have been able to comment on Theagenes and on the fall of the Megarian democracy in the *Politics*. This is no more than a supposition, but it is made more likely by the fact that Aristotle had much information to offer on Heraclea Pontica in the same work. Whether Aristotle derived his notice about Megarian comedy from Heracleides cannot be decided.

§37. While it is useful for discussing the transmission of Megarian traditions to focus our attention on Heraclea and Heracleides, Heracleides is unlikely to have been the author of the *Constitution*, which was probably the work of one of Aristotle's students. A date cannot be established for the composition of the *Constitution of the Megarians*. Indeed, it is not certain that the completion of its composition must necessarily fall within Aristotle's lifetime. A possibility as the actual author of the work is Chamaeleon, also from Heraclea Pontica.[1] As a Heraclean, he would have been aware of the same traditions as Heracleides, whose example he followed in coming to Athens. The interests of Chamaeleon, as shown by the surviving fragments of his work, equipped him to deal with Megarian traditions better than a legal specialist or an expert in cults. He wrote a treatise on Old Comedy, though in the late fourth or early third century he perhaps did not mean by the adjective **arkhaia** what we denote by "Old Comedy" (frr. 43–44). Rather, he may have dealt with the early development of the genre in general, not merely the evolution of

---

§36n1. For Heraclea, see the Chronological Table, Notes E, Q. The vigor of local history at Heraclea may be observed in the number of its practitioners: Promathidas (*FGH* 430), Amphitheos (431), Nymphis (432), Domitios Kallistratos (433), and Memnon (434). Heraclean historians occupy 43 pages of text in Jacoby, compared to 7 pages for the Megareis.

§36n2. Heracleides Ponticus (Diogenes Laertius 5.86–93): Wehrli 1953. Note that he wrote a *Peri Arkhēs* (frr. 144–145) and a *Peri Nomōn* (frr. 146–150). For Heraclea in Aristotle's *Politics*: 1304b31–34, 1305b5, 11–12, 1305b36, 1306a36–1306b1, 1327b14. In *Politics* 1304b31–34, a description of the fall of the democracy at Heraclea is directly followed by a notice of the fall of the democracy at Megara. This is perhaps an indication that these two data had the same source. Cf. Okin Ch.1 § §17–20 above.

§37n1. Wehrli 1957. The apparent absence of a biography of Theognis in Chamaeleon is striking, because he wrote lives of Hesiod (fr. 23), Alcman (frr. 24–25), Sappho (frr. 26–27), Stesichorus (frr. 28–29), Anacreon (fr. 36), Simonides (frr. 33–35), Lasos (fr. 30), Aeschylus (frr. 39–42), and Pindar (frr. 31–32).

Attic comedy down to and including Aristophanes.[2] A work *Peri Saturōn* 'On Satyr Dramas' is also known (frr. 37a–c), and a work on Thespis (fr. 38). Another of Chamaeleon's works was on the subject of intoxication (frr. 9–13), which fits with the emphasis in Plutarch on drinking and its pernicious results. The one piece of evidence bearing on the chronology of Chamaeleon does not clash with a late fourth- or early third-century date, nor does it exclude his having studied with Aristotle himself (Memnon *FGH* 434 F 7). A Heraclean could draw on Megarian political traditions, which were preserved in the Theognidea, but these Theognidean traditions had been subjected to generalizing and conventionalizing.

Megarian Ideologies and Their Literary Genres

§38. Thus, two ideologies existed in sixth-century Megara. For simplicity, let us call one democratic (or populist) and the other oligarchic, although these terms must not be given their Athenian valence. The social setting for the two ideologies varied as much as their content and generic medium. Elegy and oligarchic ideology appropriated the context of the symposium, while democratic ideology was expressed in a comic performance with its attendant religious activity. At Megara, a sense of community seems to have been dependent upon redistribution of goods through traditional means. One may think of a primitive form of patronage by the elite and a type of **kōmos** or revel in which the whole community was entertained. From this **kōmos** there bifurcated a democratic ideology expressed in the performance of comedy and an oligarchic ideology centered around the symposium.[1]

§39. How a democratic and an oligarchic ideology may have interacted at Megara can perhaps be seen in the story that Pausanias tells about the construction of the building in which the Megarian Council, the

---

§37n2. Both fragments are from Book 6. Fragment 44 refers to Hegemon of Thasos, a contemporary of Alkibiades, whose *Gigantomachy* was supposedly in performance when the Sicilian disaster of 413 was announced. Fragment 43 tells an anecdote about Anaxandridas of Rhodes, a Middle Comic poet, active after 380 (*Suda* s.v. "Kameiraia"; *IG* xiv 1098). In a work arranged chronologically, five earlier books on this scale would leave ample space for a discussion of the origins of comedy.

§38n1. In the corpus, **kōmos** (vv. 829, 940, 1046; cf. **kōmazō** [vv. 886, 1065, 1207, 1351–1352]) is analogous to **sussitos** (298, 496). Whether **sussitos** 'messmate' (v. 309) has a general meaning (= **hetairos**) is unknown. However, if Megara had officially recognized **sussitia** 'public messes' as Sparta had, it would be easy to explain how some of the material entered the corpus from Nisaean Megara as the political poetry appropriate to such a setting. In that case, elsewhere in the corpus, the term **sussition** may have been removed by a conventionalizing process.

Aisymnion, met (Pausanias 1.43.3). The structure was built over the graves of heroes. A Delphic response had advised the Megarians to take counsel with the majority. This majority was interpreted to be the dead, so that the Council House was erected upon graves.[1] This is supposed to have happened in the lifetime of Aisymnos, the eponymous founder of the office of **aisumnātās**. The councillors were expected to commune with the tutelary heroes of the **polis**. While **hoi pleones** is a euphemism for the dead (cf. Aristophanes *Ecclesiazusae* 1073; *Palatine Anthology* 7.731, 11.42), another, rather obvious, interpretation was available. To take counsel with the majority should mean to enlarge the council—either opening its membership to other social groups or increasing the number of its members. Such changes, altering the balance between an assembly and a council, are democratizing. One might imagine that a reform establishing that **probouleumata** 'preliminary proposals of a council' might be emended on the floor of the assembly could be called 'taking counsel with the majority' (cf. the Great Rhetra of Sparta [Plutarch *Lycurgus* 6.6–7]). This superficial meaning was discarded for a cryptic sense reminiscent of the insistence in the Theognidea on taking counsel only with the **agathoi** and of the emphasis on the **agathoi** as transmitters of **sophiā** from one generation to another. Only the **sophoi** can properly decode normative statements, so that it is not surprising that oligarchs at Megara would seek to explain the oracle in this way. To know, in fact, who the greater number were was the answer to a riddle, one supposedly expounded by Anacharsis (Diogenes Laertius 1.104; cf. Callimachus *Epigrams* 4 [Pfeiffer]). Another aspect of the oracle deserves note. Nagy has emphatically argued that Theognis sometimes presents himself as a hero capable of upholding **dikē** even from beyond the grave.[2] The tutelary councillors connected with the Aisymnion approximated this very sort of **phulakes** 'guardians'.

§40. Let us consider another example of ideological comment. As I have already indicated, it is unlikely that the **kōmai** of Megara can have been profoundly different from the **astu** by the late seventh century. The Theognidean description of the newly made **agathoi** who had previously inhabited the countryside and had dressed in skins is exaggerated. The image, however, is justified not by the notion that these rural aspirants to political power had in truth recently led a bestial life. Rather, such denigrating language, ostensibly

---

§39n1. Polybius 8.30.6–9 uses the same oracle to explain, somewhat less effectively, the presence of graves within the walls of Tarentum.
§39n2. See Nagy Ch.2§§64–67 above.

directed against political opponents of Theognis, could have been a reaction to their expressions of affinity with a rural or populist ideology through participation in early Megarian comedy. The skins that they wore on their sides (vv. 53–57) correspond to the costumes appropriate to animal or satyr choruses.[1] The view of themselves which proponents of this rural or populist ideology held may have found an echo in Aristotle's *Poetics*. Aristotle describes comic performers wandering around the **kōmai** because they were deprived of their rights in the city, '**atīmazomenous**' (*Poetics* 1448a36–b1). But such an act of expulsion is not historical; rather, it is a generic expression of the antagonism of the comic genre toward the city and the political men of power who were established there. This hypothesis leads to the striking possibility that the oligarchic ideology at Megara expressed by elegiac poetry responded not only to social situations created by its "populist, democratic" opponents but also to the self-representations of the populist ideology as expressed by comedy.

§41. In a properly functioning community the antagonism between rich and poor, between town-dwellers and rustics, is allayed by the incorporation of the comic performance into the life of the **polis**. Hence, in Attica comedies were performed at the city Dionysia and Lenaea, and not merely at regional celebrations in the countryside. Moreover, the acceptance by all social classes of ridicule directed at social pretension helps to integrate the **polis**. This integration is symbolized by conventional motifs of comedy such as the feast and the wedding. But when the joke is always on one social stratum, and that group's disadvantage leaves the context of the play, such deflation is a challenge to arms. Here, for the first time, we touch on what went wrong in Megarian social relations (both in Theognidean terms and in our own). Dramatic performance at Athens was subsidized through liturgies, a means of redistribution of wealth, since the well-to-do supported performances that all enjoyed. Performance of comedy at Megara seems to have gone a step further as a mechanism for redistribution. Aristotle remarks that it was customary for a **khorēgos** 'pro-

---

§40n1. I mention the satyr play with some hesitation, since some of its stock themes have no counterpart (as far as we know) in Megarian comedy (e.g., the destruction of an ogre, athletic competition), though in both genres appearances of Herakles were frequent and hospitality prominently featured (Sutton 1980.145–159). Padded dancers on Corinthian pots (Pickard-Cambridge 1962.100–101, 171–173) and the role of Pratinas of Phlious (near Corinth) in the development of the satyr play (T 1, 7, 8; F 2, 3 [Snell]; Athenaeus 14.617B) point to the vitality in the vicinity of Megara of this dramatic form in its earliest manifestations.

ducer of a play' to provide stage hangings expensively dyed in purple instead of the usual leather curtains (*Nicomachean Ethics* 1123a20-24). If the situation in Athens held true for Megara, the **khorēgos** was a wealthy man appointed by the state. The benefit to the audience of such trappings appears doubtful, but perhaps that consideration recommended the practice. In some cultures, the successful accumulate goods to be consumed in a feast. This potlatch punishes the successful for their aberrant behavior, success itself. The content of the Theognidea suggests that the elite would not have acquiesced in this sort of comic misappropriation of their **khrēmata** 'property'. In turn, the comedy that was to inhibit social aggrandizement by such provisions may have itself strayed into class aggrandizement.

§42. In societies near subsistence, it is not surprising that differences in dress (at least 15 percent of consumption) are highly symbolic of class differences. To dress "up" or "down" is a political statement. Yet, all societies experience upward and downward mobility, so that affiliation to social class by means of wealth, partially expressed by dress, creates groups that cross-cut or overlap those created by other criteria. One technique open to those anxious to freeze past social status is to legislate dress. The Spartan Helots, for instance, were compelled to wear dogskin hats and animal skins (Myron *FGH* 106 F 2). Such dress accompanied other forms of behavior opposite to the behavior of free men, like drinking to drunkenness and singing and dancing grotesquely (Plutarch *Lycurgus* 28.8-10).[1] By contrast, the Spartiate ate and drank moderately and sang the poems of Terpander, Alcman, and Spendon, of which the performance was forbidden to Helots. Furthermore, the rural dependent population of Sikyon, the **korunēphoroi** 'club-bearers', wore a rough garment called the **katōnakē** (Theopompus *FGH* 115 F 176, 311; cf. Pollux 7.68), as did slaves at Athens (Aristophanes *Ecclesiazusae* 723). Aristophanes could even have Lysistrata pretend that in freeing Athens, the Spartans had removed the **katōnakē** from Athenian backs (*Lysistrata* 1149-1156; cf. Pollux 7.68). The Helots were already in a sense performing when they sang and danced in a manner unnatural to them, much as they indulged in play-acting when they were compelled to mourn insincerely for Spartan kings (Tyrtaeus frr. 6-7 W; Herodotus 6.58.3; cf. Pausanias 4.14.5; consider the expression **dakrua Megareōn**: Chronological Table, Note A). Comedy directed such performance for its own ends. The dehumanization of animalis-

---

§42n1. See Figueira 1984.

tic dress became a disguise, a liberation from the conventions of human society. The distance established between actor and audience became a vantage point from which to mount a social counterattack.

Redistribution and Sharing among the Megarians

§43. A final series of problems manifests itself in an evaluation of Megarian traditions about Megara. These concern why Megarian local history had so little interest in either of the two ideologies dominant in the sixth century in their **polis**. Yet, to answer this question, we shall have to undertake an investigation of the distribution of material goods in Megarian society as they were perceived by the Megarians and expressed in elegy and comedy. This dominant theme in Megarian social history can be seen working its influence even before the **sunoikismos** of the community. In *Greek Questions* 17 (Plutarch *Moralia* 295B–C), the institution of the **doruxenoi** is discussed (see the Chronological Table, Notes A, B). The Megarians resisted Corinthian attempts to create conflicts between the Megarian **kōmai** by a system of mutual hospitality where captors entertained their captives until ransomed. Thus, strong community identification is a mechanism for political survival and as such is reinforced by interrelations based on reciprocity in the circulation of material goods.

§44. The tradition regarding Theagenes, Megara's only tyrant, whose career marks an important phase in the city's internal history and foreign policies, also demonstrates the importance of the state of the distribution of material goods in Megarian social and political history. We know best his involvement in Athenian history through the Cylonian affair, about which Herodotus and Thucydides inform us (Herodotus 5.71.1–2; Thucydides 1.126.3–12). About his standing in the constitutional history of Megara, less is known. Aristotle noted him among other tyrants who achieved power by the acquisition of a bodyguard from the people (*Rhetoric* 1357b30–35). Here is an indication that some form of popular assembly was operative in mid-seventh-century Megara. Theagenes therefore followed an aristocracy, not a closed oligarchy. Yet one must avoid the temptation to assume that an aristocracy of the type presented as normal in the Theognidea broke down before the rise of Theagenes. The transition from a **dikē**-inspired hereditary aristocracy to a tyranny dominant over **kakoi** is paradigmatic, not historical.[1]

---

§44n1. Cf. Nagy Ch.2§29 above.

§45. Theagenes achieved popularity by slaughtering the flocks of the rich which were trespassing by the river; so the account of Aristotle notes (*Politics* 1305a24–26). That the elite in Megarian tradition are the **euporoi** (if this term has not been introduced by the Peripatetics) suggests once again that they need not have been a hereditary aristocracy in power since the independence of the **polis**. The endogamous elite lying behind the Theognidea is a projection onto politics wherein those adopting the ideology are **agathoi** by birth, while those not embodying it are **kakoi**, either by birth or by degeneration.

§46. The identity of the river has baffled all students of Megarian history, inasmuch as there is no river in the Megarid. As a solution to this dilemma, it has been suggested that, in antiquity, when the hillsides were better wooded, streams ran toward the sea, at least in the wet season. This suggestion perhaps still overestimates the watershed available in the Megarid even before deforestation. Furthermore, Theagenes presumably slaughtered the flocks of the rich in something other than full civil war. After all, one does not win the support of one's faction in a civil war merely by leading them in fighting. In that case, popularity has to be gained first. Aristotle has just mentioned demagogues who incited the poor against the rich to achieve popularity, so that the slaughter of the flocks pertained to Theagenes' struggle to accede to power. Aristotle's language suggests that Theagenes was justified in slaughtering the flocks of the rich because of their encroachment. A traditional interpretation (for example) has been to imagine that the wealthy of Megara, who could be major producers in the woolen industry, were encroaching on the bottomland held by the other members of the community.[1] However, this entails a rather modernistic picture of a seventh-century economy and scarcely explains why it was necessary to kill the flocks. I suggest that no simple confiscation of the property of political enemies is at issue here.

§47. It is possible that the **potamos** 'river' near which Theagenes slaughtered the flocks was not actually a river but a place called Potamos. It could have taken its name from religious activity celebrated there. Potamios was a month in the calendar of the Megarian colony Kalkhedon (*GDI* 3053).[1] Months often took their name from the major festivals celebrated in them, so that one might hypothesize

---

§46n1. Oost 1973.190; Ure 1922.264–268 (for an even more modernist view).
§47n1. Hanell 1934.202.

a festival, the Potamia, in Potamios. Although the festival might have been celebrated in honor of a local river at Kalkhedon, there is a good chance (given the conservatism in these matters) that there was either a month Potamios at Megara, or, barring that, a festival Potamia. The **potamos** (or should we say Potamos) would have been a cult place where this festival took place. The land near the Potamos may have been used to produce meat for sacrifice and communal eating, but the rich may have been arrogating its use to themselves. Theagenes may have slaughtered the flocks for a sacrifice and meal. He would thus have used the sheep for their proper purpose, thereby winning favor with the rest of the community. I would see the **potamos** as an old cult place that existed at the time of the foundation of the colony of Kalkhedon (see the Chronological Table, Note E). The conflict between rich and poor during the rise of Theagenes was perhaps over evaluations of changes in the relative prosperity of the two groups. Growing prosperity among the elite was interpreted as being at the expense of the poor, and upward mobility was thought to be a theft of **khrēmata** 'property'.

§48. Another piece of evidence about Theagenes, recorded by Pausanias, can be introduced to support this hypothesis (1.41.2). At a place called **rhoos** 'stream', Theagenes diverted to the city waters flowing from the mountains and dedicated an altar there.[1] He was also credited with the erection of a fountainhouse for the use of the city of Megara (see the Chronological Table, Note F). The water available to the city of Megara was drawn from subterranean sources in the plain north of the city. The **rhoos** in its original state may have been a torrent bed with some water in it seasonally. In this primeval condition, the **rhoos** may have been equated with the **potamos**. Traces of the **rhoos** after its elaboration by Theagenes, when it drew on these subterranean waters, have been discovered, including remains of the conduit that fed the fountainhouse.[2] It is significant that most of the testimony on the career of Theagenes concerns water and its distribution among the citizens (the **potamos**, the **rhoos**, and the fountainhouse). In the Megarid, parched in the summer, access to water sources may have taken on the same importance that possession of land took in other cities. To draw water from communal sources was the preserve of the citizen.

---

§48n1. Alternatively, the story of Theagenes' slaughter of the flocks of the wealthy could have been created in the form that it has come down to us in order to provide an **aition** for the **rhoos**, for the fountainhouse of Theagenes, and for the festival Potamia.

§48n2. Muller 1981.203–207.

§49. To understand the institutional changes that Megara underwent in the sixth century, it is important to note that the Megarians fought the Athenians at least three times over Salamis (see the Chronological Table, Notes I, J, M, S). While successful initially, they seemed to have had the worst of it against Solon and Peisistratos. The latter's capture of Nisaea must have been a disaster of the first order to the Megarians (Note M). Moreover, it is possible that three wars took place between Corinth and Megara. In the first, the Megarians lost Sidous and Krommyon, perhaps to Periander (Note G). In the later wars, they seemed to have held their own, at least to the degree that they had spoils to dedicate (Note N). Near 600, the Megarians unsuccessfully fought the Samians near Perinthos (Note K). Then, at some date (perhaps not much later), they became embroiled in Euboia and fought a battle with the Milesians (Notes L, O). The Peloponnesians may also have intervened against Megara (Note P). This record of conflict urges caution in assuming that the changes in government that took place in sixth-century Megara were determined by internal constitutional developments, or that governments succeeded each other on the basis of their success in dealing with social problems. For a small city-state surrounded by larger enemies, events abroad had an overwhelming impact. Stress generated by warfare against external enemies could have intensified stasis 'conflict between social groups' in sixth-century Megara. The sentiments evoked by a city beset by its enemies may be recorded in Theognis 825–830. Here the poet laments that the land, of which the boundary can be seen from the marketplace, has been lost. Again caution is advised, since there may also have been occasions in the history of Megara's colonies that might have inspired such feelings. The poet's admonition to a Scythian (probably a Scythian slave, addressed by his master, the speaker) to cut his hair in mourning would fit well in the context of the Propontis and Black Sea colonies of the Megarians, where Scythian slaves would have been common.

§50. It is left to explain why the two Megarian ideologies, one democratic and expressed through comedy, and the other oligarchic and expressed through elegy, lost their emotive and explanatory power for fourth-century Megarians. The change may have taken place in two stages: one sixth-century (when stasis between political groups was damaging to society), the other fifth-century (when Megara lapsed into a type of passive isolationism). First, consider the ideology of democratic Megara. In Plutarch's account, the Palintokia represented a watershed (see the Chronological Table, Note Q). It is presented by him as a repayment in money of interest paid by debtors to their creditors. Yet, in the mid-sixth century, silver coinage was in its infancy.[1] The first silver coins were probably Aiginetan. Dates for them range from 580 to 550; 560 plus or minus ten years is not likely to be far wrong. Sixth- and fifth-century Megara did not have its own coinage. In the sixth century, Megara lay within the area where the Aiginetan standard predominated. The only alternative to the use of Aiginetan silver in sixth-century Megara would have been Milesian electrum, but its use in the Palintokia is improbable. The interest on agricultural loans would have been small sums, inconvenient when paid in electrum coins of high value. In any case, there was an insufficient amount of coinage in circulation to mediate the majority of the transactions taking place in a community. Thus, the Palintokia must have had a nominal character.

§51. Loans themselves in a premonetary economy deserve closer scrutiny. The Palintokia was not a measure designed to relieve a class of commercial debtors. Rather, it finds its proper place with the agrarian legislation of which the Seisakhtheia at Athens was a part.[1] The unique names of both laws served to maintain their memory, while most of archaic social legislation has been lost. No matter what mechanism the Megarians used to raise capital for commerce, craft, or slave purchase, these operations could not lead to the Palintokia; their pressure groups or constituencies were too small. Merchants, slave purchasers, and workshop owners could never have been called poor as Plutarch calls the agitators for the Palintokia. The Palintokia was meant to relieve an agricultural debtor group: they alone might dream of doing without loans in the future. Who would lend again to merchants who had demanded their interest back from their creditors? Agrarian debt in a premonetary economy was not articulated in purely economic terms. At Athens before Solon, one could be enslaved for failure to repay a loan; that is, failure to fulfill an economic agreement entailed changes in social and political status. These changes in status perhaps began with the very act of falling into debt, as the existence of the class of **hektēmoroi** 'sixth-parters' at Athens indicates. Loans were usually in foodstuffs or in seed grain, provisions for life itself. Borrowing was seldom a one-time affair, as marginal farms were repeatedly in need. In this atmosphere, loans were not quantified (in this regard, the absence of coinage is significant) and tended to become open-ended. Thus, a form of bondage was

---

§50n1. In general, see Figueira 1981.65–97.
§51n1. For the agrarian/debt legislation of Solon, see the sources cited in Martina 1968.141–146, 246, nos. 274–296, no. 487.

created with the obligations of the debtors being political, religious, and/or fiscal. Political duties might have included membership in the political following of the rich as in the case of the regional parties in Attica. Religious obligations could have involved deference and support in ritual contexts as in contributions to sacrifices where the priests took away part of the meat. Finally, obligations could have been fiscal, where regular, taxlike payments were exacted, as in participation in an Athenian naucrary, a tax unit for the provision of ships. To be a debtor was not a contractual situation but entailed a castelike status. To lend or to borrow was a hereditary role.

§52. To describe the Palintokia in these terms, however, is not to paint a totally bleak picture of economic life in sixth-century Megara before its enactment. The redistributory apparatus that I have hypothesized would have acted as a palliation. Nonetheless, against this background the radical character of the Palintokia can be seen. The dissemination of the idea of coinage made it possible to quantify the traditional services of debtors to creditors. This "interest" (presumably measured in current prices) cannot but have been arbitrary, nor was there sufficient currency available to make repayment. Hence, it is not surprising that confiscations and exiles followed. The concept of Palintokia may have been designed to tip a mechanism for redistribution over into expropriation. It is significant that in Aristotle's more general account of the fall of the Megarian democracy, he speaks of the demagogues' confiscating (the verb **dēmeuein**) the **khrēmata** 'property' of the **gnōrimoi** 'political elite' (Aristotle *Politics* 1304b36–38). The Palintokia, then, in an account obviously hostile to Megarian democracy, could be portrayed as mere expropriation. We have already seen an example of the same behavior in the expenses levied on a Megarian **khorēgos** (see above, §41). From this perspective, it becomes obvious why the Seisakhtheia seemed moderate to the ancients, while the Palintokia was extreme. The Seisakhtheia ended debtor status at a time when most creditors had long since recovered the value of their loans in real terms. The inception of money (not the prevalence of coins) allowed the Megarians not only to abolish their debtor class but to undertake a massive shift of wealth to the former debtors.

§53. When an evaluation of Megarian social history focuses on the Palintokia, the conclusion is that the Megarian democrats seem to have been the initiators of disequilibrium at Megara. Whether encroachments by the rich (like the self-aggrandizement that Theagenes had reacted against) had driven the poor, resistant to acquiescing in economic dependency, to counterattack, is unknown. It is noteworthy that Megara did not mint coins until the fourth century. Previously, the Megarians had been imitators of Corinth, insofar as they had become colonizers like their Corinthian neighbors. Corinth was producing currency in the sixth century (from 570/560?). Possibly the Megarians used the coins of their Aiginetan, Corinthian, and Athenian neighbors. But the absence of a local coinage may have retarded the fiscal development of the Megarian government and slowed its adoption of new taxes and types of expenditure (building programs, the development of a fleet, and liturgies) which recirculated the wealth of a community. The stability of the oligarchies at Aigina and Corinth may be partially attributable to these phenomena. Such stability was not achieved through the subjugation of the lower orders by an exploitative elite. The ability of the Corinthians and Aiginetans to man large fleets of triremes shows that the nonelite members of the community who provided rowers for the fleets accepted the directives of the government. Where the elite sponsored the adoption of money, traditional patterns of redistribution may have been reformulated in monetary terms.[1]

§54. I have already posited a democratic, populist agitation for a sharing of the property of the wealthy among the **dēmos**, one in which techniques of expropriation like the Palintokia may have played a part. I shall now consider the Theognidean perspective on the distribution of goods in society. It has been argued that verse 678 expresses a Megarian equivalent of what the Athenians would call **isonomiā** 'equality under the law' or 'equal reciprocity'.[1]

δασμὸς δ᾽ οὐκέτ᾽ ἴσος γίνεται ἐς τὸ μέσον.
Theognis 678

No longer is there equal division in the middle.

The phrase **isos dasmos** means equal division of political influence, like **isonomiā**. Yet, **dasmos** is primarily used in connection with the division of booty, as in its only appearance in the *Iliad* (I 166), a sense in which the verb **dateomai** is common.[2] Another usage of **dateomai** is to describe the division of an estate among heirs (*Iliad*

----

§53n1. Figueira 1981.300–310; cf. Will 1950, 1955b.
§54n1. Cerri 1969.
§54n2. *Iliad* I 125, 368, IX 138 = 280, 333, XVIII 511, XXII 120; *Odyssey* ix 42, 549. Compare the suitors' intention to divide the estate of Odysseus: ii 335, 368, iii 316 = xv 13, xvi 385, xvii 80, xx 216. Another connected use is the division of land in the foundation of a city: *Odyssey* vi 10; cf. xv 412; Hesiod fr. 233 MW.

v 158; *Odyssey* xiv 208; cf. Hesiod *WD* 37) and the division of
food for a human meal (*Odyssey* i 112, iii 66, xix 425, xx 280) or of
carrion among animals (*Iliad* xxii 354, xxiii 21; *Odyssey* xviii 87,
xxii 476). Here **dateomai** could mean 'divide among interested parties', but, given the close relationship of warfare and hunting, the
sense 'divide as booty' is not very foreign. Moreover, **dasmos** appears in the *Homeric Hymn to Demeter* 86, where the position of
Hades is described as based on the division of the **kosmos**. Similarly,
in *Theogony* 425, **dasmos** marks the position of Hekate after the
dasmos following the defeat of the Titans. In these passages, one
ought to think of a division of booty at the beginning of the reign of
Zeus.[3] The fifth-century meaning 'tribute' is an extension of the idea
of division of booty, for tribute is merely the usufruct over time of a
share in booty.[4] Nonetheless, Cerri notes correctly that the phrase **es
meson** 'in the middle' is associated with **isonomiā** in Herodotus
(3.80.2, cf. 80.6; 3.142.3).[5] The phrase **es meson**, however, need
mean nothing more than 'in public', that is, deliberatively (*Iliad*
xxiii 574; Herodotus 4.161.3). Hence, it is inevitably contrasted with
one-man rule, as demonstrated by Herodotus, but is also compatible
with the range of nontyrannical regimes. Therefore, there is a strong
possibility that Theognis 678 refers to a **dasmos** as a division of
booty. Thus, it would allude to a view that saw the socioeconomic
status quo at Megara as going back to dispositions made by the
Dorian conquerors of the Megarid. Almost any widening of political
rights, any social mobility, and any change in the composition of the
elite might disrupt this original order. If **dasmos** has the connotation
merely of 'division among interested parties', there is still an important difference between an **isos dasmos** and **isonomiā**. A **dasmos** is
imposed from above; its dynamic is generated by a leader. An **isonomiā** is a reciprocal feature of dynamic forces *within* society.

§55. A recurring pattern in the Theognidea allows us to delve further
into the oligarchic ideology of the Megarians. The corpus opens
with a strong evocation of the marriage of Kadmos, the founder of
Thebes, to Harmonia, a personification of good social order (vv. 15–
18). Thebes is the ideal counterimage to disordered Megara.[1] The

---

§54n3. For the organization of the world by Zeus: *Iliad* xv 189; Hesiod *Theogony* 112, 303, 520, 789; fr. 141.15 MW.
§54n4. Aeschylus *Persians* 586; Sophocles *Oedipus Rex* 36; *Oedipus Coloneus* 635.
Tributaries are **dasmophoroi**: Herodotus 3.97.1, 5.106.6, 6.48.2, 6.95.1, 7.51.1, 7.108.1.
§54n5. Cerri 1969.103–104.
§55n1. See Nagy Ch.2§§6–7 above.

mythological connections between Thebes and Megara (grounded in Dark Age population movements?) provide a basis for such a formulation. Moreover, Philolaos, a Corinthian émigré of the Bacchiad clan, was a legislator at Thebes. He enacted laws on procreation (cf. Theognis vv. 183–192) in order to maintain the same number of klēroi 'allotments' or 'households' (Aristotle *Politics* 1274a32–b5).[2] So the image of Thebes could be involved with institutional patterns inherited by Megara from Bacchiad Corinth. An effort to keep the number of households the same and to regulate the number of children raised mandated not only that the political class be maintained at the same number but also that the relative economic status of members of the community remain the same. Also, in light of the pederastic ideology so prominent in the second book of the Theognidea, it is striking that Aristotle visualized Philolaos as an **erastēs** 'active homosexual participant'.

§56. Thebes must have begun to cast an even greater shadow at Megara when the Thebans became the leaders of the Boiotian League (after 550).[1] Toward the end of the sixth century, Thebes was exerting pressure on Plataea, immediately to the north of the Megarid (see the Chronological Table, Note R). Democratic Megara included Tanagrans in her colony Heraclea (see Chronological Table, Note E). By 509, Tanagra belonged to the Boiotian League (Herodotus 5.79.2). By the period of the Persian Wars, Thebes was a narrow oligarchy, a **dunasteiā** (Thucydides 3.62.3). Near the end of Book I of the corpus (vv. 1209–1216), the speaker identifies himself as Aithon in **genos** 'race' or 'extraction', who inhabits Thebes in exile from his homeland (see below, §58). He goes on to retort to a female interlocutor named Arguris, who reproached him for his exile, that he is not a slave. The emphasis falls in a fashion typical of the Theognidea on inheriting the status of free man or slave. He has a city in the Lethaian Plain. Here, if Nagy is correct, the recurring figure of the exile is assimilated to a dead man.[2] The despair of the exile is poignant, but it has an added point: the world of the dead can also be

---

§55n2. Cf. Pheidon of Corinth (Aristotle *Politics* 1265b12–16; cf. 1274a31–b5), who regulated the number of households and citizens. On Philolaos: Will 1955.318. On a priori grounds, one might date Philolaos to the second half of the seventh century, after the expulsion of the Bacchiads (Cloché 1952.26). However, if he is correctly identified by Aristotle as the friend of Diokles, the Olympic victor, he is to be dated c. 728 (Buck 1979.95–96, 103).

§56n1. Jeffery 1976.78–79; Buck 1979.107–117.

§56n2. See Nagy Ch.2§§71–74 above.

equated with utopia.[3] Thus, there is an intersection between the underworld and Thebes, paradigm of reconstituted Megara.

§57. It may be possible to understand better the ideological relationship between Megara and Thebes if the parallel connection between Sparta and Crete is considered. At Sparta, primitive institutions (such as the year classes, or the **krupteiā**) were reformulated during the Dark Age and archaic period. There also, Lycurgus was evoked as the authority for successive reinstitutionalizations in a community which, especially before 550, was indeed conservative but by no means static.[1] To the Spartans, reforms were truly revolutionary, since they sought to recover the original values or consensus of the society. Yet, change cannot be exorcised from popular memory. So even conservative reinstitutionalizations generate societal tension. The Spartan attitude toward Crete was a relief mechanism. Lycurgus supposedly derived his constitution from there (Plutarch *Lycurgus* 4.1–3; Aristotle *Politics* 1271b20–27; cf. 1274a29; Polybius 6.45–46). Historically, it is improbable that the Spartans derived anything substantive from the Cretans, who continued to live in a primitive, relatively undifferentiated social order. Superficial similarities between Spartan and Cretan institutions were a matter of common inheritances. However, the similarities enabled the Spartans to hold up a mirror (Crete) to their own society. If we assume a similar impulse in the Megarians to justify social evolution by reference to some external point of comparison, the emphasis on Thebes in the Theognidea can be understood. Bacchiad Corinth was a dim memory to sixth-century Megarians; contemporary Corinth was a political opponent. Thebes was nearby, with a congenial political order. But consensus was lacking at Megara. The Megarians did not have the fertile plains of Boiotia to stabilize their society around farming.

§58. Aithon upholds his position against Arguris, who has experienced slavery, while the speaker, for all his other troubles, has not. Her name is an adaptation of the word for silver, **arguros**. The name is unattested otherwise, but compare Khrusis, the name of a courtesan (Lucian *Courtesan Dialogues* 299–301). Can Arguris be a generic figure who embodies the capacity for enslaving or for confounding social distinctions inherent in money? The servile Arguris, perhaps freed and grown rich, crudely taunts Aithon about his ancestry in a

---

§56n3. Gernet 1968.139–153.
§57n1. Cook 1962.156–158.

fashion reminiscent of a slave of comedy and of the crude invective with which Megarian Comedy is associated.

§59. In verses 903–932, the poet addresses one Demokles 'He whose **kleos** is of the **dēmos**'. He ought to represent an upholder of the populist cause. When we recall the role of the redistribution of material goods as an integrating social influence in the political behavior of the Megarian **dēmos**, and the prominence of sharing food and drink in Megarian comedy, Theognis 903–932 can be read as a rejection of these attitudes and as an admonition to Demokles against them. What is most remarkable in this section is the poet's attitude toward **khrē-mata** 'money' or 'property'. A man's total of **khrēmata** is fixed. This is troublesome because the duration of life is unknown. Accomplishing few things (**erga telōn oliga**, v. 914) is preferable if one can match his resources to his lifetime. There is no entrepreneurial spirit here. The poet is uninterested in his succession and alienated from community and family. The wealth of the rich man, whose fate is to be avoided, falls into the hands of an **epitukhōn** 'any chance person' (v. 918). The poet laments that this rich man did not give his property to someone whom the rich man might have chosen. This is an odd statement, inasmuch as Greek cities customarily legislated carefully about succession to estates. The poet is perhaps thinking of a situation where heirs with a better legal claim than the chosen person would have existed, so that testamentary freedom would not be available to the speaker. When Theognis comes to draw conclusions from the examples of the rich man at death and the beggar before death, his advice is to give the **kamatos** 'fruit of one's labor' (v. 925) to no one. The **epitukhōn** is any heir, and the person of choice is someone to whom the money is to be given in life. The ideal of the speaker is to have consumed all his resources at death. Compare Theognis 271–278, which expresses the view that the most wretched misfortune occurs when children, gaining control of their father's property, hate him (cf. 719–728). The poetry of the Theognidea is most hostile toward acquisition (vv. 145–148, 197–202), and the pursuit of **kerdos** 'profit' is a cause of public ills (vv. 39–52; cf. 83–86, 465–466). In verses 903–932, these attitudes reach an extreme formulation. Perhaps we are glimpsing the oligarchic rejection of any distribution, an egotistical reduction that sees man as consumer, not as creator or sharer.

§60. When the democratic government was overthrown at Megara, it was because the number of exiles had grown great (Aristotle *Politics* 1300a17–19). The exiles established a rule that only those who had overthrown the democracy and established the oligarchy (and presumably their descendants) could hold office. This enactment indicates a situation where few common values exist to provide a basis for cooperation in political life. Only the criterion of party affiliation can be applied (see the Chronological Table, Notes P, Q). It is not surprising that this regime was stable precisely because the Spartan alliance kept away from Megara the sort of external pressures which had probably created ideological ferment there in the sixth century.

§61. An argument has been made here to the effect that populist and oligarchic ideologies at Megara were shared by colonial Megarians, along with the generic expressions of these ideologies. Is there then any indication of a similar sequence of ideological confrontations in the colonies? Aristotle testifies to the fact that democracy at Nisaean Megara ended in a manner similar to that of the democracy at Heraclea Pontica. Presumably, the Heraclean democracy fell first; hence, his order of comparison. The democracy at Heraclea fell shortly after the foundation of the colony (*Politics* 1304b31–34), and, as we have seen, Megarian democracy probably lasted into the second half of the sixth century (see the Chronological Table, Notes N, P, Q, R). Apart from this parallel, Aristotle does not give us much information about Heraclea; not enough, that is, to test properly our theory of ideological parallelism. There are, however, several details in the *Politics* which are suggestive. At a subsequent stage of the constitutional history of Heraclea, the officeholding group numbered very few, with only one member from each family of the elite (1305b11–12). The total number of these oligarchs was quite low, because the next stage in constitutional development saw the government expanded to 600. So, the Heraclean democracy gave way to a narrow oligarchy, which, in accordance with Theognidean strictures, probably forbade exogamy of the **agathoi** with the **kakoi**. Such a feature usually accompanied single representation of elite families. The succeeding regime of 600 fell before the agitation of demagogues (1305b36). Apparently the legal apparatus had not been staffed from the entire body of citizens. Did the ruling class monopolize judgment as exponents of **dikē**, with the 600 alone serving as jurors? Another passage may give more detail about this collapse. A judgment in court on a charge of adultery against one Eurytion, both **dikaios** 'just' and **stasiōtikos** 'factional', triggered the change (*Politics* 1306a36–b1). While mere adultery may have been the substance of the charge, it is also possible that a marriage between social classes, forbidden by law, was envisaged as adultery.[1]

---

§61n1. Eventually, Megarian ideological traditions at Heraclea were extinguished. The epistolary novel *Chion of Heraclea* (*Khionos Epistolai*) describes in the form of a

§62. Some further evidence comes from Megara Hyblaea and Selinous, which again draws our attention to the similarity of ideology between colony and mother city and to the differing timing of constitutional change. An inscription, dated to shortly after 500 according to letter forms, reports provisions for the settlement at Selinous of a group of exiles from Megara.[1] It has usually been assumed that this is Megara Hyblaea, although there is no firm evidence other than the mention of Selinous. The document was recorded at Olympia on a bronze plaque, suggesting that it was a treaty between Selinous and the city of origin of the exiles—or between Selinous and the exiles themselves, envisaged as a colony. One may note that the theme of exile, prominent in the Theognidea, would have evoked a response from those Sicilian Megarians involved in this affair. Provisions about **khrēmata** 'property' appear at several points in the fragmentary document, and in one place the appropriation of property by the state is at issue. One might observe the prominence elsewhere in Megarian history of confiscation. There is also a discussion of the disposition of property after the death of a parent (cf. above, §59). More hypothetical (yet tantalizing) is the restoration **peri ano[siō]n kai [peri ki-xal]lān** 'concerning the impious and concerning highway robbers'. The last reference is reminiscent of the story of the **hamaxokulistai** 'wagon-rollers', who were exiled from Nisaean Megara for their impious attack on Peloponnesian sacred ambassadors (see the Chronological Table, Notes N, P).

§63. Megara's oligarchic government ran into trouble as soon as external pressures renewed themselves. Spartan absorption in the Helot revolt gave Corinth her opportunity to attempt to subjugate Megara (Thucydides 1.103.4; Diodorus Siculus 11.79.1–2; Plutarch *Cimon* 17.1–2). Megara appealed to Athens. War broke out between the Peloponnesians and Athenians (Thucydides 1.105.1–6, 108.2; Diodorus Siculus 11.79.3–4). The Athenians admirably upheld the cause of their Megarian ally, but the Megarian government decided to defect from the Athenians after Sparta had given indications that it would not tolerate Athenian hegemony in central Greece (Thucydi-

---

Bildungsroman the events leading up to the assassination of Klearkhos, tyrant of Heraclea, by Chion, a Heraclean youth and disciple of Plato (cf. Memnon *FGH* 434 F 1; Justin 16.5.12–18; Aelian fr. 86 [Hercher]; Diodorus Siculus 16.36.3). The motives and attitudes of Chion are presented in terms of Academic tenets with no points of contact with the Megarian antityrannical tradition attested by the Theognidea. See Düring 1951.

§62n1. Dittenberger and Purgold 1896.51–58; Roehl 1882 no. 514; Jeffery 1961. 271.

des 1.114.1–2; Diodorus Siculus 12.5.2, 6.1; Plutarch *Moralia* 402A; *Pericles* 22.1). At this point, the remarkable figure of Pythion deserves attention. When the Megarians revolted from Athens and slew the Athenian troops in their territory, Pythion saved three Athenian tribal regiments under the command of Andokides. They had become trapped in the Megarid. We learn these facts from the grave monument of Pythion, who was buried at Athens (*IG* I² 1085 = Meiggs-Lewis no. 51.5–6). Pythion, a Megarian who boasts that he fought most bravely on behalf of his **polis** (boasting of seven slain enemies, line 2), identified to such an extent with Athens that he lost his homeland. Pythion was a Megarian democrat (**eukleizōn eni dēmōi** 'having won fame among the people', line 4) and, for all we know, a patriotic Megarian, but he seems to have been a democrat first; hence, he threw in his lot with the Athenians. Moreover, he helped Andokides lead away two thousand **andrapoda** 'slaves' (line 7). If they were all Megarian, they must have been most of the slave population of the Megarid. Their loss offers an ironic postscript to archaic Megarian redistribution.

§64. Pythion was a harbinger of the future ideological struggles at Megara. By 424, during the Peloponnesian War, an oligarchy had given way to a democracy (which tried to maintain alliance with Sparta). The democracy came under pressure from a group of exiles (Thucydides 4.66–73). They had been established at first by the Spartans at Plataea, and then they had seized the Megarian port city of Pagai, from which they raided the Megarians in the city. The Megarian government then attempted to bring in the Athenians. When the Athenians failed to occupy Megara (capturing only its port of Nisaea), the exiles were restored in a general reconciliation of oligarchs and democrats. Thereafter, they executed those suspected of intrigue with Athens and set up an extreme oligarchy (Thucydides 4.74.3–4). There is justification for suspecting that at this stage democratic and oligarchic ideology in Megara no longer offered much hope for reorganizing Megarian society. The old ideologies of the sixth century did not provide the skills needed to survive in a world of implacable power blocs. After the terrible suffering of the Megarians in the Peloponnesian War, the city seems to have predicated its policy on passivity and a playing off of its stronger neighbors against each other.[1] The armies of the fourth century crossed the Megarid at will.

---

§64n1. Legon 1981.263–266, 273–274, 276, draws attention to this phenomenon.

The Megarians had become spectators in their own land. Such survival is bought at some psychological cost, in a context as pervaded with territoriality as was the life of the classical **polis**. Even the oligarchic Megareis, I suggest, were uninterested in Theognis because they could not empathize with his value system.

§65. The true successors of the sixth-century Megarian ideologues were the Athenians. The surviving references to Megarian comedy are too glancing for the debt of Attic Old Comedy to Megarian comedy to be properly gauged.[1] It is worth remembering, however, that in Aristophanes' *Wasps*, where the author sensitizes his audience to the Megarian affinities of the work, we find a sustained juxtaposition of the comic hero Philokleon against the mores of an aristocratic behavior pattern focused on the symposium.[2] On the other side of the ideological spectrum, Xenophon wrote a treatise on Theognis (Stobaeus *Florilegium* 88.14). Critias, leader of the extreme oligarchical regime of the Thirty, was an elegiac poet who imitated the Theognidean idea of the **sphrēgis** 'seal' (v. 19; Critias fr. 5 W). Plato, by quoting from it, shows his interest in the corpus (*Meno* 95D–96A; *Laws* 630A).[3] Athenian oligarchs felt so akin to archaic Megarian aristocratic poetry that it is uncertain how much of the final state of the corpus is owed to Athenian reception and mediation. The plight of the Megarians in ideological terms is not all that different from their misery in the *Acharnians* (729–835). There the Megarian sells

---

§65n1. Overzealous attempts to uphold the originality and priority of Attic comedy should not blind us to the possibility that early dramatic forms evolved at several locations in archaic Greece. The extent to which Athenian drama draws on these other forms remains a mystery (cf. Pickard-Cambridge 1962), but the imitation of literary motifs and the dissemination of institutional innovation are the rule rather than the exception during the period. Cf. Wilamowitz 1875.319–341; Breitholtz 1960.40–82; Henderson 1975.223–228.

§65n2. Note Bdelykleon's coaching of his father, Philokleon, in order to prepare him to attend a symposium (vv. 1121–1264) and the description of Philokleon's behavior at the symposium (1299–1334).

§65n3. It is difficult to evaluate the effect on the corpus (as we have it) exerted by the interest in it of antidemocratic Athenian ideologues and philosophers of the end of the fifth century. In part, the emphasis on the contrast between **agathoi** 'nobles' and **deiloi** or **kakoi** 'base' or 'poor' in the surviving Theognidea may be because other political themes were less interesting to Athenian oligarchs. The programmatic but nonpragmatic quality of the political sentiments of the Theognidea may have particularly attracted the Athenians. This hypothesis would be valid if the corpus underwent an Athenian phase in its transmission. The selection process, however, would never have been started had not topical political references already been conventionalized in the early history of the corpus.

his daughters as pigs, a code word for female genitalia. The Megarians have become passive and feminized in the face of Athenian power.[4] To adapt the language of Wilamowitz, Megarian comedy had become jokes about Megarians rather than by them.

---

§65n4. At Megara the tomb of Hippolyte, leader of the Amazons, was pointed out (Pausanias 1.41.7 = *FGH* 487 F 9). The *Megarika* reported that, when the Amazons were defeated by the Athenians under Theseus, Hippolyte, disheartened by defeat and at a loss about returning to her homeland, died from grief. The Megarians, so often defeated by the Athenians, identified with Athens' enemy, even though the enemy was in this case a woman.

6
Opposites, Reversals, and Ambiguities: The Unsettled World of Theognis

Veda Cobb-Stevens

§1. The world depicted in the Theognidean corpus is one replete with conflicts, betrayals, duplicities, and uncertainties. The history of Megara as reflected in this poetry has followed a distressing and unsettling itinerary of economic change and sociopolitical discord. The agitations of the **kakoi** 'base' have followed the rule of the **agathoi** 'noble', and implicit trust of associates has been replaced by a protracted and studied suspicion. Communication, which presumably in an earlier time could be relatively straightforward, finds its paradigm here in the **ainos** 'enigmatic utterance'. This riddling discourse, which conceals its message in the very act of transmitting it, is a type of speech most appropriate to such shifting circumstances.[1]

§2. The poems revolve around the persona of Theognis, who, regardless of his status as a historical personage, appears as both their author and the exponent of their aristocratic outlook. Yet the name of Theognis is in fact less an indication of the particular origin of the poems than of their general aristocratic provenience and political orientation.[1] The value system of the Theognidea becomes defined by constellations of certain key terms that occur in pairs of contraries, the most important of which are **agathos/kakos** (or **esthlos/deilos**), **dikē/hubris**, and **metron/koros**. Among these pairs of opposites, it is naturally the first, the contrast between **agathos** 'noble' and **kakos** 'base', that is primary. Both **dikē** 'justice' and the **metron** 'mean' are the concern of the **agathos**, whereas **hubris** 'outrage' incited by **koros** 'insatiability' is the hallmark of the **ka-**

---

§1n1. Cf. Nagy Ch.2§§1–2.

§2n1. Ford Ch.3§15. Cf. also Jaeger 1945.194 and Fränkel 1975.422. By contrast with my presentation, Jaeger accentuates the individuality of the author (p.190), while Fränkel downplays the general political orientation of the poetry.

kos.[2] Furthermore, the **agathos** is properly wealthy, but the **kakos** is more deserving of penury. As Theognis says:

καὶ γάρ τοι πλοῦτον μὲν ἔχειν ἀγαθοῖσιν ἔοικεν,
ἡ πενίη δὲ κακῷ σύμφορος ἀνδρὶ φέρειν.
Theognis 525–526

For to have wealth is fitting for the *noble* [agathoi],
But poverty is appropriate for the *base* [kakos] to endure.

Thus, the **agathos**, who is well-born, wealthy, and a responsible citizen, is in every respect the opposite of the **kakos**, who is low-born, deserving of penury, and unfit for public affairs.

§3. Yet, to say that the aristocratic temper promotes the values of **genos** 'family', wealth, and **aretē** 'excellence, achievement' or **dikē** 'justice' is not adequate as an account of such an outlook, for these values are related to one another in a quite specific way. None of the three qualities alone is sufficient to make a man truly **agathos**; rather, all three must be present. Moreover, they must be ordered in such a way as to constitute a hierarchy of values in which the highest value acts as the criterion by which to judge the others. Birth, which might be thought a priori to constitute the essence of an aristocratic value system, is certainly important in the Theognidea, as the poet's laments about the dire consequences of intermarriage testify. But it is far from sufficient by itself to make a man an **agathos**. It is much easier to beget a man, we are told, than to give him **phrenes esthlai** 'a noble mind' (vv. 429–430). Being born into the right family is merely a precondition for becoming noble. In the Theognidea, as in Homer, excellence is something that must be won by constant exertion (vv. 1027–1028).[1]

§4. Wealth, likewise, is not adequate to make a man **agathos**, nor is it valued in itself as something to be hoarded or as something that

---

§2n2. Cf., e.g., vv. 153–154, 279–282, 465–466, 611–614, 693–694, and 1171–1176.

§3n1. Legon 1981.112 puts more emphasis on birth. Donlan 1973b.63 argues that in Homer there is very little attention paid to birth at all, the determination of **aretē** being based upon actual accomplishments. It was in the seventh and sixth centuries, when the aristocratic class was challenged in its claims to leadership, that an appeal to noble birth became prominent. Yet, as Donlan points out, and as I shall argue for Theognis (§5 below), this appeal to birth was not to the mere fact of lineage itself but was based on the assumption that a noble heritage brought with it instruction in a superior morality. Cf. also Ferguson 1958.19 and Cerri 1968.12.

makes possible a life of self-indulgent dissipation. Wealth, as something that a man *has*, is a necessary condition for his being an **agathos**, just as birth is a necessary aspect of what he *is*. It is through wealth that the **agathos** is socially responsible, entertaining his friends and repaying debts, something that the **deilos** cannot do (vv. 101–112). It is also through wealth that the **agathos** is politically responsible, since he is free enough from the concerns of subsistence to be able to speak and act on behalf of the **polis**, being both persuasive in the assembly and forceful on the battlefield (vv. 173–178, 1003–1006).

§5. The highest value is that of **dikē** 'justice', along with that quality of character which embodies it, **dikaiosunē**. The importance of a noble **genos** derives not so much from birth itself as from the **genos** as the repository of instruction in **dikē**. The use of the wealth that is inherited from the **genos** is always to be guided by its strictures, a lesson that both father and mother will teach (vv. 131–132). The garnering of further wealth, honors, and achievements is not to be done by shameful or unjust deeds (vv. 29–30); and the aristocrat should choose piety and few possessions rather than extravagant riches gotten **adikōs** 'unjustly' (vv. 145–148).

§6. But if wealth is the least important of the three aristocratic values, being simply the means by which an **agathos** meets the social and political obligations of his way of life and being always subject to the requirements of **dikē**, it is nonetheless true that the poetry of the Theognidea portrays poverty as the most debilitating of misfortunes (vv. 173–178), worse even than death itself (vv. 181–182). This paradox derives from the "unsettled world" in which the aristocratic ideal is being propagated, from the fact, in short, that it is precisely an ideal and not a reality. For, as Theognis points out:

... κακοὶ δ᾽ ἀγαθῶν καθύπερθεν.
Theognis 679

... the *base* [**kakoi**] are above the *noble* [**agathoi**].

This reversal, resulting in a world where status is no longer assured and friendships are precarious, is grounded in the ascendancy of a single human motivational complex: desire for private gain and for power (vv. 45–46).[1]

---

§6n1. Cf. Jaeger 1945.201 and Adkins 1960.76.

§7. The **kakoi** are not concerned with justice or equal distribution for the common good (v. 678). They have no sense of political responsibility but are intent upon gaining every advantage for themselves alone. They thus upset the ship of state like a violent storm (vv. 667–682),[1] since their wishes, as Aristotle would say, are not constant but are "at the mercy of opposing currents like a strait of the sea" (*Nicomachean Ethics* 1167b6–7). What this unrelenting concern for one's own advantage demands in practical terms is a willingness to shift one's stance at a moment's notice, to betray a friend if this means an increase in property, or to break an alliance if this will result in a gain in political power.

§8. Verses 39–52 depict an uneasy situation in which the **hēgemones** 'leaders' have succumbed to **hubris** 'outrage' and are ruining the **dēmos** 'community'. Being leaders, these men would have enjoyed the denomination '**agathoi**'. But Theognis insists that they cannot be **agathoi** (for the **agathoi** have never yet ruined a **polis**), so they must in fact be **kakoi**.[1] The truism that **dike** 'justice' is the concern of the born **agathos** has been put to the test and is found wanting.

§9. Another passage in which the **kakoi** are said to dominate the **agathoi** is to be found immediately following verses 39–52. In this case, we find that those are now **agathoi** who have just come in from the countryside where they wore goatskins and pastured like deer, knowing neither **dikai** 'judgments' nor **nomoi** 'laws' (vv. 53–60). These people are presumably those **kakoi** (by birth) who, in periods of social and economic upheaval, were able to acquire great wealth, status, and ultimately political power. In the eyes of any traditional aristocrat, this state of affairs would have been a radical reversal indeed. It implies the erosion of that seemingly self-evident principle that it is fitting for the **agathoi** to be wealthy and for the **kakoi** to be poor (vv. 525–526)—and this reversal is one phenomenon that receives much of Theognis' ire.[1] According to the aristocratic viewpoint of the Theognidea, it gave positions of influence to those undeserving of such power and tempted those who were deserving literally to "sell out" to baser men and to their own baser motives. The poems

---

§7n1. Cf. Nagy Ch.2 for a full analysis of this passage.

§8n1. For this reading of verses 39–52, see West 1974.67–68 and Nagy Ch.2 §§14, 18, 26–38. For a different reading, see Legon 1981.112–113.

§9n1. In verses 315–316, Theognis admits that many **kakoi** are rich, whereas many **agathoi** are poor. See also verses 161–164, where the **deiloi** have an **esthlos daimōn** and the **esthloi** have a **deilos daimōn**.

paint the portrait of a man who felt the effects of this reversal both in the **polis** of Megara and in his own life. Just as in broader social terms many of the **agathoi** consented to betray their **genos** 'family line' by giving their daughters in marriage to the newly rich **kakoi** (vv. 193–196), so also Theognis found himself betrayed by his supposedly noble friends who yielded to the temptation of wealth unjustly obtained (vv. 1135–1150; cf. vv. 267–270).

§10. In a sociopolitical context in which the **kakoi** have come to dominate the **agathoi**, making wealth, not justice, the highest value, poverty will truly be the worst lot to befall an **agathos**. His friends will leave him, and not even the ties of **genos** will make his kin steadfast (vv. 299–300). Thus deserted and deprived of the means to act in a socially or politically significant way, he will naturally want to take all measures possible to restore his former economic status. But his dilemma is at once evident: what is to determine the limits of possibility? Should he do anything to regain his wealth, or should he allow himself to be guided by the demands of **dikē**? The temptation will be to try anything. Poverty, Theognis says, teaches injustice (vv. 649–652). But the true **agathos** will nonetheless forbear. In a world where the aristocratic value system is being undermined, constancy of character and endurance of the most varying circumstances become noticeably frequent injunctions (e.g., vv. 657–658, 695–696). Yet there are few who will endure and pass the test of penury without betraying their standards (vv. 83–86).[1]

§11. Since there are very few among the born **agathoi** who will endure poverty without yielding to the temptation of **adikiā** 'injustice' to regain lost wealth, it is easy to see that, from an aristocratic perspective, the sociopolitical reversal in which the **kakoi** come to dominate the **agathoi** does not represent a parallel reversal within the value system itself. To have a parallel reversal on the level of values, it would be necessary that the new sociopolitical situation establish a new value hierarchy that simply reflects the old as if in an upside-down mirror. Whereas the prior system placed **dikē** at the apex of its values, with **genos** and wealth coming after, the new system, if such were to exist, would have to place wealth at the top, under which would be subsumed **genos** and **dikē**. The result would still constitute

---

§10n1. This is in itself an important point, illustrating that moral principle which, though varying in content as to what precisely constitutes **aretē**, maintains that excellence is difficult and is to be obtained by the few—a principle central to several value systems from Homer to Aristotle.

an ordered world, albeit one ordered in a different manner. But when greed and the desire for personal advantage gain ascendancy, they do not create an alternative order but rather preclude order altogether:[1]

χρήματα δ' ἀρπάζουσι βίῃ· κόσμος δ' ἀπόλωλεν,
    δασμὸς δ' οὐκέτ' ἴσος γίνεται ἐς τὸ μέσον·
φορτηγοὶ δ' ἄρχουσι, κακοὶ δ' ἀγαθῶν καθύπερθεν.
    Theognis 677–679

They seize possessions by force and *order* [kosmos] has been destroyed.
There is no longer an equitable division [of possessions] in the common interest,
but the merchandise carriers rule, and the *base* [kakoi] are on top of the *noble* [agathoi].

§12. When one's personal gain is the highest value, then it is not simply that all other values are subordinated to this one, but that they are, in the end, sacrificed to it. The **kakos** will not hesitate to gain riches by deceit and, once wealthy, will have no qualms about mixing his **genos** with that of an **agathos**. The ruined **agathos**, desperate to regain his lost substance, will consent to double-dealing or to marriage with a prosperous, though base-born, woman. It is this self-interested pursuit of wealth which is the hallmark of any **kakos**, whether he be one of the newly rich or one of the recently impoverished. The clash of the aristocratic value system with the principled amorality of the **kakoi** is not an open confrontation of competing positions, in which the merits of one system can be rationally examined in juxtaposition with another. If any means may be employed to gain advantage for oneself, then not the least in importance is the insincere or equivocal use of traditional value terminology. That well-born aristocrats like Kyrnos could be "bastardized"[1] so easily depended in part on the appropriation by the **kakoi** of the term 'agathos' itself.

§13. During a hypothetical period when the **agathoi** both were the ruling class in the **polis** and managed more or less to embody the code of values which they espoused, the terms 'agathos' and 'kakos' could remain relatively straightforward in both their meaning and their application. But if this condition of stability is impaired, the terms also waver. In their original meaning they incorporated the

---

§11n1. Cf. Fränkel 1975.416: "'Order' (**kosmos**) was a party slogan of the aristocracy."
§12n1. Cf. Nagy Ch.2§43.

requirements of birth, economic class, and morality, which were to be found as a single complex in the same person or group. When economic or sociopolitical changes make it possible for these various marks of being **agathos** or **kakos** to occur separately or in varying combinations, then both the meaning and the application of the terms become as unsettled as the world that contains them.[1]

§14. Theognis' charge that the **kakoi** are above the **agathoi** lodges at least two distinct complaints. For Theognis is saying that (1) the economic factor of wealth is taken (by some) to be sufficient for being **agathos**, and that (2) a noble birth does not automatically guarantee a high economic status or a noble morality. In the first instance, those who were **kakoi** by birth managed to obtain the wealth and status that, ideally, are fitting only for the **agathoi**. But, according to Theognis' moral sensibilities, they did not rise to the requirements of being **agathoi**—loving **dikē** and avoiding **hubris**. Both morally and by birth, these people are decidedly **kakoi**. Only their wealth gives them any claim at all to the title of **agathoi**. In the second instance, those who were **agathoi** by birth, having had their economic status undermined by the rising **kakoi**, undermined in turn their own moral standards through a desire to regain lost wealth. The reversal in position of the **kakoi** and **agathoi**, therefore, is not a single event in Megara's history, nor does it carry with it a single semantic shift. It is, rather, the very substance of the turmoil of a **polis**: that those who were **agathoi** by birth became morally or economically **kakoi**, and that those who were **kakoi** by birth come into power above those who were by birth (and sometimes morally) **agathoi**.[1]

§15. That such a reversal of expectations could throw askew the semantics of normative discourse is not surprising and is, in fact, confirmed by Thucydides' account of the **stasis** 'conflict' that infected the Greek city-states in the context of the revolution in Corcyra:

καὶ τὴν εἰωθυῖαν ἀξίωσιν τῶν ὀνομάτων ἐς τὰ ἔργα ἀντήλλαξαν τῇ δικαι-
ώσει. τόλμα μὲν γὰρ ἀλόγιστος ἀνδρεία φιλέταιρος ἐνομίσθη, μέλλησις
δὲ προμηθὴς δειλία εὐπρεπής, τὸ δὲ σῶφρον τοῦ ἀνάνδρου πρόσχημα.
Thucydides 3.82.4

To fit in with the change of events, words, too, had to change their usual meanings. What used to be described as a thoughtless act of aggression

---

§13n1. Cf. Donlan 1973.369, Adkins 1960.76–79, and Lloyd-Jones 1971.46.
§14n1. Theognis would certainly place himself in the latter group, viz., of those who are **agathoi** both morally and by birth.

was now regarded as the courage one would expect of a party member; to think of the future and wait was merely another way of saying one was a coward; any idea of *moderation* [sōphron] was just an attempt to disguise one's unmanly character.[1]

For these disturbances, both political and linguistic, Thucydides offers a diagnosis not unlike that of Theognis regarding Megara:

πάντων δ' αὐτῶν αἴτιον ἀρχὴ ἡ διὰ πλεονεξίαν καὶ φιλοτιμίαν ...
Thucydides 3.82.8

Love of power, operating through *greed* [pleonexiā] and through *personal ambition* [philotimiā] was the cause of all these evils.

As in the unsettled world of Theognis, anyone in these situations who wanted to exhort others to hold on to the old values would find that the only language in which such exhortation was possible had been eroded at its foundations. In such circumstances, a speaker could resort to ambiguities.[2] Though Theognis is nothing if not exhortatory, he could be so only by fighting fire with fire: cultivating ambiguity in the midst of ambiguity.

§16. The **sophiē** 'skill' that the poet possesses (v. 770) involves the ability to make false things like unto true[1] and is explicitly described by the verb **ainissomai** 'make allusive utterances' (v. 681). This description concludes a long passage portraying how "we" are being carried along on a ship through a dark, stormy night, our troubles compounded by "their" deposing the good captain and refusing to bail. The passage depicts sociopolitical conflict in terms of a storm at sea that threatens the safety of a ship and those on it, employing an allusive language meant to be understood only by the **agathoi** and not by the **kakoi**, in the moral sense of these terms.[2] As a special **sophiē** 'skill' is needed to compose allusive utterances, so a special **sophiē** is needed to interpret them. The poet says that he, in practicing his skill (**sophizomai**, v. 19), places a seal upon his words so that they cannot be stolen without detection and so that no one will substitute something inferior for the genuine thing that they contain. This seal, forged by **sophiē** 'skill', is the mark or criterion that will

---

§15n1. Translation by Warner 1954. Cf. Edmunds 1975b.
§15n2. Cf. Nagy 1979.222–242 on the discourse of **ainos** in early Greek poetry.
§16n1. Cf. v. 713 and Hesiod *Theogony* 27–28, as discussed by Edmunds Ch.4 §§16–20.
§16n2. Cf. Nagy Ch.2§§1–5.

allow those who themselves had **sophiē** to distinguish the genuine verses and true message of Theognis from counterfeits.[3]

§17. But this poetry, which is addressed to a community of **philoi** 'friends' in the spirit of **philiē** 'friendship', also speaks about friendship and does so in terms quite similar to the manner in which it speaks of itself as poetry. For just as a skill is needed to distinguish true from counterfeit verses, and true from erroneous interpretations of allusive utterances, so also is skill needed to distinguish the true from the false friend. The seal put on the poetry to protect it against adulteration is like the **basanos** 'touchstone' needed to test a friend (vv. 415–418). But the skill needed to test a friend, as opposed to that needed to test currency, is difficult to attain (vv. 119–128).

§18. What is difficult, as we have seen (vv. 1027–1028), is reserved for the **agathoi**, but the base (**kakoi, deiloi**) can accomplish only what is easy (vv. 611–614). Furthermore, the base are depicted as constantly deceiving each other, because they do not distinguish the **gnōmai** 'criteria' of the **agathoi** from those of the **kakoi** (vv. 59–60).

§19. This is not to say that the base are totally nonknowing:

ὅστίς τοι δοκέει τὸν πλησίον ἴδμεναι οὐδέν,
ἀλλ᾽ αὐτὸς μοῦνος ποικίλα δήνε᾽ ἔχειν,
κεῖνός γ᾽ ἄφρων ἐστί, νόου βεβλαμμένος ἐσθλοῦ·
ἴσως γὰρ πάντες ποικίλ᾽ ἐπιστάμεθα·
ἀλλ᾽ ὁ μὲν οὐκ ἐθέλει κακοκερδείῃσιν ἕπεσθαι,
τῷ δὲ δολοπλοκίαι μᾶλλον ἄπιστοι ἅδον.
    Theognis 221–226

Whoever imagines that his neighbor knows nothing
and that he alone has versatile stratagems,
that man is without sense, deprived of an *intent* [**noos**] that is *worthy*
    [**esthlos**].
For we all know versatility equally well,
but one man will not consent to follow *base gain* [**kakokerdeiē**]
while the weaving of untrustworthy schemes is pleasing to another.

But, even if the **kakoi** are not totally nonknowing, we see that spheres of knowledge are nonetheless sharply distinguished from

---

§16n3. For a discussion of the nature of the poet's **sophiē**, see Edmunds Ch.4. For the political ramifications of Theognis' seal, see Ford Ch.3.

each other in terms of their moral worth. On the one hand, some people seek evil gain and others take pleasure in deceits (by implication, for the sake of gain). On the other hand, those who do not want to follow base gain have **gnōmē** 'good judgment' and **aidōs** 'respect' following along with them: these are the (truly) **agathoi**, and they are few among many (vv. 635–636).

§20. Aristotle makes a similar distinction in differentiating the quality of **phronēsis** 'practical wisdom' from that of mere **deinotēs** 'cleverness':

αὕτη δ᾽ ἐστὶ τοιαύτη ὥστε τὰ πρὸς τὸν ὑποτεθέντα σκοπὸν συντείνοντα δύνασθαι ταῦτα πράττειν καὶ τυγχάνειν αὐτῶν. ἂν μὲν οὖν ὁ σκοπὸς ᾖ καλός, ἐπαινετή ἐστιν. ἐὰν δὲ <u>φαῦλος</u>, πανουργία· διὸ καὶ τοὺς <u>φρονίμους</u> δεινοὺς καὶ πανούργους φαμὲν εἶναι. ἔστι δ᾽ ἡ <u>φρόνησις</u> οὐχ ἡ δύναμις, ἀλλ᾽ οὐκ ἄνευ τῆς δυνάμεως ταύτης. ἡ δ᾽ ἕξις τῷ ὄμματι τούτῳ γίνεται τῆς ψυχῆς οὐκ ἄνευ <u>ἀρετῆς</u>, ὡς εἴρηταί τε καὶ ἔστι δῆλον.
Aristotle *Nicomachean Ethics* 1144a24–31

[Cleverness] is such as to be able to do the things that tend toward the mark we have set before ourselves, and to hit it. Now if the mark be *noble* [kalos], the cleverness is laudable, but if the mark be *bad* [phaulos], the cleverness is mere smartness; hence we call even *men of practical wisdom* [phronimoi] clever or smart. *Practical wisdom* [phronēsis] is not the faculty, but it does not exist without this faculty. And this eye of the soul acquires its formed state not without the aid of *virtue* [aretē], as has been said and is plain.

Thus, just as one could be **deinos** 'clever' at getting what one wanted without being virtuous (which requires wanting the right things and taking the right means to obtain them), so those who in Theognis' opinion are truly base (whether they be **kakoi** or **agathoi** by birth) can certainly get what they want, but they neither want the right things nor take the right means to get them. The means that they do use are those of deceit and betrayal, strategies characteristic of a condition of **stasis** 'conflict' (cf. Thucydides 3.82.7). It is especially disconcerting when those who should have resisted such tactics are found to employ them. As Hans-Georg Gadamer remarks in his discussion of Aristotle's reflections on cleverness, the **deinos** is one who has all the natural talents necessary for **phronēsis** 'practical wisdom' and uses them with extraordinary facility to turn an unpromising situation to personal advantage or to maneuver deftly through daily exigencies. But this natural ability fails to be tempered by moral constraints, and it is not insignificant that the word meaning 'clever' also means 'terrible'. There is nothing so uncanny or appalling as dexterity in evil.[1]

§21. From Theognis' point of view, those who should have resisted the temptation to look only to their own advantage are the **agathoi**. The status and the standards were theirs, if not in fact naturally, then seemingly so. Yet they betrayed their own imperatives and by their actions assimilated themselves to the truly **kakoi**, becoming simply a part of the many and thereby losing their claim to be among the outstanding few.

§22. The observation that the highest value of the many is the getting of wealth finds its most forceful statement in the following lines:

πλήθει δ' ἀνθρώπων ἀρετὴ μία γίνεται ἥδε,
    πλουτεῖν· τῶν δ' ἄλλων οὐδὲν ἄρ' ἦν ὄφελος,
οὐδ' εἰ σωφροσύνην μὲν ἔχοις 'Ραδαμάνθυος αὐτοῦ,
    πλείονα δ' εἰδείης Σισύφου Αἰολίδεω,
ὅς τε καὶ ἐξ 'Αΐδεω πολυιδρίῃσιν ἀνῆλθεν
    πείσας Περσεφόνην αἱμυλίοισι λόγοις,
ἥ τε βροτοῖς παρέχει λήθην βλάπτουσα νόοιο—
    ἄλλος δ' οὔ πώ τις τοῦτό γ' ἐπεφράσατο,
ὅντινα δὴ θανάτοιο μέλαν νέφος ἀμφικαλύψῃ,

---

§20n1. Cf. Gadamer 1965.306–307. It should be noted that the word **deinotēs** does not appear at all in the Theognidea. Forms of **deinos** occur five times (vv. 92, 414, 697, 857, and 1318b), but all except the last are deemed questionable (cf. West 1972.193), having as alternate readings either **deilos** or **deilon**. This last passage (1318b) features **deina** and is one in which the poet laments his being a joy to his enemies and a vexation to his friends because of the terrible things (**deina**) he has suffered. Verses 697 and 857 similarly feature **deinos** (or **deilos**) to refer to a situation of misery or destitution, but speak not of friends' vexation but of their lack of steadfastness in such circumstances. The other two passages feature **deinos** (or **deilos**) to refer to human speech or to a human rather than to the calamities that may befall a person. Verses 87–92 exhort Kyrnos to be a trustworthy friend and not a **deinos**(?) companion, to express himself openly and honestly and not to engage in deceit. In verses 413–414, the poet affirms that he himself is trustworthy and claims that not even wine could make him say a **deinon epos** about his friend. Now in this latter passage, West does choose to read **deinon** (West 1971.194), as do Young (1961.27) and van Groningen (1966.163). This passage clearly has a sympotic reference and, as Levine (Ch.7) has shown, the symposium is a microcosm of the **polis**. One who would succumb to the influence of wine or feel dizzy in the swirl of wealth and power is one who would easily betray a friend or ally. And as the betrayal could be effected by a 'terrible word' (v. 414), it is not inappropriate that one who uttered that word also be 'terrible' (**deinos**). Given that verses 87–92 warn against such duplicitous utterances, we may feel more confident in identifying the **hetairos** (v. 91) who uses them as **deinos**: clever, manipulating, and terrifying.

ἔλθῃ δ᾿ ἐς σκιερὸν χῶρον ἀποφθιμένων,
κυανέας τε πύλας παραμείψεται, αἵ τε θανόντων
ψυχὰς εἴργουσιν καίπερ ἀναινομένας·
ἀλλ᾿ ἄρα κἀκεῖθεν πάλιν ἤλυθε Σίσυφος ἥρως
ἐς φάος ἠελίου σφῇσι πολυφροσύναις—
οὐδ᾿ εἰ ψεύδεα μὲν ποιοῖς ἐτύμοισιν ὁμοῖα,
γλῶσσαν ἔχων ἀγαθὴν Νέστορος ἀντιθέου,
ὠκύτερος δ᾿ εἴησθα πόδας ταχεῶν Ἁρπυιῶν
καὶ παίδων Βορέω, τῶν ἄφαρ εἰσὶ πόδες.
ἀλλὰ χρὴ πάντας γνώμην ταύτην καταθέσθαι,
ὡς πλοῦτος πλείστην πᾶσιν ἔχει δύναμιν.
Theognis 699-718

For the greater part of humankind there is this one *achievement*
  [aretē]:
"*Get rich* [ploutein]! There is no advantage to anything else,
not even if you had the *self-control* [sōphrosunē] of Rhadamanthys
  himself,
or knew more than Sisyphos, son of Aiolos,
who came up from Hades' house by his many resources,
having persuaded Persephone with wheedling words.
(It is she who gives forgetfulness to mortals when she takes away
  their thought.)
Before this no man had contrived it,
once the black cloud of death had covered him
and he had gone to the shadowy place of the dead,
passing through the dark gates which hold back
the souls of the dead—even though they protest.
But Sisyphos the hero came back even from there
by his many stratagems into the light of the sun."
[As most people say:
"There is no advantage to anything but wealth,]
not even if you made deceitful things be like genuine things,
having the *noble* [agathē] tongue of Nestor the godlike,
and were faster of foot than the Harpies
or the children of Boreas, whose feet are instantly swift.
But everyone should hoard up this *coin* [literally, mark or thought:
  gnōmē]:
that *wealth* [ploutos] everywhere has the greatest *power* [dunamis]."

§23. According to the many, wealth is the only **aretē** 'excellence', and
anything else is worth nothing in comparison. But according to the
poet, the **sōphrosunē** 'self-control' disdained by the many is something to be extolled:

ταῦτα μαθών, φίλ᾿ ἑταῖρε, δικαίως χρήματα ποιοῦ
σώφρονα θυμὸν ἔχων ἐκτὸς ἀτασθαλίης.

αἰεὶ τῶνδ᾽ ἐπέων μεμνημένος· εἰς δὲ τελευτὴν
αἰνήσεις μύθῳ σώφρονι πειθόμενος.
Theognis 753–756

Learn this lesson, *dear friend* [philos hetairos] and make your *riches*
[khrēmata] with *justice* [dikē]:
keep a heart that is *self-controlled* [sōphrōn] and removed from wicked-
ness,
keeping in mind these *words* [epos plural] of mine. And in the end
persuaded by my *sober* [sōphrōn] utterance, you will praise them.

The traditional aristocratic ideal of the Theognidea maintains that it is
not wealth as such that is important—wealth "at any price"—but only
wealth that has been acquired justly. In order to acquire wealth justly,
it is necessary to be steady in disposition, temperate and self-controlled, loyal to one's friends. It is also necessary to listen to and be
persuaded by words with these same sober qualities, that is, the
words of Theognis. The many, by contrast, allow themselves to be
persuaded by **khrēmata** 'riches' (v. 194), slander (v. 324), or unjust
deeds (v. 380). And the words that they utter are, like their characters, **deina**—clever, manipulating, and terrible (vv. 413–414 and 87–
92).[1]

§24. Yet, given the fact that the ignoble many have been able to
obtain positions of power, it is not simply a question of opposing their
encroachments with a straightforward aristocratic value system. Any
aristocrat—in any **polis**—who is to survive in circumstances such as
these must also cultivate flexibility and indirection. The heart that is
self-controlled must also be changeable, able to adapt to a changing
situation (vv. 213–214). The **sophiē** 'skill' that a poet needs to con-
struct his poetry and that the **philoi** need to penetrate to its real
significance is the very opposite of intransigence (v. 218). But although Theognis assumes that the truly **agathoi** will heed his sober
words, he does not assume that he will infallibly be able to identify
them. If the ideal of friendship demands steadfastness, the reality
of betrayal requires a wary vigilance, for appearances often deceive
one's **gnōmē** 'judgment' (v. 128). The cultivation of a pliant skill and
the careful exercise of judgment, along with a concern for **dikē**, are
the only defenses of the truly **agathoi**.[1]

---

§23n1. Cf. §20n1 above for a justification of this reading of verses 413–414 and
87–92.
  §24n1. Cf. Donlan Ch.9§23.

§25. A small comfort, perhaps, is the thought that the **kakoi** themselves are in even greater danger than the **agathoi** in the chaotic world for which they are responsible. The reversals that they effected were based on a single principle:

ἀλλὰ χρὴ πάντας γνώμην ταύτην καταθέσθαι,
ὡς πλοῦτος πλείστην πᾶσιν ἔχει δύναμιν.
Theognis 717–718

But everyone should hoard up this *coin* [literally, mark or thought: **gnōmē**],
that *wealth* [**ploutos**] everywhere has the greatest *power* [**dunamis**].

The **gnōmē** 'thought' that the many store up is the injunction to store up wealth. But the exclusive concern for attaining wealth by any and every means makes it impossible ever to be certain whether, as one is cheating, one is also not being cheated. As Kant pointed out, if deceit were universalized, then discourse would ultimately be impossible. Within the world of the money-seeking **kakoi**, this is in fact what has happened, for language does not express what it purports to express, and the **kakoi** know no **gnōmai** 'marks' (vv. 59–60) by which to discern what hides behind its surface.

§26. Thus, it is not simply that economic and sociopolitical reversals have given rise to a grievous ambiguity in the terms 'agathos' and 'kakos', but that deceit through ambiguity is the very means by which the reversals were effected. The **kakoi** have managed to dominate the **agathoi** by lying, cheating, pretending to be **philoi**, and adopting the language of the **agathoi**. Theognis' response to this shifting semantic context is, as we have seen, to forge his own ambiguities, in the hope that those things that are hidden for the truly **agathoi** can be deciphered by them, both because his seal is a mark of the authentic aristocratic message contained in the poetry and because the community of true **philoi** to whom it is addressed have the **sophiē** necessary for understanding the message.

§27. That this is nothing more than a hope, Theognis himself is willing to admit. He despairs of seeing justice done in his lifetime and can only aspire to return to earth for vengeance after death (vv. 341–350).[1] The **kakoi**, however, renounce even the possibility of return-

---

§27n1. Cf. Nagy Ch.2§§60–69. Noos is essential to this return (cf. §30 below).

ing from the dead: this Sisyphean feat means nothing when wealth can be obtained instead (vv. 699–712).[2] In fact, everything rejected by the **kakoi** as being valueless in comparison with wealth (vv. 699–718) can be seen as characteristic of Theognis and his poetry. The **sōphrosunē** praised by the poet is the judicious balancing of a Rhadamanthys (v. 701), a legislative pronouncement embodied not in the formal law code of the **polis** but in the elegiac poetry of its noble citizens.[3] Also like Rhadamanthys—who, as Plato points out, was not only just during his lifetime but pronounced just judgments even in Hades (*Apology* 41A–B)—Theognis' ideal of **dikē** extends beyond his own life by being embodied in his poetry.

§28. This poetry's persuasive power, for those who will remember it by putting its ideals into practice (vv. 753–756), provides for the perpetuation of those principles. Furthermore, given the unsettled world in which the poetry must sustain itself, that persuasion must take the form of 'wily words' (v. 704), words that can 'make deceitful things be like genuine' (v. 713). Yet it must be a persuasiveness at all times opposed to the ploys of the many, whose deceptions need not be even remotely like the truth. It must be a persuasiveness grounded in beauty, a beauty of form which has its source in the singing of the Muses and the Kharites, and a beauty of substance which is found in the content of their song (vv. 16–17). Through a beautiful **epos**, they teach the lesson that concern for the community of **philoi** is itself identical with the beautiful. This concern is based on a love of that which is **dikaiotaton** (most **dikaion** 'just'), itself deemed to be the most beautiful thing possible (v. 255). When the truly **agathoi** take this teaching to heart, then the beauty that the poetry both exhibits and enjoins becomes embodied in their own lives. By pre-empting standards of beauty and associating them not merely with physical appearance but with a poetry of social and political responsibility, the embattled **agathoi** have discovered a way to delimit a sphere of worth specifically their own.[1] The **kakoi** may call themselves **agathoi**, but they betray their own baseness in both word and deed. Oriented toward personal gain, their actions are exemplary of that which is **aiskhron** 'ugly' (vv. 27–30), just the opposite of the beautiful, and lead, not to the ordered well-being of the community, but to **stasis** and dissension (vv. 43–

---

§27n2. Cf. van Groningen 1966.279.
§27n3. For a discussion of the relation between Theognis and the Greek law-givers, see Nagy Ch.2§§20–25.
§28n1. Cf. Fränkel 1975.402, 418; also Donlan 1973.371.

52).[2] Their words, likewise, are lying ambiguities, mere masks of self-interest, so powerful that they can sometimes corrupt the **agathoi** themselves (vv. 305-308). But the truly **agathoi** will resist these blandishments, just as they remain steadfast in the face of poverty, and will refuse to imitate the twisted speech of the **kakoi**. If the **agathoi** must speak in riddles, they will do so with the **agathē** 'noble' tongue of Nestor (v. 714), always guided by a regard for the common good.

§29. This type of speech is the speech of praise and blame, a kind of utterance which by commemoration can preserve immortal fame, or which by deliberate silence can seize a man and drop him into oblivion.[1] Those who can speak with the noble tongue of Nestor will be able, like the original Nestor himself, to bring even the dead back to light and life.[2] For men such as Kyrnos, whom Theognis consents to remember (in this case by a mixture of praise and blame), there awaits the destiny of perpetuation throughout all of Greece (vv. 245-252). Being commemorated by poetry is like being given wings (vv. 237-239), and the one so honored, even though dead (v. 245), appears among the symposiasts at the very moment they begin their song, just like the winged children of Boreas, 'whose feet are instantly swift' (v. 716).

§30. But the forgetful **kakoi** (vv. 1112-1113; cf. vv. 105-112, 755), who do not remember the words of Theognis, are in turn not remembered by him (v. 798). Their forgetfulness is like the forgetfulness of death. Persephone grants forgetfulness as she takes away the **noos** of those who are dead (v. 705); and the **kakoi** are subject to the disastrous **hubris** that ensues when **koros** 'insatiability' comes to those without a **noos artios** 'sound mind' (vv. 153-154). Thus, their placing of wealth even above the possibility of returning from death is, more than they realize, already in effect. For though alive, they are without a sound **noos** or **gnōmē** (vv. 59-60) and are therefore no better off than if they were dead. From the perspective of an

---

§28n2. Theognis warns in several passages against doing what is **aiskhron**, something to which desire for gain will inevitably lead (v. 86). Especially noteworthy are lines 1377-1379, where **kalos** is juxtaposed with **kakotēs**, **deilos**, and **aiskhron oneidos** 'disgraceful reproach'. Cf. also vv. 29, 466, 481, 546, 608, 627, 628, 651, 899, 1150, 1177, and 1329.

§29n1. Obviously, blame need not always be silent. For an account of the relation between memory and the poetry of praise and blame, see Edmunds Ch.4.

§29n2. For the connection between **Nestōr**, **noos**, and **nostos**, see Frame 1978; also Nagy Ch.2§§68-70.

aristocratic exile, their **polis** might appear situated on the edges of **Lēthē**.[1]

§31. Yet the **polis** that the exiled poet can see on the edges of **Lēthē** is his **polis** (vv. 1215–1216), that beautiful city which preserves and is preserved by the gifts of the Muses, far beyond the lifetime of a single individual.[1] If Theognis laments that in the sphere of practical affairs the **kakoi** are above the **agathoi**, he intimates that this reversal will itself be reversed and suggests that in fact the process has already begun. If the **kakoi**, though living, exist as if dead, then the **agathoi**, though dead, can exist as if living.

§32. This triumph of the aristocratic ideal is not by itself sufficient, however. Theognis reminds Kyrnos:

ἀνδρός τοι κραδίη μινύθει μέγα πῆμα παθόντος,
Κύρν', ἀποτεινυμένου δ' αὔξεται ἐξοπίσω.
Theognis 361–362

The heart of a man diminishes when he has suffered grievous trouble, Kyrnos, but afterwards, when vengeance is had, it again grows great.

That the commemorative perpetuation of the **agathoi** be translated once more into actual political power remains the ultimate hope—and the intent—of this poetry.

---

§30n1. See Nagy Ch.2§72.
§31n1. Cf. Edmunds Ch.4§§23–24.

7
Symposium and the **Polis**

Daniel B. Levine

§1. The poetic language of the Theognidea describes the **polis** in terms of a symposium and the symposium in terms of a **polis**.[1] I shall argue that the drinking party was a microcosm and a model of the larger community. In the present discussion of how poetry connects symposium and **polis**, I shall show that this relationship was part of a common Greek poetic tradition—a tradition that survived into the fourth century B.C.

§2. The poetry of Theognis presents itself as idealized sympotic poetry (vv. 237–254). The poet boasts that he has given Kyrnos immortality through verse, and that young men at banquets will always sing of him. The poet imagines that his verses will be sung at symposia. This is not to call the entire corpus "sympotic poetry," but rather to say that the symposium is the one social context that can unite all other poetic forms that might be called to mind by the audience of the Theognidea. Such forms might include riddles, skolia, hymns, dithyrambs, occasional light verse, love poems, and admonitory or political verse—all of which would be appropriately recited at a banquet. This is not to say that in the poetry of Theognis the only exemplar of the

---

§1n1. Literally, a symposium is a 'drinking together'. Technically, at least in fifth-century Athens and later, it was the second part of a **deipnon** 'dinner party'. When the first course was cleared away—it was generally eaten without wine—a libation was poured, and a prayer offered; then the second phase of the **deipnon**, the symposium, began. From both vase paintings and literary sources we know that the symposium was an occasion of drinking, music, dance, and pleasant conversation (Hug 1931). The word **sumposion** appears twice in the Theognidea: at verse 298, where the overtalkative man is declared a symposium's bane, and at verse 496, where rules for decorum in a symposium are outlined. It was customary to choose a leader of the drinking to determine the proportion and the quantity of wine each guest should drink. The titles of these leaders were similar to those held by leaders in the **polis**: **sumposiarkhos** 'arkhōn of the symposium' and **basileus** 'king'. A feast was completed by a symposium. The two formed a unity that made a communal bond among companions: cf. Theognis verse 115, **posios kai brosios hetairoi** 'companions of drinking [i.e. symposium] and eating [i.e. **deipnon**]'.

polis is the symposium.[1] For instance, the **polis** can also be represented by a ship (vv. 667–682, 855–856) or a female about to give birth (vv. 39–52, 1081–1082b).

§3. A keynote of the Theognidea is sounded in the invocation of the Muses and the Kharites at verses 15–18. These goddesses were present at the wedding feast of Kadmos and Harmonia, where they sang:

ὅττι καλὸν φίλον ἐστί, τὸ δ' οὐ καλὸν οὐ φίλον ἐστί.
Theognis 17

What is **kalon** is **philon**, what is not **kalon** is not **philon**.

Political and social cohesion are stressed at the beginning of the Theognidea, one of the main themes of which is the importance of a well-ordered and proper **polis**.[1] The setting for the song of the Muses and the Kharites is a wedding—an occasion for communal eating and drinking. The message of social order that they bring is equally important to the feast that occasioned their song and to the **polis** where the theme of political **harmoniē** 'integration' is paramount.

§4. The following categories will emerge upon consideration of the parallels between **polis** and symposium:

1. Education: The symposium is a place of education for the citizen, preparing him to take part in public life. Inside and

---

§2n1. The relationship between symposium and **polis** is paralleled by the etymological association between **kōmos** 'revel' and **kōmē** 'village'. The word **kōmē** has been traced to a verbal root *kei- 'split, divide' (Palmer 1963.186–189). This root is also the base of the word **kōmos**, the etymological sense of which is 'group of men'. The word **dēmos** offers a good parallel. Aristotle says (*Poetics* 1448a) that the Peloponnesians call rural communities **kōmai** and that the Athenians call them **dēmoi**. The word **dēmos** is derived from the verbal root attested in **daiomai** 'divide' (Chantraine s.v. "**dēmos**"). The same root appears in the word **dais** 'banquet': where portions were divided among diners. Thus, the words **kōmē** and **dēmos** are derivatives of verbs meaning 'cut', 'divide', and the two words for settings of sympotic behavior, **kōmos** and **dais**, are, in their turn, related to words for communities. Palmer motivates the semantics by adducing typological parallels from Germanic (Palmer 1963.188). He presents the following words:

SHEAR

SHARE   SCHAR (German = 'band of men')

Palmer also notes that the same root *kei- 'split' yields in Lycian a noun meaning 'band of men', as well as an abverb meaning 'apart'. Cf. Pedersen 1949.48–49.

§3n1. Cf. Nagy Ch.2§§6–7. Cf. also Edmunds Ch.4.

outside the drinking party, one must learn from the good and avoid the bad.

2. Moderation and Order: A middle course is urged for those who will be participants in a symposium and a polity. A drinking party is an ideal setting for warnings about the dangers of disorder and excess, the lessons from which can be applied to daily life.

3. Cunning: In a symposium, as in a **polis**, one must beware of one's fellow man, who will try to deceive him. In both settings, one must exercise mental suppleness (or **mētis** 'cunning intelligence') and outwit his companions before they can fool him.

4. Utopia: The longing for **kharis** 'gratification', **terpsis** 'enjoyment', **euphrosunē** 'mirth', and **hēsukhiē** 'quietude' in the symposium reflects and parallels a longing for peace and stability in an equitable polity. The ideal sympotic setting is described as an embodiment of a Golden Age, where the Kharites still bless men with their presence.

§5. I shall begin with the category of education. Early in the corpus (vv. 27–30), the poet initiates a theme that is to continue throughout, that the poetry is to have a didactic function:

σοὶ δ᾽ ἐγὼ εὖ φρονέων ὑποθήσομαι, οἷάπερ αὐτὸς
Κύρν᾽ ἀπὸ τῶν ἀγαθῶν παῖς ἔτ᾽ ἐὼν ἔμαθον.
πέπνυσο, μηδ᾽ αἰσχροῖσιν ἐπ᾽ ἔργμασι μηδ᾽ ἀδίκοισιν
τιμὰς μηδ᾽ ἀρετὰς ἕλκεο μηδ᾽ ἄφενος.
Theognis 27–30

But with good intentions *will I lay down principles* for you concerning the
    things that I myself,
Kyrnos, *learned* from the good [**agathoi**] when I was yet a child.
Be prudent, and do not drag **tīmē** nor **aretē** nor wealth
toward shameful deeds or deeds without **dikē**.

Theognis will teach Kyrnos what he himself learned from the 'good' while he was young. From this and similar passages emerges a principle of archaic **paideiā**: aristocratic youth was educated properly by association with the **agathoi**.[1] The theme of companionship with 'good' men (**agathoi, esthloi**) in order to produce a 'good' youth recurs several times in the Theognidea, as does the corresponding advice not to befriend the 'bad' (**kakoi, deiloi**).

---

§5n1. Cf. Ford Ch.3§§14–15; see also Theognis verses 753–756.

§6. At verses 61–68, Kyrnos is urged not to make a **philos** of the **kakoi** 'bad'; instead, he should deceive them. At verses 69–72 he is counseled not to trust or plan with a **kakos**, but rather to go and plan with an **esthlos**. The injunction is repeated at verses 101–112. Let no one persuade you to be a **philos** to a **kakos** man: what use is a **deilos** man as a **philos**? It is better to befriend the **agathoi**, who remember the good deeds done for them (vv. 111–112). The next couplet reiterates the message: you should never make a **kakos** man your **philos**, but always flee him like a bad harbor (vv. 113–114). The message is repeated at verses 1165–1166. One should mix with the **agathoi** and never keep company with the **kakoi**.[1]

§7. The same theme is stressed in lines where the poet describes the sympotic setting as a place for learning goodness at the side of good men:

> ταῦτα μὲν οὕτως ἴσθι· κακοῖσι δὲ μὴ προσομίλει
> ἀνδράσιν, ἀλλ' αἰεὶ τῶν ἀγαθῶν ἔχεο·
> καὶ μετὰ τοῖσιν πῖνε καὶ ἔσθιε, καὶ μετὰ τοῖσιν
> ἵζε, καὶ ἄνδανε τοῖς, ὧν μεγάλη δύναμις.
> ἐσθλῶν μὲν γὰρ ἄπ' ἐσθλὰ μαθήσεαι· ἢν δὲ κακοῖσι
> συμμίσγῃς, ἀπολεῖς καὶ τὸν ἐόντα νόον.
> ταῦτα μαθὼν ἀγαθοῖσιν ὁμίλει, καί ποτε φήσεις
> εὖ συμβουλεύειν τοῖσι φίλοισιν ἐμέ.
> Theognis 31–38

Know that these things are so. And do not associate with **kakoi** men.
But always stick by the **agathoi**.
And sit, eat, and drink with them,
and please them whose power is great.
For you will learn **esthla** from the **esthloi**, but if you mix with the **kakoi**,
you will lose what mind [**noos**] you now have.
Learning these things, associate with the **agathoi**, and someday you will say
that I have given good advice to my **philoi**.

The poet says that the association with the 'good men' is desirable, and he makes his point more concrete by choosing the dining room as a prime location for learning (v. 33). Note also:

---

§6n1. At verses 1169–1170, **kaka** come from being a companion of a **kakos**, and at verses 305–308, a man can become **kakos** by associating with a **kakos**.

κεκλῆσθαι δ' ἐς δαῖτα, παρέζεσθαι δὲ παρ' ἐσθλὸν
ἄνδρα χρεὼν σοφίην πᾶσαν ἐπιστάμενον.
τοῦ συνιεῖν, ὁπόταν τι λέγῃ σοφόν, ὄφρα διδαχθῇς,
καὶ τοῦτ' εἰς οἶκον κέρδος ἔχων ἀπίῃς.
Theognis 563–566

It is a good thing to be invited to a banquet and to sit by an **esthlos**
man who knows all sorts of wisdom [**sophiē**].
Observe him whenever he says anything wise [**sophon**], so you might be
    taught
and go home having this as profit.

The general advice given elsewhere to associate and learn from the
good and to avoid bad men is illustrated specifically in these two
banquet scenes. The symposium is a learning place. What one does in
the **polis** is also practiced in the symposium, a microcosm of the
larger community.[1]

§8. I now proceed to the second of my four categories linking symposium and **polis**, that is, moderation and order. To Theognis, the
middle course is a mark of a man of sound **phrenes** 'mind'. Moderation and order are important in sympotic as well as nonsympotic
situations. The symposium has a paradigmatic character in exhorta-
tions on the dangers of excess and the importance of order.[1] It is a
place where the maxim **mēden agan/liēn** 'nothing excessively' has
special meaning, for the results of overindulgence in food and drink
are immediately apparent (vv. 478, 839–840; cf. vv. 219–220, 335–
336, 593–594).

§9. It is unnecessary to catalogue all passages urging moderation, but
some of the more important examples may be noted before showing
how sympotic passages parallel them. First, observe the importance of
the words **kosmos** 'order', **isos** 'equal', **meson** 'middle', **metron**
'measure', and **mēden agan** 'nothing excessively'. In the following
couplets the poet urges the middle course in politics and represents
himself as a model:

---

§7n1. Cf. Havelock 1952.100, who describes Plato's idea of education as similar.
See §§36–39 below.

§8n1. In the verses that give guidelines for a moderate symposium (467–468),
the poet makes himself the paradigm for proper behavior (475–478). Also note verses
543–546, 945–946, and 947–948, where the poet stresses the need for himself to
render **dikē** impartially, keep to the straight course, and not give in to one party or
another. He sees his task as being straight as a carpenter's rule, not veering to either
side.

μηδὲν ἄγαν ἄσχαλλε ταρασσομένων πολιητέων,
Κύρνε, μέσην δ' ἔρχευ τὴν ὁδὸν ὥσπερ ἐγώ.
Theognis 219–220

Be not over vexed at the citizens in confusion,[1]
Kyrnos, but *keep* to the *middle way*, as I do.

ἥσυχος ὥσπερ ἐγὼ μεσσὴν ὁδὸν ἔρχεο ποσσίν,
μηδετέροισι διδοὺς Κύρνε τὰ τῶν ἑτέρων.
Theognis 331–332

Calmly *keep to the middle way* with your feet *as I do*,
Kyrnos, giving to none the possessions of the others.

The middle course is again advised at verses 335–336 in the form of an injunction not to strive too much. The middle course in all things is best (**pantōn mes' arista**). Similarly, verses 401–407 suggest not to strive too much, and that **kairos** 'timeliness' is best for all men's actions. Only the **agathoi** know how to keep the **metron** 'measure' in speech and all things, as opposed to the **kakoi**, who chatter excessively (vv. 611–614). The next couplet (vv. 615–616) laments the fact that the present generation lacks a man thoroughly **agathos** and **metrios**. In verses 693–694, **koros** 'satiety' or 'insatiability' destroys many foolish men, for it is difficult to know the **metron** when **esthla** are at hand. See also verses 605–606, where **koros** is said to have destroyed more men, wanting more than their share, than has famine. The excesses of **koros** can destroy men, and those of **hubris**, cities (vv. 39–59, 541–542, 603–604, 1103–1104).

§10. Men should not be sad in times of trouble, nor rejoice too much about **agatha** 'good things'. Rather, the **agathos** man should bear all things (vv. 657–666). In matters of property one must also tread a middle course, not having too many possessions nor being too poor (vv. 555–560). In perhaps the strongest political statement lamenting the lack of order and moderation, the poet decries the loss of his possessions, deplores the condition of the **polis**, and concludes:

χρήματα δ' ἁρπάζουσι βίῃ, κόσμος δ' ἀπόλωλεν,
δασμὸς δ' οὐκέτ' ἴσος γίνεται ἐς τὸ μέσον·

§9n1. The verb **tarassō** carries with it a sense of the citizens in turmoil in the manner of a turbulent sea, an image appropriate in light of the "Ship of State" metaphor. Cf. *Odyssey* v 291; Archilochus fr. 105.1 W; Solon fr. 12.1 W = 13.1 GP; Euripides *Trojan Women* 88, 692; Aristophanes *Knights* 431. The poet is portrayed as keeping to a straight path when the citizens are stirred up.

φορτηγοὶ δ᾽ ἄρχουσι, κακοὶ δ᾽ ἀγαθῶν καθύπερθεν.
δειμαίνω, μή πως ναῦν κατὰ κῦμα πίῃ.
Theognis 677–680

They seize possessions by force, and order [kosmos] has perished.
There is no equitable distribution of possessions carried out for the good
  of everyone.
But the merchandise carriers rule and the kakoi are above the agathoi.
I fear that perhaps a wave may swallow the ship.

To summarize, moderation is a vital principle in the life of the citizen. It is recommended in terms such as **meson, metron, mēden agan, ison, kairos,** and **kosmos.**

§11. The same principles are reflected in descriptions of the symposium. Just as the poet is the exponent of the middle path in regard to the conduct of the **polis,** he is also the exponent of moderation for the drinking party. The confusion to be avoided in the symposium parallels that to be avoided in the political life of a city. Moderate drinking and excess correspond respectively to reasonable and unreasonable political attitudes. The poet is ambivalent toward wine, the symposium's sine qua non, alternately praising and blaming it.

§12. Wine is in most respects to be praised, but when it upsets one's equilibrium and causes one to get drunk and fight with an **ekhthros,** it can be antithetical to the spirit of a symposium, **akharistos** (vv. 841–842). A similar ambivalence toward wine is expressed here:

οἶνε, τὰ μέν σ᾽ αἰνῶ, τὰ δὲ μέμφομαι· οὐδέ σε πάμπαν
οὔτέ ποτ᾽ ἐχθαίρειν οὔτε φιλεῖν δύναμαι.
ἐσθλὸν καὶ κακόν ἐσσι. τίς ἄν σέ γε μωμήσαιτο,
τίς δ᾽ ἂν ἐπαινήσαι μέτρον ἔχων σοφίης;
Theognis 873–876

Wine, on the one hand I praise you, but I also blame you.
Nor am I able totally either to hate or to love you.
You are **esthlos** and **kakos.** Who,
having **metron** of **sophiē,** could blame you or praise you?

§13. Verses 1091–1094 seem to suggest an attitude toward friendship (and perhaps by extension toward Kyrnos: an *odi-et-amo* relationship) that is similar to the ambivalence toward wine just outlined.[1] Note the almost exact correspondence between verses 874 and 1092:

---

§13n1. Nagy Ch.2 §§42–47.

ἀργαλέως μοι θυμὸς ἔχει περὶ σῆς φιλότητος·
οὔτε γὰρ ἐχθαίρειν οὔτε φιλεῖν δύναμαι,
γινώσκων χαλεπὸν μὲν ὅταν φίλος ἀνδρὶ γένηται
ἐχθαίρειν, χαλεπὸν δ᾽ οὐκ ἐθέλοντα φιλεῖν.
Theognis 1091–1094

My **thūmos** is upset about your friendship,
since I can neither totally hate nor love you,
knowing that it is difficult for a man to hate a **philos**,
and it is difficult to be a **philos** to someone against his will.

Friendship harmonizes relations in the **polis** much as wine does in the symposium. Kyrnos personifies friendship for Theognis and represents the city that the poet hates and loves.

§14. Like a lover, wine can have good and bad aspects. One must avoid the extremes. The poet strives to exemplify the mean:

δισσαί τοι πόσιος κῆρες δειλοῖσι βροτοῖσιν,
δίψά τε λυσιμελὴς καὶ μέθυσις χαλεπή·
τούτων δ᾽ ἂν τὸ μέσον στρωφήσομαι, οὐδέ με πείσεις
οὔτέ τι μὴ πίνειν οὔτε λίην μεθύειν.
Theognis 837–840

There are two lots of drinking for wretched mortals:
thirst which loosens one's limbs and harsh intoxication.
Between these I will choose the mean, nor will you persuade me
either not to drink or to get too drunk.

When the mean is not sought and one drinks too much, he indulges in behavior **huper metron** 'beyond the mean'. Consider the following two passages:

ἄφρονος ἀνδρὸς ὁμῶς καὶ σώφρονος οἶνος ὅταν δὴ
πίνῃ ὑπὲρ μέτρον κοῦφον ἔθηκε νόον.
Theognis 497–498

Wine makes the mind [**noos**] of the balanced and unbalanced man evaporate
whenever it is drunk *beyond moderation*.

ἐν πυρὶ μὲν χρυσόν τε καὶ ἄργυρον ἴδριες ἄνδρες
γινώσκουσ᾽, ἀνδρὸς δ᾽ οἶνος ἔδειξε νόον,
καὶ μάλα περ πινυτοῦ, τὸν ὑπὲρ μέτρον ἤρατο πίνων,
ὥστε καταισχῦναι καὶ πρὶν ἐόντα σοφόν.
Theognis 499–502

Experts recognize gold and silver in fire,
but wine shows the **noos** of a man,
even of a very thoughtful one, when it is drunk *beyond moderation*,
so that it puts to shame even one who used to be **sophos**.

The words **meson** and **metron** in these passages show that archaic poetic tradition dealt with sympotic moderation in the same terms as it treated moderation in political affairs.

§15. The theme of **kosmos** 'proper order' shows a pattern of resonances between **polis** and symposium very like that concerning moderation. The passage already quoted (vv. 677–680) about the loss of equal shares and **kosmos** in the state (§10) has a strong parallel in a couplet dealing with wine. Note the word **kathuperthen** 'above' and the similarity of description:

ἀλλ' ὁπόταν **καθύπερθεν** ἐὼν ὑπένερθε γένηται,
τουτάκις οἴκαδ' ἴμεν παυσάμενοι πόσιος.
Theognis 843–844

But when what is *above* [**kathuperthen**] turns into what is underneath, then it is time for us to stop drinking and go home.

Overindulgence in wine causes disorder, making what was **kathuperthen** 'above' go **hupenerthe** 'under', just as **koros**, the loss of **kosmos**, and the unequal distribution of goods bring the **polis** to the point where what was below comes to be above:

φορτηγοὶ δ' ἄρχουσι, κακοὶ δ' ἀγαθῶν **καθύπερθεν**.
Theognis 679

But the merchandise carriers rule and the **kakoi** are *above* [**kathuperthen**] the **agathoi**.

§16. Such a reversal of up and down is also seen in verses 53–68, where the poet complains that the **kakoi** have become **agathoi** and the **esthloi** have become **deiloi**. The wicked do not know how to tell good from bad, because their **gnōmai** 'powers of judgment' are defective:

οὔτε κακῶν **γνώμας** εἰδότες οὔτ' ἀγαθῶν
Theognis 60

Not knowing how to distinguish [= not having *powers of judgment*] between what is **kakon** and what is **agathon**

So wine also, when drunk in excess, confounds one's **gnōmē**:

οἰνοβαρέω κεφαλὴν Ὀνομάκριτε, καί με βιᾶται
οἶνος, ἀτὰρ *γνώμης* οὐκέτ᾽ ἐγὼ ταμίης
ἡμετέρης, τὸ δὲ δῶμα περιτρέχει.
Theognis 503–505

My head is heavy with wine, Onomakritos, and wine overpowers me.
I am no longer in control of my *good judgment* [**gnōmē**],
and the room whirls about me.

The loss of **gnōmē**, the excessive use of wine, and the topsy-turvy perceptions of the drunken man are poetic analogues to intemperance and the subsequent confusion and disorder in the state.

§ 17. The long passage on the proper conduct for a symposium (vv. 467–496) has moderation as its centerpiece and the poet as its perfect exponent. Rules are proposed for the proper treatment of guests (vv. 467–474), and the poet says that when he has reached the **metron** 'measure' of wine-drinking, he goes home (vv. 475–476). The dinner party is most pleasant when one is not too sober and not too drunk (vv. 477–478). Whoever exceeds the measure of drinking (**posios metron**) loses control of himself and cannot remain master of either his speech or his actions (vv. 479–483). The message is not to drink wine **huperboladēn** 'in excess' (v. 484), to stop before getting drunk, or to stay and not drink (vv. 483–487). The compulsive drinker is condemned (vv. 487–491), and those who can drink without becoming obstreperous are praised, as the poet portrays the harmonious ideal of a symposium with **kharis** 'gratification' and without **eris** 'strife' (vv. 491–496). The message of moderation and order and the repeated use of **metron** tie this passage thematically to the political passages focusing on the notion of nothing in excess.

§ 18. One of Solon's poems dramatizes the destruction of a city by a reference to the citizens' excesses and inability to behave themselves properly at a banquet:

αὐτοὶ δὲ φθείρειν μεγάλην πόλιν ἀφραδίῃσιν
ἀστοὶ βούλονται χρήμασι πειθόμενοι,
δήμου θ᾽ ἡγεμόνων ἄδικος νόος, οἷσιν ἑτοῖμον
ὕβριος ἐκ μεγάλης ἄλγεα πολλὰ παθεῖν·
οὐ γὰρ ἐπίστανται κατέχειν κόρον οὐδὲ παρούσας
εὐφροσύνας κοσμεῖν δαιτὸς ἐν ἡσυχίῃ.
Solon fr. 4.5–10 W

But the citizens themselves, persuaded by possessions [khrēmata],
are willing to destroy the **polis** with their mindlessness,
and the mind [**noos**] of the leaders of the **dēmos** is without **dikē**.
They will soon suffer many pains as a result of their great
hubris. For they do not know how to withstand **koros**, nor how
to put in order [**kosmein**] their present mirth [**euphrosunē**] in the quietude [**hēsukhiē**] of a banquet [**dais**].

In the Theognidea, **hēsukhiē** is also a political term. For instance, the
poet refers to political peace that will not last long (v. 48) and says
that the **hēsukhos** man can act moderately as an arbiter (v. 331). As
we see from the above passage from Solon, the word can be used for
a sympotic as well as a political peace. Furthermore, a party and a
polity must both be well-ordered. In Solon, **kosmein** 'make order' is
used for the symposium. In Theognis, the poet will put **patris** 'homeland' and **polis** in order (**kosmēsō** v. 947), and the adverb **eukosmōs**
'well-ordered' describes the proper behavior at a symposium (v. 242).
The lack of **kosmos** describes the improper ordering of a city (Theognis v. 677, Solon fr. 13.11), and **eukosma** describes the personification of good legislation, **Eunomiē** (Solon fr. 4.32).

§ 19. I shall now proceed to the third of the four categories linking
symposium and **polis**, that is, the theme of cunning and deceit. One
of the poet's major concerns in the Theognidea is the dichotomy
between **glōssa** 'tongue' and **noos** 'mind', that is, between what a
man says and what he really thinks. The notion is well known from
the *Iliad*, where Achilles declares:

ἐχθρὸς γάρ μοι κεῖνος ὁμῶς Ἀΐδαο πύλῃσιν
ὅς χ' ἕτερον μὲν κεύθῃ ἐνὶ φρεσίν, ἄλλο δὲ εἴπῃ.
Iliad ix 312–313[1]

That man is as hateful to me as the gates of Hades,
who conceals one thing in his **phrenes** and says another.

The poetry of the Theognidea features numerous examples of this
theme. A preoccupation with deceiving and avoiding being deceived
is expressed in terms of both sympotic and nonsympotic behavior.
The idea appears in the following verses:

ἀλλήλους δ' ἀπατῶσιν ἐπ' ἀλλήλοισι γελῶντες,
οὔτε κακῶν γνώμας εἰδότες οὔτ' ἀγαθῶν.

---

§ 19n1. Cf. also *Odyssey* viii 165–177.

μηδένα τῶνδε φίλον ποιεῦ Πολυπαΐδη ἀστῶν
ἐκ θυμοῦ χρείης οὕνεκα μηδεμιῆς.
ἀλλὰ δόκει μὲν πᾶσιν ἀπὸ γλώσσης φίλος εἶναι,
χρῆμα δὲ συμμείξῃς μηδενὶ μηδ᾽ ὁτιοῦν
σπουδαῖον· γνώσῃ γὰρ οἰζυρῶν φρένας ἀνδρῶν,
ὥς σφιν ἐπ᾽ ἔργοισιν πίστις ἔπ᾽ οὐδεμία,
ἀλλὰ δόλους ἀπάτας τε πολυπλοκίας τ᾽ ἐφίλησαν
οὕτως ὡς ἄνδρες μηκέτι σῳζόμενοι.
Theognis 59–68

And they deceive one another, laughing at one another,
not being aware of the **gnōmai** of the **kakoi** or the **agathoi**.
Do not make anyone of these citizens your **philos**, son of Polypaos,
not on account of any need that might arise in your **thūmos**.
On the contrary, seem to be a **philos** in word,
but entrust no serious matter to any one of them.
For you know the **phrenes** of wretched men—
in their actions there is absolutely no faithfulness,
but they are the **philoi** of tricks, deceptions, and intricate plots,
just like men no longer saved.

Kyrnos is urged to be a friend only in word (v. 63) and to entrust no
serious matter to anyone because men are not trustworthy and they
love deception (vv. 64–67). Thus, a paradox arises. The youth is to
deceive the world because the world wishes to deceive him. He must
be false in order to avoid the falseness of others.

§20. The power that Theognis urges Kyrnos to take up is that of **mētis**
'cunning intelligence'. The word never appears in the Theognidea,
but I propose that 'cunning intelligence' could be subsumed into
gnōmē and **noos**. In terms of these words, the poet's frequent exhor-
tations to conceal true intentions beneath a façade in order to avoid
others' subterfuges conform to the description of **mētis** elaborated by
Detienne and Vernant.[1] This cunning is a mobile and polyvalent force
to be used to confront a multiple, changing reality. It is a weapon to
ensure victory over others who are stronger. It allows one to see
past, present, and future and is a power of deceit that operates
through disguise. **Mētis** beguiles an enemy into error and makes him
vulnerable. The terms **poikilos** 'variegated', **dolos** 'trickery', **polu-
plokos** 'complex', and **polutropos** 'versatile' often describe it. This
semantic range of **mētis**, as explicated by Detienne and Vernant,
corresponds to the advice of Theognis to Kyrnos.

§20n1. Detienne and Vernant 1978.5–21.

§21. The importance of cunning and deceit in the Theognidea—both its use and the detection of it in others—becomes obvious when we consider the following pieces of advice. Do not reveal personal affairs even to **philoi**, for few have a trustworthy **noos** (vv. 73–74). Whoever says one thing with his **glōssa** 'tongue' and has another in his **noos** 'mind' is an evil companion (vv. 91–92). Beware of someone who praises you when you are present but slanders you when your back is turned (vv. 93–94). A **hetairos** 'companion' is not good if he speaks smoothly with his **glōssa** but thinks otherwise in his **phrenes** 'mind' (vv. 95–96). Nothing is more difficult to know than the real nature of a **kibdēlos** 'counterfeit' man (vv. 117–118). It is a most difficult thing to know the **noos** of a counterfeit **philos**: you must try out (verb **peiraō**) each one like an animal, for appearances 'deceive one's **gnōmē**' (vv. 119–128). Present a **poikilon ēthos** 'variegated character' to all **philoi**, assimilating your character to that of others (vv. 213–214, 1071–1072). Be an octopus; change your complexion to fit the circumstances, for **sophiē** is more powerful than **atropiē** 'nonadaptability' and even great **aretē** (vv. 215–218, 1073–1074). Present different faces to servants and neighbors (vv. 301–302). Do not reveal yourself (vv. 359–360). Put an enemy off-guard by deceiving him with words, and then attack him when he is confounded (vv. 363–364). Keep your **noos** to yourself, but speak cunning words with the **glōssa** (vv. 365–366). Reputation (**doxa**) is inferior to experience (**peira**) about a man's character (vv. 571–572). Friends betray more easily than enemies, who are in any case kept at a distance (vv. 575–576). Do not praise a man until you know his true character, for people conceal their **kibdēlon ēthos** 'counterfeit character' (vv. 963–970).[1]

§22. The necessity for exercising cunning and the awareness that others are deceitful are themes that appear regularly in sections that depict banquet behavior. Some examples follow. Few of the many who are companions at the banquet are trustworthy in a serious matter (vv. 115–116, 643–644). A man should have good sense at public banquets, making jokes and pretending that everything escapes his notice, and outside he should be strong, recognizing everyone's character (vv. 309–312). It is wine that reveals a man's **noos**, which can remain hidden until he gets drunk (vv. 499–502). One should drink when others drink but keep to himself the fact that he has become

---

§21n1. See also verses 313–314, 415–418, 447–452, 1013–1016, 1059–1062, 1164e–1164h, and 1259–1262. Cf. Levine 1984.

sick (vv. 989–990). The sympotic and nonsympotic settings for advice on the variability of character dovetail in these two couplets:

μή μοι ἀνὴρ εἴη γλώσσῃ φίλος, ἀλλὰ καὶ ἔργῳ·
χερσίν τε σπεύδοι χρήμασί τ᾽, ἀμφότερα·
μηδὲ παρὰ κρητῆρι λόγοισιν ἐμὴν φρένα θέλγοι,
ἀλλ᾽ ἔρδων φαίνοιτ᾽ εἴ τι δύναιτ᾽ ἀγαθόν.
Theognis 979–982

Let me never have a **philos** in **glōssa** only, but also in deed;
let him be forthcoming with his actions and possessions [**khrēmata**]
both.
Let him not charm my **phrēn** with words beside the mixing bowl,
but let his goodness be revealed, if that is possible, when he acts.

The tensions present in the citizens' daily lives are carried over by them into their drinking parties. Such a circumstance is paradoxical, for the symposium is also presented as a peaceful place of escape from troubles (see §§26–27 below).

§23. The poetry of Theognis contrasts a setting where men meet to eat and drink (**en sussitoisin** v. 309) with the outside world (**thurēphi** v. 311):

ἐν μὲν <u>συσσίτοισιν</u> ἀνὴρ πεπνυμένος εἶναι,
πάντα δέ μιν λήθειν ὡς ἀπεόντα δοκοῖ,
εἰς δὲ φέροι τὰ γελοῖα· <u>θύρηφι</u> δὲ καρτερὸς εἴη,
γινώσκων ὀργὴν ἥντιν᾽ ἕκαστος ἔχει.
Theognis 309–312

At the common meal a man should be prudent and mindful,
seeming not to notice everything, as though he were not there.
And let him bring in laughter. And *outside*, let him be strong,
recognizing each man's character.

The same distinction is made when the poet describes men who are one's friends while eating and drinking (vv. 115, 643), but not when a serious matter arises (vv. 116, 644). Although the "inner" and "outer" distinctions are there, they refer only to different settings for one phenomenon. The same deception occurs and must occur in both contexts.

§24. The symposium is dangerous because it presents yet another way for a man to misrepresent himself. Just as the clever citizen must beware of cozening words in his daily political and social intercourse, so he must not relax his guard even in a symposium, where he takes his ease among an ostensibly integrated community of **philoi**. Political tension and rivalries are transferred into the symposium, which becomes, in poetic terms, a city on a small scale.

§25. I come finally to the last of the four categories linking symposium and **polis**, the theme of utopia. In the poems of the Theognidea there is an atmosphere pervaded by a longing for peace in the **polis** in order that the pleasures of reveling can be enjoyed. If the gods will smile on the city, the people can be happy, specifically because they will be able to eat, drink, talk, and sing together without care. A well-ordered **polis** allows its citizens to approximate a Golden Age experience where they happily benefit from **kharis** 'gratification', **terpsis** 'enjoyment', and the Muses:[1]

εἰρήνη καὶ πλοῦτος ἔχοι πόλιν, ὄφρα μετ' ἄλλων
κωμάζοιμι· κακοῦ δ' οὐκ ἔραμαι πολέμου.
Theognis 885–886

May peace and prosperity attend the city in order that with others
I might enjoy a revel [**kōmos**]. I do not love evil [**kakos**] war.

Peace is sought and war is hated because the former allows and the latter inhibits the pleasures of food, drink, and companionship.

§26. The same sentiment is expressed in two other, longer passages (vv. 757–764, 773–788). Both are addressed to gods and ask for protection of the **polis** against the Persians; they represent a state of peace by the evocation of the citizens at a drinking party, and treat war and **stasis** 'civil strife' as hostile to sympotic tranquillity. Only in a peaceful city without troubles, says the poet, can men enjoy **kharis** and **euphrosunē**, music, food, and dance:

Ζεὺς μὲν τῆσδε πόληος ὑπειρέχοι αἰθέρι ναίων
αἰεὶ δεξιτερὴν χεῖρ' ἐπ' ἀπημοσύνῃ·
ἄλλοι τ' ἀθάνατοι μάκαρες θεοί· αὐτὰρ Ἀπόλλων
ὀρθώσαι γλῶσσαν καὶ νόον ἡμέτερον·
φόρμιγξ δ' αὖ φθέγγοιθ' ἱερὸν μέλος ἠδὲ καὶ αὐλός·
ἡμεῖς δὲ σπονδὰς θεοῖσιν ἀρεσσάμενοι
πίνωμεν χαρίεντα μετ' ἀλλήλοισι λέγοντες,
μηδὲν τὸν Μήδων δειδιότες πόλεμον.
Theognis 757–764

§25n1. See §29 below on the Golden Age of man in Hesiod (*Works and Days* 109–120) and its multiform, the city of **dikē** (*Works and Days* 225–237).

May Zeus who dwells in the aether hold over this city
always his right hand to keep away troubles,
and so too the other immortal blessed gods. And Apollo
keep straight our tongue and mind.
And lyre, play a sacral melody, and the reed also.
And let us make our libations to the gods
and drink as we have **kharis**-filled conversation with one another,
fearing not the war of the Medes.

§27. The emphasis on the city is even greater in a longer passage,
verses 773–788, which is a prayer to Apollo. Apollo is the god most
closely associated with banquets and their joys, as well as being a
protector of the **polis** and its citizens. Note the iteration of the word
polis at verses 773, 776, and 782, and the final mention of fatherland
at 788. This passage also contains a contrast between musical instru-
ments and celebration on the one hand, and fear of the Persians on
the other. There is, moreover, a fear of **stasis** 'civil strife' in the
form of dissension among the Greeks. In verses 757–764 quoted
above, **kharis**-filled conversation is an important part of the enjoyment of the drinking party in a city at peace (v. 763), and in the
following passage, **terpsis** 'enjoyment' is also an important aspect of
the banquet (v. 778) and the fatherland alike (v. 787):

Φοῖβε ἄναξ, αὐτὸς μὲν ἐπύργωσας πόλιν ἄκρην,
  Ἀλκαθόῳ Πέλοπος παιδὶ χαριζόμενος·
αὐτὸς δὲ στρατὸν ὑβριστὴν Μήδων ἀπέρυκε
  τῆσδε πόλευς, ἵνα σοι λαοὶ ἐν εὐφροσύνῃ
ἦρος ἐπερχομένου κλειτὰς πέμπωσ᾽ ἑκατόμβας
  τερπόμενοι κιθάρῃ καὶ ἐρατῇ θαλίῃ
παιάνων τε χοροῖς ἰαχῇσί τε σὸν περὶ βωμόν.
  ἦ γὰρ ἔγωγε δέδοικ᾽ ἀφραδίην ἐσορῶν
καὶ στάσιν Ἑλλήνων λαοφθόρον· ἀλλὰ σὺ Φοῖβε
  ἵλαος ἡμετέρην τήνδε φύλασσε πόλιν.
ἦλθον μὲν γὰρ ἔγωγε καὶ εἰς Σικελήν ποτε γαῖαν,
  ἦλθον δ᾽ Εὐβοίης ἀμπελόεν πεδίον,
Σπάρτην τ᾽ Εὐρώτα δονακοτρόφου ἀγλαὸν ἄστυ,
  καί μ᾽ ἐφίλευν προφρόνως πάντες ἐπερχόμενον·
ἀλλ᾽ οὔτις μοι τέρψις ἐπὶ φρένας ἦλθεν ἐκείνων·
  οὕτως οὐδὲν ἄρ᾽ ἦν φίλτερον ἄλλο πάτρης.
    Theognis 773–788

Lord Phoibos, you yourself have founded the citadel of the **polis**,
giving **kharis** to Alkathoos, Pelops' son.
Now keep away from this **polis** the **hubris**-filled army of the Medes,
so that in **euphrosunē** the people
at the coming of spring might send you **kleos**-worthy hecatombs,

having **terpsis** in the **kithara** and in the lovely banquet
and in dancing the paian and in shouts of joy around your altar.
For indeed I fear the lack of **phrenes**
and people-destroying **stasis** of the Hellenes when I see it. But you,
    Phoibos,
being gracious, protect this our **polis**.
For I have been once to the land of Sicily,
and to the vine-rich plain of Euboia,
and to Sparta, the glorious city on the reed-nourishing Eurotas.
And they all, with forward **phrenes**, made me their **philos** when I came.
But no **terpsis** came over my **phrenes** as a result of association with
    those people,
since there is nothing more near and dear than one's own fatherland.

The aversion to war and the desire for peace and harmony in which to
enjoy the pleasures of sympotic, delights is expressed in terms of a
yearning for a Golden Age existence, that is, a desire for the pleasures
of a state without war, without **stasis**, and without hatreds or fears.

§28. It is noteworthy that Hesiod's description of the Golden Age
(*Works and Days* 109–120) incorporates some of the themes present
in Theognis. The **thūmos** of the Golden Age people is without care
(v. 112); they are separated from labors and hardships (v. 113); old
age never comes upon them (v. 114); their hands and feet remain
strong as they enjoy **terpsis** in a banquet separated from all bad
things (vv. 114–115). They are **hēsukhoi** 'serene' and **philoi** to the
blessed gods (vv. 119–120).[1] In other words, the men of the Hesiodic
Golden Age are living in a country perpetually at peace, and they
enjoy the pleasures of the symposium in the full vigor of life. Hesiod
presents the city of **dikē**, a recreation of the Golden Age, as a parallel
idealization (*Works and Days* 225–237). Where **dikē** is honored, the
polis prospers, as do its people (vv. 225–227). Peace attends the
land, and Zeus never sends war upon them (vv. 228–229). Their
lives are easy and untroubled; they have plenty to eat and do not
have to sail on ships (vv. 230–237). This is also the Theognidean
ideal, expressed in both sympotic and political terms.[2]

§29. In six verses about wine—the intended context of which is unclear (vv. 879–884)—the same theme comes out in the description of

---

§28n1. The implication here is that they dine with gods. For **hesukhiē** as an
aspect of the symposium, see Solon fr. 4.10 W and Pindar *N*. 9.48: **hēsukhiā de philei
sumposion** 'quietude loves a symposium'. Also above, §§25–27. Cf. Nagy Ch.2§47.
    §28n2. See §§34–35 below.

the old man Theotimos 'he who has tīmē from the god'. It is fitting that wine, to be used for an occasion where troubles are to be forgotten, should be produced by one who, like Hesiod's men of the Golden Age (v. 119), is a **philos** to the gods:

πῖν' οἶνον, τὸν ἐμοὶ κορυφῆς ὗπο Τηϋγέτοιο
ἄμπελοι ἤνεγκαν τὰς ἐφύτευσ' ὁ γέρων
οὔρεος ἐν βήσσῃσι θεοῖσι φίλος Θεότιμος,
ἐκ Πλατανιστοῦντος ψυχρὸν ὕδωρ ἐπάγων.
τοῦ πίνων ἀπὸ μὲν χαλεπὰς σκεδάσεις μελεδώνας,
θωρηχθεὶς δ' ἔσεαι πολλὸν ἐλαφρότερος.
Theognis 879–884

Drink wine, which for me below the peak of Taygetos
vines bore, vines which the old man nourished
in the mountains' hollows, god-beloved Theotimos,
drawing cold water from the well Platanistous.
Drinking this, you will scatter your troublesome cares,
and when you are tipsy, you will be more carefree.

§30. An important aspect of both the **polis** and the symposium is **kharis** 'grace, gratification, favor'. The longing for the pleasures of a banquet expresses a desire to see a city endowed with this harmony, represented by the personification of **kharis** in the plural, the Kharites (Theognis vv. 15–18). So too the quick passing of youth is deplored because it takes away the ability to enjoy drinking parties and love, that is, to indulge in the gifts of the Muses and the Kharites. The importance of **kharis** as regards the **polis** has been noted in verses 757–764 (§26) and 773–786 (§27): the city should be at peace so that people may enjoy **kharis** in the drinking party. Apollo has granted **kharis** to the hero of the city and should straighten the tongue and mind of citizens and allow them peacefully to enjoy the pleasures of drinking.

§31. Elsewhere (vv. 1135–1150), the poet says that only the goddess **Elpis** 'Hope' remains among mankind, calling to mind Hesiod's story of Pandora and the fall of man from a blessed former existence. The poem continues with a list of the other goddesses who have left, including **Pistis** 'Trust', **Sōphrosunē** 'Moderation', and finally the Kharites (vv. 1137–1142). The loss of the Kharites is placed just before the enumeration of man's failings, to show the moral, social, and political importance of these goddesses for people's dealings with one another.

§32. It is therefore not surprising that **kharis** and the pleasures of a banquet in which **kharis** prevails should occur so frequently in Theognis. The poetry expresses a longing for youth, for it is then that

kharis is most enjoyed—in a harmonious gathering of **philoi** enjoying music, wine, and fellowship. The longing for a state of harmony is approximated by constant references to hatred of advancing age—a standard topos in archaic Greek poetry—and the pleasure one can get in the symposium and **kōmos** 'revel' in the context of fleeting youth and a longing to have **kharis, terpsis**, music, companionship, **euphrosunē**, sex, food, and wine.

§33. In sum, the archaic poet's descriptions of communal eating and drinking parallel his descriptions of the **polis**. In both sympotic and political contexts there is a longing for peace and pleasure, as well as injunctions to learn good things from the noble while avoiding the base, to exercise **mētis** 'cunning intelligence', and to observe moderation. The symposium is a microcosm of the state.

Appendix 1: Aristophanes and the Symposium

§34. The symposium was only one of the contexts in which socially important eating and drinking took place. It is easy to contrast with symposia those occasions where participants were of both sexes, a greater range of ages was involved, or representatives of different social classes were present. The latter category would include wedding feasts, rural feasts (picnics), and sacrificial meals. The paedagogic and aristocratic character of elegy naturally gives little insight into these occasions, although other genres seem to have done so. As an indication of a comic poet's mediation of these themes, we may consider Aristophanes' *Acharnians*, which treats the peaceful **polis** as though it were a banquet. A basic theme of the *Acharnians* is the longing for **eirēnē** 'peace' embodied by the main character of the play, whose name Dikaiopolis 'Just (from **dikē**) City' implies that the city at peace exemplifies justice. When he has made a treaty with Athens' enemies, Dikaiopolis enjoys all sorts of foods (v. 975). The chorus describes war as a bad dinner guest (vv. 978–986). Peace is illustrated by a **deipnon** 'feast' (vv. 987–1002) that everyone wants to share (vv. 1003 ff.). Even the Athenian Lamakhos, whose very name (La-makhos) reminds us of warfare, in the end wants the feast rather than war. Yet, reluctant, he is forced to give up wine, food, and sex in order to pursue hostilities (vv. 1071–1083). The play ends with war's proponent painfully wounded while the symbol of the peaceful **polis** has won the wine-drinking prize (vv. 1197–1232).

§35. It can be shown that, in the *Acharnians*, wine is the foundation and substance of peace, as in Dikaiopolis' literalizing of the metaphorical when, for instance, he intends to drink the **spondai** 'treaties' or 'libations' (v. 199)![1] Elsewhere, Aristophanes describes Peace as a goddess "most loving of the vine" (*Peace* v. 307, cf. vv. 520, 596–597, 706–708).[2]

Appendix 2: The Symposium as a Paradigm of the Polis in Plato

§36. Plato, in the first two books of the *Laws*, insists that community and common eating and drinking are closely associated and makes the symposium a model for the establishment of an ideal community. Plato drew on the poetic tradition represented by Theognis, whom he quoted (vv. 77–78) in the *Laws* (630A), his fullest treatment of the symposium and the city.

§37. In the *Republic* (562D), Plato speaks of a generic democracy as "thirsty" for freedom and coming upon bad **oinokhooi** 'wine-pourers' for leaders and thus "getting drunk" [**methusthēi**] from freedom in excess as though they had drunk unmixed wine (**akrātou**). This metaphorical description of an intemperate democracy is repeated by Plutarch (*Greek Questions* 18 [*Moralia* 295C–D]), who refers to Plato's statement in regard to Megara's period of democracy. Reflecting the philosopher's diction, he mentions the corruption of the Megarians by wine-pouring demagogues (**dēmagōgōn oinokhoountōn**) who give the citizens an **akrāton** 'unmixed' taste of freedom. He goes on to say that the poor entered the rich men's houses and demanded to be wined and dined in sumptuous fashion. When they did not get what they wanted, they resorted to **biē** 'brute force' and **hubris** 'outrage'. Both authors treat citizens who have had too much freedom in the **polis** as banqueters who have indulged excessively in wine. The intemperance of their political actions is compared to overindulgence at a banquet, much like the intemperate leaders of the **dēmos** in Solon (fr. 4.9–10, see above §18). Whether or not they were directly influenced by the Theognidea, both Plato and Plutarch were writing under the influence of a literary tradition that equated citizens and revelers, a tradition clearly evident in the Theognidea.

§38. The political-sympotic traditions in Theognis and Plato are tied together more strongly by the word **basanos** 'touchstone'. It occurs three times in a short space in Plato's *Laws* (649D–650B) in refer-

---

§35n1. Edmunds 1980, esp. p.5.
§35n2. Edmunds 1980.20.

ence to the use of a symposium as a place where 'playful testing' of a man's character can take place. The term **basanos** is employed in Theognis also in the same sense, to express a test of a person's true worth. The poet protests that when he is tested he is found true (vv. 415–418, 447–452, 1164e–h) and that the **basanos** would be a good way to see whether a man deserves a good reputation (vv. 1105–1106). The use of the so-called "Lydian stone" to test gold was a poetic trope for the testing of the inner nature of men (cf. Khilon in Diogenes Laertius 1.71; Adespota Elegiaca 22 W = Stobaeus 1.8.15; Pindar *P.* 10.67, *N.* 8.20, fr. 122.16 SM; Bacchylides fr. 14 SM; Sophocles *Oedipus Tyrannus* 510). One might recall here how Theognis emphasizes the need to find a man's true worth and also to hide one's own true self in both sympotic and political contexts. Plato's exposition is entirely consonant with traditional thinking.

§ 39. At the end of the second book of the *Laws* (674A), Plato concludes his description of the model for a city by saying that wine should properly be used by the state to create good citizens. The state should control wine production and set up rules for its use. He makes a list of drinking ages (666D). For youths under 18 years, no wine is allowed. From 18–30, wine is allowed in moderation, but intoxication is prohibited. For those 40 and over, drunkenness is allowed—to soften the disposition. (No rule is listed for those between 30 and 40.) The stricture against drinking by young men, as well as Plato's conservative attitude in general, reminds one of Theognis:

> ὦ παῖ, μὴ κώμαζε, γέροντι δὲ πείθεο ἀνδρί·
> οὔτοι κωμάζειν σύμφορον ἀνδρὶ νέῳ.
> Theognis 1351–1352

Boy, do not indulge in a revel [**kōmos**], but obey your elder.
It is not proper for a young man to indulge in a **kōmos**.

8
Eros and the **Polis** in Theognis Book II

John M. Lewis

§1. As we now find it, the Theognidean corpus is divided into two books, the second of which appears to have been formed from an integral text by a fairly mechanical process of culling out passages with an erotic content and relocating them at the end of the text. In his reconstruction of the history of the transmission of the Theognidea, Martin L. West has offered a plausible account of the excerptor's motive and procedure in so doing, together with a probable date (c. A.D. 900) for his activities.[1]

§2. West's account of the formation of Book II is in keeping with his observation that "there is nothing in [that book] that looks later than the fifth century B.C."[1] Given West's hypothesis of a rearrangement within the corpus, it would be surprising if this were not the case. Massimo Vetta's recently published commentary on Book II substantiates West's observations in some detail. Vetta demonstrates that the passages in Book II, like those in Book I, show evidence of having been composed in a sympotic context, and, further, that they share fully in the vocabulary, stylistic traits, generic types, and sociopolitical themes of the passages in Book I.[2] Vetta also makes it clear that it is impossible to consider the erotic content of the passages in Book II apart from their relation to the thematic concerns and compositional purposes of the Theognidea as a whole. More precisely, the **paiderastiā** 'love of boys' in them constitutes an important ideological and practical dimension of aristocratic **paideiā** 'education' in archaic Megara.

---

§1n1. West 1974.43–45. Note also that the term Book II will be used only for the sake of convenience and without implications about the history and transmission of the corpus. N.B.: Some of the more prominent Greek words discussed in this chapter will be at times cited without a gloss. All such words, however, can be found in the Glossary at the end of this volume.

§2n1. West p.43.

§2n2. Vetta 1980.xi.

§3. As its title indicates, the aim of this chapter is to explore the inter-relationship of erotic and political elements in Book II of the Theogni-dea. I shall begin with the erotic.

§4. Some passages in Book II are what might be termed strictly erotic, in that they contain occurrences of the names or epithets of Eros and Aphrodite, the two deities who presided over the erotic experience, both emotional and physical. In three of the erotic passages, 1231–1234, 1323–1326, and 1386–1389, the name or epithet of the deity appears in the vocative, so that each is, formally at least, a hymnic prayer. As inspection of two of these will show, the prayerlike charac-ter of the language extends beyond the vocative to include certain features of syntax and style as well. Take first the opening passages of Book II:

σχέτλι' Ἔρως, Μανίαι σ' ἐπιθηνήσαντο λαβοῦσαι·
ἐκ σέθεν ὤλετο μὲν Ἰλίου ἀκρόπολις,
ὤλετο δ' Αἰγείδης Θησεὺς μέγας, ὤλετο δ' Αἴας
ἐσθλὸς Ὀιλιάδης ᾗσιν ἀτασθαλίαις.
Theognis 1231–1234

Obstinate *Eros*, Madnesses took *you* up and suckled you:
through *you* the high stronghold of Ilium *perished*;
and the son of Aigeus, great Theseus, *perished*; and Ajax *perished*,
that *noble* [esthlos] man, son of Oileus—and each by reason of his
recklessness.

Here the triple repetition of **ōleto** 'perished' and the double one of **se** ... **sethen** 'you ... through you' help indicate the prayerlike charac-ter of the passage: they are instances of ascriptions or repetitions found in Greek prayer and indeed distributed throughout the world. The nature of the god is revealed and celebrated in a series of short parallel statements about him. In a passage addressed to Cyprus-born Aphrodite, the language of prayer takes the form of a series of brief requests or petitions:

Κυπρογένη, παῦσόν με πόνων, σκέδασον δὲ μερίμνας
θυμοβόρους, στρέψον δ' αὖθις ἐς εὐφροσύνας·
μερμήρας δ' ἀπόπαυε κακάς, δὸς δ' εὔφρονι θυμῷ
μέτρ' ἥβης τελέσαντ' ἔργματα σωφροσύνης.
Theognis 1323–1326

Cyprus-born, *put a stop to* my pains, *scatter* the cares
that gnaw at my **thūmos**, *turn* them again to moments of **euphrosunē**.
Grant me *a respite* from *evil* troubles, *grant* that with a merry **thūmos**

I may accomplish deeds of **sōphrosunē** when I have traversed the span of my youth.

I have underscored verb forms in the imperative representing short petitions, which can be paralleled in prayers.[1] Ascription and petition, in which worshipers are put in mind of the god's power and then seek to draw the benign aspect of that power to themselves, are often associated. They are both ways of creating and maintaining the link between mortals and gods. As such, they belong to the pragmatic sphere of religious language.

§5. The other variety of strictly erotic passage is not addressed to Eros or Aphrodite but rather tells us something about the actions of one of those deities. These are **logoi** 'utterances' about the gods, which supply mythological paradigms purporting to explain or justify the vicissitudes of mortal life in terms of divine action. Included are a passage describing the arrival of Eros: 1275–1278; three passages that contain references to the **dōra** 'gifts' of Aphrodite: 1283–1294, 1327–1334, and 1381–1385; one that refers to her **erga** 'works': 1305–1310; and one that celebrates her deliverance of the speaker from longing: 1337–1340. A related mythological paradigm is found in 1341–1350, which recounts the rape of Ganymede by Zeus.[1]

§6. While these passages are erotic in a strict sense, almost all of Book II is erotic in another sense because it treats human experience under the influence of eros. The erotic passages in Book II are virtually all pederastic, i.e., dealing with the conventions of erotic relationships between older and adolescent males, in later times highly structured and institutionalized. Eventually, the terms for the older and younger participants in such relationships became **erastēs** 'lover' and **erōmenos** 'beloved' respectively, which henceforward I shall use for the sake of brevity.

§7. It is possible to divide this group of erotic passages into two categories and to invoke the presence of the vocative as a criterion for

---

§4n1. See Vetta 1980.xxviii for other hymnic-prayer passages in Theognis and the *Carmina Convivialia*. The discussion of the hymnic-prayer pattern in relation to Sappho fr. 1 V/LP in Page 1955.16–17 contains a useful selection from the rich secondary material.

§5n1. Vetta 1980.119–120 summarizes the controversies over the dating of this passage, the subsequent references to Ganymede, and the relevance of the myth to the program of self-justification for an **erastēs**.

distinction. Nineteen passages contain the vocative "(O) boy" [(ō) pai], the favored form of address by erastēs to erōmenos. These passages are, like the hymnic prayers discussed in §4 above, pragmatic; that is, they represent speech acts that could, with or without the substitution of a proper name for (ō) pai, be used in an actual erotic relationship by an erastēs seeking to create, maintain, or dissolve such a relationship. In addition to these passages, there is only one in Book II containing the vocative: Kurne, 1353–1356. This proper name, so common in Book I, occurs here in a passage that describes the bitter effect of eros on the erastēs who experiences it. Lacking the urgency of command or entreaty, this passage is distinct from the passages of the (ō) pai group.

§8. Four passages in Book II contain second person forms without vocatives. Three of these are certainly erotic in import: 1241–1242, 1363–1364, and 1373–1374. Aside from its inclusion in Book II, the character of 1239–1240 (perhaps to be grouped with 1238a–b) is unclear. In all four passages the speaker adopts a stance of authority in respect to his addressee: he warns, commands, or reproves. So, if these passages are erotic, they are spoken by an erastēs, not an erōmenos, as are all the passages with a vocative. That this should be so ought not to surprise us, for it is in keeping with the ideal of pederastic paideiā. Instruction is a major benefit offered by the erastēs to the erōmenos (cf. 1235, 1321), and in all these passages the speaker instructs.

§9. The remaining erotic passages may be classified by a negative criterion: they do not contain occurrences of the second person, with or without the vocative. For this reason, they can be regarded as nonpragmatic meditations on or contemplations of erotic relationships. In six of these, the erastēs describes what it is like to love, or no longer to love, an erōmenos: 1255–1256, 1335–1336, 1337–1340, 1357–1360, 1369–1372, and 1375–1376. The first and fourth of these examples contain an occurrence of the verb philein 'to be philos to' or 'to love' in construction or compounded with pais 'boy', while the remaining four contain the verb erān 'to desire', 'to love', or a derivative thereof, in more or less close construction with pais. Thematically related to this group are two passages in which such collocations do not occur, one on what a boy's noos 'intuition' is like (1267–1270) and one on what his kharis 'gratitude' is like (1367–1370).

§10. Thus far, I have accounted for 150 out of 166 verses in Book II. Of the eight passages unaccounted for, four are doublets of distichs occurring in Book I. Three of these contain occurrences of **philos** or one of its derivatives, while one (1278c–d) is the opening distich of the notoriously obscure passage 949–954, which has been seen variously as political or erotic. Three others form a group on the loss of friendship or the threat of future enmity, and so have a possible erotic application. The last informs us that the man is **olbios** 'fortunate' who has boys that are **philoi**, horses, dogs, and **xenoi** 'guest-friends'.[1] That all but one of the doubtfully erotic passages in Book II should contain a form or a derivative of **philos** indicates the uncertainty built into this family of words. When is a **philos** just a friend, and when is he a sexual partner? The compiler of Book II undoubtedly could not or would not always distinguish.

§11. Having completed my survey of erotic passages in Book II of the Theognidea, and having noted the distinction between pragmatic and nonpragmatic passages, I now turn to a consideration of the political aspects of eroticism in Theognis Book II. My starting point, however, is a passage not from Book II but from Book I:

> τόλμα θυμὲ κακοῖσιν ὅμως ἄτλητα πεπονθώς·
> δειλῶν τοι κραδίη γίνεται ὀξυτέρη.
> μηδὲ σύ γ᾽ ἀπρήκτοισιν ἐπ᾽ ἔργμασιν ἄλγος ἀέξων
> αὔχει μηδ᾽ αἴσχεα· μηδὲ φίλους ἀνία,
> μηδ᾽ ἐχθροὺς εὔφραινε. θεῶν δ᾽ εἱμαρμένα δῶρα
> οὐκ ἂν ῥηϊδίως θνητὸς ἀνὴρ προφύγοι,
> οὔτ᾽ ἂν πορφυρέης καταδὺς ἐς πυθμένα λίμνης,
> οὔθ᾽ ὅταν αὐτὸν ἔχῃ Τάρταρος ἠερόεις.
> Theognis 1029–1036

Bear up, **thūmos**, under misfortunes, even though you are suffering
    unbearable things [**atlēta**].
Look, the heart of the worthless is very quick to anger.
Do not make much of your grief [**algos**] over unperformed (or unper-
    formable) [**aprēkta**] deeds,
boasting about them, nor yet make much of shameful things done, nor
    cause pain to your **philoi**
nor give your enemies [**ekhthroi**] cause to rejoice. Not easily
may a mortal man escape the destined [**heimarmena**] gifts of the gods,
no, not if he sinks to the bottom of the stormy sea,
nor when shadowy Tartaros holds him fast.

---

§10n1. As is well known, Plato *Lysis* 242E takes **philoi** as qualifying all the substantives in conjunction with **paides**. Some commentators on Theognis have followed Plato; for a summary of the arguments adduced on both sides of the question, see Vetta 1980.60–61.

I may conveniently start here, since Book II has no passage that is so reflective of the political content of the corpus.

§12. The speaker's troubles are general and unspecified, but the attitude conveyed is noteworthy. On the surface it seems heroic, even provisionally Odyssean, in that it opens with an imperative **tolmā** 'bear up' related to the epithet **polutlās** 'much-enduring' so often applied in the Homeric poems to Odysseus, the hero who **polla ... en pontōi pathen algea hon kata thūmon** 'suffered many griefs in his **thūmos** in the open sea' (*Odyssey* i 4). The exhortation to bear up in the Theognidean passage is an unconditional one, for the speaker tells his **thūmos** to bear up under misfortunes even though he is suffering **atlēta** 'unbearable things', a word derived from the same verbal root as the imperative at the head of the line (**tol-mā ... a-tlē-ta**). Again like Odysseus, whose patient bearing up under the insults of the suitors provides much of the dramatic tension of the *Odyssey*, the Theognidean speaker here enjoins his **thūmos** to be slow to outward expressions of distress, for such self-control will distinguish his conduct as sharply as possible from that of the **deiloi** 'wretched' (1030). The latter are verbally incontinent, a frequent theme in Book I (cf., e.g., 611–614). Although 1029–1036 is not truly a riddle (cf. 261–266, 1229–1230), by leaving the heroic resonances of the speaker's attitude unexpressed, it involves an act of the imagination similar to that used in encoding and decoding a riddle. In this sense, **ainos** as praise poetry and as riddle converge in an act of self-praise.[1] A riddling claim to be like Odysseus might well have had a political valence, linking the speaker and his audience with the heroes of epic and marking them off from the **deiloi** 'wretched', thus providing them a claim of entitlement to political power.

§13. I shall continue my analysis of Theognis 1029–1036 with a consideration of the opposition **philos/ekhthros** 'friend/enemy' and of the notion of **heimarmena dōra** 'destined gifts'. As it turns out, these two themes have an inner connection. A warning against the failure to act justly, to give to **philoi** and **ekhthroi** their due, can be expressed: **mēde philous aniā/mēd' ekhthrous euphraine** 'do not pain your friends, nor give your enemies pleasure'. To each class one owes something, pleasure to one's friends and pain to one's enemies. There is another way of making the same point, as can be seen from Solon's prayer to Mnemosyne that he may

---

§12n1. For related discussions of **ainos** in this volume, see especially Nagy Ch.2 §§2–8 and Edmunds Ch.4 §§13–22.

εἶναι δὲ γλυκὺν ὧδε φίλοις, ἐχθροῖσι δὲ πικρόν,
τοῖσι μὲν αἰδοῖον, τοῖσι δὲ δεινὸν ἰδεῖν.
Solon fr. 13.5–6 W

be *sweet* to **philoi** but *bitter* to **ekhthroi**,
to the former a thing of reverence to see, to the latter a thing to be
feared.

Noteworthy in this distich is the appeal to a double antithetical image,
with the hexameter drawing on the sense of taste, the pentameter on
sight. The association of **glukus** 'sweet' with **philos** appears in Athena's exhortation in the *Iliad* to the Achaeans to fight.

τοῖσι δ' ἄφαρ πόλεμος γλυκίων γένετ' ἠὲ νέεσθαι
ἐν νηυσὶ γλαφυρῆσι φίλην ἐς πατρίδα γαῖαν.
Iliad ii 453–454

Then forthwith battle was *sweeter* [**glukiōn**] than to return
in their hollow ships to *their own* [**philē**] native land.

Homecoming, the return to one's homeland, **philē** in part because it
is one's own and because one's **philoi** reside there, may be sweet,
but under the goddess's inspiration battle is sweeter. The association
of **glukus** with **philos** occurs also in the *Odyssey*, when Odysseus
prefaces his account of his adventures with this gnomic saying:

ὡς οὐδὲν γλύκιον ἧς πατρίδος οὐδὲ τοκήων
γίγνεται, εἴ περ καί τις ἀπόπροθι πίονα οἶκον
γαίῃ ἐν ἀλλοδαπῇ ναίει ἀπάνευθε τοκήων.
Odyssey ix 34–36

So there is nothing *sweeter* [**glukion**] than one's native land and parents,
even if one were to inhabit a rich house afar off
in another country, apart from those parents.

In this passage, the place of **philos** is taken by the reflexive pronoun
hēs 'one's own', a semantic equivalent. A sympotic context for the
sweetness arising from **philos** relationships may be found in Pindar.

γλυκεῖα δὲ φρὴν καὶ συμπόταισιν ὁμιλεῖν
μελισσᾶν ἀμείβεται τρητὸν πόνον.
Pindar *P.* 6.52–54

His *mind* [**phrēn**] is *sweet* [**glukeia**], and holding converse with his
fellow symposiasts
he surpasses the honeybee in its chambered work.

Thus, the company of one's friends is a sweet experience, worthy of a 'sweet mind', which leads to sweet behavior.

§14. By the same token, **pikros** 'bitter' often occurs where friendship is denied or enmity is asserted. When Odysseus, disguised as a beggar, appears in his own house, the suitor Antinoos reviles him:

τίς δαίμων τόδε πῆμα προσήγαγε, δαιτὸς ἀνίην;
στῆθ' οὕτως ἐς μέσσον, ἐμῆς ἀπάνευθε τραπέζης,
μὴ τάχα πικρὴν Αἴγυπτον καὶ Κύπρον ἵκηαι.
    Odyssey xvii 446–448

What god has brought hither this annoyance, an **aniē** at the feast?
Stand there, in the middle, far from my table,
lest you speedily come to a *bitter* [**pikros**] Egypt and Cyprus.

Note that one's native land is **philē**, but a distant country is bitter. To Antinoos, Odysseus is an **aniē** 'pain', unworthy of a place of honor at the banquet. Antinoos threateningly implies that if this beggar does not keep his place, for him Ithaca will become **pikros** as faraway Egypt had been to him. Geographic separation leads to enmity: those distant from you are probably **ekhthroi**. As protection against encircling **ekhthroi**, the institutions of **philoxeniā** 'hospitality' assimilated outsiders to **philoi**. Against this background, we can appreciate assertions that the suitors will find a **pikrogamos** 'bitter marriage' when Odysseus returns home (*Odyssey* i 266, iv 346, xvii 137). It is a **gamos** that will indeed be the opposite of what is anticipated in marrying, that is, a marriage that leads to death at the hands of **ekhthroi**.

§15. Returning to Solon fr. 13.5, one can now see more clearly what he means. To be **glukus** 'sweet' to one's **philoi** is to produce in them the same effect as home, parents, or a good symposium, in short, **euphrosunē** 'merriment'. In contrast, to be **pikros** 'bitter' to one's **ekhthroi** is to be an **aniē** 'pain' to them, to cause them pain, loss, and, if possible, death.

§16. As noted above, the sensory appeal in the Solon passage is a double one: first to taste and then to sight. A similar double sensory appeal, this time to taste and then to touch, is found in Theognis:

πικρὸς καὶ γλυκὺς ἴσθι καὶ ἁρπαλέος καὶ ἀπηνὴς
λάτρισι καὶ δμωσὶν γείτοσί τ' ἀγχιθύροις.
    Theognis 301–302

be *bitter* [**pikros**] and *sweet* [**glukus**], *pleasing to touch* [**harpaleos**] and *hard* [**apēnēs**]
to hirelings and to household slaves and to the neighbors near your door.

Pleasant or difficult behavior is given a tactile dimension here in advice on behavior toward those who are not your **philoi** but with whom you are in daily contact. This couplet is apparently related to those urging Kyrnos to assume a changeable disposition toward such persons. Only one's **philoi** have the right to expect that you will be uniformly **glukus** 'sweet' to them. To summarize:

Status	philos ['friend']	non-philos [non-'friend'] (hireling, slave, or neighbor)	ekhthros ['enemy']
Behavior	glukus ['sweet'] harpaleos ['pleasing to touch']	glukus/pikros ['sweet'/'bitter'] harpaleos/apēnēs ['pleasing to touch'/ 'hard']	pikros ['bitter'] apēnēs ['hard']
State caused by behavior	euphrosunē ['merriment']		aniē ['pain']

§ 17. It is significant that the hexameter of the distich just cited occurs also in an erotic passage, in Book II:

πικρὸς καὶ γλυκύς ἐστι καὶ ἁρπαλέος καὶ ἀπηνὴς
ὄφρα τέλειος ἔῃ Κύρνε νέοισιν ἔρως.
ἢν μὲν γὰρ τελέσῃ, γλυκὺ γίνεται· ἢν δὲ διώκων
μὴ τελέσῃ, πάντων τοῦτ' ἀνιηρότατον.
Theognis 1353–1356

Bitter [**pikros**] and *sweet* [**glukus**], *pleasing to touch* [**harpaleos**] and *hard* [**apēnēs**]
is *sexual desire* [**erōs**] to youths, Kyrnos, until it reaches its goal.
If you bring it to its goal, it becomes *sweet*, but if you chase it
and cannot bring it to its goal, it is of all things *the most full of pain* [**aniē**].

In light of the system I have observed, the passage takes on a precise meaning. If the object of the speaker's **erōs** spurns his advances and treats him as an **ekhthros** would, then that **erōs** tastes bitter and feels hard to him, but if the desired boy accepts the suitor's advances, treating him as a **philos** would, that same **erōs** tastes sweet and feels good to the touch.[1]

§18. If possible, as Theognis 561–562 reminds us, we ought to take from our **ekhthroi** good things, so causing them **aniē**, and give these goods to our **philoi**, engendering **euphrosunē**.[1] What is treated negatively as prohibitions in 561–562 is treated positively elsewhere:

ἔν μοι ἔπειτα πέσοι μέγας οὐρανὸς εὐρὺς ὕπερθεν
χάλκεος, ἀνθρώπων δεῖμα παλαιγενέων,
εἰ μὴ ἐγὼ τοῖσιν μὲν ἐπαρκέσω οἵ με φιλεῦσιν,
τοῖς δ' ἐχθροῖς ἀνίη καὶ μέγα πῆμ' ἔσομαι.
Theognis 869–872

May the great broad bronze sky fall on me from above
—a thing feared by men of old—
If I do not help those who are *friends* [**philoi**] to me,
But to my *enemies* [**ekhthroi**] I will be a *pain* [**aniē**] and a great grief to boot!

§19. To fail in the just distribution of **aniē** to **ekhthroi** and **euphrosunē** to **philoi** is to become **deilos** 'wretched' or 'worthless':

ὤ μοι ἐγὼ δειλός· καὶ δὴ κατάχαρμα μὲν ἐχθροῖς,
τοῖς δὲ φίλοισι πόνος δειλὰ παθὼν γενόμην.
Theognis 1107–1108 = 1318a–b

O *wretched* [**deilos**] that I am! Because I have suffered *wretched* [**deila**] things
I have become a thing of joy to my *enemies* [**ekhthroi**] and a burden to my *friends* [**philoi**].

Here the **deila** the speaker has suffered make him a **deilos**, who inflicts **ponos** 'pain', a word semantically equivalent to **aniē**. Far from being able to take away their joy from his **ekhthroi**, he has become someone at whose expense they enjoy pleasure. A **deilos** can no longer participate in that system of giving and taking, free among friends and forced among enemies, which creates and sustains rela-

---

§17n1. On a specialized sense of **apēnēs** in Aristophanes ('sexually frustrating'), see Vetta 1980.126.

§18n1. On the importance of gift exchange to the maintenance of **philos** and **xenos** relations, see Finley 1977.64–69; on the duty of repaying in kind the unkind deeds of one's **ekhthroi**, see Finley p.77 (the blood feud). The subject of reciprocity is treated elsewhere in this volume (Donlan Ch.9§3, with note to Benveniste on **philos**).

tionships between **philoi** and **ekhthroi**. In social terms, **aniē** is the discomfort caused by another behaving as an **ekhthros**, whether he be a true **ekhthros** or a supposed **philos**. The discomfort is particularly intense where the social code enjoins the opposite, that is, from one's friends. That such a predicament can have a pederastic context is seen from the repetition of 1107–1108 in Book II as 1318a–b.

§20. It is this last type of **aniē** that receives much attention in the Theognidea. In 75–76 Kyrnos is advised to put his faith in few men in an important undertaking lest he reap an **anēkeston** . . . **aniēn** 'incurable . . . pain'. Again, in Theognis 257–260 the mare finds it an **aniē** that she has a **kakos** man for a rider. Finally, the exile whose plight is considered in 209–210 finds that the greatest cause of **aniē** is that he has no **philos** and **pistos hetairos** 'trustworthy companion'.[1] A majority of the passages in the corpus dealing with **philoi** turn out to have as their subject persons who are no **philoi** at all, who seem, on the basis of their actions, more like **ekhthroi**. Society, that is, the network of relationships of **philoi**, the parallel institution of relations of **xenoi**, the family (cf. Theognis 271–278 on filial ingratitude), and beyond these, the **ekhthroi**, can all be sources of **aniē**. Therefore, the pain caused by social tension can be understood to lie at the heart of the evils to be endured in Theognis 1029–1036 (quoted at §11).

§21. In Theognis 1029–1036, however, the painful experiences of the speaker are seen as divinely ordained. The gods, too, as either **philoi** or **ekhthroi**, may enter into relations with particular mortals.[1] Their immortality makes them in every way superior to men, so that a sense of disparity between gods and mortals, along with the notion of divine gift-giving, pervades the passage:

... θεῶν δ' εἱμαρμένα δῶρα
οὐκ ἂν ῥηϊδίως θνητὸς ἀνὴρ προφύγοι.
Theognis 1033–1034

... not easily may *mortal* [**thnētos**] man escape
the *destined* [**heimarmena**] *gifts* [**dōra**] of the gods.

"Not easily" turns out to be a litotes, since mortals cannot escape the destined gifts at all. Compare the passages in epic where actions

---

§20n1. For a full account of the difficulties encountered by the Theognidean aristocrat in his quest for the **philos kai pistos hetairos**, see Donlan Ch.9.

§21n1. So Peleus was **philos** to the immortal gods, Hesiod fr. 211.3 MW; so Bellerophon, though initially favored of Zeus, became hated by the gods, *Iliad* VI 200.

difficult or impossible for men are described as easy for gods.[2] Recall that earlier the passage spoke of not making too much of actions that were **aprēkta** 'unperformed' or 'unperformable' and set this against the words of Aphrodite to Hera as Hera sets out to seduce Zeus:

>   ... οὐδέ σέ φημι
> ἄπρηκτόν γε νέεσθαι, ὅ τι φρεσὶ σῇσι μενοινᾷς.
> *Iliad* xiv 220–221

> ... I do not think that
> you, at least, will return with that *unaccomplished* [**aprēkton**] which you
> intend to do in your *mind* [**phrenes**].

§ 22. Given the inequality between gods and mortals, one crucial element of any **philos** relationship is lacking between them, reciprocity. Gods and men are so unequal in what they have to give, there can be no question of those equal returns that maintain status. The gods, then, are **philoi** to whom they please at their pleasure, and their dealings with mortals are only in a limited and analogical way like the dealings of mortals with one another. In the terms of Sumner, the gods form neither an out-group with whom we can fight, nor an in-group with whom we can carry out fair distributions.[1] They stand outside both **philos** and **ekhthros** relations in the strictest sense:

> οὔτις ἄποινα διδοὺς θάνατον φύγοι οὐδὲ βαρεῖαν
> δυστυχίην, εἰ μὴ μοῖρ᾽ ἐπὶ τέρμα βάλοι,
> οὐδ᾽ ἂν δυσφροσύνας, ὅτε δὴ θεὸς ἄλγεα πέμπῃ,
> θνητὸς ἀνὴρ δώροις βουλόμενος προφυγεῖν.
> Theognis 1187–1190

> No one can escape death by paying a *ransom* [**apoina**] nor heavy
> bad luck, unless *fate* [**moira**] set a limit to it,
> nor, when a god sends him *pains* [**algea**], may a *mortal*,
> wishing to forestall death by giving *gifts*, escape *distress* in his *mind*
> [**phrenes**].

Dōra 'gifts' are what you give to your **philoi**. They are currency, the exchange of which sustains those relationships. The idea that **dōra** are for **philoi** is reinforced by the idea of volition in **boulomenos** (1190)

---

§21n2. Note that the uprooting of the magical moly is hard for a mortal man to do, but the gods can do everything (*Odyssey* x 303–304). A formula in the *Iliad* reminds us that Zeus can easily put to flight a brave warrior (e.g., *Iliad* xvii 178).

§22n1. Sumner's earlier terms for these groups were "we-group" and "others-group" (Sumner 1906.12); the more familiar terms "in-group" and "out-group" were introduced in his 1911 essay on war (Sumner 1963.35).

and of initiative or gratuity in the **pro** of **prophugein**. **Apoina** 'ransom' or 'compensation' are offered to someone who has possession of something of yours, keeping it from you as an **ekhthros** would. **Apoina** are thus the kind of compensation offered to an **ekhthros** in order to avoid or terminate his enmity. **Apoina** (just as **dōra**) are regular and regulative parts of the social order. But when mortal men deal with the gods or with those shadowy powers, death and fate, they cannot employ human means of interrelating. In consequence, the world remains a risky and unpredictable place governed by beings whose intentions are unfathomable. It is a fine thing to be **philos** to the gods, as Theotimos was in Theognis 881 or as the speaker in 653 finally wishes to be, but there are few who achieve this happy condition.

§23. The speaker, then, his social behavior constrained by his inability to know whether his fellow citizens are **philoi** or **ekhthroi** masquerading as **philoi**, turns his attention to the gods, only to find that there, too, he confronts inscrutable behavior. Against this doubly dark background, we may now consider more closely the notion of **theōn dōra** 'gifts of the gods', so that we may rightly interpret the gifts of Aphrodite. Let us start with the single instance in Theognis of a god's gift to another god, that of Zeus to Aphrodite:

Κυπρογενὲς Κυθέρεια δολοπλόκε, σοὶ τί περισσὸν
Ζεὺς τόδε τιμήσας <u>δῶρον</u> ἔδωκεν ἔχειν;
δαμνᾷς δ' ἀνθρώπων πυκινὰς <u>φρένας</u>, οὐδέ τίς ἐστιν
οὕτως ἴφθιμος καὶ <u>σοφὸς</u> ὥστε φυγεῖν.
Theognis 1386–1389

Cyprus-born, Cytherean, weaver of deceits! What is this *outstanding gift* [dōron] that Zeus, honoring you, gave you to have?
You tame the stout **phrenes** of men, nor is there any
so strong or so *skilled* as to escape you.

When a god confers a gift, he gives honor, a situation that holds good for mortals. (Consider the name **Theotīmos** 'he who has received honor [tīmē] from the god' in Theognis 881.)

§24. In this light, let us consider the formula **makar eudaimōn te kai olbios** 'blessed and fortunate and happy' (Theognis 1013), used to describe a man endowed with the gifts of the gods. The man it celebrates is **philos** to the gods, and thus **makar**, denoted by an epithet properly theirs, and so a participant in their bliss.[1] Because of his

---

§24n1. See *LSJ* s.v. "makar."

olbos 'wealth' granted by the gods (cf. Theognis 165–166, 373–392, 865–868), he can participate in the reciprocities of **philos** relationships in the sphere of mortal life, including pederasty (Theognis 1253–1254, 1335–1336, 1375–1376). He is not like the **deiloi**, without property to exchange or power to create **euphrosunē** for his **philoi** or **aniē** for his **ekhthroi**. To the former he is **glukus**, to the latter he is **pikros**. At the same time he is aware that **philoi** are often false and that the gifts of the gods are sometimes evil (e.g., destructive old age [Theognis 271–272]). His experience in the social world is unstable and threatened by disorder because **philoi** are not always trustworthy and the gods often bestow gifts of wealth and power on **deiloi**. As a member of an embattled circle of aristocratic **philoi**, he as an **erastēs** invites his **erōmenos** to join the fellowship of this elite.

§25. The fellowship defines itself in terms that fuse political and erotic themes:

οὐκ ἐθέλω σε κακῶς ἔρδειν, οὐδ᾽ εἴ μοι ἄμεινον
πρὸς θεῶν ἀθανάτων ἔσσεται ὦ καλὲ παῖ.
οὐ γὰρ ἁμαρτωλαῖσιν ἐπὶ σμικραῖσι κάθημαι·
τῶν δὲ καλῶν παίδων οὐ τίσις οὐδ᾽ ἀδίκων.[1]
Theognis 1279–1282

I have no intention of treating you *badly*, not even if it would be better for me,
O beautiful boy, in my relations with the immortal gods.
No, it is not over petty faults that I sit in judgment quietly.
But beautiful boys get no punishment even when they are without **dikē**.

Here is revealed an impasse between the claims of the community and those of eros. The **erastēs** has been injured by the **erōmenos**, and the gods' sense of justice requires that he seek satisfaction. Failure to punish the **erōmenos** amounts to a violation of the proper code of conduct among **philoi** and exposes the **erastēs** to the anger of the gods. Yet as the last line indicates, a beautiful boy never gets punished for his misdeeds, because he is protected by his beauty, which is one component of his youth, itself a gift of the gods (cf. Theognis 271–272). Eros creates disorder. Consider the opening passage of Book II:

σχέτλι᾽ Ἔρως, Μανίαι σ᾽ ἐτιθηνήσαντο λαβοῦσαι·
ἐκ σέθεν ὤλετο μὲν Ἰλίου ἀκρόπολις,

---

§25n1. This reading is based on an emendation, for which see the discussion of Vetta 1980.76–77.

ὤλετο δ' Αἰγείδης Θησεὺς μέγας, ὤλετο δ' Αἴας
ἐσθλὸς 'Οιλιάδης ἧσιν ἀτασθαλίαις.
Theognis 1231–1234

Obstinate *Eros*, Madnesses took you up and suckled you:
through you the high stronghold of Ilium perished.
And the son of Aigeus, great Theseus, perished; and Ajax perished,
that *noble* [esthlos] man, son of Oileus, each by reason of his recklessness.

This passage contains a miniature Theogony, wherein Eros is nursed by the Maniai 'Madnesses'. Moreover, the series of exempla (Troy, Theseus, Ajax) illustrates violent disregard of social convention under the influence of Eros, rather as madness sometimes leads warriors to make war on their own kindred.[2] It was Paris' abduction of Helen that violated the marriage tie and the relationship between guest and host that led to the destruction of Troy. Theseus joined forces with Perithoos in an attempted rape of Persephone, a direct threat to the boundaries between living and dead, gods and men, as well as a violation of a marriage. Ajax son of Oileus made a sexual assault upon Cassandra, a priestess of Apollo. In each story, Eros incited mortals to offend against human and divine order, so that the god is called **skhetlios** 'cruel' or 'obstinate' for inciting others to **atasthaliai** 'acts of recklessness'.[3] Eros is **skhetlios** not just because he causes suffering in his victims but because he inspires them with a disruptive cruelty similar to his own. In this he is like a warrior in a battle frenzy whose condition is denoted by **hubris**.

§26. Note this other Theognidean passage on **hubris**:

ὕβρις καὶ Μάγνητας ἀπώλεσε καὶ Κολοφῶνα
καὶ Σμύρνην· πάντως Κύρνε καὶ ὔμμ' ἀπολεῖ.
Theognis 1103–1104

Arrogance [hubris] destroyed both Magnesia and Colophon and Smyrna. Kyrnos, to be sure, it will destroy you, too.

This distich has been associated with the one preceding it:[1]

---

§25n2. For a discussion of this theme, see Dumézil 1970, esp. pp.105–107 on the sins of the warrior against the three functions and 133–137 on the initial combat of Cúchulainn.

§25n3. West 1974.165 emends 1234 to read ἧσιν ἀτασθαλίαις on the grounds that the text as we have it speaks blasphemously when it attributes to the god a class of actions that properly can be performed only by mortals. Vetta pp.42–43 argues in favor of the manuscript reading: σῆσιν.

§26n1. Harrison 1902.157 followed by Young 1961.

ὅστις σοι βούλευσεν ἐμεῦ πέρι, καί σ' ἐκέλευσεν
οἴχεσθαι προλιπόνθ' ἡμετέρην φιλίην ...
Theognis 1101–1102

Whoever counseled you about me and bade you
go and leave my **philiē** ...

By implication, betrayal of **philiē** is **hubris** of the same sort as that which destroys cities. While this juxtaposition may at first seem forced, it nonetheless fits a theme characteristic of the Theognidea: that a **polis** survives because its **esthloi** are **philoi**, partaking of an eros that is without **hubris**.[2] In the first of the two distichs, the boy's affections have strayed because his mind cannot resist the persuasion of others. The connection between this and the second of the two distichs becomes clearer when we note another warning against persuasion by false friends:

μήποτε τὸν παρεόντα μεθεὶς <u>φίλον</u> ἄλλον ἐρεύνα
<u>δειλῶν</u> ἀνθρώπων ῥήμασι πειθόμενος.
πολλάκι τοι παρ' ἐμοὶ κατὰ σοῦ λέξουσι μάταια,
καὶ παρὰ σοὶ κατ' ἐμοῦ· τῶν δὲ σὺ μὴ ξυνίει.
Theognis 1238a–1240

Never dismiss your present *friend* [**philos**] and go hunting another,
persuaded by the words of *worthless* [**deiloi**] men.
For often they will lay idle charges against you in my presence,
and against me in yours: do not listen to them.

Such an impressionable mind is not **artios** 'well put together' (cf. Theognis 153–154) and becomes a breeding ground for acts of **hubris**. What links eros and **hubris**, then, is that they both act to dissolve social bonds. It is not surprising, therefore, that the compiler of Book II was led to include 1101–1102 among the pederastic poems, where it appears as 1278a–b.

§27. Although eros and **hubris** act on society in the same fashion, eros is different in one important regard. It is personified as early as Hesiod (*Theogony* 120–122): for the effect of Eros on the minds of men, Hesiod uses the verb **damnazō** 'tame' (122). Compare Athena's spear in the *Iliad*, by which she **damnēsi** 'masters' ranks of men (*Iliad* v 746). The same word is used for breaking horses and marrying a woman to a man. Especially relevant to us is its use to express sex-

---

§26n2. Cf. van Groningen 1966.405.

ual conquest, as in the *Iliad*, where Hera asks Aphrodite for love and desire, by which she **damnāi** 'masters' immortals and mortals alike (xiv 199). The same image of Aphrodite appears in Theognis 1386–1389 (§23 above). Both the *Theogony* and Theognis picture the deity as subduing mortals through their minds (**noos, boulē, phrenes**).

§28. A parallel expression appears in Book II:

> ὦ παῖ, ἄκουσον ἐμεῦ δαμάσας φρένας· οὔτοι ἀπειθῆ
> μῦθον ἐρῶ τῇ σῇ καρδίῃ οὐδ' ἄχαριν.
> ἀλλὰ τλῆθι νόῳ συνιεῖν ἔπος· οὔτοι ἀνάγκη
> τοῦτ' ἔρδειν ὅτι σοι μὴ καταθύμιον ᾖ.
> Theognis 1235–1238

Boy, listen to me, *subduing* [damasās] your **phrenes**. I will tell you a tale *not unpersuasive nor without gratification* [kharis] for your heart.
Bring yourself to understand this **epos** in your **noos**: it is *not* necessary to do the thing that is *not what agrees with your disposition* [thūmos].

This passage is one of persuasion, in which an **erastēs** invites a boy to accept an agreeable proposal, perhaps to become an **erōmenos**. Verses 1299–1304 and 1365–1366 of Theognis invite a boy to listen to or to grant a favor to the speaker in similar language. In the passage at hand (1235–1238), however, the phrase **akouson emeu damasās phrenas** is quite ambiguous. If we take **emeu** '(of) me' as the object of **akouson** 'hear' (an imperative), we have 'listen to me, subduing your **phrenes**' (the translation above). If **emeu** is used possessively with **phrenes**, we have 'listen, you who have subdued my **phrenes**'. The **phrenes** have become the mind of the **erastēs** overcome by the boy's beauty.[1] In either case, we see humans initiating acts like the subduing initiated by the activity of the gods. If the boy is being asked to subdue his **phrenes**, it may be because a new infatuation is threatening to overcome him. The **erastēs**, probably in vain, asks the **erōmenos** to resist this influence.

§29. The speaker's invitation to the boy to listen suggests that the message about to be imparted by the speaker will bring the boy's behavior into balance with his **thūmos**. Therefore, the speaker's injunction has a calming effect, in part suggested by the delaying effect that the series of negations (**outoi** ... **oud'** ... **outoi** ... **mē**) might convey. The violent subjugation initiated by the divine force of

---

§28n1. For a treatment of the syntactic problems in v. 1235, see Vetta 1980.44–45.

Eros leads in the end to a **philos** relationship between **erastēs** and **erōmenos**. They are now no longer a threat to the social order.

§30. This process of socialization is symbolized by the marriage of Atalanta:

> ὦ παῖ, μή μ᾽ ἀδίκει· ἔτι σοι κα<τα>θύμιος εἶναι
> βούλομαι, εὐφροσύνῃ τοῦτο συνεὶς ἀγαθῇ.
> οὐ γάρ τοί με δόλῳ παρελεύσεαι οὐδ᾽ ἀπατήσεις·
> νικήσας γὰρ ἔχεις τὸ πλέον ἐξοπίσω,
> ἀλλά σ᾽ ἐγὼ τρώσω φεύγοντά με, ὥς ποτέ φασιν
> Ἰασίου κούρην παρθένον Ἰασίην
> ὡραίην περ ἐοῦσαν ἀναινομένην γάμον ἀνδρῶν
> φεύγειν· ζωσαμένη δ᾽ ἔργ᾽ ἀτέλεστα τέλει
> πατρὸς νοσφισθεῖσα δόμων ξανθὴ Ἀταλάντη·
> ᾤχετο δ᾽ ὑψηλὰς εἰς κορυφὰς ὀρέων
> φεύγουσ᾽ ἱμερόεντα γάμον, χρυσῆς Ἀφροδίτης
> δῶρα· τέλος δ᾽ ἔγνω καὶ μάλ᾽ ἀναινομένη.
> Theognis 1283-1294

Boy, do not treat me without **dikē**—I still wish to be
what agrees with your **thūmos**—perceiving this with good complaisance
   [**euphrosunē**].
You will not slip by me guilefully, nor will you deceive me.
You have won in the past and will do so more often than not in the
   future,
but I will wound you as you try to get away from me as they say once
   happened to
the daughter of Iasios, the girl Iasie.
Though she was of a ripe age for love, she said no to marrying with men
and fled. Her girdle still fastened, blonde Atalanta tried to fulfill
things that were not to be fulfilled. She left the house of her father
and went off to the peaks of lofty mountains,
fleeing from the bliss of marriage, *gifts* of golden
Aphrodite. But in the end she came to know, for all her saying no
   before.

The passage conflates two aspects of the myth of Atalanta. In vv. 1283-1287 an **erastēs** threatens to take vengeance on his **erōmenos** for unjust behavior, while citing the case of Atalanta. In 1287-1294, the focus is on Atalanta's flight to escape marriage, only to yield ultimately, just as the boy will yield to his **erastēs**.

§31. It is the second of these aspects that interests us. The salient characteristic of Atalanta both in the story of her races with her suitors and in the hunting of the Calydonian Boar is that she refuses marriage. In the latter story, love-struck Meleager awards her the spoils of the hunt, which touches off a feud that destroys his household and family, an exemplum of the destructiveness of love like those in Theognis 1231-1234.[1] We see eros appearing in two aspects. If refused, as by Atalanta initially, social bonds are not renewed, and there is a reversion to the presocial existence in the wilderness. Eros, however, poses a continual threat to existing social ties, as exemplified by Meleager.

§32. I shall say something more about the first of these two aspects. Atalanta's flight 'from the house of her father' is a flight from the place of domestication, a rejection of the prescribed role of women for the life of a warrior. 'Girdled', she performs **erg' atelesta** 'vain exploits', the term for rebellion against one's role which Marcel Detienne has elucidated.[1] In the *Ehoiai*, we learn that Atalanta fled from marriage **andrōn . . . alphēstāōn** 'with **alphēstēs** men' (fr. 73.5 MW). The word **alphēstēs** may be glossed as 'grain-eating', related to **alphi**, **alphiton** 'barley-groats'.[2] Thus, Atalanta left the place of cereal cultivation, hence the place of civilized human beings, and assimilated herself to creatures of the wilderness like Centaurs, who are **ōmophagoi** 'eaters of raw flesh'.[3] Consider these verses addressed to Kyrnos:

δειμαίνω μὴ τήνδε πόλιν Πολυπαΐδη ὕβρις
ἤ περ Κενταύρους ὠμοφάγους ὀλέσῃ.
Theognis 541-542

I am afraid, O son of Polypaos, that *outrage* [hubris] will destroy this
city,
the very outrage that destroyed the Centaurs, *eaters of raw flesh*
[ōmophagoi].

---

§31n1. For the story of the Calydonian Boar, see Ovid *Metamorphoses* 8.260–546; for Atalanta's flight to avoid marriage (here motivated by an oracle) and the footrace with the suitors, cf. *Metamorphoses* 10.560–570. Noteworthy in the latter passage is the fulfillment of the oracle: Atalanta, persuaded by the suddenly amorous Hippomenes to lie with him in a precinct sacred to Cybele, finds herself and her husband transformed into a pair of lions. Thereafter *pro thalamis celebrant silvas* 'they frequent forests rather than the marriage-chamber' (*Metamorphoses* 10.703): their marriage gone awry, the wedded pair returns to the wilderness. I am indebted to Andrew Ford for calling my attention to the relevance of the whole myth of Atalanta for my reading of Theognis 1283–1294, as well as for many other suggestions here silently incorporated into my text.
§32n1. Detienne 1979.31–32.
§32n2. Cf. Chantraine 1968.67.
§32n3. Cf. Nagy Ch.2§39.

When at length Atalanta accepts **himeroenta gamon** 'delightful marriage', the **khrūsēs Aphroditēs dōra** 'gifts of golden Aphrodite', she returns to civilization in her husband's house. This is her **telos** 'fulfillment', in place of **erg' atelesta**. She moves away from houses, grain fields, and social institutions toward a Centaurlike or Amazonian existence on the margin of society and then, tamed by eros, accepts marriage. Atalanta, who became a huntress beyond civilization, becomes the quarry for a different kind of hunter, one who, inspired by eros, seeks to reincorporate her into human society. The would-be **erastēs** of Theognis 1283–1294 presents the story of Atalanta as a paradigm for his own approach to the **erōmenos**.

§33. A similar passage may serve as a further illustration:

ὦ παῖ, μέχρι τίνος με προφεύξεαι; ὥς σε διώκων
  δίζημ᾽· ἀλλά τί μοι τέρμα γένοιτο κιχεῖν
σῆς ὀργῆς· σὺ δὲ μάργον ἔχων καὶ ἀγήνορα θυμὸν
  φεύγεις ἰκτίνου σχέτλιον ἦθος ἔχων.
ἀλλ᾽ ἐπίμεινον, ἐμοὶ δὲ δίδου χάριν· οὐκέτι δηρὸν
  ἕξεις Κυπρογενοῦς δῶρον ἰοστεφάνου.
  Theognis 1299–1304 Vetta

Boy, how long will you continue to flee me? How I chase you,
seeking you out! May I find some *limit* [**terma**]
to *your temperament* [reading **sēs orgēs**]! But you, with your greedy and
  too hardy **thūmos**,
take flight, you with the *self-willed* [**skhetlios**] *temperament* of a kite.
But stay where you are and grant me **kharis**. Not for much longer
will you have the gift of her that was Cyprus-born, the violet-crowned.

Vetta takes **terma**, translated 'limit' above, to refer to the goal-marker in a race, so that the hunting image is combined with an athletic one, as in the case of Atalanta. Again, the **erastēs** is the pursuer, the **erōmenos** the pursued. But just as the pursued Atalanta was a huntress herself, so here the **erōmenos** is a hunter in ethos, as he has the temperament of a predatory bird. In the wilderness, where the erotic hunt takes place, the natures of pursuer and pursued intermingle.

§34. The time is short during which a boy is fit to play the role of an **erōmenos**.[1] The gifts of Aphrodite will not be his to enjoy once he

---

§34n1. Vetta 1980.89–90 discusses this topos and cites references from Greek and Latin erotic literature.

has come to the end of adolescence. In this respect, the position of the prospective **erōmenos** contrasts in the sharpest possible way with that of Atalanta. For her the acceptance of the gifts of Aphrodite in marriage marks her arrival at the **telos** 'goal' of child-bearing and domestic life. For the boy, however, acceptance of the invitation of **paidophiliē** leads to a temporary status, ostensibly one of subordination for the purpose of **paideiā**, which in a few years will be converted into its complementary role when he becomes an **erastēs** in his turn.

§35. There is another paradigm in mythology for the erotic hunt:

παιδοφιλεῖν δέ τι τερπνόν, ἐπεί ποτε καὶ Γανυμήδους
  ἤρατο καὶ Κρονίδης ἀθανάτων βασιλεύς,
ἁρπάξας δ' ἐς Ὄλυμπον ἀνήγαγε καί μιν ἔθηκεν
  δαίμονα, παιδείης ἄνθος ἔχοντ' ἐρατόν.
οὕτω μὴ θαύμαζε Σιμωνίδη, οὕνεκα κἀγὼ
  ἐξεφάνην καλοῦ παιδὸς ἔρωτι δαμείς.
Theognis 1345-1350

The *love of boys* [**paidophilein**] is something to take pleasure in, since
  even Zeus,
king of the immortals, once upon a time loved Ganymede,
and snatching him up carried him to Olympos and made him
a **daimōn** while he still had the lovely bloom of youth.
So do not be surprised, Simonides, that I too
have been shown [**exphanēn**], *tamed* [**dameis**] by **erōs** for a beautiful
  boy.

Here, as in 1283–1294, the **erastēs** is characterized as a hunter, and there is an allusion to the gift of the gods, the **anthos paideiēs** 'bloom of youth'. Note too the ambiguity of role linking hunter and hunted, which culminates in the assertion that the hunter is 'tamed by eros'. If the emendation **exphanēn** at Theognis 1350 is correct, we are directed from the world of myth to the here and now of the speaker. The **erastēs** and **erōmenos**, reenacting the myth of Zeus and Ganymede, play out their roles under the eyes of their fellow citizens, their **philoi** and **ekhthroi**, a fact that elicits the speaker's explanation to Simonides.[1] The corpus provides several other instances of this theme, the closest being 1341–1344 (a passage often linked with 1345–1350). I shall return to it below.

---

§35n1. For a discussion of this vocative and the problems it has caused those concerned with the authenticity of poems in the Theognidea, see Vetta pp.121–123.

§36. One more passage needs to be cited in my discussion of this motif. Verses 949–954 struck the excerptor as erotic in import, and the first distich appeared in Book ɪɪ as 1278c–d. K. J. Dover suggests lexical reasons for supporting this opinion:[1]

νεβρὸν ὑπὲξ ἐλάφοιο λέων ὣς ἀλκὶ πεποιθὼς
ποσσὶ ματαμάρψας αἵματος οὐκ ἔπιον.
Theognis 949–950 = 1278c–d

Like a lion trusting in his strength, I have snatched with my claws
the fawn from the doe—but I did not drink his blood.

The formulaic **leōn hōs alki pepoithōs** 'like a lion trusting in its strength' occurs in the Homeric poems, for example, *Odyssey* vi 130. It belongs to a class of formulas used to compare warriors to various predatory animals. When Menelaos, learning of the conduct of the suitors of Penelope, becomes incensed, he predicts their fate at the hands of Odysseus (*Odyssey* iv 333–340). The suitors are characterized as men without **alkē** 'strength', in the face of the strength of Odysseus. The lion of Theognis, trusting in his strength, creates a striking contrast when he does not drink the fawn's blood. Another use of the lion motif may be cited, this one in the words of a prophetic figure who appears to the Peisistratid Hipparchus on the eve of his assassination:

τλῆθι λέων ἄτλητα παθὼν τετληότι θυμῷ.
οὐδεὶς ἀνθρώπων ἀδικῶν τίσιν οὐκ ἀποτίσει.
Herodotus 5.56.1

Endure [**tlēthi**], O lion, the *unendurable* [**atlēta**] with a *patient* [**tetlēoti**] **thūmos**:
No man who *acts without justice* [**dikē**] will fail to pay the *penalty* [**tisis**].

In both Theognis and Herodotos the image of the lion illuminates heroic restraint, which suggests an interpretation of 949–954 that emphasizes a difference between hunting and the erotic hunt. The former has as its object killing the quarry, the latter to bring the quarry into the network of **philos** relations. As such, **paidophilein** is a prerogative of the **agathoi**, for the **deiloi** do not have the self-control to respect its conventions, lacking the **thūmos** to endure. Hence, beside the image of destructive eros in 1231–1234, Theognis 949–954 sets the image of temperate eros developed out of images of heroic self-control such as we find in Theognis 1028–1036.

---

§36n1. See Dover 1978.58 for including Theognis 949–962 among the erotica.

§ 37. The process of eros traced here emerges in response to a social problem, the need to control erotic feelings, which, while necessary to form social bonds, are potentially disruptive of society. The process (seen most clearly in the Atalanta passage) is one of double movement. First, the object of eros is marginalized, that is, located in a space beyond society, where it is legitimate for another to hunt him. Next, the feelings of the erotic object are tamed, domesticated, and, if he grants his suitor **kharis**, channeled into the institution of **paidophiliē**, in which the hunter repays him with **paideiā** 'instruction'. So the boy reenters society in a reciprocal relationship as an **erōmenos**. This serves the community by transmitting values from one generation to another. Self-control, as in Theognis 1029–1036, is high on the list of these values. In Theognis 1351–1352, for example, where the **pais** is warned not to **kōmazein** 'revel', self-control is stressed, which, in combination with the vocative **pai**, is responsible for the inclusion of the passage in Book II.[1] The erotic relationship contributes to aristocratic **euphrosunē** (cf. Theognis 1255–1256), making the participants, especially the **erastēs**, **olbioi**, and **makares** (see Theognis 1253–1254, 1335– 1336, 1375–1376), akin to the gods.

§ 38. The association of pederasty with other institutions of the aristocracy reaffirms the opposition between **agathoi** and **deiloi**, an emphasis of the Theognidea. The faithless **erōmenos** has been made so by consorting with **deiloi** (cf. 1238a–1240, 1243–1244, 1311–1318), so that his defection amounts to a passing over to what was to Theognis an anti- or at least a nonaristocratic faction. The **erastēs**, by contrast, is pictured as faithful even in absence (Theognis 1363–1364), a model of heroic (or aristocratic) constancy. If we adopt the emendation of **sainōn** to **s' ainōn** (accepted by West and Vetta), verses 1327–1328 assert that the **erastēs** will never cease praising his **erōmenos**, even if he is fated to die. The thought here sounds hyperbolical. Yet in the light of the political character of the group of **philoi** to which the **erastēs** and **erōmenos** belong, Theognis 237–254, in which Kyrnos is told that he will be **essomenoisin aoidē** 'a song to those who will live after us' (251), suggests that it need not be so. The **erastēs** will go on praising his **erōmenos** after death through the medium of song in the mouths of later aristocratic singers as long as the community of **philoi** survives.

---

§ 37n1. For **kōmos** and its special reference to the sympotic situation, see Levine Ch.7.

§39. Such at least is the ideal completion of the process I have traced. In what sort of society is this **philos** relationship situated? Obviously, that to which the political poems of Book I have introduced us, where there is scarcely a **pistos hetairos** 'trusted companion', where every **philos** relationship is pregnant with defection and betrayal, where concealing one's thoughts is prudent, and where the **deiloi** are everywhere in the ascendancy. This is a society in which every new friendship brings its risks (note my discussion at §35 of Theognis 1345–1350). Consider next the following passage:

αἰαῖ, παιδὸς ἐρῶ ἁπαλόχροος, ὅς με φίλοισιν
πᾶσι μάλ᾽ ἐκφαίνει κοὐκ ἐθέλοντος ἐμοῦ.
τλήσομαι οὐ κρύψας ἀεκούσι<α> πολλὰ βίαια·
οὐ γὰρ ἐπ᾽ αἰκελίῳ παιδὶ <u>δαμεὶς ἐφάνην</u>.
                                                            Theognis 1341–1344

Alas, I love a boy with tender skin, who exposes me
to all my **philoi**, though I am unwilling.
I will endure [**tlēsomai**], not hiding the many *acts of violence* I suffered
against my will.
At least *I have been revealed* [**ephanēn**] as the conquest [**dameis**] of a not
unseemly boy.

The **erastēs** in this passage, tamed by eros, yet enduring the acts of violence of his **erōmenos** against him, acts that are in fact the usual behavior of **ekhthroi**, accepts as part of the price exacted from him by eros the public knowledge of the wrongs done him. Elsewhere too we note the pressure exerted on any **philos** relationship by the counsels of others, for example in 1238a–1240, 1278a–b. One passage, 1295–1298, seeks to link the boy's **philiē** to the powers watching over human social relations. Here the anger of the gods takes vengeance on violations of the social order such as betrayal of the **philos** relationship (1297). The **baxis** 'gossip' of men is also a check on improper behavior, as in any "shame culture."[1]

§40. Despite these powerful sanctions, the **philos** relationship often comes to an end. The bond is broken, and insofar as it is broken rather than ended by the maturation of the **erōmenos**, the community undergoes loss. The Theognidean corpus explores various responses to this rupture, including a balancing of the goods and ills of **paidophiliē** (1369–1372), assertions of the joys of freedom from the relationship (1337–1340, 1377–1380), an imprecation on the defect-

---

§39n1. On "shame cultures," see Dodds 1951.17–18.

ing erōmenos (1317–1318), and declarations that a philos relationship no longer exists, sometimes coupled with an assertion of future enmity (1243–1244, 1245–1246, 1247–1248). Most frequently cited as cause is strayed affection, the appearance of an allos philos 'other friend' to whom the erōmenos attaches himself. He is usually visualized as one of the deiloi into whose hands the whole city has fallen (cf. Theognis 53–60, where lāoi . . . alloi 'other folk' are the new elite). The deiloi are said to be led by wild men on the margins of civilized life (Theognis 53–68), whose ascendancy will destroy the polis (like Centaurs, cf. Theognis 541–542), a hegemony strengthened by the formation of philos relationships by defecting erōmenoi.[1] The hubris of the deiloi may be compared with the appeal of the erastēs, who cites the parallel of Atalanta to his erōmenos.

§41. This account of Theognidean paidophiliē has uncovered a complex pattern, with a background in a hierarchically ordered cosmos, where immortal gods nevertheless have interrelations with men. The aristocracy, linked to the gods by philiē and divine descent, participates only to a limited extent in divine well-being. Yet the boundary between the aristocracy, the agathoi, and the deiloi is as clear as that between gods and mortals. Eros emerges as an ambiguous god, working both good and ill in the social sphere. Taming the phrenes of men, he incites them to form philos relationships with one another, making possible through paideiā/paiderastiā the transmission of values from one generation to the next. The formation of these relations follows mythological paradigms, involving first a marginalization of the boy and then his reincorporation into the community. But Eros is also a breeder of hubris who puts bonds already formed under strain. Faithless eros contributes to that confusion of agathoi and deiloi so often complained of in the corpus, and leading to the destruction of cities. Eros is responsible, then, not merely for the fulfillment of an ideal state of affairs, but also its passing away. From generation to generation, the silent erōmenos became in due season the vocal erastēs until the archaic aristocracy, together with its system of values, gave way before new social forces, necessitating a

---

§40n1. *Editors' note:* We may imagine that, in reality, aristocrats (esthloi) competed for erōmenoi, while fickle youths could switch from one erastēs to another and thus move from one aristocratic faction to another. An ideology where each faction could claim to be *the* elite would not only explain life; it could also explain away the troubling facets of living, in this case by banishing diversity from its field of attention and by differentiating groups whose claims to traditional authority were only marginally different.

reconceptualization of eros in human life. The social significance of **paiderastiā** underwent change, as indicated by Aristophanic comedy.[1] In the dialogues of Plato, with their subtle mocking of aristocratic pretensions, and in the erotic epigrams of the twelfth book of the Anthology, the outlines of a new social range for pederasty can be discerned.

---

§41n1. In general see Vetta's cautious approach to the problem of double entendre in the Theognidea. The position taken in this chapter is consistent with Vetta's cautions. Having demonstrated that the Theognidean **paideiā / paiderastiā** is fully integrated into the central values of aristocratic society, he goes on to suggest that, during the sixth century, these values were losing their position of centrality. This process of devaluation would lead in time to marginalization of the once central values, hence to their subjection to ridicule (a common tactic for peripheralizing certain forms of behavior, as observed in Aristophanes).

9
Pistos Philos Hetairos

Walter Donlan

§1. In the earliest example of archaic poetry, the Homeric epics, the ties that bind men in friendship appear as strong and inviolable. It is taken for granted that friends (**philoi**) and companions (**hetairoi**) are loyal and trustworthy.[1]

§2. At a critical point in the *Iliad*, the Embassy of Book IX, Achilles comes close to betrayal of his **philoi** by refusing to help them when they seek his aid. Ajax (the exemplar of the loyal comrade) complains that Achilles

> ... οὐδὲ μετατρέπεται φιλότητος ἑταίρων
> τῆς ᾗ μιν παρὰ νηυσὶν ἐτίομεν ἔξοχον ἄλλων.
> *Iliad* IX 630–631

... has no regard for the friendship [**philotēs**] of his **hetairoi**,
with which we honored [= verb **tiō**] him by the ships far above all the
others.

This is unusual behavior and is considered such. In the normalizing tale of Meleager, related by Phoenix to "all my **philoi**" (*Iliad* IX 528), not even Meleager's **hetairoi**, who were 'truest and dearest [**kednota-toi kai philtatoi**] of all' (586), were able to persuade him. As Gregory Nagy points out, however, his **hetairoi** are second only to Meleager's wife in the ranking of affinities—above mother, sisters, father, priests, elders. In fact, eventually, it is the death of Patroklos, **polu philtatos hetairos** 'the most **philos hetairos** by far' (*Iliad* XVII 411, 655), that

---

§1n1. E.g., **pistos hetairos**: *Iliad* XV 331, 437; XVI 174; XVII 500, 557, 589; XVIII 235, 460; *Odyssey* XV 539. The much more common epithet of **hetairos** is **eriēros** (heteroclitic plural **eriēres**), which is used exclusively of **hetairos** in the *Iliad*, and always in the *Odyssey*, except in three instances where it is an epithet of **aoidos** 'singer, poet'. **Eriēros** is apparently derived from **arariskō** 'join, attach' and may be glossed as 'strongly attached'. N.B.: some of the more prominent Greek words discussed in this chapter will at times be cited without a gloss. All such words, however, can be found in the Glossary at the end of this volume.

induces Achilles to recognize his social obligation to his **philoi**.[1] Achilles' failure of friendship is temporary, an exception to accepted standards of the group.[2]

§3. For the protoaristocrats of the Greek Dark Age, no bond, not even that of blood relationship, was more reliable than the bonds between **philoi** (friends), **hetairoi** (companions), and **xeinoi** (friends who live outside the tribal group). Emile Benveniste has demonstrated that in origin and essence 'friendship' is a structural element of early Greek society, since it refers to the relations of an individual with the members of his group: kin, retainers, friends (including guest-friends). The personal, affectionate aspect of **philotēs** proceeds from the social, institutional bond and eventually exceeds it, but at no time does the word **philos** lose its ancient rootedness in the institutional sphere.[1] **Hetairos** (companion), as Benveniste also shows, is from an Indo-European root *swe (indicating 'one's own') from which comes also Greek **etēs** 'kinsman, relation'. Both **philos** and **hetairos**, therefore, imply from earliest times "a bond of a social character of kinship or sentiment."[2] Embedded as it is in societal integration, friendship is by nature simple and straightforward.

§4. In the Theognidea, however, friendship is problematical. A very large number of verses in the collection are concerned with friendship—political, personal, and erotic. There is little discernible difference in language, theme, and tone among what appear to the modern observer as quite different forms of the friendship bond. A striking feature of the passages on friendship is their consistently negative quality, evident in the typology that follows below. Verses that have to do with friendship fit more or less neatly into three main groupings: complaints, advice, and observations.

---

§2n1. See Nagy 1979.103–111 for an extended analysis of the Meleager story and of heroic **philotēs**.

§2n2. **Apistos** in the *Odyssey* always means 'unbelieving', 'not trusting' (*Odyssey* xiv 150, 391; xxiii 72). In *Iliad* III 106 the sons of Priam are 'arrogant', 'overbearing' (**huperphialoi**), and **apistoi**; the reference is to oaths (105). Hecuba, in *Iliad* XXIV 207, calls Achilles 'savage' (**ōmēstēs**) and **apistos**, referring to his lack of pity and of a sense of shame and honor (**aidōs**). Once **apistos** is linked to **hetairos**; in *Iliad* XXIII 63 Hera berates Apollo for preferring mortal Hector to god-born Achilles, although Apollo had attended the wedding feast of Peleus and Thetis with his lyre: thus he is '**hetairos** of evil men [**kakoi**], always faithless [**apistos**]'.

§3n1. Benveniste 1973.277–288.

§3n2. Benveniste p.271. The behavior expressed by the verb **phileō** "always has an obligatory character and always implies reciprocity" (p.280); cf. p.426.

§5. A. *Complaints.*

A 1. Poet complains that friends have betrayed him, deceived him, or acted duplicitously toward him: 253–254, 575–576, 599–602, 811–813, 851–852, 861–862, 967–970, 1097–1100, 1101–1102 = 1278a–b, 1243–1244, 1263–1266, 1311–1318, 1361–1362; cf. 271–278, 1241–1242, 1245–1246, 1377–1380.

B. *Advice.*

B 1. Poet advises not to betray a friend or not to be duplicitous toward a friend: 87–90 = 1082c–f, 323–324, 399–400, 1083–1084, 1151–1152 = 1238a–b, 1283–1294.

B 2. Poet warns against a duplicitous friend: 91–92, 93–96, 333–334, 963–966, 979–982, 1239–1240.

B 3. Poet advises to be a duplicitous friend: 63–65, 73–74, 213–218, 309–312, 1071–1074; cf. 301–302, 313–314.

B 4. Poet advises to trust no one or to trust only a few: 61–68, 75–76, 283–286.

B 5. Poet advises never to be a friend to, nor to trust, a **kakos** man: 69–72, 101–104, 105–112, 113–114, 305–308; cf. 1238a–1240.

C. *Observations.*

C 1. Poet observes that trustworthy friends are few in difficult or trying circumstances: 77–78, 79–82, 115–116, 209–210, 299–300, 332a–b, 643–644, 645–646, 697–698, 857–860, 929–930; cf. 83–86, 97–100 = 1164a–d.

C 2. Poet comments that it is difficult to tell a false friend from a true one: 119–128, 641–642, 963–970, 1219–1220; cf. 117–118, 221–226, 571–572, 1016.

C 3. Poet asserts that he is a trustworthy friend (having been tested): 415–418 = 1164e–h, 447–452, 529–530, 869–872, 1104a–1106; cf. 237–254, 511–522, 1079–1080, 1087–1090, 1311–1318, 1363–1364.

§6. A thematic pattern is evident, which leads to certain observations. First, friendship as an institutional phenomenon is assumed; there is, therefore, a continuous connection with the epic tradition. A break with that tradition is obvious, however, for the institution is perceived as being very fragile. In effect, unalloyed friendship does not exist—ambivalence, deception, and betrayal are common elements of the relationship, either present in it or lurking in the background. What appears in Theognis is a form of friendship that is qualitatively different from the traditional ideal: wary, suspicious, even hostile; loyalty and fidelity are no longer automatic reflexes. Nevertheless, the idealized form itself remains a constant; the poetic tradition knows what friendship ought to be like, while at the same time it knows what friendship has become. This is evident in the passages gathered in C 3, above, which include the more positive lines on friendship in the corpus, inasmuch as the poet asserts that he conforms to the traditional expectation that **philoi** and **hetairoi** be faithful and loyal to one another.[1] But even here, the emphasis on testing and the stated or implied notion that betrayal is a recurrent and common element in friendship show clearly the awareness of great disparity between ideal and reality.

§7. One possible explanation is that, historically, the institution of friendship had changed; although, as a conceptual category in the mind of poet and audience, it retained its traditional configuration. Another way of saying this is that the traditional poetic theme and diction, which described a traditional social institution as a simple one-to-one equivalence, continued in use to describe a radically altered, much more complicated, set of relational ties, in which the correspondences between concept and reality were neither direct nor satisfactory.

§8. Before this possibility can be confronted, it is first necessary to see in what respects friendship in the Theognidea is problematical. In the analysis that follows, no differentiation is made among the various kinds of friendship: political, personal, and erotic. The poet's bitterest lament is that his friends (**philoi**) have betrayed (verb **prodidōmi**) him (vv. 575, 812; cf. 861), a thing that is likened to death itself (811–812). Once, he says that he has never betrayed a friend and faithful companion (**philos kai pistos hetairos**: 529). This is the extreme negative statement about friendship; being betrayed is second only to death, and betrayal is associated with a slavish nature (530).

§9. The key attribute of a friend and companion (one that is consistently applied to friendship in the epic) is the quality of being faithful or worthy of trust (**pistos**), and it is this quality that has been lost or is lacking among **philoi / hetairoi**.[1] In what amounts to a gnomic summary statement about the current absence of trustworthiness, Theog-

---

§6n1. Among these may also be included those lines that are purely erotic (see Lewis Ch.8) and those that are variants of the familiar topos: love your friends, hate your enemies (e.g., 337–340, 561–562, 869–872, 1032–1033, 1087–1090), which have parallels in the verses of other archaic poets.

§9n1. See Benveniste 1973.84–100 on "personal loyalty."

nis complains that Faith (**Pistis**), 'the great goddess', has abandoned earth for Olympus, together with **Sōphrosunē** and the Kharites. The result is that there are no longer oaths that are **pistoi** and just (**dikaioi**), nor is there reverent awe of the gods. The generation of pious (**eusebeis**) men has perished, and men no longer know (verb **gignōskō**) customary law (**themistes**) and pious observances (1135–1142).

§10. This pessimistic view is restated in a number of ways, specifically in regard to friends and comrades. Few **philoi** have a trustworthy mind (**pistos noos**: 74, 698); the poet seeks in vain for a **pistos hetairos** free of deception (**dolos**) like himself (415–416 = 1164e–f); Kyrnos is advised that he will find few men who are **hetairoi pistoi** (79–80); someone is told that he will find few kin (**kēdemones**) who are **pistoi hetairoi** (645); a former friend is told that he has a deceptive nature (**ēthos dolion**), which is contrary to **pistis** (1244).

§11. It is with this theme that an analysis proper of the archaic poet's vision of a traditional institution gone awry begins. For around the central notion, that **pistis** has vanished and few **philoi/hetairoi** are **pistoi**, clusters a constellation of associated ideas that dramatize in depth and detail the ethical and moral confusion of aristocrats in a situation where old and cherished certainties are perceived as yielding—inexorably, and with a speed that must have seemed demonically swift to the archaic mind—to new realities.

§12. No truly precise historical statements can be made about Theognis the poet or about the collection that has come down under his name. The theory advanced by Nagy about the poet and the corpus of poetry has the merit of obviating many difficulties, compositional and historical, inherent in the Theognidea. To paraphrase: the Theognidea are a local poetic tradition, extending over a century or more (from the late seventh to the early fifth centuries B.C.), most of the particular epichoric elements of which were obliterated in its dissemination as pan-Hellenic poetry.[1] We can then imagine how "Theognis," as a local "witness," experienced squabblings among aristocratic corporations for hegemony, the rise and fall of the tyrant Theagenes, a "moderate oligarchy," uprisings of the poor against the rich, and a semianarchic "democracy," which was succeeded by a second "moderate oligarchy." We can even imagine how he must have "seen" colonization, the growth of overseas trade and commerce, which

---

§12n1. Nagy Ch.2§§14–16.

brought new wealth and styles to a backward agrarian district. He must also have "seen" the rise of Megara as a sea power, its urbanization and increased population, and its adventures overseas and wars with neighbors. In short, the subject matter of "Theognis," as a local poet, must have been much like the subject matter of countless other local poetic traditions.

§13. As part of the "cumulative synthesis of Megarian poetic traditions," and in their refinement as a pan-Hellenic tradition, Theognis' reflections on friendship belong both to the Megarian experience and to the wider world of Hellenic city-states (poleis). They are a distillation of archaic aristocratic alienation in a time of flux, when the complexities of a society in change had rendered epic friendship a nostalgic and formal vision contained only in the poetic memory.

§14. An expressed awareness that the institutional and affective bonds presumed in the relationships of philoi, hetairoi, and xeinoi had degenerated is not unique to the Theognidean corpus. In the poetic tradition associated with the name of Hesiod, similar ideas find utterance. In *Works and Days* 174–201, the present is described as a debased age of inferior men; in the time to come, kin, xeinoi, and hetairoi will no longer live in the same reciprocity (expressed by the adjective homoiios) 'as before'. Men will not have the proper awe of the gods, oaths and justice will be despised, the doer of evil and hubris will be honored. The kakos man will harm the better man, 'speaking with crooked words', forswearing his oath; and finally, respect and loyalty (Aidōs), along with righteous indignation (Nemesis), will depart from earth to Olympus. In both theme and diction, Hesiod's description of the race of Iron Men corresponds closely to the Theognidean passage cited above (vv. 1135–1142, §9).

§15. Clearly, there is a tradition in archaic Greek poetry, traceable from Homer on, which is concerned with the deterioration of the institutional ties that knit the community of men together. The temporary failure of Achilles to respond to the demands of philotēs has echoes elsewhere in the epic, notably in the reversal by the aristocratic suitors of the *Odyssey* of the norms of behavior demanded in the guest-host relationship, the loyalty of the lesser chiefs to the house of the paramount chief, and the etiquette of feasts, in which those reciprocal obligations find concrete expression. The themes surrounding the breakdown of friendship, which I shall examine in detail in Theognis, have responsions in other poets of the seventh and sixth centuries as well, but nowhere else is the crisis of friendship presented so fully (one is tempted to say so systematically) or so pessimistically as it is in the Theognidea.

§16. From a diachronic, that is, a conventionally historical, perspective, it is important to note that the theme of the rupture of the conventional integrative ties is perceived as an anomalous deviation in Homer. It is central to the dialectic in the *Works and Days* between what Nagy calls the **polis** of **dikē** and the **polis** of **hubris** in which, eventually, **dikē** will triumph.[1] Although he laments the deterioration of the inherited values, Hesiod is ultimately hopeful about the reintegration of these same values, appropriately symbolized by the possibility of reconciliation with his brother Perses, his faith in the vindication of **dikē**, the hope of harmonious association between rulers and ruled, and his generally positive attitude toward relations between **philoi** and **hetairoi** (see, e.g., *Works and Days* 432–472, 706–723). The obsessive and deeply pessimistic attitude toward friendship in the Theognidea, in contrast, appears to reflect the belief that the social universe once integrated by blood, affinal, and close personal ties (the kinship community) is now threatened with disintegration.

§17. Accordingly, it is important to note the context in which the threatened ship is dramatized in Theognis. To begin, the observation that few **philoi** out of many have a **pistos noos** 'trustworthy mind' occurs in a couplet (vv. 73–74), the first line of which advises the addressee not to share his business (**prēxis**) completely with all his **philoi**. Elsewhere, we find this elaboration:

εὖ μὲν ἔχοντος ἐμοῦ πολλοὶ φίλοι· ἢν δέ τι δειλὸν
συγκύρσῃ, παῦροι πιστὸν ἔχουσι νόον.
Theognis 697–698

When I am doing well, I have many **philoi**. But if something bad happens, few have a **pistos noos**.

So also in 79–82, few men are **pistoi hetairoi** in 'difficult matters' (**khalepa prēgmata**), or (in 645–646) 'in great misfortune' (**megalēi amēkhaniēi**). The theme is restated numerous times: no one is **philos kai pistos hetairos** to an exile (209–210, 332a–b). Many men are **hetairoi** in banquets, but few in 'a matter of importance' (**spoudaion prēgma**: 115–116, 643–644). No one, not even a brother, is a **philos** when evil (**kakon**) comes (299–300); **philoi** turn away when

---

§16n1. Nagy 1982.57–66.

one is in difficulty (ti deilon ekhōn) but show him philotēs when he is doing well (857–860). If you are rich, you have many philoi, but few if you are poor (929–930). Clearly, in Theognis, steadfast loyalty in friends and companions is contingent. Misfortune, exile, and poverty weaken or dissolve the bonds of friendship. More significantly, friendship becomes problematical when 'a matter of importance' (spoudaion prēgma) is at stake (115–116, 643–644).

§18. It may be asserted that spoudaion prēgma has as its primary reference political alliance. In Greek society philos and hetairos were essentially social categories. More precisely, as Benveniste has shown, personal friendship and political friendship are not to be distinguished. In the closely knit aristocratic world posited by the poetry of Theognis, all ties (including those of blood and marriage) would be conceived of in terms of groups, so that the personal dimension—including the erotic—and factional membership went *pari passu*. Psychological stresses would have been unavoidable when any one man was linked to numerous "others" (and *their* groups) in a complex network of shifting factional loyalties. The paramount problem was determination of some sure and dependable basis of fidelity by which today's friend would not be revealed as tomorrow's enemy. Unfortunately, such ideologically sure and dependable loyalties were in practice elusive. In an agonistic culture, success counts for most; it is inexpedient to be allied with a loser. Poverty, exile, and other accidents of fortune attenuate the ties of friendship among men struggling to be at the top of the heap. 'A matter of importance' was fraught with uncertainty:

πιστὸς ἀνὴρ χρυσοῦ τε καὶ ἀργύρου ἀντερύσασθαι
ἄξιος ἐν χαλεπῇ Κύρνε διχοστασίῃ.
Theognis 77–78

A pistos man is worth his weight in gold and silver,
Kyrnos, in a difficult factional split [khalepē dikhostasiē].

§19. The ancient ideal of enduring loyalty and trust remains the (unstated) background against which the archaic poet, who is moralist and teacher both, attempts to deal with present realities. First and foremost is the problem of knowing. Counterfeit (kibdēlos) gold and silver are easy to discern (and the loss is easy to bear), but the false (psudros) noos and deceitful heart (dolion ētor) of a philos is the most counterfeit of all, and the most painful to discover (119–124). Nothing is more difficult to know than a kibdēlos man, nor more important (117–118). It is difficult for an ekhthros to deceive (verb exapataō) his foe, but 'It is easy, Kyrnos, for a philos to deceive [exapataō] a **philos'** (1219–1220). An enemy is like rocks that stick up from the sea, easy to avoid: 'It is my **philoi** who betray me' (575–576). A man is fortunate if he dies before having to 'test [verb **exetazō**] what **noos** his **philoi** have' (1013–1016).

§20. It is only by experience that we know who are loyal friends and who are not:

οὐδὲ γὰρ εἰδείης ἀνδρὸς <u>νόον</u> οὔτε γυναικός,
  πρὶν πειρηθείης ὥσπερ ὑποζυγίου,
οὐδέ κεν εἰκάσσαις ὥσπερ ποτ᾽ ἐς ὥριον ἐλθών·
  πολλάκι γὰρ <u>γνώμην</u> ἐξαπατῶσ᾽ <u>ἰδέαι</u>.
Theognis 125–128 Young

For you would not know the **noos** of a man or a woman
until you try it as you would a yoked animal;
nor would you make a guess as you do sometimes when you go in
  among crops in season.
For *outward appearances* [**ideai**] often deceive [verb **exapataō**] the *ability to know* [**gnomē**].

The trustworthy friend knows that when he is tested against the **basanos** 'touchstone', he is found true (417–418 = 1164g–h; 447–452), but because intent is hidden within, sure knowledge comes only with result:

οὔτοί κ᾽ εἰδείης οὔτ᾽ εὔνουν οὔτε τὸν ἐχθρόν,
  εἰ μὴ <u>σπουδαίου πρήγματος</u> ἀντιτύχοις.
Theognis 641–642

In truth you would not know a man who has a friendly **noos** [= one who is **eunoos**] nor an **ekhthros**
unless you encounter him in *a matter of importance* [**spoudaion prēgma**].

<u>δόξα</u> μὲν ἀνθρώποισι <u>κακὸν</u> μέγα, <u>πεῖρα</u> δ᾽ ἄριστον·
  πολλοὶ <u>ἀπείρητοι</u> <u>δόξαν</u> ἔχουσ᾽ <u>ἀγαθῶν</u>.
Theognis 571–572 = 1104a–b

Reputation [**doxa**] is a great **kakon** for men; *trial* [**peira**] is best.
Many men who are *untried* [**apeirētoi**] have the **doxa** of **agathoi**.

§21. Friends deceive friends with words. Theognis complains that he has given Kyrnos immortal fame (**kleos aphthiton**),

... αὐτὰρ ἐγὼν ὀλίγης παρὰ σεῦ οὐ τυγχάνω αἰδοῦς,
  ἀλλ᾽ ὥσπερ μικρὸν παῖδα λόγοις μ᾽ ἀπατᾷς.
Theognis 253–254

... but I do not get even a little loyalty [aidōs] from you;
rather you deceive [verb apataō] me with words [logoi] as if I were
some small boy.

The poet prays to Zeus to destroy the man who

... τὸν ἑταῖρον
μαλθακὰ κωτίλλων ἐξαπατᾶν ἐθέλει.
Theognis 851–852

... wants to deceive [verb exapataō] his hetairos, beguiling him with
soft words.

Theognis tells Kyrnos that if Kyrnos loves (verb phileō) him and if
his noos is pistos 'trustworthy', he should not love him with words
(epea), with a noos and phrenes that are intentioned otherwise, for

... ὃς δὲ μιῇ γλώσσῃ δίχ᾽ ἔχει νόον, οὗτος ἑταῖρος
δειλὸς Κύρν᾽· ἐχθρὸς βέλτερος ἢ φίλος ὤν.
Theognis 91–92; cf. 1082c–f[1]

He who with one tongue has his noos going two ways,
that man is a terrible hetairos, Kyrnos. He is better an ekhthros than a
philos.

§22. The way to know beforehand who is a true friend and who is
false is to know a man's character and the workings of his mind—for
faithfulness is a matter of character. A betraying friend is one

... ἦθος ἔχων δόλιον, πίστεος ἀντίτυπον.
Theognis 1244

... who has a character [ēthos] that is deceitful [dolion] and the opposite
of pistis.

The poet tells a friend who has 'cheated [verb kleptō] our friendship
[philiē]' to associate with other men 'who know your noos better
than I' (595–600). A deceitful friend who praises you to your face
and slanders you behind your back, saying good things with his
tongue and thinking quite different things in his phrenes, is not a
good (esthlos) hetairos philos:

---

§21n1. Cf. vv. 399–400, where the poet advises to be loyal (aideomai) to philoi
and to 'flee man-destroying oaths'. On the close and constant connection between
philos and aidōs in Homer, see Benveniste 1973.277–278, who shows that aidōs represents the same notion of relational fidelity to the group. See also Theognis 607–610,
1083–1084, 1238a–1240.

ἀλλ' εἴη τοιοῦτος ἐμοὶ φίλος, ὃς τὸν ἑταῖρον
γινώσκων ὀργὴν καὶ βαρὺν ὄντα φέρει
ἀντὶ κασιγνήτου. σὺ δέ μοι φίλε ταῦτ' ἐνὶ θυμῷ
φράζεο, καί ποτέ μου μνήσεαι ἐξοπίσω.
Theognis 97–100; cf. 1164a–d

But may my **philos** be such a man, being aware of
the temperament of his **hetairos** and bearing with him, even when he is
troublesome,
as if he were his brother. You, my **philos**! Give thought
to these things in your **thūmos** and, at some time in the future, you will
remember me.

μήποτ' ἐπαινήσῃς, πρὶν ἂν εἰδῇς ἄνδρα σαφηνέως,
ὀργὴν καὶ ῥυθμὸν καὶ τρόπον ὅστις ἂν ᾖ.
πολλοί τοι κίβδηλον ἐπίκλοπον ἦθος ἔχοντες
κρύπτουσ', ἐνθέμενοι θυμὸν ἐφημέριον·
τούτων δ' ἐκφαίνει πάντως χρόνος ἦθος ἑκάστου.
καὶ γὰρ ἐγὼν γνώμης πολλὸν ἄρ' ἐκτὸς ἔβην·
ἔφθην αἰνήσας πρὶν σοῦ κατὰ πάντα δαῆναι
ἤθεα· νῦν δ' ἤδη νηῦς ἅθ' ἑκὰς διέχω.
Theognis 963–970

Do not praise a man before you know him clearly,
that is, his character [**orgē**], habits, and personality.
Many men, having a false [**kibdēlon**] and thievish [**epiklopon**] **ēthos**,
hide it, taking on their everyday **thūmos** within themselves.
Time reveals the character [**ēthos**] of each one of all these men.
And even I went far astray in my judgment [**gnōmē**], since
I acted too soon in praising you before I completely
knew your character [**ēthea**], but now already I am a ship keeping my
distance.

As has been noted, the aristocratic obsession with the loyalty of
friends is not confined to Theognis. Consider, for example, these
verses from the Attic Skolia:

εἴθ' ἐξῆν ὁποῖός τις ἦν ἕκαστος
τὸ στῆθος διελόντ', ἔπειτα τὸν νοῦν
ἐσιδόντα, κλείσαντα πάλιν,
ἄνδρα φίλον νομίζειν ἀδόλῳ φρενί.
Carmina Convivialia fr. 889 Page

Would that it were possible to open up each man's chest
just as he really was, and look at his **noos**
and close it up again, and think he was a **philos** man with
undeceitful [= without **dolos**] **phrēn**.

ὅστις ἄνδρα φίλον μὴ προδίδωσιν, μεγάλην ἔχει
τιμὴν ἔν τε βροτοῖς ἔν τε θεοῖσιν κατ' ἐμὸν νόον.
Carmina Convivialia fr. 908 Page (cf. 892, 903)

Whoever does not betray [verb **prodidōmi**] a **philos** man has great
tīmē among both mortals and the gods, according to my **noos**.

§23. An insoluble moral problem has been revealed. Friends betray
friends. They do this, not openly (like **ekhthroi**), but by deceit—the
detection of which depends on knowledge of a man's mind and
character. Since this is effectively impossible, betrayal is discovered
only by trial, which means discovery after betrayal. There is no solution to this problem. The cautious man can take certain steps that will
avoid some of the dangers of false friendship. One should never be a
friend (verb **phileō**) to a **kakos** man, for there is no advantage in
having a base (**deilos**) man as a **philos**:

οὔτ' ἄν σ' ἐκ χαλεποῖο πόνου ῥύσαιτο καὶ ἄτης,
οὔτέ κεν ἐσθλὸν ἔχων τοῦ μεταδοῦν ἐθέλοι.
Theognis 103–104

He would not save you from sore trouble and from ruin,
nor be willing to share anything good if he has it.

μήποτε τὸν κακὸν ἄνδρα φίλον ποιεῖσθαι ἑταῖρον,
ἀλλ' αἰεὶ φεύγειν ὥστε κακὸν λιμένα.
Theognis 113–114

Never make a **kakos** man a **philos hetairos**,
but always flee him like a bad harbor.[1]

This advice is of the same nature as the recurring didactic topos
which advises to avoid the **kakoi** and to associate only with **agathoi**.[2]
By shunning contact with **kakoi/deiloi** (social and moral inferiors)
who are, by nature, incapable of the refined ethical behavior of **agathoi**, the aristocrat is at least able to escape the most obvious source
of bad effects from perverted friendships. So, too, if a man takes care
not to betray or to deceive his friends (B 1, C 3, above, §5) and is
on guard against false friends (A 1, B 2, above), the potential for
damage is diminished. These are, nevertheless, puny defensive measures, and they run up against the primary stumbling block of the impossibility of knowledge beforehand (C 2, above).

---

§23n1. See B 5 (above, §5); also 105–112, 1151–1152, 1169–1170, 1377–1380.
§23n2. Cf. 29–38, 563–566, 792, 1165–1168.

§ 24. The only sure way to avoid betrayal is to be a **philos** to no one or to very few:

μηδένα τῶνδε φίλον ποιεῦ Πολυπαΐδη ἀστῶν
ἐκ θυμοῦ χρείης οὕνεκα μηδεμιῆς.
Theognis 61–62

Do not make any one of these citizens your **philos**, son of Polypaos,
in your **thūmos**—no matter what the need may be.

παύροισιν πίσυνος μεγάλ᾽ ἀνδράσιν ἔργ᾽ ἐπιχείρει,
μή ποτ᾽ ἀνήκεστον Κύρνε λάβῃς ἀνίην.
Theognis 75–76

Be trustful [**pisunos**] toward few men when you attempt great deeds
[**megala erga**],
so that you, Kyrnos, may never receive an incurable hurt.

ἀστῶν μηδενὶ πιστὸς ἐὼν πόδα τῶνδε πρόβαινε,
μηθ᾽ ὅρκῳ πίσυνος μήτε φιλημοσύνῃ,
μηδ᾽ εἰ Ζῆν᾽ ἐθέλῃ παρέχειν βασιλῆα μέγιστον
ἔγγυον ἀθανάτων πιστὰ τιθεῖν ἐθέλων.
Theognis 283–286

Take not one step, trustful [**pistos**], on behalf of these citizens,
and do not be trustful [**pisunos**] of their oaths or their claims to be your
philoi.
Not even if they want to offer Zeus, great king of the gods,
as their guarantor when they offer you surety [**pista**].

§ 25. In fact, one should be a duplicitous friend to friends:

ἀλλὰ δόκει μὲν πᾶσιν ἀπὸ γλώσσης φίλος εἶναι,
χρῆμα δὲ συμμείξῃς μηδενὶ μηδ᾽ ὁτιοῦν
σπουδαῖον.
Theognis 63–65

But seem to be a **philos** to all with your tongue,
but do not associate with anyone in any matter of importance
[**khrēma spoudaion**] at all.

θυμέ, φίλους κατὰ πάντας ἐπίστρεφε ποικίλον ἦθος,
ὀργὴν συμμίσγων ἥντιν᾽ ἕκαστος ἔχει.
πουλύπου ὀργὴν ἴσχε πολυπλόκου, ὃς ποτὶ πέτρῃ,
τῇ προσομιλήσῃ, τοῖος ἰδεῖν ἐφάνη.
νῦν μὲν τῇδ᾽ ἐφέπου, τοτὲ δ᾽ ἀλλοῖος χρόα γίνου.
κρέσσων τοι σοφίη γίνεται ἀτροπίης.
Theognis 213–218; cf. 1071–1074

My **thūmos**, keep turning and showing a new side of your versatile
    nature [**poikilon ēthos**] to all your **philoi**,
keep matching your temperament [**orgē**] to theirs.
Have the **orgē** of a complex octopus,
who always looks like whatever rock he has just clung to.
Now be like this; then, at another time, become someone else in your
    coloring.
Skill is stronger than resourcelessness.[1]

§26. But such an extreme negative attitude runs counter to the whole
ethic of archaic friendship. At this point it is necessary to return to an
earlier observation (see §15). Friendship is problematical in 'matters
of importance' or in misfortune (like poverty and exile), not in the
everyday sphere of sympotic fellowship. Thus, many men are **philoi**
when it comes to eating and drinking, but few in a 'matter of importance' (**spoudaion prēgma**: 115–116, 643–644). At public banquets
the wise man (**pepnūmenos**) acts with insouciance, but "outside" he
must be strong, seeking to know each man's **orgē** 'temperament'
(309–312). As for verses 979–982, I propose the following interpretation. A man should not be a **philos** in tongue only but in
deed (**ergon**) also; he must express his care (verb **speudō**; cf. the
adjective **spoudaio-** 'important') with hands and possessions (**khrēmata**) both:

μηδὲ παρὰ κρητῆρι λόγοισιν ἐμὴν φρένα θέλγοι,
    ἀλλ' ἔρδων φαίνοιτ' εἴ τι δύναιτ' ἀγαθόν.
Theognis 981–982

Do not let him charm my **phrēn** with words [**logoi**] beside the mixing
    bowl,
but let him reveal himself as an **agathon** thing when he acts [verb **erdō**],
    if he can do anything.

§27. When **philoi hetairoi** associate over their cups, deception and
duplicity are relatively harmless, regulated by the narrow confines of
the sympotic occasion. In 'matters of importance', those that have to
do with the wider society, with the life of the citizen in the **polis** (the
sphere that includes the ups and downs of prosperity, status, and
factions), the game is much more serious. Nevertheless, the inside
world of the symposium and the outside world of the **polis** appear as
parallel. As Daniel Levine argues, the sympotic setting is a model or
metaphor of the larger community, a symbol of the "city on a small

---

§25n1. See B 3, B 4 (above, §5): cf. also 313–314.

scale."[1] Association in everyday fellowship with **agathoi** constitutes an education for the aristocratic youth of the community. In sympotic gatherings such a youth learns not only the civic lessons appropriate to his social station (correct behavior with respect to men and the gods, moderation) but also how to recognize the **pistos** and the **apistos hetairos**. The formal/informal setting of the symposium, where 'wine shows the **noos** of a man' (500), and a drunken man is 'no longer master of tongue or **noos**' (480), is a laboratory for investigation of men's intentions. The symposium, like a miniature **agorā**, is an exchange of words, a kind of crucible where a man's character can be revealed or hidden.[2] The symposium—and the body of poetry itself, which is sung in symposia—coalesces as a formal metaphor for the **polis**.

§28. The symbol of the symposium is also active at another, higher level. As Levine shows (Ch.7§4), the often expressed "longing for **kharis** 'gratification', **terpsis** 'enjoyment', **euphrosunē** 'mirth', and **hēsukhiē** 'quietude' in the symposium reflects and parallels a longing for peace and stability in an equitable polity." The properly conducted symposium thus stands for a "Golden Age" of prosperity, peace, internal harmony, and good fellowship (cf. **euphrōn thūmos**, 765; **euphrosunōs**, 766; **euphrosunē**, 776). In the context of the symposium, Apollo is asked to 'make straight our tongue and **noos**' (760), that is, to reconcile the opposition between speech and intention.

§29. But the idealized milieu of the properly conducted feast, in which **philoi** associate in perfect harmony, has no counterpart in the **polis** outside, the real world of factional violence and betrayal, of **aphradiē** 'mindlessness' and **stasis lāophthoros** 'people-destroying civil conflict' (778–782). The symposium is a fairly congruent paideutic model of real-life stresses and tensions, but as a utopian (Levine) model, the kind of harmony desirable and attainable in such settings (effectively symbolized by the theme of moderation in drinking)[1] cannot be approximated in the **polis**, although the participants are the same **philoi**

---

§27n1. Levine Ch.7§24.

§27n2. Levine writes (§24): "The symposium is dangerous because it presents yet another way for a man to misrepresent himself. Just as the clever citizen must beware of cozening words in his daily political and social intercourse, so he must not relax his guard even in a symposium, where he takes his ease among an ostensibly integrated community of **philoi**."

§29n1. See Theognis 211–212, 467–496, 509–510, 837–840, 873–876. On moderation in general, see Levine Ch.7§§8–18.

hetairoi. **Thaliē** 'celebration' and **kōmos** 'revel' are not, after all, the **polis** writ small, because what happens at symposia, banquets, and feasts is carefully controlled by the rigidly prescribed rules of such gatherings in the first place; and, in the second place, if discord results, for example from too much wine, no great damage is done: the revelers simply go home to sleep it off (841–844, 503–508). As a descriptive and prescriptive analogue of the **polis**, the symposium is not perfectly satisfactory; moreover, it fails to cohere precisely at the crucial juncture between what ought to be and what is. The **polis** should be like a well-ordered symposium (cf. **eukosmōs**, 242), but it is not.

§ 30. It is clear, however, that the archaic poet is questing for a "key," for some universally valid symbol that will not only explain, but will also mediate, the bewildering real-life paradox that **philoi hetairoi**, traditionally (indeed, by definition) faithful and loyal, in fact act oppositely. So, too, the ambivalence inherent in Theognis' erotic relationship with Kyrnos is analogous to the political situation in Megara (or in any **polis**) in which **philoi** betray **philoi**. Kyrnos gives little loyalty (**aidōs**) to Theognis and deceives him with words (253–254). Verses 87–92 (cf. 1082c–1084), partially quoted above, § 21, which include the major themes of the problematical nature of friendship, apply perfectly to **philoi** as lovers or to **philoi** as political associates. For Nagy, Kyrnos (like Theognis) is a "generic" figure, who is "typical of the debased elite of Megara."[1]

§ 31. The tension between Theognis and Kyrnos, according to Nagy, stands for the relationship of teacher and lawgiver to the community and for the civic relationship between **philoi**. Yet the quarrel (**neikos**: 90, 1082f) between Theognis and Kyrnos "never becomes overt," as Nagy says. "The bond of being **philoi** that exists between Theognis and Kyrnos—as well as all Megara by extension—is never completely severed."[1] As an analogue of the political relationship between **philoi**, the theme of erotic love is, in some respects, a more forceful one than the symposium; it captures more forcefully the dominant opposition between tongue and mind, word and intent; and it expresses the fundamental soundness of the institution itself. Kyrnos is "debased," to be sure, but he is still the beloved. As an institution, **philiā** must continue to exist, for there is no alternative available to the archaic polity, nor one conceivable to the archaic mind.

---

§ 30n1. Nagy Ch.2 § § 42–43.
§ 31n1. Nagy Ch.2 § 44.

§32. Nevertheless, the real-world situation of betrayal and deception among **philoi** in the **polis** contains one element that is lacking in its poetic and symbolic counterparts—the **spoudaion prēgma** 'matter of importance'. The symbols of the **neikos** 'quarrel' of lovers and the **eris** 'strife' of banquets cannot support the weight of **stasis** 'social conflict' in the community, where the stakes are life, property, status, and the orderly existence of the **polis** itself. This can be expressed another way. The causes and results of conflict among **philoi hetairoi** at banquets and in bed are circumscribed by the forms themselves of these associations, which forms dictate the limits of poetic metaphor. But the causes and results of civic **stasis** are much more complex, for they relate not only to interactions between men but to the dynamics of a social order in flux. Intermarriage and alliances between **agathoi** and **kakoi** are represented as causing the ruin of the aristocratic class (183–196). This state of affairs is blamed in part on the notion that the **kakoi** have gained wealth (149–150, 321–322, 865–867, 1117–1118). Men who are regarded as socially inferior, the **kakoi**, now hold political power (53–60, 289–292, 679, 1109–1114).

§33. But, more than anything else, the desire for gain (**kerdos**) is blamed as the factor most responsible for the overturn of the traditional values held by the archaic aristocracy.[1] That, and the economic reversals suffered by some of the nobles (511–522, 525–526, 667–682, 1115–1116), placing them at a political disadvantage, are presented as the key elements in the erosion of trust among **philoi hetairoi**.

§34. Two passages from Theognis shed light on the social situation that is a background to the poet's despair about **philiā**. The first of these has already been presented in our volume [Theognis 39–52, Greek text quoted by Nagy Ch.2§27]:

> Kyrnos, this **polis** is pregnant, and I fear that it will give birth to a man
> who will be a straightener of our **kakē hubris**.
> The citizens here are still moderate [**sōphrones**], but the leaders
>   [**hēgemones**]
> have veered so much as to fall into depravity [= **kakotēs**].
> Never yet, Kyrnos, have **agathoi** men ruined any **polis**,

---

§33n1. See Theognis 50, 83–86, 197–202, 221–226, 227–232, 465–466, 523–524, 607–610, 833–836. Nagy (Ch.2§§42–43) conjectures that the name **Kurnos**, the generic debased aristocrat, means 'bastard' (hence, 'base', equivalent to **kakos**), and the name of his father, **Polupāos**, means 'he who has acquired much'.

but when the **kakoi** decide to behave with **hubris**,
and when they ruin the **dēmos** and render judgments [= **dikai**] in favor
of men [or things] without **dikē**,
for the sake of personal **kerdea** and for the sake of power [**kratos**],
do not expect that **polis** to be peaceful for long,
not even if it is now in a state of great serenity [**hēsukhiē**],
when these things become **phila** to **kakoi** men,
namely, gain [**kerdea**] entailing **kakon** for the **dēmos**.
For from these things arise discord [**staseis**], intestine killings,
and monarchs. May this **polis** never decide to adopt these things!

§35. The **hēgemones** are aristocratic leaders; Theognis calls them **kakoi**, significantly. The prediction of a 'straightener of our **hubris**', and the **kakotēs** into which the leaders have 'fallen', are most plausibly explained in terms of factional aristocratic disputes and aristocratic highhandedness. In behaving with **hubris** they commit the two political crimes most frequently alleged in the archaic age—'to destroy the **dēmos**' and 'render judgments with injustice'. These crimes are caused by the archaic age's (all ages') most common sin, the seeking of profit and power. The consequences to the still peaceful **polis** of a further, greater degree of greed (which goes together with loss to the **dēmos**), is the familiar archaic catalogue of public disasters: factional quarrels, murders committed against men of the same kinship group, and the emergence of one faction as supreme.

§36. This is a 'matter of importance' (**spoudaion prēgma**), indeed. In the narrow, closely knit upper class of Megara, these **agathoi**—demoted to **kakoi** because of their moral shortcomings—constitute the small pool from which the poet's **philoi hetairoi** are drawn. The social situation lamented by the poet, namely factional discord and the inevitable internecine killing that attends it, are what turn **philoi** into **ekhthroi** and force friends to betray friends.

§37. We come, then, to the second of the two passages that shed light on the social situation. This passage too has already been presented, earlier on in our volume [Theognis 667–682, Greek text quoted by Nagy Ch.2§1]:

If I had my possessions [**khrēmata**], Simonides,
I would not be distressed as I am now while I am together with the **agathoi**.
But now they [my **khrēmata**] have passed me by, despite my awareness,
and I am speechless
from lack of **khrēmata**, though I would be better aware than many,

[aware] that we are now being carried along, with white sails lowered,
beyond the seas of Melos, through the dark night.
And they are unwilling to bail, and the sea washes over
both sides of the ship. It is a difficult thing for anyone
to be saved, such things they are doing. They have deposed the
    esthlos helmsman
who was skillfully standing guard.
They seize **khrēmata** by force [**biē**], and order [**kosmos**] has been
    destroyed.
The division is no longer an equitable division, in the common
    interest,
but the carriers of merchandise rule, and the **kakoi** are above
    the **agathoi**.
I am afraid that perhaps a wave will swallow the ship.
Let these things be allusive utterances hidden by me for the **agathoi**.
One could be aware of even future **kakon**, if one is **sophos**.

§38. In this passage, anguished by the loss of his possessions, the poet complains again of **stasis** in the **polis**. On this occasion the 'carriers of merchandise are ruling', and the '**kakoi** are on top of the **agathoi**'. This is another example of a 'matter of importance' (**spoudaion prēgma**): the greed of those in power has destroyed order (**kosmos**) in the **polis** and threatens it with ruin. The deposing of the 'noble helmsman' (675–676), the seizing of property by force, which results in unequal distribution of wealth, and the eversion of the usual pattern of rule in the archaic **polis** suggest that the Theognidean aristocracy has relinquished political and economic power to a group below them. In any case, the reversal of traditional ordered stability, dramatically illustrated by the loss of the poet's **khrēmata**, is another instance of the debasement of the **agathoi**. The Ship of State metaphor, in which the ship is engulfed by a sudden storm, is an appropriate symbol of the sudden mutability of fortune in an age of rapid social change, economic and political:

> ... καὶ ἐκ κακοῦ ἐσθλὸν ἔγεντο
> καὶ κακὸν ἐξ ἀγαθοῦ· καί τε πενιχρὸς ἀνὴρ
> αἶψα μάλ᾽ ἐπλούτησε, καὶ ὃς μάλα πολλὰ πέπαται
> ἐξαπίνης ἀπὸ πάντ᾽ οὖν ὤλεσε νυκτὶ μιῇ·
> καὶ σώφρων ἥμαρτε, καὶ ἄφρονι πολλάκι δόξα
> ἕσπετο, καὶ τιμῆς καὶ κακὸς ὢν ἔλαχεν.
>   Theognis 661–666

> ... Even from **kakon**, **esthlon** can come;
> and **kakon** from **esthlon**. Even a poor man
> has quite quickly become rich; and he who has acquired many things
> suddenly loses everything in a night.

As the **sōphrōn** goes astray, so too fame often comes to the one without
phrenes,
and the one who is **kakos** nonetheless comes into possession of honor
[**tīmē**].

§39. According to Nagy, in the Theognidea, "the poet is speaking to
an ostensibly integral community of **philoi** that is the **polis** of Megara."[1] Still, just as **kakoi** become **agathoi** and **agathoi** are debased to
kakoi, through circumstances and moral error, so also the same
circumstances—especially the insatiable quest for **kerdos** 'profit'—
cause **philoi** to betray each other:

πίστει χρήματ᾽ ὄλεσσα, ἀπιστίῃ δ᾽ ἐσάωσα·
γνώμη δ᾽ ἀργαλέη γίνεται ἀμφοτέρων.
πάντα τάδ᾽ ἐν κοράκεσσι καὶ ἐν φθόρῳ· οὐδέ τις ἥμιν
αἴτιος ἀθανάτων Κύρνε θεῶν μακάρων,
ἀλλ᾽ ἀνδρῶν τε βίη καὶ κέρδεα δειλὰ καὶ ὕβρις
πολλῶν ἐξ ἀγαθῶν ἐς κακότητ᾽ ἔβαλεν.
                            Theognis 831–836

Because of my good faith [**pistis**], I lost my possessions [**khrēmata**], and
    I got them back through lack of good faith [**apistiē**].
The knowledge [**gnōme**] of both is bitter.[2]
Everything here has gone to the ravens and perdition. And
not one of the immortal and blessed gods is responsible to us for this,
    Kyrnos,
but the violence [**biē**] of men and their base gains [**kerdea**] and their
    hubris
have plummeted them from much nobility [**agatha**] into debasement
    [**kakotēs**].

[Theognis 649–652, Greek text quoted by Nagy Ch.2§70]:

Ah, wretched Poverty! Why do you weigh upon my shoulders
and debase both my body and my **noos**?
Forcibly and against my will, you teach me many shameful things [**aiskhra**],
    though I am one among men who understands what are **esthla** and beau-
tiful [**kala**].[3]

---

§39n1. Nagy Ch.2§5.
§39n2. *Editors' note:* The collocation here of gnōmē 'knowledge', derivative of
gīnōskō, with the theme of loss and recovery of possessions [khrēmata], reinforces the
interpretation offered by Nagy (Ch.2§4) of gīnōskō at Theognis 669/670/682.
§39n3. See Theognis 226, where doloplokiai apistoi 'faithless weavings of wiles'
are equated with kakokerdeiai 'base deeds of kerdos'. Cf. also 595–602, where a

§40. Since the perversion of the traditional bonds of friendship is blamed by Theognidean poetry on social and economic circumstances that are portrayed as irresistible and that cause, by their very nature, infidelity and betrayal, the integrated community of **philoi** becomes more and more of an impossiblity.

§41. If we return to Theognis' gnomic summary with which my analysis began (vv. 1135–1142, above, §9), this point becomes clear. All the benign forces and effects that are conducive to harmony, order, and loyalty in the community of **philoi**—whether it is represented as the fellowship of the symposium, the association of lovers, or the **polis** itself—are enumerated, and their departure from earth is lamented. The things that have forced the absence of these integrative, harmonizing powers are clearly stated. They are quite familiar to us by now: deceptive speech, injustice, impiety, greed, and the formation of dishonorable alliances (**aiskhra sumbola**: 1147–1150). A similar catalogue is found in a passage that is both overtly political and also fixes the blame on the **kakoi**, who have 'become leaders with their outrageous laws [**ektrapeloi nomoi**]': in this state of affairs loyalty and respect (**aidōs**) have perished, and their opposites, shameless disregard (**anaideiē**) and **hubris**, have conquered **dikē** and now rule over the land (289–292).

§42. Only the 'good goddess Hope' is left; and in Hope alone, to whom men should sacrifice 'first and last', lies the possibility of the return of **Pistis, Sōphrosunē**, the Kharites, oaths that are trustworthy and just [**horkoi pistoi dikaioi**], norms [**themistes**], and observances of piety [**eusebiai**]: a slender solace, but the only one available to mankind now (Theognis 1135–1150). The reciprocal trust that binds **philoi**, '**Pistis**, the great goddess', has been erased by historical circumstances that have forced a radical reshaping of the institution of friendship. But because the ancient institution of friendship is the only instrument of societal integration possible (or imaginable) in the archaic polity, the poet (teacher/lawgiver/tradition) clings to it and manipulates its symbolism in an effort to mediate the contradictions of a disintegrating social order in which the very dynamic that holds the society together and gives it stability is the dynamic that is destroying it.

---

philos hetairos has become **ekhthros** and **apistos** because he has 'acted like a thief in our friendship': now he is a cold and shifty (**poikilos**) snake. At the beginning of the passage the poet complains that there is '**koros** of everything except wealth [**ploutos**]' (596).

§43. The hope for the restoration of the **pistos philos hetairos** is a psychological necessity—not only because in reality **philiā** is the sole historical mechanism of social unity, but also because archaic poetic diction possessed no other means of expressing the notion of the integrative community. The poetic expression that presents the positive (but not tensionless) visions of the harmonious symposium and the lover (unfaithful, but still beloved) as symbols of the **polis** presupposes a fundamental reliance on the **pistos philos hetairos** as an eternally enduring institution. If these models seem to fail ultimately, it is because the poet recognizes (but cannot reconcile) powerful new social forces that threaten to invalidate, make obsolete, that basic presupposition.

Appendix
Language, Meter, and Sense in Theognis
(The Role of **agathos** 'noble, good')

Nathan A. Greenberg

§1. No apology is needed for examining the adjective **agathos** 'noble, good' in archaic Greek elegy, especially in view of what Theognis himself affirms about the values encoded in his elegiac poetry: he learned these values, the poet says, when he was still a boy, from the **agathoi** 'noble' (Theognis 28). My examination of **agathos** will be of a preliminary sort, since my major interest here is not so much in the word's meaning as in its deployment in the poetry of Theognis and the other elegiac poets, notably Archilochus, Callinus, Mimnermus, Solon, Tyrtaeus, and Xenophanes.[1] It is quite a common word in extant elegy, occurring on the average once in about sixteen verses. This frequency should be compared with that in Homer, once in about 190 verses. Such a datum is significant in itself and is a gross indication of the sharp differences between archaic elegy and, say, Homeric epos. In this connection, I adduce the thesis of Pietro Giannini that there are formulaic expressions not only in the hexameter lines of the elegiac couplet (which is taken for granted) but in the pentameter line as well.[2] Giannini's method is clear, and the claims for it modestly put,[3] but his inquiry also raises serious matters of discussion that will be taken up here in due course.

§2. Giannini's method consists largely of searching for repeated pairs of words in the hemistichs, either first or second, of the pentameter

---

§1n1. The citations are from the edition of M. L. West. For the technical terms used in this chapter, see the Introduction, §§8–9.

§1n2. Giannini 1973 uses the phrase "espressioni formulari" in his title. Other phrases are "la fraseologia epica" (p.7) and "schematizzazioni espressive" (p.9). It is stated (p.9) that the "elemento formulare" is found with greater frequency in the hexameter line of the elegiac couplet.

§1n3. Giannini claims to put forward mainly a collection of data, "una presentazione dei fenomeni."

lines in the extant elegiac corpus. Consider his first three lists of citations under the entry **agathos**.¹

Collocations of **agathos** 'noble' and **kakos** 'base':

*καὶ κακὸς ἐξ ἀγαθοῦ	Theognis 190²
οὐ κακὸς ἀλλ᾽ ἀγαθός	Theognis 212
τὸν κακὸν ἄνδρ᾽ ἀγαθόν	Theognis 438
οὐ κακόν, ἀλλ᾽ ἀγαθός	Theognis 510³
*καὶ κακὸν ἐξ ἀγαθοῦ	Theognis 662
καὶ κακὸς ἄνδρ᾽ ἀγαθόν	Theognis 972

Collocations of **agathos** 'noble' and **anēr** 'man':

*οὐ γὰρ ἀνὴρ ἀγαθός	Tyrtaeus 9.10
*οὗτος ἀνὴρ ἀγαθός	Tyrtaeus 9.20
*πᾶς δέ τ᾽ ἀνὴρ ἀγαθός	Theognis 148
αὐτὸς ἀνὴρ ἀγαθός	Theognis 930

Collocations of **agathos** preceded by forms of **ekhō** 'have' in iambic metrical shape (˘ —):⁴

δόξαν ἔχειν ἀγαθὴν	Solon 1.4
αἰὲν ἔχειν ἀγαθόν	Xenophanes 1.24
δόξαν ἔχουσ᾽ ἀγαθῶν	Theognis 572
*γλῶσσαν ἔχων ἀγαθὴν	Theognis 714
δόξαν ἔχουσ᾽ ἀγαθοί	Theognis 1104b

§3. Lists like these may appear impressive, but they can also be deceptive. As everyone knows, concordances give a warped view of a poet's style. But this aside, the major question is what is demonstrated, supported, or suggested by such lists. Giannini speaks, as noted above, of epic phraseology and formulaic expressions; but this is vague, perhaps purposely so, for he is quite aware that elegiac verse is not formulaic in the way that the verse of Homer is.¹ Real-

---

§2n1. Giannini pp.13–18.

§2n2. The asterisk is used to indicate citations of the first hemistich of the pentameter line.

§2n3. Note, however, the reading in West's text: ἀλλ᾽ ἀγαθόν.

§2n4. Giannini omits Theognis 112 but includes it later (p.47) in the listing under **mnēma**. Giannini's remaining lists for **agathos** (pp.15–16) are more questionable and are omitted here from consideration. They consist of instances of **agathos** preceded by a preposition or a monosyllabic conjunction, of **agathos** preceded by an attribute at the beginning of the hemistich (two instances), and of **agathos** preceded by an article at the beginning of the hemistich (two instances).

§3n1. Giannini recognizes (p.71) that formulaic economy is lacking in elegy, that is, that the elegiac poets do not always say the same things with the same words.

izing that one cannot utilize Parry's principle of economy, he falls
back upon the frailer support of repetition,[2] and not even verbatim
repetition, but repetition with modification.[3] Yet repetition in and of
itself is insufficient. It must be shown that repetition is significant.

§4. My point is a simple one. The words **agathos** 'noble', **kakos**
'base', **aner** 'man', and **ekhō** 'have' are so common in the elegiac
corpus that it is no surprise to find them occasionally in collocation.
Almost ninety of the nearly 1400 verses in Theognis contain a form
of **agathos**, and forms of **kakos** occur about 120 times. If the words
were randomly scattered through the text (which is, of course, not
the case), we should expect to find about eight lines in which both
words occur.[1] There is, however, a very palpable semantic link, and
we find in fact that there are twenty-nine such verses. Thirteen of
these collocations occur in the hexameter line of the elegiac couplet.
Of the sixteen instances in the pentameter, nine have the words in
separate hemistichs. Giannini has cited the remaining six, which I
have listed above, and noted the seventh (Theognis 172) as an
exception (because **agathos** precedes **kakos**).[2] Finally, only five of
these seven occur in the final hemistich. In sum, collocations of the
words are too generally distributed for their occurrence to be meaningful. Most noteworthy, however, are the sixty lines where **agathos**
occurs without **kakos** and the ninety lines where the reverse is true.

§5. There are thirty occurrences in Theognis of the nominative singular of **aner**. Four of these are in lines containing a form of **agathos**,
but twenty-six are not,[1] and two of the remainder do not appear in
the same hemistich.

This is a paraphrase of the famous definition of Parry 1971.13: "The formula can be
defined as an expression regularly used, under the same metrical conditions, to express
an essential idea."

§3n2. Giannini p.10, if I understand him correctly, says that repetition guarantees the formulaic character of an expression. "Il criterio di individuazione delle espressioni e la ripetizione, che garantisce una loro autonomia di carattere formulare." This
seems to confuse a necessary criterion with a sufficient one.

§3n3. Giannini p.11 refers briefly to the complicated topics of "formula types"
and "structural formulae."

§4n1. The calculation for this simple approach: given 1400 verses in Theognis,
the expected number of verses containing both words is

$$90/1400 \times 120/1400 \times 1400 = 7.7$$

§4n2. It is noteworthy that **kakos** precedes in six of the seven cases. I discuss
this below.

§5n1. The four cases include the two cited by Giannini as well as Theognis 319
(a hexameter line) and 662, where the words occur in separate halves of the verse.

§6. Forms of the word **ekhō** occur more than 120 times. If we restrict ourselves to forms of the iambic (◡ —) metrical shape, that number is reduced to about seventy.[1] If again we were to assume that **ekhō** is randomly distributed (once again a dubious assumption), we should expect to find about four lines containing both words. In fact there are five.[2] There are over sixty lines with **ekhō** where this is not the case, and more than eighty with **agathos**.

§7. Do the above findings indicate that the collocations cited by Giannini are not formulaic? Much of the answer depends on what is meant by "formulaic"—a thorny matter, as all students of Homer know. As it happens, the word **agathos** figures in one expression that has been considered formulaic by almost any criterion. The word in the nominative singular occurs forty-eight times in the *Iliad* and ten times in the *Odyssey*. In thirty-five of the cases in the *Iliad* and eight in the *Odyssey*, it occurs in the ornamental epithet

βοὴν ἀγαθὸς Μενέλαος / Διομήδης

Menelaos / Diomedes, good at the war-cry.

Similarly, the word **boēn** 'at the war-cry' appears in the phrase forty-six times out of a total of fifty appearances in the epics.[1] It should be clear that this phrase will weather unscathed the sort of statistical attack launched above on the elegiac collocations.

§8. While there are other features of the Homeric phrase which we have come to think of as formulaic, for example, its fixed position within the line and the association with a proper name,[1] I am particu-

---

Note that the form **agathos** (nominative singular masculine) occurs only five times in Theognis. Two of these five are associated with **anēr**. There is a methodological difficulty in deciding whether to limit consideration to single forms of a paradigm. Note, for example, that two of the six citations for **kakos/agathos** contain the word **andr'**.

§6n1. It would be possible to increase the number to about 110 by using elided particles to establish position, but none of Giannini's citations contains this device.

§6n2. The five cases include the three cited by Giannini as well as Theognis 525 (a hexameter verse) and Theognis 614 (where the words are in separate hemistichs).

§7n1. Some complication in the figures is due to the fact that the fixed phrase occurs five times with **agathos** and the proper name in the accusative. The inexact term "formula" is problematic, and I shall henceforth tend to avoid using it. See the good discussion of the formula in Edwards 1971.40–73.

§8n1. Parry 1971.93 placed this phrase among the group of "generic epithets" because they are applied to more than one hero in Homer. Note also, as does Parry

larly interested here in the fact that the words **agathos** and especially **boēn** occur far more often together than separately. This is simply not the case so far as these citations from elegy are concerned.[2]

§9. Parry's view was that once such a fixed combination as **boēn agathos Menelãos** 'Menelaos, good at the war-cry' has evolved, the poet or singer uses the expression as a convenient mnemonic device for filling out the verse.[1] The theory held that little attention is paid to the meaning of the constituent words of the expression or to the expression as a whole, and thus we have an explanation for the use of such expressions in allegedly unsuitable environments, or for various metrical irregularities (where they are carelessly or hurriedly inserted into the verse). While this reasoning remains generally persuasive, there are occasions, as argued by the critics,[2] where the ornamental element is responsive to the immediate context. With the forty-one times that the phrase is used to fill out the last half of the verse as a basis for comparison, I shall inspect the five variant instances in the *Iliad* where **agathos** occupies the same metrical position in the line. It is at least arguable that some of these variants are responsive to the context.

§10. πολλάκι γάρ οἱ ἔειπε γέρων ἀγαθὸς Πολύιδος
    Iliad xiii 666

    since many times the **agathos** old man Polyidos had told him

Is it justified to assume that Polyidos is pointedly not **boēn agathos** 'good at the war-cry'? The word **gerōn** 'old man' replaces **boēn** neatly. Consider the other four instances:

    Θρηίκιοι· τὸν δέ σφιν ἄνακτ' ἀγαθὸς Διομήδης
    Iliad x 559

    [these horses come] from Thrace, and **agathos** Diomedes killed their
    master

---

pp.93–94, that Menelaos and Diomedes do not share the adjectives **xanthos** 'blond' and **krateros** 'powerful', but these in turn are shared with other heroes.

§8n2. See §5n1 above, where I cite the fact that the form **agathos** occurs only five times in Theognis. Two of the five occur with **anēr**. That is coming close to my notion of a fixed phrase.

§9n1. Hainsworth 1968.35n3 says correctly that the Homeric formula is not the same thing as a cliché. Lord too protests (1960.4) that "the formulas are not the ossified clichés which they have the reputation of being."

§9n2. Whallon 1969.1–70; Austin 1975.11–80.

οὓς ἑτάρους ὀλέκοντα βοὴν ἀγαθὸς βάλεν Αἴας
Iliad xv 249

boēn agathos Ajax struck [me] as I slaughtered his companions

Ἕκτωρ δὴ παρὰ νηυσὶ βοὴν ἀγαθὸς πολεμίζει
Iliad xiii 123

for **boēn agathos** Hektor is fighting beside our ships

Ἀτρεΐδαι; ἐπεὶ ὅς τις ἀνὴρ ἀγαθὸς καὶ ἐχέφρων . . .
Iliad ix 341

[do only] the sons of Atreus [love their wives]? Since any man who is **agathos** and careful . . .

These four verses are all interesting cases of varying the traditional phrase. In *Iliad* x 559, **anakt'** 'king' replaces **boēn** 'at the war-cry', but syntactically more is happening, since **anakt'** is the direct object of a verb to come in the next line. In *Iliad* xv 249, the second citation, Ajax gets the epithet for the only time in the epic, along with the verb **balen** 'struck'. So too in *Iliad* xiii 123, Hector in detached position receives the epithet. The most interesting is the last, *Iliad* ix 341, where little if anything remains of the phrase unless one is willing to believe that Achilles has deliberately challenged the social ideal underlying the phrase with the new collocation **anēr agathos** 'a man who is noble', a collocation unique in the *Iliad* but one seen several times in elegy.

§11. Since a slight variation of the phrase also occurs with **agathos** and the proper name in the accusative singular (four times in the *Iliad* and once in the *Odyssey*), there is some basis for inspecting cases of **agathon**, that is, **agathos** 'noble, good' in the masculine accusative, when they occur in the same metrical position:

Πάμμονα τ' Ἀντίφονόν τε βοὴν ἀγαθόν τε Πολίτην . . .
Iliad xxiv 250

Pammon and Antiphonos, and **boēn agathos** Polites . . .

Ἕκτορα δ' ἐφράσσαντο βοὴν ἀγαθὸν καὶ ἑταίρους
Iliad xv 671

they noticed **boēn agathos** Hektor and his companions

σὺν κεινῇσιν νηυσί, λιπὼν ἀγαθὸν Μενέλαον
Iliad iv 181

with ships empty, leaving behind **agathos** Menelaos

The above three citations continue to illustrate ways of varying the phrase. In *Iliad* xxiv 250, Polites is honored by the epithet, and a detached Hector is once again so described in *Iliad* xv 671. The word **lipōn** 'leaving' replaces **boēn** in *Iliad* iv 181, and this may be a pointed substitution, given the context of Agamemnon's anticipating the future boasting of a Trojan over the corpse of Menelaos.

§12. It seems reasonable to suppose that in all of the above cases, the fixed or standardized phrase was somehow resident in the poet's mind and in the minds of the hearers. It is noteworthy that such fixed phrases tend to come at the end of the Homeric line, as though the poet, having once launched himself into the line, is in some fashion compelled by his medium to use the unique expression that fills out the line. Speculation of this sort appears to have been an important part of the impressive intuitive leap that engendered Parry's formulaic theory. A great deal has been written on the subject, and it cannot be reviewed here.[1] I note only that there continue to be problems in extending the idea of the formula to other aspects of Homeric poetry.[2] The conclusion to be drawn appears to be that, while uniformities are certainly noticeable, the idea of compulsion is an inference that goes too far. The poet is not compelled to use such fixed phrases. He is able to vary them at will, play changes upon them, or omit them altogether. He may often seem to use them as metrical "fillers," but not always. Rather, the fixed phrase seems to constitute a help, an aid in the mysterious process of oral composition, but that is a difficult matter. As Hainsworth puts it, there is a tension between what is aesthetically effective and what is technically useful,[3] and the poet's choice in any single instance is not always clear.

§13. The great and enduring result of Parry's work is that we have come to understand better how poetry functions in societies where writing is nonexistent or rare. But even if one could define formulae with greater precision, and even if one could spread the formulaic net so as to encompass all Homer and other early Greek poetry too, the

---

§12n1. For a recent survey, see Fenik 1978 passim.

§12n2. Most convincing have been extensions of the formulaic system to combinations of noun and adjective or adjectival phrase. Parry 1971.109–117 explores extensions to such substantives as ships, horses, and shields. Whallon 1969.34–54 discusses fully the phrases with shields. Austin 1975.11–80 has an important discussion of the major epithets.

§12n3. Hainsworth 1978.48.

set of inferences that went along with Parry's theory would not necessarily apply in all instances. The processes of oral composition are more varied than at first supposed. There is room for poetic ingenuity under any hypothesis, and room for the ongoing development and improvement of oral traditional poetry. Even if we look in vain elsewhere for the sort of fixed phrases embodied in the epic epithet, however, there is no need to jettison Parry's insights on the social and cultural settings out of which oral traditional poetry arises. It has become clear that we do not need literacy to produce epic poetry and *a fortiori* the shorter pieces of elegiac poetry. Granted, the fixed phrase in its strictest sense is a feature of Homeric epic.[1] But wherever the epithets of heroes and gods do not abound, the fixed phrase is not readily found.

§ 14. Remaining instances of **agathon** in this metrical position in Homer seem remote from the status of fixed phrase, in part because of a semantic shift:

χρὴ μῦθον Δαναοῖσι καὶ οὐκ ἀγαθόν περ ἐόντα
Iliad ix 627

[if we] must tell this story, though it is not **agathos**, to the Danaans

Here it is a **mūthos**, rather than a man, that is not **agathos**.[1] The shift toward the abstract is clearer in the next two citations:

ὅττι τοι ἐν μεγάροισι κακόν τ' ἀγαθόν τε τέτυκται
Odyssey iv 392

what **kakon** and what **agathon** has been done in your halls

τὸν πέρι Μοῦσ' ἐφίλησε, δίδου δ' ἀγαθόν τε κακόν τε·
Odyssey viii 63

whom the Muse loved above all, and gave him both **agathon** and **kakon**

The forms are now neuters used as generalized substantives. The next three lines, from Hesiod, along with the last line cited above, seem to suggest a different standardized or fixed phrase:

---

§ 13n1. Young 1967 passim argues that formulae in Homer are a matter of style rather than compulsion, that they are a feature of the genre.

§ 14n1. The expression **agathos per eōn** occurs four times in the *Iliad* (i 131 = xix 155, i 275, xv 185) at a different position in the line. This is one more example of the variation of set phrases.

γεινομένοισι διδοῦσιν ἔχειν ἀγαθόν τε κακόν τε,
Hesiod *Theogony* 219
They give men as they are born **agathon** and **kakon** to have,

ὥς οἱ συμφράσσαιτο θεὰ ἀγαθόν τε κακόν τε.
Hesiod *Theogony* 900
that the goddess might plan for him both **agathon** and **kakon**.

θνητοῖς ἀνθρώποισιν ἔχειν ἀγαθόν τε κακόν τε.
Hesiod *Theogony* 906
[They give] mortal men **agathon** and **kakon** to have.

In a shifted metrical position, I cite also:

Ζεὺς ἀγαθόν τε κακόν τε διδοῖ· δύναται γὰρ ἅπαντα
Odyssey iv 237
Zeus gives **agathon** and **kakon**, for he can do anything

With the proper position, but with a shift back to the masculine nominative:

θνητοὶ δ᾽ ὧδε νοεῦμεν ὁμῶς ἀγαθός τε κακός τε
Solon 1.33
so we mortal men think, **agathos** and **kakos** alike

The evidence for the fixed status of the phrase **agathon te kakon te** is not as massive as that for **boēn agathos Diomēdēs**, given the comparative frequencies, but the form **agathon** appears only three times in Hesiod, in just the lines cited above. Thus the evidence is slim, and my position would be more secure if the expression also occurred forty-eight times, but what evidence there is suggests that the words constitute a formula or standardized phrase in Hesiod. And if in Hesiod, may it not also be a fixed phrase in the lines cited from the *Odyssey* and in the modified occurrence in Solon?

§ 15. If we accept the phrase **agathon te kakon te** as a formula, is it not also lurking in the background of the lines cited by Giannini (§2 above)? It is also suggestive that when the terms "good" and "bad" are paired in English, "good" always precedes, unless some special effect is sought. It is noteworthy, therefore, that in six of the seven hemistichs in Theognis which contain the pair, **kakos** precedes. Compare:

γίνεται ἀνθρώποις οὔτ' ἀγάθ' οὔτε κακά.
Theognis 172

[Without the gods] men have neither **agatha** nor **kaka**.

This is the verse omitted by Giannini, but, paradoxically, the one closest to the fixed phrase. It occurs in a couplet of serious tone enjoining prayer to the gods, but even so there is a rhetorical twist in putting the words into the negative, and a touch of *para prosdokian* in the implicit notion of the finale, that one must pray to the gods to receive evils.

§16. πίνῃ ἐπισταμένως, οὐ κακὸς ἀλλ' ἀγαθός.
Theognis 212

[If someone] drinks expertly, he is not **kakos** but **agathos**.

πίνῃ ἐπισταμένως, οὐ κακὸν ἀλλ' ἀγαθόν.
Theognis 510

[If someone] drinks expertly, it is not a **kakon** thing but an **agathon** thing.

πολλάκι τοι νικᾷ καὶ κακὸς ἄνδρ' ἀγαθόν.
Theognis 972

Even a **kakos** man, you see, has many times beaten an **agathos**.

The above verses deal with the drinking of wine. In each case, there is again a bit of rhetorical pointing. Drinking wine in excess is bad, but in moderation it is not only not bad but even good. The third citation makes the point that, while winning prizes is ordinarily good, this is not so in a wine-drinking contest.

§17. κἄπρηξαν μέντοί τι· καὶ ἐκ κακοῦ ἐσθλὸν ἔγεντο
καὶ κακὸν ἐξ ἀγαθοῦ· καί τε πενιχρὸς ἀνὴρ . . .
Theognis 661–662

[The gods] have really caused something to happen! Something **esthlon**
[synonym of **agathon**] comes out of a **kakon**,
and a **kakon** out of an **agathon**. A poor man, too . . .

χρήματα μὲν τιμῶσι· καὶ ἐκ κακοῦ ἐσθλὸς ἔγημε
καὶ κακὸς ἐξ ἀγαθοῦ· πλοῦτος ἔμειξε γένος.
Theognis 189–190

People honor property. The **esthlos** marries the daughter of a **kakos**,
while the **kakos** marries the daughter of an **agathos**; wealth has mixed
up the lineage.

These two citations echo each other and constitute the two occasions when the collocation occurs in the first hemistich. It may be that one is a multiform of the other, where **egento** 'comes about' is replaced by **egēme** 'married'. The one remarks on the unexpected nature of things, of unexpected transformations from good to bad and vice versa. The other is from the famous poem on breeding, where the application of animal husbandry to humans sounds a provocative note. The motif of breeding is continued in Theognis verses 429–438, cited by Plato, which culminate in the following:

> ... πειθόμενος μύθοισι σαόφροσιν· ἀλλὰ διδάσκων
> οὔποτε ποιήσει τὸν κακὸν ἄνδρ' ἀγαθόν.
> Theognis 437–438
>
> ... instructed in tales of self-control. Even by teaching
> one will never make a **kakos** man **agathos**.

Once again there is a rhetorical point in placing **kakon** before **agathon**. This observation may be strengthened by citing the two last passages where **kakos** precedes **agathos**:

> ... κακὸς ἢ ἀγαθός· Ζεὺς δ' ἔμπης πάντ' ἰθύνει·
> *Iliad* XVII 632
>
> [neither] **kakos** nor **agathos** [miss]; Zeus straightens them all equally.

Here Ajax complains that the enemy's weapons are divinely aimed, that neither bad nor good ever misses. Is the poet playing with the naïveté of the bluff Ajax? Then there is the single occurrence of the form **agathos** in Hesiod:

> πῆμα κακὸς γείτων, ὅσσον τ' ἀγαθὸς μέγ' ὄνειαρ·
> Hesiod *Works and Days* 346
>
> a **kakos** neighbor is as much a trouble as an **agathos** one is a blessing.

Rhetorical contrast and gnomic tone characterize the line—as they tend to characterize the pentameter lines cited above. We are not dealing with a fixed phrase, but such lines may be making a pointed allusion to the fixed phrase, and so we have here variations on a theme and the use of rhetorical contrast.

§ 18. Fixed phrases like **boēn agathos Diomēdēs** 'Diomedes, good at the war-cry' are not found in every line in Homer, but they embody nonetheless a very important feature of that poetry. Elegiac poetry too has its peculiarities. The elegiac couplet makes unusual formal demands in allowing no resolution of — ˘ ˘ as — — in the second hemistich of the pentameter. I suspect, without knowing any way of confirming or refuting the suspicion, that such strict formal constraint plays a role analogous to that of the constraints within the epic line. By being so strict, the close of the elegiac couplet is proclaimed by a predictable rhythm not unlike the predictable rhythmical pattern — ˘ ˘ — ⌒ at the end of the hexameter.[1] The formal constraint of the hexameter line is reinforced by the tendency of Homeric fixed phrases to take up the final feet of the line. The elegiac couplet functions in some ways as a longer unit than the epic hexameter, with its metrical closure occurring at the end of the pentameter and, I suspect, with a preponderance of sentences ending at that point. As a result, the effects of the Homeric fixed phrase, designed to draw the hexameter line to a close, are perhaps avoided or simply did not develop in the elegiac medium. Rather than end the thought with the hexameter, the hexameter line is used, often, to set the stage, to induce a set of expectations, which the pentameter line is designed to satisfy with closure of sense, with rhetorical point, wit, and contrast. Often the pentameter plays one hemistich against the other. There is a tendency for wordplay in the pentameter—rhyming, for example,[2] and an accompanying tendency, therefore, for the hexameter to be colorless for contrastive purposes. A few examples entailing contrasts of **agathos** and **kakos** can be no more than suggestive:

οὐδέ τις ἀνθρώπων ἐργάζεται ἐν φρεσὶν εἰδὼς
ἐς τέλος εἴτ᾽ ἀγαθὸν γίνεται εἴτε κακόν.
Theognis 135–136

No man, with his wits about him, can bring
a deed to fulfillment, whether it be **agathon** or **kakon**.

οὐδεὶς ἀνθρώπων οὔτ᾽ ὄλβιος οὔτε πενιχρὸς
οὔτε κακὸς νόσφιν δαίμονος οὔτ᾽ ἀγαθός.
Theognis 165–166

No man is rich or poor,
kakos or **agathos**, without a guiding force.

---

§18n1. In comparison, it is noteworthy that the Latin hexameter demands, in addition to a dactylic fifth foot, coincidence of metrical ictus and prose stress in the last two feet of the line.
§18n2. Nagy 1974.100.

Κύρν', ἀγαθὸς μὲν ἀνὴρ γνώμην ἔχει ἔμπεδον αἰεί,
τολμᾷ δ' ἔν τε κακοῖς κείμενος ἔν τ' ἀγαθοῖς.
Theognis 319–320

Kyrnos, the **agathos** man has permanent good judgment,
and he endures in **kaka** [neuter plural] situations as well as in **agatha**.

ἀλλὰ Ζεῦ τέλεσόν μοι 'Ολύμπιε καίριον εὐχήν·
δὸς δέ μοι ἀντὶ κακῶν καί τι παθεῖν ἀγαθόν.
Theognis 341–342

Zeus, Olympian, bring my timely prayer to fulfillment!
Give me something **agathon** to experience in place of **kaka** things.

The pointed use of words and the display of wit are not inappropriate to the sympotic atmosphere of much elegiac poetry.[3] Playfulness at the symposium was not confined to **kottabos**.

§19. We cannot consider here every occurrence of **agathos** and **agathon** in epic and elegy, let alone the usage of the adjective in the plural and in the other cases, although such discussion would be useful. It is, for example, noteworthy that the nominative plural **agathoi** does not occur in Homer or Hesiod but does occur ten times in elegy. In answer to the hypothetical objection that the form is somehow unacceptable in hexameter, I note that seven of the nine instances in Theognis are in the hexameter verses of the couplet. It would seem that it is the social grouping that is foreign to Homer and Hesiod.[1]

§20. I turn instead to a consideration of the instances of **agathos** in the aggregate, with particular attention to the positions within the lines where the forms occur. A notation for metrical position will be helpful. I schematize the elegiac couplet as follows:

(1) − ⏓ (2) − ⏓ (3) − ⏓ (4) − ⏓ (5) − ⏑⏑ (6) − ⏓
(7) − ⏓ (8) − ⏓ (9) − (10) − ⏑⏑ (11) − ⏑⏑ (12) ⏓.

In the phrase **boēn agathos Diomēdēs**, for example, the word **agathos** takes up the last two short syllables of the fourth foot and the first long of the fifth. I schematize its scansion as ⏑ ⏑ (5) −. Since we are dealing only with forms of anapaestic shape (⏑ ⏑ −), I shall give the name "Position 5" to the metrical position of **agathos** in the phrase.

---

§18n3. See Levine Ch.7.
§19n1. See Donlan Ch.9.

It will be obvious that forms of **agathos**, theoretically at least, can appear at Positions 2, 3, 4, 5, 6 in the hexameter and at Positions 8, 9, 11, 12 in the pentameter.

§21. I present first the distribution of the forms **agathos** and **agathon** in "epic" (*Iliad*, *Odyssey*, *Homeric Hymns*, Hesiod) and in elegy (Archilochus, Callinus, Tyrtaeus, Mimnermus, Solon, Xenophanes, Theognis).

agathos / agathon

Position	2	3	4	5	6	8	9	11	12
Epic	6	13	9	65	2				
Elegy	4	2	5	3		4	6		10

The figures are not large enough to carry much conviction, aside from the number 65 at Position 5 in epic. This is of course due to the presence there of the fixed phrase. But even if we discount the 48 instances of the phrase, 17 cases remain, still the largest entry in the table. As we have seen, a goodly number are adaptations or reminiscences of the phrase that places **agathos / -on** so massively at Position 5. There is no such equivalent phrase in elegiac, and the attraction of forms to that position is also lacking. Secondly, the next most populated spot in the epic hexameter is Position 3, where **agathos / -on** rounds out the most common caesura. This is not the case in the elegiac hexameter. Instead, 16 of the total of 34 instances in elegy are concentrated at Positions 9 and 12, where word end must occur and where there is a higher demand, perhaps, for significant words of anapaestic shape.

§22. Some aspects of the aggregate distribution are clarified by the data for all forms of **agathos**, including those tabulated above.

agathos — all forms

Position	2	3	4	5	6	8	9	11	12
Epic	19	36	13	69	10				
Elegy	11	14	8	7	5	7	22	6	22

Once again discounting the massive presence of the fixed phrase at Position 5 in epic, we find now that Position 3 is the favorite for the hexameter in both epic and elegy, but less markedly so in the latter. The favored positions in elegy continue to be Positions 9 and 12. Note that the pentameter contains about 55 percent of the instances of the forms of **agathos** in elegy.

§23. A final set of considerations takes us back to the list of collocations of **agathos** 'noble, good' with forms of **ekhō** 'have'. According to Giannini,[1] hexameter phrases can be utilized in the pentameter in the following ways:

a. Hexameter phrases from verse-beginning to major caesura are identical in meter to the pentameter hemistich and can be transferred without change. (I have found no such case involving **agathos.**)

b. Phrases from the latter half of the hexameter line can be transferred after modification of ending or of word order (again, no example with **agathos**).

c. Transfers can be made through the addition of an iambic word, and three examples (none involving **agathos**)[2] are cited that use forms of the verb **ekhō**. I tabulate summarily the findings for three forms of **ekhō**.

ekhei, ekhein, ekhōn

Position	2	3	4	5	6	8	9	11	12
Epic									
ekhei	11	4	32	1					
ekhein	5	2	13						
ekhōn	35	28	45	1					
Total	51	34	90	2					
Elegy									
ekhei	1	1	6			1	1	4	18
ekhein			8				2	3	11
ekhōn	1		1	1		7	4	3	9
Total	2	1	15	1		8	7	10	38

If we keep in mind that the attested epic corpus is about twenty times the size of the elegiac, it is clear that the forms of **ekhō** are not underrepresented, even in the hexameter lines of the elegiac couplet.[3] The localization of the forms to the fourth foot of the hexameter in both epic and elegy is also noteworthy. What is truly startling, however, is the very large number of occurrences in the elegiac pentameter as compared with the elegiac hexameter. From my tabu-

---

§23n1. Giannini 1973.63.

§23n2. This is Giannini's contribution. None of the three examples cited involves Homeric phrases.

§23n3. For completeness, note in addition that **ehkei** in correption, filling the last two short syllables of the fourth foot, occurs 18 times in epic and twice in elegy.

lation above of the forms of **agathos** it will be seen that of the 102 occurrences in elegy, 45 occur in the hexameter and 57 in the pentameter, close enough to the null hypothesis of an equal division. The given forms of **ekhō** are split 19 to 63. I have no explanation for the very large proportion in the pentameter. Perhaps the function of these forms is to enable the adaptation of epic phrases into the pentameter, as Giannini implies, but my cursory inspection has not borne this out.

§24. We have at our disposal no protocol of the inner workings of the poet's or singer's mind as he switched from singing in hexameters to elegiacs. But we may at least surmise that it would be analogous to a situation where bilingual speakers switch from one language to another. If they are truly bilingual, they assume a different cultural stance and take on a different set of speech habits. There is a way of saying things in elegiacs that is different from the way things are said in hexameters. One of the byproducts of that switch may be that, consciously or not, words of anapaestic shape like **agathos** will tend to be reserved, displaced, postponed, summoned up to fill those parts of the pentameter, that is, Positions 9 and 12, where the formal constraints demand word ending. More elaborate analysis of the deployment of various metrical word-shapes in both hexameter and elegiac is needed before any of this can be stated with confidence.

§25. If the preliminary and tentative conclusions outlined above are substantiated, they will tend to confirm what has been hypothesized on other grounds by Nagy,[1] that is, that elegy is not simply an adaptation of epic hexameter with the tailoring of hexameter expressions to fit the pentameter. Instead, the language of elegy, like the language of hexameter, is a structured systematic *plenum* in its own right. As such, variations at one point affect other points in the structure. If elegy has a comparatively high demand for anapaestic words at Positions 9 and 12, it will tend to be comparatively more sparing of these at other points such as Position 3. An important corollary may be that we should not think of elegy as derived from the hexameter. It is different, and it has its own rules; we should therefore not be surprised if it does not exhibit the set phrases characteristic of the epic hexameter.

---

§25n1. Nagy 1974.99–101, 1979b.628.

Chronological Table
Archaic Megara, 800–500 B.C.

Thomas J. Figueira

This table has been compiled with a specific goal in mind, namely to organize chronologically the data available on the history of Megara during the archaic period. It is my hope that the table will prove useful wherever historical events are discussed in this volume and will serve as a reminder to the reader that the evolution of the Theognidea was open to influences, now irrecoverable or nearly so, from other **poleis**. Naturally, my views on the generic, ideological, and pan-Megarian character of the Theognidea entail that much of the reading of specific, externally-attested political situations into the corpus is to be discarded. The table, therefore, should be read together with Ch. 5, where the relationship of Theognis and Megarian society is investigated. On the basis of the arguments to be presented below, it will become striking how much can be known about archaic Megara and its chronology, once a *biographical* reading of the corpus is avoided. I should like to draw the reader's attention to the following works, which I have found especially useful in compiling this chronology: Hammond 1954; Highbarger 1927; Legon 1981; Oost 1973; and Salmon 1972.

Before 750	Megarians under intermittent Corinthian control (A)
c. 750	Five **kōmai** system before **sunoikismos** (B)
750–725	Megara Hyblaea founded; Megarian **sunoikismos** and independence (B, C)
725–700	Recovery of Megarian territory by Orsippos (D)
712/11	Foundation of Astakos (??) (E)
685	Foundation of Kalkhedon (E)
Early seventh century	Foundation of Selymbria (E)
669	Foundation of Byzantion (?) (E)
650–625	Foundation of Selinous by Megara Hyblaea and Megara (C, E)
640/630–600	Theagenes tyrant in Megara (F)
628/7	Alternative date for Byzantion; reinforcement of city (??) (E)

625–600	Corinthians capture Sidous and Krommyon from Megara (G)
625–600	Beginning of confrontation between Athens and Megara (H)
Before 600	Megarians occupy Salamis (I, S)
Before 600	Exile of Dorykleians from Megara (J)
c. 600	Naval warfare between Megarians and Samians at Perinthos (K)
c. 600–595	Athenians recapture Salamis (I)
600–582	Megarians troubled by warfare in Euboia (L)
590–570	Megarians reoccupy Salamis during Athenian stasis (I, M)
570–565	Peisistratid capture of Nisaea and Salamis (?) (I, M)
575–550	Megara at war with Corinth (N)
575–550	War between Megarians and Miletos (O)
560	Foundation of Heraclea Pontica (E)
550–510	Peloponnesian intervention against Megara (N, P)
545–510	Megara at war with Corinth (??) (N, O)
544/1	Floruit of Theognis; Palintokiā or fall of Megarian Democracy (?) (Q)
c. 510	Alliance of Megara with Sparta (R); Sparta awards Salamis to Athens (S)

*A (before 750) An important piece of evidence about Corinthian hegemony over Megara is Plutarch's description (based on the Constitution of the Megarians) of the connotation of the Megarian term doruxenos (Greek Questions 17). In Attic usage the word means a military ally (Aeschylus Choephoroi 562; Sophocles OC 632), but it can also denote the tie that unites a warrior with his captured enemy (Suda s.v. "doruxenos"; Eustathius on Iliad III 205–207, p. 405). Plutarch gives to it this latter meaning, with the added explanation that this type of xeniā was created when Megarians were taken prisoner by other Megarians and were entertained by their captors until they were ransomed. The historical setting for the custom is a time when the five kōmai 'villages' constituting Megara fought each other. The Corinthians fomented these conflicts. This situation suggests an early date, before Megarian sunoikismos, when each of the five kōmai was a separate political entity. A date before sunoikismos is congruent with the convention (mentioned by Plutarch) that those working the land were not to be molested. This suggests a date before the adoption by the Megarians of the hoplite phalanx. The effectiveness of hoplite warfare depended in large part on threats to an enemy's farmland, forcing him to a set battle in defense. The preservation of a tradition about the **doruxenoi** may be attributed to a situation in which Megarian aristocrats sought to uphold a heritage of individual combat in the face of political claims based on participation in the phalanx (see Note J below).

It would be most interesting to know by what means the Corinthians were able to incite the Megarians against each other. Gift-giving (through guest-friendship), which selectively bypassed the leading village at any one time, might induce a weaker village to tackle this leader. The Megarian system of ransom and mutual hospitality would have been a well-designed antidote to Corinthian interference.

Further evidence for early Megarian subjection to Corinth is predominantly proverbial and centers around explanations for the expression **Dios Korinthos** 'Corinth of Zeus' and a sometimes connected expression **dakrua Megareōn** 'Megarian tears' (used for insincere mourning). The antiquity of **Dios Korinthos** is not to be doubted. The expression was known to Pindar (*N.* 7.106), and the scholia to this line offer an explanation congruent with the sense of the text (scholia Pindar *N.* 7.155a–b; cf. scholia Plato *Euthydemus* 292E; *Suda* s.v. "**Dios Korinthos**").

The fullest account is given in scholia Pindar *N.* 7.155b, which is based on the Atthidographer Demon, who lived c. 300 and wrote a work *On Proverbs* (*FGH* 327 F 19, cf. F 4). The Megarians, inhabitants of a colony of Corinth, were forced to obey the stronger Corinthians and to provide mourners for the funerals of members of Corinth's ruling Bacchiad clan. That Megara was an **apoikiā** is a motif suggesting the perspective of Corinth, which refused to recognize Megarian independence. Corinth aspired to hegemony over its colonies, unusual for the classical period (Graham 1983.233–234, cf. 118–153). Corinthian **hubris** reached such a point that the Megarians revolted. A Corinthian embassy came to remonstrate with them and stated that **Dios Korinthos** would be angered if the revolt went unpunished. These remarks drove the Megarians into a rage, and they attacked the ambassadors. When further reinforcements arrived from Corinth and a battle was fought, the Megarians, victorious, pursued their beaten enemy with cries of **Dios Korinthos**. Demon uses the anecdote to illustrate Corinthian arrogance.

The story was a popular one, appearing in differing versions, as can be seen in the variants offered in a scholion to Aristophanes (scholia *Frogs* 439). In another scholion to Pindar (*N.* 7.155a), the phrase **Dios Korinthos** is brought into an explanation of the proverb **dekhe-**

tai kai bōlon Alētēs 'Aletes receives the clod of earth' (cf. Hesychius s.v. "Dios Korinthos"). This proverb is explained by the story of the Dorian occupation of Corinth. As can be seen from the version of the Dios Korinthos story based on Demon, the phrase Megareōn dakrua could be worked into the same explanatory complex. The phrase does not appear, but its explanation is implicit (cf. Suda s.v. "Megareōn dakrua"). In the scholion, the provision for the Megarians' attending Bacchiad funerals is made into a piece of Corinthian policy. In another version, the proverb is particularized. A Megarian king Klytios, otherwise unknown, has married his daughter to Bakkhios, a Corinthian (Zenobius 5.8). When the daughter dies, Klytios forces Megarian mourners to go to Corinth. This story is not very different, inasmuch as Bakkhios was the royal ancestor from whom the Bacchiad clan claimed their descent and authority. The variant, rather than explaining Megareōn dakrua, gives a rationale for the custom of enforced mourning by the Megarians. One might well imagine a Corinthian arguing for the justice of such a requirement by pointing to its origin in a voluntary act of a Megarian king. The same cannot be said for another version of the story, which explains Megarian tears as tears for their own kings (Diogenianus 6.34). This is banalizing, and it removes all point from the proverb. It is perhaps merely the result of careless abbreviation. Hammond (1954.97) believes that the source for the explanations of these proverbs was Aristotle's Constitution of the Megarians.

It is not necessary to judge the authenticity of explanations of such cryptic expressions. It is sufficient to observe that such explanations could have been plausibly stated only if Corinthian control of Megara was granted by most Greeks. The forced attendance of the Megarians at Bacchiad funerals indicates that they were the personal subjects of the Bacchiad clan, whose adult male members constituted the Corinthian government. This meshes with what is known about the closed oligarchy at Corinth and with an eighth-century date (the Bacchiads ruled 748–657). Herodotus reports a similar institution at Sparta, where the Helots were compelled to attend the funerals of Spartan kings (heroized after death) and to make highly formalized shows of mourning (Herodotus 6.58.2–3; Pausanias 4.14.4). Such an institution exists in order to create feelings of dependency, forcing the subjects to dissociate their outward behavior from their inner feelings, and to emphasize distinctions between the elite, for whom grief is strictly controlled, and the dependents, for whom immoderate behavior is mandated. The Megarian and Spartan customs appear to be parallel adaptations created to institutionalize dependency roles. Intrinsic to the data on Corinthian designs on the Megarid is the underlying resistance of the Megarians. Corinthian hegemony may have been only fitfully brought to bear. There is no reason to think that the relations between the two cities implicit in the proverbial stories and those involving the **doruxenoi** are irreconcilable or must be chronologically removed from each other.

*B (c. 750) Plutarch's discussion of Megarian **doruxenoi** provides valuable information about the constituent units of Megara after **sunoikismos**. As for the period before **sunoikismos**, the five original **kōmai** 'villages' were inhabited by the Heraeis, Piraeis, Megareis, Kynosoureis, and Tripodiskioi. First, note that these five divisions differ from the five towns that the Megarians held to have been listed in the Catalogue of Ships as grouped with the contingent of Ajax (Strabo 9.1.10 C394). Two of the **kōmai** involve no difficulties in their location. The Megareis are to be associated with the later **polis** center of Megara, which presumably, because of its political importance, gave its name to the whole community. The Tripodiskioi are undoubtedly from the town of that name, to the west and inland of the city of Megara on the east slopes of Geraneia (cf. Thucydides 4.70.1–2). One of the **kōmai**, moreover, that of the Heraeis, has been localized in the Perachora Peninsula. The name "Heraeis" is to be connected with the Heraeum at the tip of the peninsula.

Early Megarian occupation of Perachora has been associated by Hammond with the stages of cult activity in the worship of Hera at that site (Hammond 1954.93–102). For Hammond the cult of Hera Akraia was succeeded by the cult of Hera Limenia c. 725, a change contemporary with the abandonment of the temple near the harbor and the movement of the cult to a site further inland. Hammond wished to see this transition as marking the occupation of the Perachora Peninsula by the Corinthians. His attempts to bring to bear archaeological data have come under attack by Salmon (1972), who shows that the sites are probably part of the same cult and that activity continued at the earlier sanctuary near the harbor. Therefore, the neat division of activity at Perachora into Megarian and Corinthian periods cannot be true.

However, while the archaeological record fails to support Hammond's contention that Megarian control of Perachora ended in the late seventh century, Salmon's view that Megarian influence at the site was dominant before the foundation of Corinth is equally problematical. The continuing fivefold division of the Megarian state and the continued use of at least one of the **kōmai** names (Kynosoureis: *IG* iv² 42.18) argue that the traditions of the five **kōmai** were still very much alive at the time of the creation of the **polis** of Megara.

Salmon would put the loss of Perachora so early that such continuity would be hard to explain. For political units below the level of the tribe, such continuities, spanning the Dark Age, are unparalleled. Moreover, the proverbial traditions that refer to Megarian subjection to Corinth in the archaic period would have to be discarded.

If Dark Age Megarians were under strong Corinthian influence, as the anecdotes cited above argue, their ritual behavior might well have been indistinguishable from that of the Corinthians. It may well be that the inhabitants of the Perachora Peninsula had been (when compared to other Megarians) particularly under Corinthian influence, so that in a sense the Corinthians had continuous control of the cult of Hera at Perachora. Nevertheless, the nature of this control may well have changed. Before the independence of the Megarians, Corinthian hegemony over the peninsula was expressed through dominance over the Heraeis. After Megarian independence the Heraeis (or a sizeable number of them) withdrew from the peninsula to territory under Megarian control, thus giving the Corinthians a more direct control of Perachora. They may have chosen at this time to build a new temple to express their greater interest in the cult.

Hence Corinthian colonists could establish a cult of Hera Akraia at Corcyra (founded c. 735) shortly after its foundation (Salmon 1972.181–182, 202; Kalligas 1969). It is also possible that cults of Hera in Megarian colonies, established on promontories, were cults of Hera Akraia, as Hammond has suggested (Hammond 1954.98), but this reorganization does not mean that independent Megarians had ever really held this peninsula, so close to Corinth's harbor town, Lekhaion. It does mean that the inhabitants of the peninsula could be described as Megarians at a moment when all the Megarians were dominated by Corinth. The inhabitants saw themselves as Megarians, and the habitation of a place so near Corinth by self-proclaimed Megarians contributes to a redefinition of what the term "Megarian" implied in the eighth century. Megarians inhabited the predominantly marginal agricultural land to the north and east of Corinth. The newly autonomous **polis** of Megara probably never exerted authority over the southern portions of this area. Therefore, it is fallacious to visualize the foundation of Megara as a pure **sunoikismos**. The term "in-gathering" better describes this phenomenon. Those who identified themselves as Megarian revolted from Bacchiad rule, but they could not manage to hold on to all the territory where an appreciable portion of the population was Megarian.

The location of the Piraeis has been put on the Megarian border with Corinth because here is the location of Peiraion, which is mentioned in the context of the Corinthian War (Xenophon *Hellenica*

4.5.1). It has been placed on the northeastern shore of the Perachora Peninsula near the Isthmus (Sakellariou and Faraklas 1972.22, figs. 17a, b), and it has even been equated with the entire region of northern and eastern Perachora (Wiseman 1978.32–33). Hammond associates the name with the adjective **peraios** 'opposite' and believes it to be a term used generally (in the Bronze Age!) for Greeks of the Peloponnesus. Salmon argues that only the region of Perachora (which he would reserve for the Heraeis) and the area south of the Isthmus near Kenkhreai might seem to be opposite to Megarians, from Krommyon eastward (Salmon 1972.195–196). There is no reason, however, to accept the assumption of Salmon that the peninsula could not have contained two **kōmai**. The connection with **peraios** 'opposite' need not mean that they must have received their names from a vantage point within the Megarid. Megara as an independent **polis** need not have existed at the time of the naming. Yet Salmon is troubled by the lexical difficulty in equating Piraeis with **peraios** 'opposite'. He introduces a verbal communication of G. Huxley, who noted a Cape Spiraion in the southeast Corinthia (Thucydides 8.10.3; cf. Ptolemy *Geography* 3.14.33; Pliny *Natural History* 4.12.57; Salmon compares *P. Oxy.* 1247.42 [Thucydides 8.6.3–11.2], where the cape is either Speiraion or Peiraion). Salmon notes a Spiraion in a third-century Epidaurian inscription (*IG* iv² 71.4, 18) for a place in the border region of the Corinthia and Epidauria. Thus, there is a possibility that the Piraeis, perhaps Spiraeis to be correct, may be associated with Cape Spiraion (cf. Wiseman 1978.33, 41n109, 136–140). So the Piraeis might be associated with the southern Megarid. How far south their territory extended is unknown, as we do not know whether they occupied places like Sidous and Krommyon on the Isthmus and also the area around Kenkhreai, Solugeia, and Cape Spiraion, this last bordering on Epidauros. There is no reason, however, to think that the Piraeis lost their land before the foundation of Corinth. If a connection with Cape Spiraion is maintained, they could have been extruded from their southern holdings in stages, finally losing Sidous and Krommyon in the late seventh century.

The Kynosoureis have been generally associated with the northwestern Megarid (e.g., Halliday 1928.98). The peninsula southwest of Aigosthena could well appear as a **kunosourā** 'dog's tail' (a common name for a peninsula). Sakellariou and Faraklas, citing the Spartan village of Kynosoura, believe that the name "Kynosoureis" need not describe a topographical feature of the Megarid (1972.22–23). They opt rather for the procedure of finding a habitation site, the name of which is unknown, and thereby locate the Kynosoureis in the northeast Megarid along the border with Eleusis.

That, subsequently, the fivefold division was continued for constitutional organization (e.g., the five **stratēgoi, polemarkhoi, aisumnātai, dāmiourgoi**) suggests that consolidation of population may have taken place.[1] Hammond notes a decree (*IG* VII 1 [c. 300]) that juxtaposes city and **kōmē** (Hammond 1954.95). The older **kōmai** were possibly incorporated into a civic order based on **hekatostues** 'hundreds'. Kynosoura was a **hekatostus** in the third century (*IG* IV² 42.18).

Megara conceptualized itself on the paradigm of the five **kōmai**. The verse that the Megarians wished to claim as part of the Homeric Catalogue of Ships also presents Megara as being a union of five villages (Strabo 9.1.10 C394). This group (Salamis, Polikhna, Aigiroussa, Nisaea, and Tripodes) portrays the actual situation (the original five **kōmai** may have continued to exist in constitutional terms) in the late seventh and sixth centuries. Among the Megarian communities, Salamis is included, although probably not absorbed into Megara before the last third of the seventh century. On this list Tripodes may stand as a variant (one is tempted to say deliberate archaism) for Tripodiskioi (cf. Pausanias 1.39.5). Nisaea could be the port of that name, but it also could be an archaism for Megara (cf. Pindar *P.* 9.91; *N.* 5.46; Euripides *HF* 954). Polikhna, a diminutive of **polis**, which can mean fort, cannot be placed. Conceivably, it could be another variant for Megara (E. Kirsten *RE* 21.2.1371–1372). But if Polikhna is to be envisaged as a fort, it may have been located on the slopes of Geraneia along Megara's border with Corinth, or, even better, where the Perachora Peninsula joins the Isthmus near the site of the Corinthian fort of Oinoe (Xenophon *Hellenica* 4.5.5; Strabo 8.6.22 C380; see also Wiseman 1978.28–32). Aigiroussa was also known as Aigeiros (Stephanus Byzantius s.v. "**Aigeiroussa**"; cf. Theopompus *FGH* 115 F 241). It is to be identified with Aigeiroi, where the impious Megarians called 'wagon-rollers' (Plutarch *Greek Questions* 59 [*Moralia* 304D–F]) ambushed a Peloponnesian sacred embassy on its way to Delphi. This incident is supposed to have taken place on the shores of a lake. The only remaining lake in the area, Vouliagmeni, is south on Perachora, but a lake that would have been northeast of Pagai is hypothesized by Hammond as the setting (Hammond 1954b; cf. Sakellariou and Faraklas 1972.32–33, figs. 15a, b; Wiseman 1978.26–27 against a location near Akra Mavrolimni on the Corinthian Gulf south of Pagai). None of these villages can be put

---

*Bn1. Svenbro 1982 sees the fivefold division in the ground plan of Megara Hyblaea, where districts may radiate out from the agora, as derived from the five **kōmai**.

farther south than the territory actually held in the fifth century by the Megarians. These relatively modest claims make sense when it is remembered that this list is meant to make credible a claim to Salamis. Whatever the true feelings of the Megarians may have been about territories lost to Corinth, the inclusion of current possessions of Corinth in this group would only serve to undercut a claim to Salamis. Whether this verse is contemporary with Solon or merely with the late sixth-century Spartan arbitration (see Note S below), the Megarians were limited to their fifth-century boundaries at the time of its application to the dispute.

*C (750–725) To establish a date for Megarian independence from Corinth, it is necessary to consider the checkered career of the Megarian colonists in Sicily. According to Thucydides, they originally settled at Trotilon, on the shore to the east of Leontini (Thucydides 6.4.1; Gomme *HCT* 4.215–216). To Thucydides, the Megarians became associated with the Khalkidian colonists who founded Leontini. In another tradition, they were associated with the Khalkidian colonists of Naxos (Ephorus *FGH* 70 F 137; Strabo 6.2.2 C267). The link between Megarian and Khalkidian colonists is significant if the ties between Khalkis and Corinth are remembered. Corinth and Khalkis acted cooperatively in their colonization in the West. The Corinthians expelled Eretrian colonists from Corcyra (Plutarch *Greek Questions* 11 [*Moralia* 293A–B]). Topographically, Syracuse stands in a complementary relationship to the Khalkidian colonies, and it contains place names redolent of Euboia (e.g., Arethusa), suggesting that the site was scouted by Euboians. Therefore, it is unlikely that the Megarians would have been included in a Khalkidian venture if they were at odds with the Corinthians. The role played by the Megarians at Leontini is also noteworthy. The Megarians were to subjugate the indigenous Sicels on behalf of the colonists (Polyaenus 5.5; cf. Strabo 6.2.2 C267). In time, the Megarians were expelled by the Leontinians and founded a settlement at Thapsos. From there they may eventually have been expelled by the Syracusans. Next, they made a more permanent foundation at Megara Hyblaea with the support of the Sicel king Hyblon, who betrayed (?) (**prodontos**) the land to them. In interpreting this episode, it is important to note that composite colonies were the rule rather than the exception (Figueira 1981.192–202). The Megarians at Leontini were probably meant to be content with subordinate status, perhaps indicated by their employment as shock troops against the natives (oaths inhibiting the Leontinians themselves are cited in Polyaenus). When they founded their own settlement, they took the surprising step of taking the name of their mother city for their new colony, necessitating the byname of Hyblaea. This act of naming is unusual (cf. the derivation of the name "Lokroi") in the early period of Greek colonization.

Thucydides says that Leontini was founded five years after Syracuse (734–733, a date supported also by the Eusebian chronographic tradition). Therefore, Megara Hyblaea would have been settled (after the successive moves of the Megarians) around 729–725. If Megara and Syracuse were approximately contemporary, then it is not hard to see why the Sicels aided the Megarians as potential allies against the Corinthians at Syracuse.[1]

The Megarians were not free agents in Sicily. It may be that even in their settlement of Trotilon, they were acting as auxiliaries of the Khalkidians. Those Megarians who were induced to join a Khalkidian colonial venture probably recognized the authority of the Bacchiad government at Corinth. So too did the inhabitants of the upland village of Tenea provide the bulk of the settlers at Syracuse, founded by the Bacchiad Archias (Strabo 8.6.22 C380). Otherwise one must assume that the Megarians were pioneers and became colonizers almost before they had a Corinthian example in Syracuse to follow. The breakdown of cooperation between the Khalkidians and the Megarians mirrors the state of relations between the Megarians and Corinth. With the circumstances of the colonization of Megara Hyblaea in mind, one is less surprised that Megara and Megara Hyblaea have the same name. The Megarians in Sicily chose the name of Megara for their new foundation because Megara in Greece was barely (if at all) established as an independent **polis**. Like the Euboian colonists of Cumae, who named their city after a town dominated by Khalkis (Stephanus Byzantius s.v. "**Kumē**"), the Megarians in Sicily took their colony name from some part of their mother city, in this case the name of Megara, their home district in the **polis** of Corinth. The Megarians in Sicily founded Megara Hyblaea between 750 and 725. The commonly accepted date for Orsippos, who recovered some territory for independent Megara, is after 720, so that Megara was independent by the last quarter of the eighth century. By

---

*Cn1. A higher date, c. 750, has been argued on archaeological grounds for Megara Hyblaea (Vallet and Villard 1952). They adduce in support that Megara Hyblaea's colony in western Sicily, Selinous, traditionally said to be founded 100 years after Megara Hyblaea, is to be dated before 650 (Thucydides 6.4.2–3: Vallet and Villard 1958). The chronology of Ephorus on Megara Hyblaea (Strabo 6.2.2 C267; cf. [Scymnus] 270–282) and on Selinous (Diodorus Siculus 13.59.4) should be preferred to Thucydides, perhaps misled here by his source Antiochus of Syracuse. Yet, after a period of general acceptance, this higher chronology for Megara Hyblaea is now widely discounted (Graham 1982.103–104).

the first quarter of the seventh century, the Megarians are traditionally said to have been colonizing in the Propontis. Therefore, the movements for independence both by the Megarians of the Isthmus and those in Sicily were roughly contemporary (cf. Legon 1981.75). We cannot be certain about which group made its break first. Nevertheless, if war was being fought by Khalkis and its ally Corinth against Eretria over the Lelantine Plain (see, in brief, Jeffery 1976.64–67), the timing of the **sunoikismos** and rebellion of the Megarians might be explained. It is noteworthy that the Megarians never by themselves colonized in the western Mediterranean again but confined their efforts to the East where Miletos, Eretria's ally, was beginning to become the dominant colonizing, if not commercial, state. That Megara and Megara Hyblaea were coevals helps to explain how the Theognidea could be the product of both cities (see Ch.5 §§19, 21, 35, 61–62). The foundation of both communities had the same political context, so that their institutional histories thereafter may have been more nearly parallel than was customary between colony and mother city.

*D (725–700) A Megarian general named Orsippos captured territory from one of Megara's neighbors (Pausanias 1.44.1). This accomplishment is commemorated by an epigram inscribed on the base of his statue. The epigram is known both from literary sources and from a late (second century A.D.) inscription found at Megara, certainly a copy of an earlier inscription probably seen by Pausanias (*IG* VII 52; for vv. 1–2, 4–6, cf. scholia Thucydides 1.6.5).[1] The epigram and the statue were erected by the Megarians in obedience to a Delphic response. The epigram states that Orsippos defended the boundaries of Megara in the face of enemies appropriating a piece of territory. Both Pausanias and the epigram record that Orsippos won the **stadion** race at Olympia. He was reportedly the first of the Greeks to run ungirt. This detail may be juxtaposed with Thucydides' statement that the Spartans were the first to practice athletics naked (1.6.5). Other sources suggest that Orsippos ran ungirt accidentally (*Etymologicum Magnum* s.v. "**gumnasia**"; cf. Pausanias 1.44.1).

The priority of Orsippos as the first naked Olympic victor is not without challenge. A connected problem is reconciling the two tradi-

---

**Dn1. Verse 1 differs slightly in orthography (*IG* VII 52: Orripos; scholia Thucydides 1.6.5: Orsippos) and in wording, which suggests several variants antedating even the earlier inscription. All the variants perhaps derive from an epigram of Simonides (Boeckh 1874.4.173–182), suggesting a time c. 530–468 for the Megarians' revival of the heroic honors of Orsippos.*

tions about his date. According to the chronographer Julius Africanus, preserved in Eusebius (*Chronica* p.91 [Karst]; cf. Hesychius s.v. "zōsato"), Orsippos won the **stadion** in 720, but Akanthos, a Spartan, won the **dolikhos** ungirt. This is not merely a textual error, as Dionysius of Halicarnassus credited Akanthos with the first victory ungirt (*Antiquitates Romanae* 7.72.3; cf. Pausanias 5.8.6; Philostratus *De gymnastica* 12). An apparent confusion of Orsippos and Akanthos can be read in the *Etymologicum Magnum*, which speaks of Orsippos the Spartan. A more troubling variant detail is also provided by Homeric scholia (*Iliad* XXIII 683 B'; Eustathius on *Iliad* XXIII 683) and dated by an Athenian archon date. According to the scholia, running naked was enjoined by decree at Olympia when Orsippos, encumbered in a race by his loincloth, died. Moreover, Orsippos could well be dated to 652/1 (*Etymologicum Magnum*; scholia *Iliad* XXIII 683 D). In any case, a confusion over Orsippos' date is hard to understand, if he won the **stadion**, since victors in this event provided eponyms for each Olympiad, and their canonical list was well known (cf. Jacoby *FGH Komm.* 3b 399–400; *Noten* 236–237).

Any statement on Orsippos, then, must be conjectural. The date at which running ungirt at Olympia began seems better established than the name of the inaugurator of the practice and its circumstances. It is possible that, to defend a Megarian claim, Orsippos, a Megarian victor in 652/1, was moved to 720. Yet one is reluctant to posit two men named Orsippos, one a victim in 720 and another a victor in 652, not only a priori, but also because the discrepancy in dates might result from a confusion between Hippomenes the ten-year archon (723/2–713/2) and the unknown archon of 652/1. I prefer to think that an anti-Megarian commentator (an Atthidographer?), faced with irreconcilable traditions about Orsippos and Akanthos, made Orsippos the first naked (albeit accidentally) runner—only to make him perish in a mishap so that Akanthos could claim priority in the next race, the **dolikhos**. That anyone would have bothered to compose a variant with Orsippos as a victim indicates Orsippos' place in Megarian patriotic tradition.

If the facts about the athletic accomplishments of Orsippos are irrecoverable, it is still profitable to return to the attitudes toward him of later Megarians. To them he was undoubtedly a great military figure. At an eighth- or even seventh-century date, it is probably more sensible to see Corinth as his adversary rather than Athens or Boiotia (Legon 1981.62–63). In fact, recovery of land cut off (verb: **apotemnō**; cf. *Palatine Anthology* 7.720) by a neighbor may have been a code phrase for hostilities against Corinth, since much land that had once been occupied by the Megarians was now in Corinthian hands.

However, if the legend of Orsippos was for the most part fabricated in the sixth or fifth century (in connection with the receipt of a Delphic response), the identity of his opponents might have acquired significance only from this later context. From the standpoint of sixth- or fifth-century Megara, Athens becomes a more credible alternative to Corinth, and this may explain why a tradition existed that Orsippos died at Olympia.

After his death, Orsippos was given heroic honors and was buried within the walls of the city, as the inscription instructs us. Thus, he was treated like the oecist of a colony. The extraordinary character of this honor may suggest that Nisaean Megara was in a real sense as much a colony of the Megarians as was Megara Hyblaea or Byzantion. Orsippos received the same honors after death as Koroibos, who founded the Megarian town of Tripodiskioi (Pausanias 1.43.8; cf. *Palatine Anthology* 7.154).[2] The tombs within the city sacralized and politicized its territory (Bohringer 1980). When later Megarians had recourse to Delphi, they were exhorted to revive or strengthen honors to Orsippos. Such a response may have been especially appropriate if the later Megarians were facing a threat similar to that confronted by Orsippos, namely Corinthian hostility. What with sixth-century Argive military help to Megara, the coupling of Orsippos with the Argive Koroibos may be significant. It is, in any case, proper to look for a late sixth- or fifth-century date for the Delphic response, as well as for the epigram (note the possibility that Simonides was its author). These honors fit an Orsippos of the late 700s. Nevertheless, it is possible that he was active in the mid-seventh century. At that time Corinth was weak, because the Bacchiads were unpopular, at odds with Argos, and soon to be expelled by Kypselos.

*E (eighth and seventh century) The fact that Megara became a colonizing state deserves to be stressed. After independence, Megara does not seem to have moved in a line of evolution different from its former **hēgemōn**, Corinth. Instead, its evolution is parallel. By contrast, Aigina, already a complement rather than a mirror image of its erstwhile **hēgemones** Argos and Epidauros, experienced an accelerated divergence from their social and economic patterns (Figueira

---

*Dn2. We can class among "founding heroes" buried in the city the anonymous heroes buried in the Aisymnion (Pausanias 1.43.3) and those who fell in the Persian Wars (Pausanias 1.43.3; cf. Tod 1 no. 20 for a reinscription of the memorial with an epigram attributed to Simonides). The tomb of the Argive king Adrastos was also claimed by the Megarians (Dieuchidas *FGH* 485 F 3). For the placement of the tombs and archaeological remains: Muller 1981.218–222.

1981.166–192). The most apparent similarity between Corinth and Megara was the tradition of colonization of both states. Megara colonized in its own right and cosponsored foundations with its colonies.

Megarian Primary and Secondary Colonial Foundations

Colony	Region	Cosponsors	Date	Source
Megara Hyblaea	E. Sicily		750–725	See Note C above
Astakos	S. Shore Propontis	Kalkhedon (Charon *FGH* 262 F 6)	712/11	Memnon *FGH* 434 F 12 Eusebius *Ol.* 17.2 at Jerome (p.91b [Helm]); *Ol.* 18.3 (p.183 [Karst])
Kalkhedon	E. Shore Bosporus		685 17 years before Byzantion	Eusebius *Ol.* 23.3 at Jerome (p.93b [Helm]) Herodotus 4.144
Selymbria	N. Shore Propontis		before Byzantion	[Scymnus] 715
Byzantion	W. Shore Bosporus		660–658	Eusebius *Ol.* 30.2 at Jerome (p.94b [Helm]; p.185 [Karst])
			628/25	Johannes Lydus *De magistratibus* 3.70
Selinous	S.W. Sicily	Megara Hyblaea	650–625	See Note C above
Heraclea Pontica	S. Shore Black Sea	Boiotians	560	[Scymnus] 972–973
Mesambria	W. Shore Black Sea	Byzantion Kalkhedon	before 516	Herodotus 4.93; 6.33.2 [Scymnus] 741–742; cf. 760

Whether the Megarians had any part in sixth- or fifth-century Heraclean colonization is unknown (Panelos, Kallatis in the sixth century; Khersonesos in the fifth). The received chronology of Megarian colonies cannot be trusted.[1] Note that Kalkhedon is said to have participated in colonizing Astakos, whose traditional date precedes Kalkhedon's, and that several dates are handed down for Byzantion. Most of the colonies in the Propontis and the Black Sea have seen little excavation. At Byzantion, where later building effaced much of the earliest levels, Corinthian pottery of the late seventh century is the earliest material discovered to date. It would not be surprising if future excavation led to a down-dating of Megara's colonies in this area (Boardman 1980.238–246; Graham 1982.118–121, 160–162). If the Megarians were truly listed on the Thalassocracy List preserved in Diodorus (7 fr. 11), as Burn suggests (reading "Megareis" for "Kares": Burn 1927), they would occupy the period c. 666–599. This would suggest that Megarian colonization (excepting Megara Hyblaea) took place after c. 666 and that the thalassocracy ended with the defeat at Perinthos.

While Megara may have lost territory to the Corinthians in the eighth and seventh centuries, I find it improbable that overpopulation of the remaining Megarian territory was the most important factor in Megarian colonization. Megarian population could have followed the normal Greek pattern in rising between the seventh and the mid-fifth century. Throughout Greece in the seventh century there was much colonization, and, on the whole, generally little in the fifth century. To colonize was, for the most part, a sign of vitality. The chronology of the Megarian colonies does not suggest that population pressures predominated. At least one generation, possibly two, separated Megara Hyblaea from the seventh-century colonies in the Propontis. Surely the refugees from Perachora must have been absorbed or have perished from want long before the seventh-century wave of colonies got under way (Legon 1981.75–81). The presence of Boiotians from Tanagra at the sixth-century Megarian colony of Heraclea indicates that a Megarian **apoikiā** need not have been exclusively composed of Megarians.[2]

---

*En1. The exception is Mesambria, where archaeology supplements the literary evidence: Ognenova 1960; Hoddinott 1975.41–49.

*En2. Heraclea: Ephorus *FGH* 70 F 44; Justin 16.3.4–8; Euphorion fr. 78 [Powell]; Nymphis *FGH* 432 F 3; Apollonius Rhodius 2.846–849 and scholia; Pausanias 5.26.7; Diodorus Siculus 14.31; [Scymnus] 972–973. Note Hesychius *FGH* 390 F 1.16 on the cult of Amphiaraos. See Burstein 1976.15–18. There are also traditions about Byzantion which assign that city to other founding states: Constantine Porphyrogenitus *De thematibus* 1.43 (Dorian colony); Ammianus Marcellinus 22.8.8 (Athenian colony); Velleius Paterculus 2.7.7 (Milesian colony); Dionysius Byzantius *Anaplus Bosphori* W 8 (Corinthian colony). There may also be traces of Boiotian constitutional survivals in Byzantion, but the text is unclear (Diodorus Siculus 14.12.3). Cf., on Astakos, Memnon *FGH* 434 F 12.

Here it is appropriate to recapitulate my views expressed elsewhere on the rationale for colonization (Figueira 1981.192–202). Colonial powers sought to encapsulate citizens of their own city as a ruling elite surrounded by second-class citizens and dependent classes made up of immigrants from other **poleis** as well as natives. For Megara, a pool of those anxious to emigrate may have been available in nearby Boiotia. One more possible background detail ought to be noted regarding Megarian colonization, namely the role of Miletos. Miletos was the friend of an enemy of Corinth, Eretria, and the enemy of a friend of Corinth, Samos. Megara and Miletos predominated as the Hellenizers of the shores of the Propontis and the Black Sea (Boardman 1980.238–246). Their shared enmity for Corinth and the common area for their colonization could indicate that their activity overseas was coordinated.

*F (640/630–600) Few chronological data are known about Theagenes. However, he must have been in power at the time of his son-in-law's coup d'état at Athens. Kylon's uprising was in an Olympic year (636, 632, or 628; see Okin Ch.1 § § 2–3). He had been Olympic victor in 640. It is known that Theagenes did not found a tyrant dynasty. Aristotle does not list him among the long individual tyrannies (*Politics* 1315b11–39). If he meant his list to be complete and he had Theagenes in mind, then Theagenes cannot have ruled for as many as eighteen years. He is usually assumed to have followed an aristocratic or oligarchic government.[1]

The record of Megarian colonization may tell us something about the dates for Theagenes. If Theagenes had followed the model of the Kypselids to his south, he would have set up members of his own family or, in their absence, henchmen in the newly founded colonies. One should expect some trace to have been left of them, as in the case of the Kypselid foundations. The foundation of Byzantion is usually dated to c. 660–657, but a later date of 628 is also attested (Johannes Lydus *De magistratibus* 3.70). One may believe either that 628 is the correct date for the foundation of Byzantion or that only a reinforcement to the colony was dispatched at that date. All Megarian colonies in the Propontis are dated by Roebuck on the basis of the scant available data to 650–625 (1959.114). They were in any case in place by the time of the conflict with the Samians at Perinthos. It is, therefore, possible that seventh-century Megarian colonization ebbed

---

*Fn1. Labarbe 1972.236–243 has Theagenes usurping a democracy and himself followed by a moderate democracy and finally an extreme democracy.

around 630–625. One might speculate, then, that Theagenes took power by c. 630 and that his supremacy began a hiatus in Megarian colonization. Perhaps the internal policy of Theagenes compensated for the suspension of colonization in some unknown manner. If colonization, as seen from the perspective of poor Megarians, was a form of patronage by the elite, its end may signal the first fissure in Megarian social integration (see Figueira Ch.5 §§ 50–65). Later Megarians believed that their city's fountainhouse and aqueduct were the work of Theagenes (Pausanias 1.40.1, cf. 1.41.2). This date for the fountainhouse has not been borne out by archaeology, which would put the surviving remains in the late sixth or early fifth century (before 480; Gruben 1964.41). We know little otherwise about the foreign policy of Theagenes except that he believed Kylon's attempt to seize power at Athens important enough to support him with Megarian troops (Thucydides 1.126.5). Theagenes gave way to the so-called regime of sōphrosunē, assumed to be a moderate oligarchy (Legon 1981.104–105, 112–115), but, in fact, of an indistinct character in the surviving evidence. Even its claim to moderation merely serves to make of it a foil for the succeeding, much maligned democracy. It does not appear to be an unreasonable conjecture that Theagenes is hardly likely to have weathered the crises of the Solonian capture of Salamis and the defeat of the expeditionary force dispatched against Perinthos. Arguments from silence (as always, weak) suggest that Theagenes was no longer in power at the time of these events.

*G (625–600) One may infer from Strabo that at some point the Megarians lost Krommyon to the Corinthians (8.6.22 C380; cf. Xenophon *Hellenica* 4.4.13, 4.5.19). Krommyon could be described as a border area between the Ionians and the Dorians before the Dorianization of Megara (Strabo 9.1.6 C392), that is, a border area between Megara and Corinth. Sidous was also at some stage Megarian, since Stephanus of Byzantion describes it as a kōmē of the Corinthia and also a harbor of the Megarid (s.v. "Sidous"). I assume, perhaps arbitrarily, that it was the **polis** of the Megarians that lost the two towns, not the Megarians at the beginning of their independence. Perhaps Orsippos had upheld Megarian rule over them. If I am correct that these two locations were not included in the Megarian list in the Homeric Catalogue of Ships (see Note B above), they must have been lost before the period of the Spartan arbitration of Salamis (c. 510?), and perhaps before the Solonian effort to recapture Salamis c. 600, which possibly prompted the Megarian claim that their boundaries were validated by the testimony of Homer. At first the Saronic

Gulf had been less important to the Corinthians than the Corinthian Gulf, which their city directly adjoined. The **diolkos**, the grooved track along which wagons and perhaps undercarriages for carrying warships could be drawn, was built at the beginning of the sixth century (Verdelis 1956; cf. Cook 1979.152–153). Kenkhreai must have become critically important to the Corinthians at this time. The information that Periander possessed squadrons of triremes on both seas (Nicolaus of Damascus *FGH* 90 F 58) is important for determining a date for the loss of Sidous and Krommyon. The Megarian loss of this area should be before 600, and, given the importance to Periander of Kenkhreai (near the eastern terminus of the **diolkos**), one might guess further that this Corinthian conquest may have taken place early in his reign—his accession was c. 629–628 (Sakellariou and Faraklas 1971.62; cf. Wiseman 1978.18, 38n17). By the late sixth century, the inscriptions from the area of Krommyon employ an alphabet that has its closest affinities to the Corinthian rather than to the Megarian letter style (Salmon 1972.196n227).

*H (625–600) The beginnings of the confrontation between Athens and Megara are most likely to have ensued after Athens had incorporated Eleusis and thus had given the two cities a common and disputed border. Significantly, a struggle with Megara over Eleusis was put in the time of Theseus.[1] Furthermore, the Megarians celebrated games in honor of Diokles, an Eleusinian ruler who fled to Megara (just as Eurysakes came from Salamis to Athens) (scholia Theocritus 12.27–33f; cf. Theocritus 12.27–33; Aristophanes *Acharnians* 774 with scholia; *Hymn to Demeter* 153, 474; scholia Pindar *N.* 3.145; see Highbarger 1927.57–58). Yet, other mythological evidence strongly suggests that the Athenians of the classical period believed that early Eleusis and Athens had themselves come into military confrontation (Thucydides 2.15; Pausanias 1.27.4, 1.38.3; see Mylonas 1961.24–29). In the Homeric *Hymn to Demeter*, we seem to glimpse a stage in the evolution of the Eleusinian cult at which Athenian influence did not yet predominate (e.g., the **Kērux** 'Herald', later an important official at Eleusis, is not introduced; Richardson 1974.7–10). While it is customary to date the *Hymn* (followed by Athenian control of the sanctuary) to the second half of the seventh century (Mylonas

---

*Hn1. Theseus' capture of Eleusis from Megara: Plutarch *Theseus* 10.4, cf. 25.5. Compare the legend of the division of Attica (including the Megarid) among the sons of Pandion: scholia Aristophanes *Lysistrata* 58; *Wasps* 1223; Sophocles fr. 24 Radt. Eleusis may have been included in the Megarid: Andron *FGH* 10 F 14; cf. Philochorus *FGH* 328 F 107.

1961.63–64), its most recent editor sees no *terminus ante quem* before 550, when Athens began to show greater interest in the Eleusinian hero Eumolpos and when the Hall of the Mysteries was rebuilt (under the sponsorship of Peisistratos?) with an orientation establishing that Eleusis was under Athenian control (Richardson 1974.9–10). An earlier date for the *Hymn* and for the end of independence for Eleusis depends on a passage in Herodotus (1.30.5). Here Solon rates as the most happy of men Tellos of Athens, who fell in a battle against the Eleusinians: **genomenēs gar Athēnaioisi makhēs pros tous astugeitonas en Eleusini boēthēsās** . . . , 'As a battle took place for the Athenians against [their] neighbors in Eleusis, [Tellos], coming as an ally . . . '. Although there has been some discussion of the interpretation of this phrase, an examination of parallel phraseology suggests the following. The phrase **genomenēs** . . . **Eleusini** constitutes a unit, and **boēthēsās** is to be construed absolutely. The word **pros** should mean 'against' (cf. 1.39.2 [esp.]; 4.111.1; 5.49.8; 7.226.2; see Powell 1938.320–321).

Placing much weight on this piece of evidence is, however, made difficult by the chronological improbability that Solon and Croesus as king can ever have held such a discussion. The confrontation of Solon and Croesus is an elaboration of conventional themes appropriate to a wise man's advice to a hubristic potentate. The tradition is to be classed along with other apocryphal material in Herodotus associated with the careers of the Seven Sages. It is possible that an earlier variant of the story (one more sensitive to chronology) had some other Lydian or barbarian ruler as the beneficiary of Solon's advice. The question to be raised, then, is whether the authors or compilers of earlier variants would have appended a seventh-century conflict between Athens and Eleusis as an incidental detail. From the context one may infer that Tellos was at least a contemporary of Solon (having several grandchildren at the time of his death). Solon was born not later than 640 (Sosicrates at Diogenes Laertius 1.62; cf. Phainias F 21 [Wehrli]), so that Tellos could have fought the Eleusinians in the late seventh or early sixth century. Unfortunately, it is therefore impossible to determine whether the Athenians first had cause for grievance with the Megarians over Salamis or over Eleusis. A more superficially sensible sequence would be that the first break with the Megarians occurred over the border with Eleusis, but there is no reason to believe that such a chronology is necessarily or arguably true.

The standard charge later leveled by the Athenians against Megara was that the Megarians encroached upon land sacred to Demeter, the Hiera Orgas (e.g., Thucydides 1.139.2). That the dispute between the two states resolved itself into these terms indicates its early archaic origin. To incorporate the territory of a community into a unity under the protection of the gods, its borders were sacralized. Thus the ephebes swore by the borders of Attica (Tod 2 no. 204.20). Where external threats to a community were most intense (i.e., disputed borders), the land in question became especially holy and was left fallow to signify this.

*I (before 600) The evidence of epic seems to suggest that Salamis was inhabited by a small community dependent on seafaring, perhaps in the form of piracy, but the Salaminioi seem to have exempted Athens from attack, alone of their neighbors (Hesiod fr. 204.46–51 MW; cf. Strabo 9.1.11 C395). At some moment, presumably before 600, the Megarians took Salamis. They claimed that Salamis was a Megarian village in the Catalogue of Ships (Strabo 9.1.10 C394). For Megara, the possession of Salamis kept open Megara's access to the outside world by sea, and its arable land was valuable in and of itself. It is possible that Theagenes undertook this aggression. It is also possible that Salamis was an alternative field for Megarian expansion, so that Megarian possession of Salamis may be connected with a possible cessation of Megarian colonization c. 630–625. If there is anything to Athenian claims that they incorporated the Salaminians into their society (see Note S below), the Megarians perhaps expelled the Salaminians and settled the island themselves. In the Megarian version of the Solonian capture of the island, the Megarian settlers on Salamis are called **klēroukhoi** 'lot-holders'. The term ought to mean that they had replaced the original settlers, if it is used analogously to the concept of later Athenian cleruchies.

Plutarch states that the Athenians fought a long, difficult, and unsuccessful war with the Megarians over Salamis. Pausanias could be shown the beaks of warships taken from the Athenians in combat over Salamis (Pausanias 1.40.5). The Athenians reached the point of prohibiting the mention of Salamis on pain of death (Plutarch *Solon* 8–10). At this point, Solon intervened. Feigning madness, he went as a herald to the Agora and delivered his elegy exhorting the Athenians to recapture the island.[1] Plutarch gives two accounts of the

---

*In1. For Solon and Salamis in general: Aristotle *Rhetoric* 1375b29–30; Strabo 9.1.10–11 C394–395; Aeschines 1.25; Demosthenes 19.252; [Demosthenes] 61.49; Diogenes Laertius 1.46; Libanius *Declamationes* 1.152. It is possible that the history of Athenian confrontation with Megara may involve the socioeconomic aspirations of different segments of the Athenian population. Further discussion would be inappropriate here, but see, for example, Hopper 1961.210–215. Compare the modernizing account of French 1957.

capture of Salamis. In the first, the Megarians are lured from Salamis by a false deserter who urged them to kidnap a group of Athenian women celebrating a festival of Demeter at Cape Kolias. It is interesting to note in this Megarian sacrilege Demeter's first appearance in the conflict between Athens and Megara. The alacrity with which the Megarians on Salamis rose to the lure of piracy may suggest that Megarian piratical raids were no small threat to Athens. The Megarians manned a **ploion** 'vessel', but they were met by youths disguised as women and were slain. The Athenians then occupied Salamis, left bereft of defenders (cf. Polyaenus 1.20.1–2; Aelian *Varia Historia* 7.19). Plutarch suggests that this is the most popular account. Yet its content is hard to square with its context. An attempt to kidnap Athenian women for ransom could be taken to suggest that Athens and Megara were already at war. Yet Solon is supposed to have roused the Athenians at a time when they had abandoned Salamis. Moreover, it is difficult to understand why there were not more Megarians (than a shipload) established on Salamis as settlers, as the Megarian version asserted. Equally troubling is the presence of Peisistratos at Solon's side in the campaign. Peisistratos, born c. 605–600, can hardly have been a leading officer before 575 (Davies 1971.445). There is, moreover, independent testimony on the Peisistratid campaign against Megara in which he captured Nisaea (Herodotus 1.59.4).

Although the sources for Plutarch's chronology in the *Life of Solon* are most obscure, he evidently believed that the Solonian capture of Salamis (which to Plutarch made the statesman famous) was early in Solon's career. It was before the First Sacred War, and by inference before the purification of Athens by Epimenides and the Solonic reforms. The difficulty caused by the report of Peisistratos' participation in the affair with Solon could be partially obviated by following the early fifth-century date for Epimenides (Plato *Laws* 642D) and by redating the constitutional reforms of Solon to c. 580 (Hignett 1952.316–321). Such a process of dating would allow for the participation of a rather young Peisistratos. Yet, the priority of the Salamis campaign to the Sacred War can be taken to mean (if Plutarch's order is correct) that Peisistratos cannot have been Solon's collaborator. The First Sacred War involved fighting in the 590s and 580s (Krisa fell in 591/90: Hypothesis b, d to Pindar *P.*; *Marmor Parium* 37 [Jacoby]). This led to a reorganization of the Pythian festival in 586 while further changes were made in 582 (Pausanias 10.7.4–7; *Marmor Parium* 38). Solon withdrew from Athens for ten years after his legislation. On his return he adopted a passive stance, stirring himself (if Plutarch, basing himself on the *Atthis*, is correct) only to resist Peisistratos at the last moment (Plutarch *Solon* 30). This suggests an early campaign for Salamis. The same confusion between Solon and Peisistratos as adversaries of Megara over Salamis is seen in the differences among the Megareis concerning which of these two Athenians made interpolations in Homer in order to strengthen the affiliation of Ajax to Attica (Dieuchidas *FGH* 485 F 6; Hereas *FGH* 486 F 1). Clearly, it was calculations like those just presented that led Aristotle to affirm that Peisistratos had not collaborated in the capture of Salamis (*Constitution of the Athenians* 17.2). Solon could then be brought in because many Athenians became reluctant to credit the tyrant dynasty with so great a service to the state.

That Solon and not Peisistratos is the interloper in Plutarch's first account may be demonstrated by the version of the same story given most completely by Aeneas Tacticus (4.8–11; cf. Frontinus *Strategematica* 2.9.9; Justin 2.8.1–6). This tradition specifically assigns the incident to Peisistratos during his generalship. The Megarians set out to kidnap a group of Athenian women celebrating the Thesmophoria at Eleusis. They were ambushed and killed by Peisistratos, who had learned of their plot. Bringing soldiers in the Megarian ships, Peisistratos sailed into a harbor near the city. When prominent Megarians approached the ships, they were taken prisoner or slain. To a certain extent, this version differs from Plutarch by both simplification and elaboration. While in the story reported by Plutarch the Athenian women were celebrating the sacrifice to Demeter at Cape Kolias, in this variant, the less specific and more pan-Hellenic term **thesmophoria** is used. No Athenian celebration of the Thesmophoria is known for Eleusis—the main celebration was in the suburbs of Athens. The account of Aeneas exaggerates insofar as the Megarians have now come in many ships, although Polyaenus and Aelian report several and two ships, respectively. Further simplification is seen in the absence of an explanation of how Peisistratos learned about the Megarian plot. Yet, at the same time, where Plutarch merely reports the capture of Salamis after the ambuscade, the tradition attributing the incident to Peisistratos gives an account of the subsequent attack.

The motif of men disguised as women has been replaced in Aeneas and the others by the less striking sequence having Athenians manning Megarian ships and thus being disguised as Megarians, while their women were disguised as prisoners. That such similar trickery plays a role at two different stages in the same episode is unlikely, and the theme may be a borrowed one. The original story may have avoided the improbable detail wherein Peisistratos risks the lives of prominent Athenian women. Rather, the same young men who had played the part of the celebrants in Plutarch may have continued their masquerade on the Megarian ships. The location of the discomfiture of the Megarians is not fully specified, that is, according to Aeneas, it is merely a place at some distance from the city, and, according to Justin, the port. Legon may well be right that this is meant to represent the capture of Nisaea (1981.137). Yet the fact that the Megarian officials are described as having advanced from the city to meet the ships suggests an anchorage rather than a port town like Nisaea. Curiously, it is Plutarch's second version of Solon's capture of Salamis which is parallel here. In it, the city that is mentioned ought to be a settlement on Salamis, so that possibly the phrase **ta Megara** in Aeneas is meant to mean only Megarian territory and could stand for a settlement on Salamis. If such wording was in Plutarch's source, the fact that Aeneas' account has its denouement occurring at Megara would be explicable. The shifting of the sacrifice of the Athenian women from Cape Kolias to Eleusis is probably to be considered an outgrowth of such confusion. An ambush at Eleusis would bring Peisistratos near Megara and so would make more sense than Cape Kolias if Nisaea was to be the eventual destination. In Aeneas, Peisistratos makes his attack on the Megarian leaders before nightfall on the day of his ambush of their ships. I suspect that these changes were not made by Aeneas, who only simplified the story. He cites it in an excursus to illustrate his category of **sussēma** 'prearranged signals'.

The version reported by Aeneas (early fourth century?) maintained the role of Peisistratos as leader but changed the setting to Eleusis (perhaps to adapt the story to narrate a capture of Nisaea) and changed the part that disguise played. These alterations may have been in part based on a conflation of this anecdote with the other story of the capture of Salamis related by Plutarch. The early predominance of this version may explain why Daimakhos (early fourth century) of Plataia stated that fighting against Megara was not Solon's accomplishment (Plutarch *Comparatio Solonis et Publicolae* [4] [*FGH* 65 F 7]). The evolution of the story may have occurred along these lines: an original story describing the Peisistratid capture of Nisaea or Salamis was altered to allow the participation of Solon by Plutarch's source, perhaps an Atthidographer or a biographer dependent upon an *Atthis*. Even if it concerned Nisaea originally, Salamis now became the story's subject. Aelian, who attributes the capture to Solon, describes the conclusion of the incident in the same manner as Aeneas but sets the slaughter of the Megarians on Salamis. In later Atthidography, when Solon tended to usurp the accomplishments of other statesmen—compare the fate of Kleisthenes as the founder of the democracy—the story was assigned to him.

There were losses and perhaps recaptures of Salamis in the period after Solon (whether accounts of these events have survived or not). Plutarch reports the loss of Nisaea and Salamis in the post-Kylonian turmoil (*Solon* 12.5). Since, however, only one capture of Nisaea is known, the Peisistratid one, Plutarch has probably confused the pre- and post-Solonian periods of **stasis**. Nisaea and Salamis were both lost at some time before Peisistratos firmly established himself.

Plutarch's second version is a better choice for the Solonian capture (*Solon* 9: Legon 1981.127). Solon takes with him 500 young men who will be **kurioi tou politeumatos** 'authoritative in the body-politic'. This grant of political status ought to mean that Salamis was not simply to be incorporated into Attica but was to have a separate identity. The **kurioi** were to be full citizens of a new political entity on Salamis, probably envisaged as an **apoikiā** 'colony'. Note that the later Athenian dispensation for the island does not coincide with Solon's provisions, which were perhaps superseded by a later Megarian capture (see Note J below). Solon invoked the aid of the heroes Periphemos and Kyrkreos. The pattern the capture takes is framed as an aetiology for sacrifices to these heroes which were undertaken thereafter (*Solon* 9.1). Yet both these heroes are remarkable for their absence from later literature. Periphemos appears nowhere else. Kyrkreos was the son-in-law of Skiron (Plutarch *Theseus* 10.2–3). His affiliation with Salamis and Megara is thus secure, and this fact was admitted by the Megareis (*Theseus* 10.3 = *FGH* 487 F 1). Thus the struggle between Atthidographers and Megareis both to appropriate heroes (e.g., Nisos) and to impose upon them a particular moral evaluation (e.g., Skiron) is at work here.

In Plutarch's second account, the effort to capture Salamis is sanctioned by a Delphic response that says that the heroes were buried looking toward the setting sun. This detail coincides with the arguments used by the Athenians before the Spartan arbitrators (Plutarch *Solon* 10.4) and suggests that the oracle dates no later than the late sixth century, when Salamis seems to have been awarded to Athens by Sparta (see Note S below). The attribution of these Delphic responses to Solon is perhaps also no later than that date. The **hērōon** of Kyrkreos was built only after the Battle of Salamis (Pausanias 1.36.1), at the urging of a Delphic response (cf. Aeschylus *Persians* 570; Sophocles fr. 579 Radt). One is impressed once more with the stillborn quality of Solon's provisions for Salamis as reported by Plutarch.

Solon captured a Megarian ship sent out to scout for an attacking Athenian force. He filled it with the bravest of his men, who approached the **polis** on the island. The rest of his force made a general attack, whereupon the crew of the captured ship seized the city. In this story, disguise and treachery play the same role as they do in the Aeneas (Peisistratid) variant of the other story of the capture of Salamis. Here this motif had an aetiological point, in that it explained a mimetic invasion of Cape Skiradion, the western promontory of Salamis, by a single ship. This ritual was celebrated near a temple of Enyalios, supposedly founded by Solon. An Attic red-figure cup may bear a representation of this cult act (Petersen 1917). It is the work of the potter Hieron, and Beazley attributes the decoration to the Telephos Painter, a follower of Makron (1942.542; cf. Beazley 1963.816–817). The Telephos Painter was active in the 460s (Boardman 1975.195–196), so that the pot would bring nothing to my investigation of this story save confirmation of the existence of this tradition of the Solonian capture before 450 (something attested by the cult of Kyrkreos after Salamis). The fact that only one warship was involved and that this was a triakonter (rather than a pentekonter or trireme) points toward an early date and an improvised sortie. The capture of the island is also an impromptu measure appropriate to a situation where Solon convinced the Athenians by his elegy to take action. He immediately gathered volunteers and attacked the island. The Megarians on the island were a settlement, and they were unprepared for the surprise attack. Both of these features suggest that Megara was complacent in its control of the island.

To conclude, the first capture of Salamis reported by Plutarch should belong to Peisistratos. Plutarch's second story represents the Solonian capture, the first Athenian occupation of the island. Yet all we can do is to attempt to recover the original traditions, which nevertheless cannot be vouched for as historical. The first story permits no judgment of its factuality. It might represent either sound tradition contained in an Atthidographer or plausible conjecture by later Athenians. The second account, however, preserves several odd details about the Solonian provisions for Salamis. Its use of oracles calls to mind the Athenian justification for their ownership of Salamis in the late sixth century.[2] At the same time, the use of the disguise motif and of aetiology to explain the mimetic invasion may be apocryphal.

*J (before 600) The Athenian versions of the loss of Salamis do not accommodate the Megarian account, which had the island betrayed by a group of Megarian exiles called the Dorykleians (Pausanias 1.40.5

---

*In2. The phrase that describes Solon's activities upon arriving on Salamis may also be mentioned. Solon anchors at a promontory (or breakwater) looking toward Euboia. As practical topography this is meaningless, but it is possibly acceptable as the cryptic language of an oracular response that Solon deciphered to refer to Salamis.

= *FGH* 487 F 12). They made their way to the Megarian settlers on Salamis and then betrayed the island to the Athenians. Pausanias' notice is very terse. Though no details are in common, the context of the account in Plutarch which we believe to be Solonian is nearer to it. The Megarian story has a notion of betrayal, to be compared with surprise in the Athenian story. The Solonian and Megarian captures have as their background the occupation of Salamis by settlers. **Dorukleioi** means 'famous for the spear' (cf. **dourikleitos** [e.g., *Iliad* v 55, 578]; **douriklutos** [e.g., *Iliad* ii 645, xvi 26; Archilochus fr. 3]). **Dorukleioi** is an odd name for a **genos**, a phratry, or a political subgroup. The Dorykleians may have been a warrior brotherhood expelled from Megara. There has been almost unanimous credibility accorded to the Athenian versions of the loss of Salamis (Piccirilli 1975.131–133). Yet it is less important to affirm either the Athenian or the Megarian traditions about Salamis than to observe some features about the context of the story. There is no reason to doubt that the Dorukleioi existed or that they had been exiled from Megara. The Megarians were trying to add plausibility to their face-saving story about the Athenian conquest of Salamis. This goal would scarcely have been served by the invention of an improbable-seeming group of exiles.

If warrior bands (= **hetaireiai**?) had conducted Megarian military operations, it might partially explain the emphasis on **philoi** in Theognis. Elsewhere, at Sparta and Ephesus, Tyrtaeus (fr. 10–12) and Callinus (fr. 1) sang the virtues of the hoplites, steadfast in maintaining the phalanx. At Megara, the Theognidea are more concerned with careful gauging of the temperament of **philoi** (vv. 93–100, 213–216, 309–312 [n.b. v. 309: **sussitoisin**], 963–970, 1071–1074, 1163–1164h; see also Levine Ch.7, Donlan Ch.9). In the fighting of aristocratic bands, trust between comrades and the ability to predict the reactions of the one fighting nearby are more important than immersion of the individual personality in group fighting. If the Dorykleians acquiesced in Solon's capture of Salamis, certain conclusions can be drawn. They were exiled either by Theagenes or less probably by the regime said by Plutarch to have been characterized by **sōphrosunē** 'moderation', and not by the democracy—unless the democracy is to be put early, c. 600 (see Note F above, Notes K, Q below). In any case, the theme of exile so evident in the Theognidea does not have to be grounded in the historical plight of a single group of exiles, namely those following the Palintokia. The fate of the Dorykleians suggests that banishments occurred more than once in the intense political infighting of archaic Megara. Therefore the exile-passages of the Theognidea were perhaps to some extent conventional (e.g., 209–210, 332a–334, 1209–1216).

*K (c. 600) Plutarch in the *Greek Questions* (57) provides an explanation for the name of a building at Samos, the "Hall of Fetters" (Plutarch *Moralia* 303E–304C). When the Samians founded their colony at Perinthos, they came into conflict with the Megarians in the Propontis presumably because the Megarians found Perinthos threatening to their colonies there. A fleet dispatched by the ruling aristocracy of Samos, the **Geōmoroi**, defeated the Megarians at Perinthos. However, the commanders of the fleet decided to overthrow the regime at Samos and enlisted the help of the Megarians in doing so. The Megarians were introduced to the council house on Samos with fetters rigged for escape. Once in the presence of the members of the government, the Megarians threw aside their rigged bonds and assassinated them. The new Samian government offered the 600 Megarian prisoners citizenship. I shall assume that Okin is correct and that the source for this story is Samian local historical tradition, possibly Duris of Samos (see Okin Ch.1 § 4–8). The political background of this confrontation is not hard to envisage. Samos had been an ally of Corinth, so that it is possible that the hostility between the Samians and the Megarians had a previous history (Thucydides 1.13.3). When Periander changed the pattern of alliances in the Aegean by establishing friendship with Thrasyboulos, tyrant of Miletos, it was likely that all other powers had to make adjustments (Herodotus 1.20; 5.92ζ2–η1; Diogenes Laertius 1.95; Aristotle *Politics* 1311a20–22). Therefore, a bout of hostilities between Megara and Samos followed by rapprochement between the two states is not surprising. The change in Corinthian alliance patterns from friendship with Samos to alliance with Miletos was not later than 605–604.[1] Consequently, at the end of Periander's life (in one version of the story), the Samians intercepted a group of Corcyraean noble youths sent by Periander to Alyattes of Lydia for castration (Herodotus 3.48.2–4).

Perinthos was founded in 602, according to the traditional chronology (Strabo 7 fr. 56; Jerome *Chronica* 98b [Helm]). It is perhaps the Samian propensity for piracy (e.g., Herodotus 3.39.3, 3.47.1–3; Meiggs-Lewis no. 16) which directly prompted Megarian concern for

---

*Kn1. The first token of Periander's friendship with Thrasyboulos is information sent to Miletos about a Delphic response given to king Alyattes of Lydia when he sought to counteract the plague afflicting his people (Herodotus 1.20). The sacrilege supposedly responsible for the plague occurred in the sixth campaign of Alyattes against Miletos. Herodotus dates his accession to 617, but this figure very possibly should be corrected to 612 (Kaletsch 1958.34–39). A dedication of the pharaoh Necho, presumably made in peacetime at Miletos, points to a date before 605 for peace between Lydia and Miletos following Periander's intervention on behalf of the Milesians (Pedley 1968.53).

the lines of communication to their colonies, the nearest of which was Selymbria. If the date of the alliance between Periander and Thrasyboulos was before 605, one would be reluctant to opt for a date for this maritime conflict between Samos and Megara much after the foundation of Perinthos. The fact that the Samians offered the Megarian assassins citizenship is intriguing. The attraction in using the Megarians had presumably been that, since they were outsiders, even enemies, the blood guilt intrinsic to the murder of the **Geōmoroi** would not pollute the Samian community. Yet the Samians, by the offer of citizenship, were in a sense assimilating the guilt that they may have sought to avoid. Perhaps the Megarians could not return home, either because their actions on Samos would be interpreted negatively by the Megarian government or because their behavior did not wipe the slate clean of the defeat at Perinthos (cf. Burn 1967.219). The Megarian democracy is the least likely of the Megarian governments to have been in power at this point. Such a democracy might well have honored the assassins of the arch-aristocratic **Geōmoroi** (cf. Legon 1981.122).[2]

*L (600–585) It is possible that a military confrontation, the knowledge of which we owe to the Theognidea, may belong to the same interstate context to which the conflict with the Samians over Perinthos and the fighting with the Milesians may be attributed (see Note F above; Note O below).

οἴ μοι ἀναλκίης· ἀπὸ μὲν Κήρινθος ὄλωλεν,
Ληλάντου δ' ἀγαθὸν κείρεται οἰνόπεδον·
οἱ δ' ἀγαθοὶ φεύγουσι, πόλιν δὲ κακοὶ διέπουσιν.
ὡς δὴ Κυψελιδῶν Ζεὺς ὀλέσειε γένος.
Theognis 891–894

Alas for my weakness; Kerinthos is destroyed
and the good vineland of the river Lelas is ravaged.
The **agathoi** [nobles] are in flight; the **kakoi** [base] manage the city.
Would that Zeus may destroy the race of the Kypselids.[1]

---

*Kn2. It is possible that the engineering work at Samos of the Megarian Eupalinos, who designed the great water tunnel, attests to a later stage of the same friendship (Herodotus 3.60.1–3), perhaps in the time of Polykrates, c. 538–522 (cf. Aristotle *Politics* 1313b24).

*Ln1. The manuscripts have the unmetrical and meaningless **Kupselizōn** (A) or **Kupsellizon** (OXI). Recent editors follow the emendation of Herrmann which is printed in our text. Ellis 1910.45 prefers **Kupsele son**. Cf. Busolt 1893.1.650–651n6; Harrison 1902.286–294.

The poet bewails his weakness and mourns the sack of Kerinthos in Euboia. He goes on to complain of the ravaging of the Lelantine Plain and closes by hurling imprecations at the Kypselids. The historical context for the passage is a flare-up of hostility between Khalkis and Eretria over the Lelantine Plain. Although the best context for the major conflict between Khalkis and Eretria which we call the Lelantine War is the late eighth century, the fighting mentioned in this passage need not be dated so early (cf. Herodotus 5.99.1).[2] The dispute over the plain may not have had a final settlement, at least so long as Khalkis and Eretria remained capable of contesting its ownership through a resumption of hostilities. The Megarians have been thought of as allies of the Eretrians because of the previous friendship between Khalkis and Corinth attested by the Corinthian expulsion of Eretrian colonists from Corcyra (Plutarch *Greek Questions* 11 [*Moralia* 293A–B]) and the possible collaboration of these two states in colonization (see Note C above). Nevertheless, from its location, Kerinthos appears to lie in the Khalkidian sphere of influence in Euboia. Whether the Lelantine Plain, the destruction of which the poet laments, was in the hands of Khalkis or Eretria cannot with certainty be determined. Boardman believes, based on the quantity and quality of Khalkidian and Eretrian pottery, that Eretria held the upper hand over Khalkis in the seventh century and the first half of the sixth century (Boardman 1957.27–29). But pottery finds or even indications of wealth and poverty are hardly indicative of military success. Alignments become clearer, however, when we consider late sixth-century alliances. Khalkis was an ally of Thebes and the Boiotian League (Herodotus 5.74.2), with whom the Khalkidians (perhaps c. 506) had minted common monetary issues. Eretria, however, had good relations with Athens, demonstrated by its support for Peisistratos (*Constitution of the Athenians* 15.2), common aid to the Ionians (Herodotus 5.99.1), Athenian help to Eretria in 490 (Herodotus 6.100), and marriage links with the Alcmaeonids (Aristophanes *Clouds* 46–48; cf. *Acharnians* 614; scholia Aristophanes *Clouds* 46a, 48b, 800).

This pattern of interstate relations makes it probable that a sixth-century Megara would find its sympathies lying with Khalkis rather than Eretria. So if Kerinthos was aligned with Khalkis, the poet's solicitude for that city is understandable. A date after 600 for these hostilities is reasonable, when the similarity to the sequence of events involving the Megarian relationship to Miletos is noted. If the military

---

*L n2. Burn 1929.

alignment of Eretria-Miletos-Megara against Khalkis-Samos-Corinth reflects eighth- and early seventh-century international politics, then it is possible that Periander's shift in Corinthian alliance from Samos to Miletos can be paralleled by a shift from Khalkis to Eretria. Such a change would put Corinth on the same side as Athens, for whom Periander arbitrated the possession of Sigeion to the detriment of Mytilene (Herodotus 5.95.2; cf. Apollodorus *FGH* 244 F 27), and with whose leading family, the Philaiads, the Kypselids intermarried (Herodotus 6.35.1; 6.128.2). Jeffery notes that Periander planted the colony of Poteidaia on the peninsula of Pallene in the Khalkidike in c. 600 (Nicolaus of Damascus *FGH* 90 F 59; Jeffery 1976.66, 70). This may have been an infringement upon the territory of the Khalkidians of the north, who had sent help against Eretria on behalf of their mother city, Khalkis, c. 700 (Plutarch *Dialogue on Love* 17 [*Moralia* 761A] = Aristotle fr. 98). It may be remarked that the same alignment can be seen in central Greece on the evidence of the suitors of Agariste, the daughter of Kleisthenes of Sikyon (Herodotus 6.127). Among them were two Athenians, Megakles and Hippokleides, of whom the latter was initially favored because of his marriage connections with the Kypselids of Corinth; Lysanias of Eretria; Leokedes, an Argive of the Heraklid royal house (probably in exile from his homeland; cf. Meiggs-Lewis no. 9); and Diakoridas, of the Scopad family from Krannon in Thessaly. Kleomakhos, one of the Ekhekratids of Pharsalos, rivals of the Scopads, had helped Khalkis in fighting against Eretria (Plutarch *Dialogue on Love* 17 [*Moralia* 760E–761A]). One may note that Sikyon was apparently friendly with Athens at this time (both states had fought on the side of Delphi in the First Sacred War: Hypothesis to Pindar *N.* 9; Pausanias 2.9.6, 10.37.6; Polyaenus 3.5). Moreover, the Argive government, which fought against Kleisthenes of Sikyon, had probably helped Megara against Corinth (see Note N below).

Not only is the destruction at Kerinthos and on the Lelantine Plain bewailed, but, in typical Theognidean language, the flight of the **agathoi** and the political supremacy of the **kakoi** are lamented. An attested sequence of events in archaic Khalkis might have made such language apposite. A tyrant, Phoxos—his name is probably a nickname, note Thersites **phoxos ... kephalēn** 'pointed ... in the head' (*Iliad* II 219)—took power with the **gnōrimoi** only to give way shortly to the **dēmos** (Aristotle *Politics* 1304a29–31). Another tyrant, Antileon, was succeeded by an oligarchy (*Politics* 1316a31–32).

But it is important to note that this section of the Theognidea begins with a plaint of weakness. It is presumably Megarian weakness that is at issue, and it may be that Corinthian military activity hindered the Megarians from coming to the aid of their Euboian allies. It is therefore possible that the section should find its place as a reference to the war between Megara and Corinth in which eventually the Megarians were to achieve some victories, with the help of Argos. Periander in the latter part of his reign (c. 600–588/85) is an obvious candidate for the Kypselid responsible. Yet, for the Kypselids, it is also possible that the short-lived successor of Periander, Psammetikhos (and his relatives), might be suggested. Psammetikhos lost power in Corinth in 581. However, the formula of execration of the Kypselids is traditional (cf. *Suda* s.v. **"Kupselidōn anathema en Olumpiāi"**: **exōlēs eiē Kupselidōn geneā**). The Kypselids were held accursed through the marriage with Melissa, daughter of Prokles, the tyrant of Epidauros. Prokles had married a daughter of Aristokrates, king of the Arkadians, who had betrayed the Messenians and been cursed for it (Pausanias 4.22.7; Callisthenes *FGH* 124 F 23).

*M (570–565) If there had been a Peisistratid capture of Salamis, there must have been a preceding loss after the Solonian capture. One might guess that war between the two states broke out once more, perhaps when the Athenians were distracted by the internal strife of the 580s or 570s. Peisistratos' capture of Salamis would belong before his first tyranny (no earlier than 561) and is to be connected with his seizure of Nisaea. The capture of Nisaea, which is mentioned by Herodotus (1.59.4), gained more renown for Peisistratos, as it presumably was a much more serious setback for Megara. Conceivably, the recapture of Salamis might be included in the "other great deeds" attributed to Peisistratos by Herodotus. Yet Salamis could also have been lost during one of the periods of Peisistratos' absences from power after his initial assumption of the tyranny. Peisistratos as tyrant might then have recaptured Salamis. Hence the recapture of Salamis would not be dated by the Peisistratid capture of Nisaea (570–565). His good neighbor policy, predicated perhaps on a disinclination to bring together the Athenian army en masse, ought to be one consideration in preferring a date c. 570–565 for both the recapture of Salamis and the capture of Nisaea. Contemporaneous attacks on both places would explain how a capture of Nisaea came to be confused with a capture of Salamis (if, in fact, it was: see Note I above). This dating would allow Peisistratos to have achieved his exploits against Megara while allowing a few years' time to accommodate his activities at the head of the Hill Party before his accession to power. The Peisistratid capture of Nisaea should perhaps be considered a particularly successful raid. It is unlikely that the Athenians could have kept Nisaea, probably unwalled at this time (see Note I above). It could not have been held without fortifications, nor could reinforcements from

Athens have reached Nisaea to save it from recapture because the Athenians did not possess a standing fleet with a capacity for swift mobilization (cf. Herodotus 6.89).

*N (575–550, 545–510) Megarian conflicts with Corinth in the sixth century are prey to conjecture. Given the material about the early subjection of Megara to Corinth and about the career of Orsippos, and the evidence for Corinthian aggression against Megara in the fifth century, it is not surprising that Corinth and Megara fought in the sixth century. The Megarian treasury at Olympia was built out of spoils taken from the Corinthians (Pausanias 6.19.12–14). Pausanias says that the treasury was built some years after the battle with the Corinthians, but either a numeral (50 or 500?) or the adjective 'many' qualifying 'years' has fallen from his text (Hitzig 1901.506, 636). A two-stage process is at work here, as the treasury contained earlier offerings. Pausanias believes that the spoils from which the treasury was built were taken in the reign of Phorbas, a life-archon at Athens. He is said by Pausanias to have reigned both before the annual archonship at Athens and before the Eleans kept records of the Olympiads, namely in the tenth century (e.g., 952–924: Jerome *Chronica* 74a–76a [Helm]). That any war between these two cities was so early is extremely unlikely, nor is one likely to have been remembered.

It is odd that the name of Phorbas, an Athenian, is used to date a Megarian/Corinthian war. An archon date suggests a written source, perhaps one that is Atthidographical or derived from the *Atthis*, but why such a source would have even treated this war is hard to visualize. Megarian local historians did not use archon dates, as far as we can tell from the scanty extant material. The Megareis hardly would have wished to date anything by an archon date, given their antipathy toward Athens. An alternative explanation would be that Pausanias identified a Phorbas associated with the Megarian treasury as the Athenian life-archon rather than as a Megarian of the same name unknown to him. Perhaps the name was inscribed on the treasury or something connected with it. Note the use of **hēgoumai** 'I believe' for his introduction of the dating by Phorbas. The next question to be raised is whether Pausanias introduced the idea that the conflict took place before the Eleans kept records for any reason other than to illustrate that the war and Phorbas were both early. In other words, did he know somehow that the Eleans could not date the war between the Megarians and the Corinthians, or the spoils in the Megarian treasury, or even the beginning of the building of the treasury itself?

If this last supposition is correct, it is possible that the reason why the records of the Eleans were in default was that the war took place at a time when the Pisatans had usurped management of Olympia. Damophon, son of the Pisatan tyrant Pantaleon, usurped the conduct of the Olympian Games in 588, according to Pausanias (6.22.2–4). His brother, Pyrrhos, carried on the struggle after Damophon's death. Other testimonia (e.g., Strabo 8.3.30 C355) on Olympia record a more complex pattern of conflict over the sanctuary than the three anolympiads (748, 644, 588) of Pausanias. It is possible that the war between Corinth and Megara took place in the period after 588, when the Eleans were not securely in control of Olympia. Depending on how long one makes Pisatan control of the sanctuary last, one may date other things concerning the Megarian treasury (e.g., dedications or spoils) in such a context.

According to Pausanias, the Argives helped the Megarians in this war. Argive hostility to Corinth makes sense. Corinth under Periander had intervened in the Argolic Akte against Prokles of Epidauros (Herodotus 3.52.7). In some stories, the Argive tyrant Pheidon fell during a civil war at Corinth (Nicolaus of Damascus *FGH* 90 F 35; cf. Plutarch *Love Stories* 2 [*Moralia* 772D–773B]; scholia Apollonius Rhodius 4.1212); whether in support of the Bacchiads or against them is uncertain. Yet Argos cannot have helped Megara in the second half of the sixth century. In c. 546, Argos had been defeated by the Spartans in the Battle of Champions and had been stripped of Kynouria, the Thyreatis, and perhaps Kythera (Herodotus 1.82). Argos then fell into internal confusion. The Argive tyrant Perilaos may have come to power at this time (Pausanias 2.23.7; cf. 2.20.7; Herodotus 1.82.8). Also, the Argives may have been inhibited from further action by a fifty-year truce with Sparta. They could not have helped Megara against Corinth without arousing Spartan suspicion, especially inasmuch as Corinth's alliance with Sparta antedates 525 (Herodotus 3.46–50).

Rather, Argive participation belongs to the string of earlier Argive moves meant to redress the power balance in the northeast Peloponnesus (Figueira 1983.27–28). After the Argive decline associated with the successors of Pheidon (Plutarch *How to Profit from One's Enemies* 6 [*Moralia* 89E]; Pausanias 2.19.2), the Argives rebounded with the destruction of Nauplia (Pausanias 4.24.4, 4.27.8, 4.35.2), the expulsion of the Spartan garrison at Halieis, activity in the area of Epidauros, and support of Aigina against Athens (Herodotus 5.86.4; see also Jameson 1969). These events can be dated between 615 and 590. It is possible that the Argive help to Megara (albeit probably some years later) belongs in this same succession. The fighting might belong to the same complex of warfare as the Euboian hostilities lamented by Theognis (see Note L above).

The pedimental sculptures of the Megarian treasury date that structure to the last quarter of the sixth century, perhaps even to the last decade, and a date in the first decade of the fifth century would not be impossible (Bol 1974). Pausanias states that earlier dedications were kept in the Megarian treasury (Pausanias 6.19.14). He assigns these to the Spartan sculptor Dontas, a pupil of the Sikyonians Skyllis and Dipoinis. Elsewhere, however, Pausanias calls this artist Medon rather than Dontas (5.17.2). The name Medon is attested elsewhere, while Dontas is not. It remains for us to consider why Pausanias wanted to date the dedications created by Medon/Dontas earlier than the treasury. Although he may well have believed that Daidalos was a very early figure, so that his pupils Skyllis and Dipoinis (and thereby Medon) were also early, it is far-fetched to think that he felt compelled for this reason to date the dedications to the tenth century. Perhaps Pausanias envisaged this sequence: (1) war during the life-archonship of Phorbas; (2) dedications by Medon/Dontas; (3) Megarian treasury: thus, the early dedications are merely older than the treasury, not earlier than a war he believed to be very early (cf. Meyer 1954.332, 633).

Skyllis and Dipoinis had a *floruit* of c. 580 (Pliny *Natural History* 36.4.9–10). Their pupil should have had his *floruit* in the thirty years after theirs and may have worked for the Megarians around the middle of the sixth century. The artist Medon/Dontas, the participation of the Argives, and perhaps the occurrence of this war during a period of confusion at Olympia all seem to point toward a conflict in the second quarter of the sixth century. Whether we should hypothesize two wars in this period, one nearer to 580 (when the Eleans were in trouble at Olympia) and the other after mid-century, in order to lessen the hiatus between the war and the late sixth-century treasury built from its spoils, is worth considering. As Megara was not a rich **polis**, it is possible that the more usual pattern of slow building prevailed for this structure. Thus, a second war with Corinth could be as much as a generation before a treasury finished c. 510. The completion of the treasury might then have been urged by the Megarian alliance with Sparta, which, for the moment, vouchsafed Megara protection against Corinth and Athens (see Note R below).

*O (575–550) It would not be surprising if Miletos, friendly to Corinth after 600, came into conflict with Megara, Corinth's inveterate enemy. A polyandrion at Miletos bore an inscribed epigram (Peek *GV* 1 no. 33) that recorded that the dead within had fallen in a victory over Megara (L. Robert, *BE* [1967] = *REG* 80 no. 528, pp.536–538; cf. Peek 1966). The epigram is Hellenistic (c. 200). Its author may have composed another Milesian epigram, the one dedicated to Lichas (Hiller von Gaertringen 1926 no. 107). It is unlikely that this conflict preceded the friendship of Periander and Thrasyboulos. A conflict between Megara and Miletos is also unlikely to have happened without any other trace after 500, when Greek foreign affairs become better attested. What can be learned from the content of the epigram suggests an archaic date for the conflict. The Milesian dead are said to have upheld the example of their forefathers, who, with their warships, had explored the Black Sea, founding colonies there, and had established the city of Naukratis in Egypt. These boasts may indicate that the geographical context for the conflict was somewhere in the areas of colonization at the fringes of the Greek world. While such themes were undoubtedly traditional in Milesian commemorative poetry, it is possible that the author was in part inspired by a previous epigram contemporary with the polyandrion. When the polyandrion was refurbished, a new epigram was commissioned to replace the original one that was used as a source.

Nonetheless, the foundation of Heraclea may give us an approximate indication of date. Heraclea was a homologue of Sinope, in that each city was situated to control a natural trade route across the Black Sea (Boardman 1980.254–255). Sinope dominated the shortest crossing to the Crimea, while Heraclea was placed at one of the south coast's few other good harbors. Just as the Milesian colonies of the northern and western shores of the Black Sea were emplaced after the foundation of Sinope, the Megarian colony of Mesambria (perhaps with the collaboration of Byzantion and Kalkhedon) and the Heraclean colonies of Panelos, Kallatis, and Khersonnesos were founded on the northern and western shores after the foundation of Heraclea. While Sinope seems to have been founded in the late seventh century (Cook 1946.77), and the other Milesian colonies may have been founded in the first half of the sixth century, the Megarians had settled the eastern end of the Propontis, leaving the Black Sea to the Milesians. As might be expected, the poet of the epigram saw the Megarians as the aggressors in the fighting. Although the context lends itself to patriotic exaggeration, it is worth noting that the epigram suggests that the fighting was on a considerable scale. The Megarians had not colonized in the Black Sea before Heraclea (c. 560: see Note E above). It is thus possible that the foundation of that city was meant as deliberately competitive to Miletos and took place in a period of hostility between the two states. Such a period could have been inaugurated by the rapprochement between Periander and Thrasyboulos and also by Megarian aid to the Samian generals against their government (see Note K above). Thus, any time after 600 could accommodate fighting between Megara and Miletos. If the boast of having founded Naukratis, established shortly before 600 (Austin 1970.22–24; von Bissing 1951), belonged to an earlier epigram on the polyandrion, the episode must be after 600. The second quarter of the sixth century is a possible broad time frame, since fighting between these two states at that time would coincide with the foundation of Heraclea.

*P (550–510) Plutarch *Greek Questions* 59 (*Moralia* 304E–F) is our only source on the clan of the 'wagon-rollers'. They earned their name from an attack on a Peloponnesian **theōriā** 'sacred embassy', encamped in wagons with their families, on its way to Delphi. That a **genos** can ever have been officially called **hamaxokulistai** 'wagon-rollers' is doubtful, if **genos** is to be understood in the sense that it had in Athens, that is, 'clan'. Nor is it clear how the **thrasutatoi** 'boldest' of the Megarians responsible for the crime became a family group. Moreover, while it is possible that a sacred embassy might be accompanied by their families, I can think of no parallel. The anecdote is aetiological and could be designed to explain the name 'wagon-rollers', or some name sounding enough like this term to corroborate the anecdote. Thus, in this interpretation, no great trust ought to be placed in the details of the story.

Yet, if **genos** can mean 'class' or 'caste' here (see Figueira 1984b), another line of analysis is available. It is known from Aristotle that the oligarchic government that succeeded Megara's democracy restricted officeholding to those who had returned from exile with the oligarchs and had fought the **dēmos** (*Politics* 1300a17–19), and not on the basis of the usual criteria of birth or wealth. Those barred from political power could have been a **genos** of 'wagon-rollers' tainted by sacrilege, if by this is meant the descendants of those resisting the oligarchic coup, possessing a status exactly the opposite of the descendants of the exiles. They would be like the **enageis** 'cursed' descendants of the destroyers of the Kylonians at Athens (Herodotus 5.70.2–72.1; Thucydides 1.126.2–127.1; *Constitution of the Athenians* 1; *Suda* s.v. "**Kulōneion agos**," "**Periklēs**" [1179]; Diogenes Laertius 1.110; Plutarch *Solon* 12.2–9). These Athenians were subject to repeated attacks on their civil rights and political position because of the conduct of their ancestors.

The account of the 'wagon-rollers' as it is found in Plutarch would have been preserved for its continuing relevance to partisan politics. The anecdote shares the antidemocratic bias of other passages from its source, the *Constitution of the Megarians*. It may be dated by the mention of the incident's occurring during the Megarian democracy (see Note Q below). That retaliation was undertaken by the Amphictyony against the guilty suggests a date after the First Sacred War. The term **theōriā** is customarily used for an official embassy. The designation 'Peloponnesian' describing it should mean that it was dispatched by Sparta and its allies, as no other collectivity bore the title 'Peloponnesian'.

One may doubt that the Megarian government was unable to punish the malefactors because of the democracy's prevailing anarchy. The democracy moved against its aristocratic enemies, banishing them (Aristotle *Politics* 1304b34–39). Here it probably chose not to intervene. The presence in a Peloponnesian embassy of Corinthians, archenemies of Megara, might be reason enough for such a decision, even if the Megarians did not happen to be fighting the Corinthians at the moment. Megara may have considered itself at permanent war with Corinth (cf. Aristotle *Politics* 1280b13–15). The Amphictyones did not usually act against individuals, holding their city responsible for them (Halliday 1928.220). The Amphictyones did not have the military force to intervene in the Megarid (especially if the Megarians were friendly with Boiotia, which shielded them from the Amphictyonic states to the north: see Note E above). Force applied by the Amphictyony in the Isthmus could only have come from Sparta. Therefore, the story may be interpreted as Peloponnesian retaliation sanctioned by Delphi.

Undoubtedly, some military action was involved. Some of the 'wagon-rollers' were put to death. Others were exiled, which argues that the Megarian government was brought to acquiesce in their punishment. Several contexts are possible. The punishment of the 'wagon-rollers' could be associated with a war between Megara and Corinth, the latter supported by Sparta. The Megarians were defeated, with the chastisement of the 'wagon-rollers' as part of the settlement. Yet Megara seems to have held its own in sixth-century fighting with Corinth (see Note N above). The Peloponnesians may, however, have intervened against the Megarian democracy, as the investigation of the term **genos** above has suggested. They helped to establish an oligarchy that affirmed or completed the punishment of the 'wagon-rollers'. A further extrapolation might indicate that the best setting for these events would be the moment at which Megara allied itself with Sparta (see Note R below). The massacre of the **theōriā** was a pretext for Spartan help to the exiled Megarian oligarchs. Delphi played a similar role in sanctioning Spartan military activity in the intervention against the Peisistratids (Herodotus 5.63.1; *Constitution of the Athenians* 19.4).

*Q (544/1) The Megarian democracy was in power when Heraclea was founded c. 560 (Aristotle *Politics* 1304b31–32; cf. 1305b34–37; see also Note E above). Megarian comedy originated during the Megarian democracy (Aristotle *Poetics* 1448a30–32). The *Marmor Parium* dates the beginnings of comedy between 580 and 560 (*FGH* 239 A 39). The democracy may therefore have been in existence as early as 580. Given the weak biographical tradition about Theognis (see Ch.5§§15–18), it is likely that the date of 544/1 for his *floruit* is an ancient conjecture (*Suda* s.v. "**Theognis**"; Jerome *Chronica* 103b [Helm]; Eusebius *Chronica* p.189 [Karst]). The conjecture was based on some date otherwise known from Megarian history. It is likely that Theognis was inserted at a critical juncture in what little was known in the classical period of Megarian political history. Some constitutional change, the collapse of Megara's democracy or the Palintokia (perhaps seen as the cause of the collapse), may be suggested. Perhaps the Palintokia is the preferable choice as the event to be dated to 544/1. The later that the Megarian democracy stayed in power, the more likely it is that its downfall included the intervention of the Peloponnesians against the 'wagon-rollers' (see Note P above). A date of 544/1 for the Palintokia puts the measure about a generation after the earliest date for the first minting of silver coinage in mainland Greece by the Aiginetans, c. 580 (see Ch.5§50; Figueira 1981.88–97). Moreover, dates as late as 550 have been suggested for its advent. Although it existed earlier, silver coinage became prevalent only after 530; fractional coinage, not until even later. Estimates about the speed at which silver coinage can have made a psychological impact on the Megarian **dēmos** are beyond our capacity to reach. Yet a date in the 540s appears early rather than late from this perspective. A Megarian awareness of electrum coinage may not in itself have been sufficient to trigger the attitudes toward debt seen in the Palintokia. The fall of the democracy was effected by returning exiles (Aristotle *Politics* 1304b35–39; cf. also 1300a15–20). There are passages in the Theognidea that mention exile and return from exile (e.g., vv. 332a–332b, 333–334, 1214; see also Note J above). Although conventional in nature, they may have prompted ancient chronographers to place in 544/1 what would have been a critical moment in the supposed biography of the poet, his exile after the Palintokia. How late in the sixth century Megarian democracy lasted is unknown, but clearly it was no brief interlude in the institutional history of that city (cf. Legon 1981.134). I see no *prima facie* reasons why it cannot have lasted into the last quarter of the century.

*R (c. 510) In their intervention against the Peisistratids and later against the Kleisthenic government, Spartan armies moved through the Megarid (Herodotus 5.64–65; cf. 5.72.1, 74.2). Therefore, either

Megara was already an ally of Sparta by 510 or Sparta violated Megarian sovereignty repeatedly without leaving a trace of these acts in our sources. Whether a *terminus ante quem* for this alliance can be dated earlier depends on the interpretation of events surrounding the inauguration of the Athenian alliance with Plataia. Thucydides dates the first alliance between Athens and Plataia to 519 (Thucydides 3.68.5; Herodotus 6.108.1–6). The details of the joining together of these two states are related by Herodotus. The Plataians originally approached Kleomenes, who was in the neighborhood. To have been near Plataia, a Spartan army most probably would have passed through the Megarid. It is possible that Kleomenes was in the area because he had brought Megara into the Spartan alliance (Legon 1981.141–145; cf. Piccirilli 1973.725–730). Kleomenes directed the Plataian request to Athens. When the alliance was made, war broke out between Thebes, with designs on Plataia, and Athens. The Athenians were victorious. The Corinthians were also on the scene, and they arbitrated between the two parties.

The presence of the Corinthians is curious. Kleomenes scarcely would have brought them along to convince the Megarians to become allies of Sparta. However, the details of the story have led scholars since Grote to emend the date to 509.[1] At this time Kleomenes and the Corinthians could be near Plataia because they were intervening in Attica. With the redating of the Plataian alliance with Athens to 509, a Megarian alliance with Sparta c. 519 is no longer necessary as a rationale for the Spartan presence in central Greece in 519. 509 becomes the *terminus ante quem* for the Megarian alliance with Sparta, but a *terminus post quem* is lacking. Nevertheless, there is no reason to put the Megarian alliance with Sparta before the Spartan expulsion of the Peisistratids. The fact that the first Spartan attempt against the Peisistratids under Ankhimolios reached Attica by sea (perhaps on Corinthian ships) may suggest that Megara was not yet an ally of Sparta. The Megarid was closed to the Spartans in the company of their allies from Corinth, the archenemies of Megara. Nonetheless, Kleomenes could have forcibly brought Megara into the Peloponnesian League by expelling the democrats and helping to

---

[*]Rn1. Grote 1888.3.385n4. One may note in addition that the Thebans and the Peisistratids were allies (Herodotus 1.61.3; *Constitution of the Athenians* 15.2) and that a Thessalian force could come to the aid of the Peisistratids, perforce by land (Herodotus 5.63.3–64.2; *Constitution of the Athenians* 19.5). Amit 1970 believes that the existence of a narrow oligarchy (cf. Thucydides 3.62.3) at Thebes would have prompted the Plataians to seek an alliance with post-Peisistratid Athens rather than with Peisistratid Athens (cf. Buck 1979.112–114).

install an oligarchic government of exiles with Corinthian aid (see Note Q above). Megara (under its oligarchy?) allied itself with Sparta only after the first expedition. Kleomenes was therefore able to march through the Megarid and to free Athens.

The Megarian oligarchy may have joined Sparta on the understanding that Salamis would be arbitrated but might still have been too dependent on Sparta to press its case. The newly liberated Athenians would scarcely be in a position to resist any Spartan decision. Whether moved by Realpolitik or the strength of the Athenian case, the Spartans decided against the Megarians (see Note S below). If Corinthian behavior in the 460s (when the Corinthians took advantage of Spartan distraction to make war on Megara [Thucydides 1.103.4; Diodorus Siculus 11.79.2; Plutarch *Cimon* 17.2-3]) is any indication of their general policy toward Megara, Corinth may not have recognized that Megara was an independent **polis**. Corinthian acquiescence in a Megarian alliance with Sparta is most reasonable in c. 510, when Corinth may have been anxious to liberate Athens from Hippias. Hippias' rapprochement with Persia threatened the establishment of Athens as a Medizing state in the immediate vicinity of Corinth.[2] Corinth, however, might have bridled had Sparta strengthened Megara through arbitration at the expense of Athens.

*S (c. 510) Plutarch concludes his narrative on the Salamis dispute with a description of the arguments that Solon purportedly used to sway Spartan arbitrators to concede the Athenian right to own Salamis (*Solon* 10; Aelian *Varia Historia* 7.19). The arguments were from the Homeric Catalogue of Ships, supporting the contention that Philaios and Eurysakes, sons of Ajax, had emigrated to Athens (*Iliad* ii 557-558), and from the orientation in their graves of those buried on Salamis (cf. Hereas *FGH* 486 F 4). Delphic responses also supported the Athenian claims by asserting that Salamis was Ionian. Plutarch reports, in addition, the counterarguments of the Megarians. Strabo reports another of the arguments deployed: the priestess of Athena Polias used only foreign cheese, including cheese from Salamis (9.1.10-11 C394-395). The Athenians countered by observing that the identification of cheese as foreign extended to other offshore islands undeniably Athenian. Later elaboration by Megareis and Atthidographers may have garbled the traditions they received. However, while the argument from mythological affinity to political sovereignty may be archaic, the reasoning from local customs (burial rites

---

*Rn2. In general, see Wickert 1961.19, 59–60.

and the dietary taboos of the priestess) is crude anthropology. The idea is that different states have different **nomoi** 'conventions', which remain static. Perhaps such arguments belong better in the late sixth century, but such a judgment can only be subjective.

Solon insisted upon the Ionian character of Athens, calling Attica the eldest land of Ionia (fr. 4a.2). For Salamis, the Delphic responses make a similar claim, so that such arguments on behalf of Athenian ownership of Salamis could go back to Solon. The intervention of Delphi on the side of the Athenians will fit any time after Solon's participation in the Sacred War, for which Athens may have been conceded the Ionian vote in the Amphictyony. One's impression from the account of Plutarch is that the Spartan arbitration definitively settled the status of Salamis, ensuring the prominence of the story (along with the names of the Spartan arbitrators) in popular memory. Yet there was fighting with Megara, probably over Salamis, under the command of Peisistratos. The use by the Alcmaeonids of oracles in their struggle against the Peisistratids shows the continued influence of Athens at Delphi (Herodotus 5.62.2–63.2). The Peisistratids, however, made use of Onomakritos, in his own right a skilled manipulator of religious pedigrees for political decisions (Herodotus 7.6.3). Perhaps Alcmaeonid influence at Delphi prevented Peisistratos from similar use of that oracle. The arbitration, therefore, is unlikely to have been of the Peisistratid period.

Sparta was unlikely to have been chosen at a time when it was allied with Megara, unless some corresponding tie existed with Athens also. This point is especially telling when one notes that the Spartan arbitrators were said to have been moved by arguments that Salamis was Ionian and thus Athenian. Thereby they were siding with Ionians against their fellow Dorians of Megara. So a dating of the Spartan arbitration to an early period (that of Solon, for instance), when neither Megara nor Athens was particularly close to Sparta, is not to be preferred to a later date when both cities had some equal, countervailing affinity. There is, however, a good reason for believing that the Spartan arbitration came toward the end of the sixth century (Beloch 1912–1927.1.2.312–314). Of the five arbitrators (Kritolaidas, Amompharetos, Hypsekhidas, Anaxilas, and Kleomenes), Kleomenes may be the famous king of that name, and Amompharetos is perhaps the senior officer whom Pausanias found so recalcitrant at Plataia in 479 (Herodotus 9.53–57, 71.2, 85.1 [where the identification as an **irēn** 'youth' is suspect: How and Wells 1912.2.325]; Plutarch *Aristeides* 17.3). The Delphic oracles would then be inspired by the Alcmaeonids. While the Spartans had ties of **xeniā** with the Peisistratids (Herodotus 5.90.1), these did not deter them from expelling the tyrants from Athens. After the expulsion (510), Athens for a short period maintained good relations with Sparta, until political hegemony was lost decisively by Isagoras, Kleomenes' friend (510–508/7). Kleomenes would have been aware of the potential instability in an increased role for the Athenian dēmos, if he had already intervened against the Megarian democrats. By awarding Salamis to Athens, he may have sought to strengthen Isagoras in the face of the populist agitation of Kleisthenes. At this time Delphi would have held no favor for the Megarians if the story reported by Plutarch (*Greek Questions* 59) that the Megarian 'wagon-rollers' had waylaid visitors on their way to Delphi is true (Legon 1981.133; see also Note P above).

A late sixth-century inscription, post-Peisistratid, must also be taken into account (Meiggs-Lewis no. 14).[1] It makes provisions for Athenian settlers on Salamis in their mobilization for war and stipulates restrictions on the leasing of their property. It is probable that Salamis was the first Athenian cleruchy (scholia Pindar *N.* 2.19; cf. *IG* II² 30b.6). It is to be dated before the cleruchy at Khalkis, established in 506 (Herodotus 5.77.2). Nonetheless, understanding of it is hampered by uncertainty over whether the inscription reports a reorganization or an organization of the community. Yet it is striking that affairs needed to be settled at so late a date. The inhabitants of Salamis belonged to all ten tribes, as the island was not divided into demes. Since Salamis directly adjoins Attica, this may suggest that the organization of Salamis was after the Kleisthenic reforms. Yet it also may have been because the Athenians needed to keep the ownership of Salamis separate on account of religious scruples, on the grounds that the island descended to them through Philaios and Eurysakes. Consequently, the Spartans could have awarded Salamis to the Athenians after the liberation of Athens from the Peisistratids, but before Kleisthenes' reform of the tribes. Afterwards, when Sparta had become hostile to Athens, the Athenians may have anticipated further Megarian aggression toward Salamis and may have sought to regularize certain features of the island's governance and defense with this in view (Meiggs-Lewis no. 14.3, 9).

The incorporation of former inhabitants of Salamis into Attica is also involved in this question. When the Megarians seized the island originally, the inhabitants fled to Attica. Solon, c. 600, led a force of volunteers that recaptured the island (see Note I above). The 500 youths who participated perhaps became citizens of this new Athe-

---

*Sn1. In general see Wade-Gery 1946; Guarducci 1948.

nian Salamis, an entity akin to a colony (a **politeuma** in Plutarch), but Salamis was then lost, to be recovered once more by Peisistratos. The third-century decree that discusses the phratry of the Salaminioi divides them into two groups (*LSCG Suppl.* no. 19).[2] One is concentrated in the Sounion area and the other spread among seven of the nine other tribes, although concentrated in the vicinity of the **hērōon** of Eurysakes in Melite, a suburb of the city.

That the Salaminioi were originally inhabitants of Salamis is shown by their practice of the cult of Athena Skiros (*LSCG Suppl.* no. 19.10, 41–45, 93; *IG* II[2] 1232; cf. Philochorus *FGH* 328 F 14, 15), with its connections to the Megarid (Praxion *FGH* 484 F 1; Dieuchidas 6b Piccirilli). It is noteworthy that the majority of the phratry of the Salaminioi had been in Athens during the sixth century, since they seem to have lived in Attica long enough before the Kleisthenic reforms for about half of them to have scattered from an original place of settlement in the Sounion area. They had never been definitively reestablished on the island after Solon. The Athenian state made contributions to the cult activity of the Salaminioi in accordance with enactments contained on the **kurbeis**. The **kurbeis** contained the laws of Solon, so that state participation in subsidy of the religious activity of the Salaminioi may go back to Solon's time (*LSCG Suppl.* no. 19.86). Their dominance in the cults of Pandrosos and Aglauros (*LSCG Suppl.* no. 19.11–12, 45) and in the festival of the Oskhophoria (*LSCG Suppl.* no. 19.20–24, 48–50) suggests an early establishment in Attica.

It is noteworthy that Plutarch records a loss of Nisaea and Salamis but connects it with **stasis** in Athens in the time of Solon (*Solon* 12.5). Since Peisistratos captured Nisaea, these events could have happened during the **stasis** attendant upon Peisistratos' exiles and returns to power. Whether the island was allowed to revert to Megara under Peisistratos, an unlikely event, was left vacant in these years, or was treated as an appanage of the Peisistratid family, is uncertain. In the last case, they could have given their followers estates there. Any of these possibilities would explain why an arbitration was sought by either Megara or Athens at the end of the sixth century. Also explicable would be the Athenian need to reorganize Salamis toward the end of the century. Discontinuity seems to have marked Athenian control of Salamis in the sixth century, as indicated by the fact that the later cleruchs do not appear to have been merely the descendants of the original inhabitants of the island, the Salaminioi.

---

*Sn2. See Ferguson 1938; Nilsson 1938; Guarducci 1948b.

Glossary of Greek Words

(Some words that are less frequently cited but regularly glossed, such as **sphrēgis** 'seal', are excluded from this list; m./f./n. = masculine/ feminine/neuter; pl. = plural.)

agathos (m.), **agathē** (f.), **agathon** (n.), **agathoi** (m.pl.), **agatha** (n.pl.) 'good, noble'; synonym of **esthlos**

aidōs 'shame, sense of shame, sense of consideration for others, respect and loyalty'

ainos: designates an enigmatic or allusive form of discourse, deserving of a reward; praise; enigma, riddle; fable; public resolution

aiskhros (m.), **aiskhron** (n.) 'shameful, dishonorable, ugly'

amēkhaniē 'resourcelessness, powerlessness'

aniē 'pain'

apēnēs 'hard'

aretē: designates striving to achieve a noble goal; achievement of a noble goal; achievement; excellence

biē 'force, violence'

daimōn, daimones (pl.): designates a supernatural force (= god or hero); spirit; lot in life

deilos (m.), **deilon** (n.), **deiloi** (m.pl.) 'wretched'; synonym of **kakos**

dēmos 'district, population of a district (minus its leaders); community'

dikē, dikai (pl.) 'judgment; justice'; **dikaios** (m.), **dikaion** (n.) 'just'; **dikaiosunē** 'justice'

ekhthros (m.), **ekhthrē** (f.), **ekhthroi** (m.pl.) 'enemy'

epos, epea/epē (pl.) 'utterance, expression, poetic utterance'

erastēs 'lover' (in a relationship of **paiderastiā**)

erōmenos 'beloved' (in a relationship of **paiderastiā**)

esthlos (m.), **esthlē** (f.), **esthlon** (n.), **esthloi** (m.pl.), **esthlai** (f.pl.), **esthla** (n.pl.) 'genuine, good'; synonym of **agathos**

ēthos, ēthea (pl.) 'nature, temperament, character'

euphrosunē 'mirth, merriment'

genos 'stock' (in the sense of 'breeding'); 'family-line; family; generation'

gignōskō (gīnōskō) 'be aware, know, perceive'

glukus 'sweet'

gnōmē 'awareness, knowledge, ability to know; codification of knowledge; criterion; good judgment'

harpaleos 'pleasing to touch'
hēgemōn, hēgemones (pl.) 'leader'
hēsukhos 'serene'; **hesukhiē** 'state of being **hēsukhos**; quietude'
hetairos, hetairoi (pl.) 'companion, comrade'
hubris 'outrage' (opposite of **dikē**)
kakos (m.), **kakē** (f.), **kakon** (n.), **kakoi** (m.pl.), **kakai** (f.pl.), **kaka** (n.pl.) 'bad, evil, base, worthless, ignoble'; **kakotēs** 'state of being **kakos**; debasement'
kalos (m.), **kalon** (n.) 'beautiful'
kerdos, kerdea (pl.) 'gain, profit; desire for gain, profit; craft employed for gain, profit'
kharis, kharites (pl.) 'reciprocity, give-and-take; initiation of a reciprocal relationship; the pleasure derived from reciprocity, from a reciprocal relationship; gratification; gratitude'
khrēma 'thing, matter'
khrēmata (pl. of **khrēma**) 'possessions, property'
kleos, klea (pl.) 'glory, fame' (especially as conferred by poetry)
kōmos: designates a celebrating group of men or boys; celebration, revel
koros 'being satiated, satiation; satiety; being insatiable, insatiability'
kosmos 'arrangement, order, law and order, the social order, the universal order'
kubernētēs 'pilot, helmsman'
mēnis: designates a supernatural kind of anger
metron 'measure, mean, moderation'; **metrios** 'moderate'
neikos 'quarrel, dispute, feud'
nemesis: designates the process whereby everyone gets what he or she deserves; righteous indignation that calls for this process; retribution
nomos 'custom; law'
noos: designates realm of consciousness, of rational functions; intuition, perception; intent, intention; mind; principle that reintegrates **thūmos** (or **menos**, a partial synonym) and **psūkhē** after death
nostos 'homecoming, return; song about homecoming'
orgē 'temperament, character'
paideiā 'education, instruction'
paiderastiā 'love of boys'
pais 'boy'
philos (m.), **philē** (f.), **philon** (n.), **philoi** (m.pl.), **phila** (n.pl.) 'friend' (as noun), 'dear, near and dear, belonging to self' (as adjective); **philiē** (**philiā**)/**philotēs** 'state of being **philos**'
phrēn, phrenes (pl.): designates the physical localization of the **thūmos**; thinking or feeling; mind; heart

pistis 'faith, trustworthiness'
pistos (m.), **pistoi** (m.pl.) 'faithful, trustworthy'
pisunos 'trustful, trusting'
polis, poleis (pl.) 'city, city-state'
pontos 'sea'
prēgma, prēgmata (pl.) 'thing, matter'
psūkhē, psūkhai (pl.): synonym of **thūmos** (or **menos**) at the moment of death; conveyor of identity after death
sophos (m.), **sophon** (n.), **sophoi** (m.pl.) 'skilled, skilled in understanding poetry, wise'; **sophiē** 'quality of being **sophos**'
sōphrōn (**saophrōn**), **sōphrones** (pl.) 'with sound/safe **phrenes**; moderate; balanced; sober; self-controlled'; **sōphrosunē** 'state or quality of being **sōphrōn**'
stasis, stasies/staseis (pl.) '[social/civic] conflict, discord; feud'
sunoikismos 'confederation'
terpsis 'enjoyment'
themis, themistes (pl.) 'customary law; norm; divine law'
thūmos: designates realm of consciousness, of rational and emotional functions; mind; heart
tīmē 'honor, honor paid to a supernatural force by way of ritual'
xenos (**xeinos**), **xenoi** (pl.) 'guest-stranger; guest; stranger'

Bibliography

Adkins, A. W. H. 1960. *Merit and Responsibility: A Study in Greek Values.* Oxford.

Amit, M. 1970. "La date de l'alliance entre Athènes et Platées." *L'Antiquité Classique* 39:414–426.

Anti, C. 1920. "Athena marina e alata." *Monumenti Antichi: Reale Accademia dei Lincei.* 26:270–318.

Apostolius. *See CPG.*

Austin, M. M. 1970. *Greece and Egypt in the Archaic Age. Proceedings of the Cambridge Philological Society* Suppl. 2.

Austin, N. 1975. *Archery at the Dark of the Moon: Poetic Problems in Homer's Odyssey.* Berkeley and Los Angeles.

BE. See Robert 1938–.

Beazley, J. D. 1942. *Attic Red-Figure Vase-Painters.* Oxford.

————. 1963. *Attic Red-Figure Vase-Painters.* 2d ed. 2 vols. Oxford.

Beloch, K. J. 1888. "Theognis' Vaterstadt." *Jahrbuch für klassischen Philologie* 11:729–733.

————. 1912–1927. *Griechische Geschichte.* Berlin.

Benveniste, E. 1969. *Le vocabulaire des institutions indo-européennes.* I. *Economie, parenté, société.* II. *Pouvoir, droit, religion.* Paris = *Indo-European Language and Society.* Translated by E. Palmer. London, 1973.

Bergren, A. L. T. 1975. *The Etymology and Usage of* ΠΕΙΡΑΡ *in Early Greek Poetry.* American Classical Studies, no. 2. American Philological Association.

von Bissing, F. W. 1951. "Naukratis." *Bulletin de la Société Royale d'Alexandrie* 39:33–82.

Bloch, H. 1940. "Herakleides Lembos and His *Epitome* of Aristotle's *Politeiai.*" *Transactions of the American Philological Association* 71:27–39.

————. 1940b. "Studies in the Historiography of the Fourth Century." *Harvard Studies in Classical Philology* Suppl. Vol.:303–376.

Boardman, J. 1957. "Early Euboean Pottery." *British School at Athens, Annual* 52:1–29.

————. 1975. *Athenian Red Figure Vases: The Archaic Period, A Handbook.* London.

————. 1980. *The Greeks Overseas.* 3d ed. London.

Boeckh, A. 1874. "De epigrammate in Orsippum Megarensem lapide servato [C.I.G. n. 1050]." *Opuscula.* Vol. 4, 173–183. Leipzig.

Bohringer, F. 1980. "Mégare: Traditions mythiques, espace sacré et naissance de la cité." *L'Antiquité Classique* 49:5–22.

Bol, P. C. 1974. "Die Giebelskulpturen der Schatzhauses von Megara." *Mitteilungen des Deutschen Archäologischen Instituts, Athenische Abteilung* 89:65–74.

Breitholtz, L. 1960. *Die Dorische Farce.* Stockholm.

Bremmer, J. 1983. *The Early Greek Concept of the Soul.* Princeton.

Buck, R. J. 1979. *A History of Boeotia*. Edmonton.

Burn, A. R. 1927. "Greek Sea-Power, 776–540." *Journal of Hellenic Studies* 47:165–177.

———. 1929. "The So-Called 'Trade-Leagues' in Early Greek History and the Lelantine War." *Journal of Hellenic Studies* 49:14–37.

———. 1960. *The Lyric Age of Greece*. London. Reprinted 1967.

Burstein, S. M. 1976. *Outpost of Hellenism: The Emergence of Heraclea on the Black Sea*. University of California Publications, Classical Studies 14. Berkeley.

Busolt, G. 1893. *Griechische Geschichte*. Gotha.

Carrière, J. 1948. *Théognis de Mégare: Etude sur le recueil élégiaque attribué à ce poète*. Paris.

Cerri, G. 1968. "La terminologia sociopolitica di Teognide: 1. L'opposizione semantica tra *agathos-esthlos* e *kakos-deilos*." *Quaderni Urbinati di Cultura Classica* 6:7–32.

———. 1969. "*Isos dasmos* come equivalente di *isonomia* nella silloge teognidea." *Quaderni Urbinati di Cultura Classica* 8:97–104.

CGF. See Kaibel 1899.

Chantraine, P. 1968, 1970, 1975, 1977, 1980. *Dictionnaire étymologique de la langue grecque* I, II, III, IV–1, IV–2. Paris.

Clay, D. 1970. "Fragmentum Adespotum 976." *Transactions of the American Philological Association* 101:119–129.

Cloché, P. 1952. *Thèbes de Béotie*. Louvain.

Coldstream, J. N. 1977. *Geometric Greece*. London.

Collitz, H.; Bechtel, F.; and Hoffmann, O., eds. 1884–1915. *Sammlung der griechischen Dialekt-Inschriften*. Göttingen.

Connor, W. R. 1962. "Charinus' Megarean Decree." *American Journal of Philology* 83:225–246.

———. 1970. "Charinus' Megarean Decree Again." *Revue des Etudes Grecques* 83:305–308.

Cook, R. M. 1946. "Ionia and Greece in the Eighth and Seventh Centuries." *Journal of Hellenic Studies* 66:67–98.

———. 1962. "Spartan History and Archaeology." *Classical Quarterly* 56 = n.s. 12:156–158.

———. 1971. "ΕΠΟΙΗΣΕΝ on Greek Vases." *Journal of Hellenic Studies* 91:137–138.

———. 1979. "Archaic Greek Trade: Three Conjectures." *Journal of Hellenic Studies* 99:152–155.

CPG. See von Leutsch and Schneidewin 1839–1851.

Crahay, R. 1956. *La littérature oraculaire chez Hérodote*. Paris.

Davidson, O. M. 1983. "The Crown-Bestower in the Iranian Book of Kings." Ph.D. diss., Princeton University.

Davies, J. K. 1971. *Athenian Propertied Families, 600–300 B.C.* Oxford.

Davison, J. A. 1955. "Peisistratus and Homer." *Transactions of the American Philological Association* 86:1–21.

———. 1955b. "Quotations and Allusions in Early Greek Poetry." *Eranos* 53:125–140.

————. 1958. "Notes on the Panathenaia." *Journal of Hellenic Studies* 78:23–41 = 1968:28–69.

————. 1959. "Dieuchidas of Megara." *Classical Quarterly* 53 = n.s. 9:216–222.

————. 1968. *From Archilochus to Pindar: Papers on Greek Literature of the Archaic Period.* London.

Day, J., and Chambers, M. H. 1962. *Aristotle's History of Athenian Democracy.* Berkeley and Los Angeles.

Detienne, M. 1972. *Les jardins d'Adonis: La mythologie des aromates en Grèce.* Paris = *The Gardens of Adonis.* Translated by J. Lloyd. Sussex, 1977.

————. 1973. *Les maîtres de vérité dans la Grèce archaïque.* 2d ed. Paris.

————. 1977. *Dionysos mis à mort.* Paris = *Dionysos Slain.* Translated by L. Muellner and M. Muellner. Baltimore, 1979.

Detienne, M., and Vernant, J.-P. 1974. *Les ruses de l'intelligence: La* ΜΗΤΙΣ *des Grecs.* Paris = *Cunning Intelligence in Greek Culture and Society.* Translated by J. Lloyd. Sussex, 1978.

Diels, H., and Kranz, W., eds. 1951–1952. *Die Fragmente der Vorsokratiker.* 6th ed. Berlin.

Dilts, M. R., ed. and tr. 1971. *Heraclidis Lembi Excerpta Politiarum.* Durham, N.C.

Diogenianus. *See CPG.*

Dittenberger, W., ed. 1915–1924. *Sylloge Inscriptionum Graecarum.* 3d ed. Leipzig.

Dittenberger, W., and Purgold, K., eds. 1896. *Die Inschriften von Olympia.* Olympia 5. Berlin.

DK. *See* Diels and Kranz 1951–1952.

Dodds, E. R. 1951. *The Greeks and the Irrational.* Berkeley and Los Angeles.

————, ed. 1960. *Euripides: Bacchae.* 2d ed. Oxford.

Donlan, W. 1970. "Changes and Shifts in the Meaning of Demos." *La Parola del Passato* 135:381–395.

————. 1973. "The Origin of ΚΑΛΟΣ ΚΑΓΑΘΟΣ." *American Journal of Philology* 94:365–374.

————. 1973b. "The Role of *Eugeneia* in the Aristocratic Self-Image during the Fifth Century B.C." In *Classics and the Classical Tradition: Essays Presented to Robert E. Dengler,* 63–78. University Park, Pa.

Döring, K. 1972. *Die Megariker: Kommentierte Sammlung der Testimonien.* Amsterdam.

Dover, K. J. 1966. "Anthemocritus and the Megarians." *American Journal of Philology* 87:203–209.

————. 1978. *Greek Homosexuality.* Cambridge, Mass.

Dumézil, G. 1969. *Heur et malheur du guerrier.* Paris = *The Destiny of the Warrior.* Translated by A. Hiltebeitel. Chicago, 1970.

Durante, M. 1960. "Ricerche sulla preistoria della lingua poetica greca: La terminologia relativa alla creazione poetica." *Atti della Accademia Nazionale dei Lincei, Rendiconti, Classe di Scienze morali, storiche e filologiche* 15:231–249.

Düring, I. 1951. *Chion of Heraclea: A Novel in Letters.* Göteborg. *Acta Universitatis Goteburgensis* 57/5.

Edmunds, L. 1975. *Chance and Intelligence in Thucydides*. Cambridge, Mass.
————. 1975b. "Thucydides' Ethics as Reflected in the Description of Stasis (3.82–83)." *Harvard Studies in Classical Philology* 79:73–92.
————. 1980. "Aristophanes' *Acharnians*." *Yale Classical Studies* 26:1–41.
Edwards, G. P. 1971. *The Language of Hesiod in Its Traditional Context*. Publications of the Philological Society 22. Oxford.
Ellis, R. 1910. "Adversaria VI." *Journal of Philology* 31:45.
Else, G. F. 1957. *Aristotle's Poetics: The Argument*. Cambridge, Mass.
FdD = *Fouilles de Delphes*. Ecole Française d'Athènes. Paris. 1902–.
Fenik, B. C., ed. 1978. *Homer: Tradition and Invention*. Cincinnati Classical Studies. n.s. II. Leiden.
Ferguson, J. 1958. *Moral Values in the Ancient World*. London.
Ferguson, W. S. 1938. "The Salaminioi of the Heptaphylai and Sounion." *Hesperia* 7:1–74.
FGH. See Jacoby 1923–.
FHG. See Müller 1841–1872.
Figueira, T. J. 1977. "Aegina and Athens in the Archaic and Classical Periods—a Socio-Political Investigation." Ph.D. diss., University of Pennsylvania.
————. 1981. *Aegina*. New York.
————. 1983. "Aeginetan Independence." *Classical Journal* 79:8–29.
————. 1984. "Mess Rations and Subsistence at Sparta." *Transactions of the American Philological Association* 114:87–109.
————. 1984b. "The Ten *Archontes* of 579/8 at Athens." *Hesperia* 53:447–473.
Finley, M. I. 1968. "Sparta." In *Problèmes de la guerre en Grèce ancienne*, edited by J.-P. Vernant, 143–160. Paris.
————. 1977. *The World of Odysseus*. 2d ed. New York.
Ford, A. L. 1981. "Early Greek Terms for Poetry: Aoidē, Epos, Poiēsis." Ph.D. diss., Yale University.
Fornara, C. W. 1968. "The 'Tradition' about the Murder of Hipparchus." *Historia* 17:400–425.
Forrest, W. G. 1969. "The Tradition of Hippias' Expulsion from Athens." *Greek Roman and Byzantine Studies* 10:277–286.
Forssman, B. 1980. "Hethitisch *kurka–*." *Zeitschrift für Vergleichende Sprachforschung* 94:70–74.
Foucault, M. 1977. *Language, Counter-Memory, Practice: Selected Essays and Interviews*. Edited by D. Bouchard. Translated by D. Bouchard and S. Simon. Ithaca.
Fraenkel, E. 1920 (1924). "Zur Form der AINOI." *Rheinisches Museum für Philologie* 73:366–370.
Frame, D. 1978. *The Myth of Return in Early Greek Epic*. New Haven.
Fränkel, H. 1975. *Early Greek Poetry and Philosophy*. Translated by M. Hadas and J. Willis. New York.
French, A. 1957. "Solon and the Megarian Question." *Journal of Hellenic Studies* 77:238–246.
Friedländer, P. 1969. *Plato*. Translated from the German by H. Meyerhoff. New York = *Platon: Seinswahrheit und Lebenswirklichkeit*. 2d ed. 1954. Berlin.

Friedländer, P., and Hoffleit, H. B., eds. 1948. *Epigrammata: Greek Inscriptions in Verse from the Beginnings to the Persian Wars*. Berkeley and Los Angeles.

Frisk, H. 1960–1970. *Griechisches etymologisches Wörterbuch*. Heidelberg.

Gadamer, H.-G. 1965. *Wahrheit und Methode*. Tübingen.

GDI. See Collitz, Bechtel, and Hoffmann 1884–1915.

Gentili, B. 1977. "Addendum: A proposito dei vv. 253–254 di Teognide." *Quaderni Urbinati di Cultura Classica* 26:115–116.

Gentili, B., and Prato, C., eds. 1979. *Poetae Elegiaci* I. Leipzig.

Gerber, D., ed. 1970. *Euterpe*. Amsterdam.

Gernet, L. 1968. *Anthropologie de la Grèce antique*. Paris = *The Anthropology of Ancient Greece*. Translated by J. Hamilton and B. Nagy. Baltimore, 1981.

Giannini, P. 1973. "Espressioni formulari nell' elegia greca arcaica." *Quaderni Urbinati di Cultura Classica* 16:7–78.

Giessen, K. 1901. "Plutarchs Quaestiones graecae und Aristoteles' Politien." *Philologus* 60:446–471.

Gladigow, B. 1965. *Sophia und Kosmos: Untersuchungen zur Frühgeschichte von ΣΟΦΟΣ und ΣΟΦΙΗ. Spudasmata* I. Hildesheim.

Gomme, A. W., Andrewes, A., and Dover, K. J. 1945–1981. *A Historical Commentary on Thucydides*. 5 vols. Oxford.

Graham, A. J. 1982. "The Colonial Expansion of Greece." In *The Cambridge Ancient History*. 3d ed., vol. 3.1, edited by J. Boardman and N. G. L. Hammond, 83–162. Cambridge.

———. 1983. *Colony and Mother City in Ancient Greece*. 2d ed. Chicago.

Greene, W. C. 1944. *Moira*. Cambridge, Mass.

Gronewald, M. 1975. "Theognis 255 und *Pap.Oxy.* 2380." *Zeitschrift für Papyrologie und Epigraphik* 19:178–179.

van Groningen, B. A., ed. 1966. *Theognis: Le premier livre*. Amsterdam: Verhandelingen der koninklijke Nederlandse Akademie van Wetenschappen, afd. Letterkunde, n.s. 72/1.

Grote, G. 1888. *A History of Greece*. London.

Gruben, G. 1964. "Das Quellhaus von Megara." *Archaiologikon Deltion* 19.A: 37–41.

Guarducci, M. 1948. "Il decreto Ateniese per Salamina." *Rivista di Filologia e d'Istruzione Classica* 76:238–243.

———. 1948b. "L'origine e le vicende del ΓΕΝΟΣ attico dei Salaminii." *Rivista di Filologia e d'Istruzione Classica* 76:223–237.

Gudeman, A. 1934. *Aristoteles: ΠΕΡΙ ΠΟΙΗΤΙΚΗΣ*. Berlin.

Guthrie, W. K. C. 1969. *A History of Greek Philosophy* 3: *The Fifth-Century Enlightenment*. Cambridge.

GV. See Peek 1955.

Haavio, M. 1959. "A running stream they dare na cross." *Studia Fennica* 8:125–142.

Hainsworth, J. B. 1968. *The Flexibility of the Homeric Formula*. Oxford.

———. 1978. "Good and Bad Formulae." In Fenik 1978, 41–50.

Halliday, W. R. 1928. *The Greek Questions of Plutarch with a New Translation and Commentary*. Oxford.

Hammond, N. G. L. 1954. "The Heraeum at Perachora and Corinthian Encroachment." *British School at Athens, Annual* 49:93–102.

———. 1954b. "The Main Road from Boeotia to the Peloponnese through the Northern Megarid." *British School at Athens, Annual* 49:103–122.

Hanell, K. 1934. *Megarische Studien*. Lund.

Harrison, E. 1902. *Studies in Theognis*. Cambridge.

Harvey, A. E. 1955. "The Classification of Greek Lyric Poetry." *Classical Quarterly* 49 = n.s. 5:157–175.

Hasler, F. S. 1959. *Untersuchungen zu Theognis*. Winterthur.

Havelock, E. A. 1952. "Why Was Socrates Tried?" In *Studies in Honor of Gilbert Norwood*, edited by M. White, 95–109. Toronto.

———. 1982. *The Literate Revolution in Greece and Its Cultural Consequences*. Princeton.

HCT. See Gomme, Andrewes, and Dover 1945–1981.

Helm, R., ed. 1956. *Die Chronik des Hieronymus. Eusebius Werke*. Vol. 7. Berlin.

Henderson, J. 1975. *The Maculate Muse*. New Haven.

Henrichs, A. 1976. "Despoina Kybele: Ein Beitrag zur religiösen Namenkunde." *Harvard Studies in Classical Philology* 80:253–286.

Hercher, R., ed. 1866. *Claudii Aeliani: Varia Historia, Epistulae, Fragmenta*. Leipzig.

Highbarger, E. L. 1927. *The History and Civilization of Ancient Megara*. Baltimore.

———. 1937. "Theognis and the Persian Wars." *Transactions of the American Philological Association* 68:88–111.

Hignett, C. 1952. *A History of the Athenian Constitution*. Oxford.

Hiller von Gaertringen, F., ed. 1926. *Historische Griechische Epigramme*. Berlin.

Hitzig, H. 1901. *Pausaniae Descriptio Graeciae*. II. Leipzig.

Hoddinott, R. F. 1975. *Bulgaria in Antiquity: An Archaeological Introduction*. New York.

Hopper, R. J. 1961. "'Plain', 'Hill', and 'Shore' in Early Athens." *British School at Athens, Annual* 56:189–219.

How, W. W., and Wells, J. 1912. *A Commentary on Herodotus, with Introduction and Appendixes*. Oxford.

Hudson-Williams, T., ed. 1910. *The Elegies of Theognis*. London.

Hug, A. 1931. "Symposion." *Pauly-Wissowa Realencyclopädie* 2. Reihe, 7. Halbband. 1266–1270.

IG = *Inscriptiones Graecae*. Berlin. 1873–.

Immisch, O. 1933. "Die Sphragis des Theognis." *Rheinisches Museum für Philologie* 82:278–304.

Jacoby, F. 1904. *Das Marmor Parium*. Berlin.

———. 1923–. *Die Fragmente der griechischen Historiker*. Leiden.

———. 1949. *Atthis: The Local Chronicles of Ancient Athens*. Oxford.

Jaeger, W. 1945. *Paideia: The Ideals of Greek Culture*. Translated by G. Highet. New York.

Jameson, M. H. 1969. "Excavations at Porto Cheli and Vicinity. Preliminary Report, I: Halieis, 1962–1968." *Hesperia* 38:311–342.

Jeffery, L. H. 1961. *The Local Scripts of Archaic Greece*. Oxford.

————. 1976. *Archaic Greece: The City-States c. 700–500 B.C.* London.

Kaibel, G., ed. 1878. *Epigrammata Graeca.* Berlin.

————, ed. 1899. *Comicorum Graecorum Fragmenta.* Berlin.

Kaletsch, H. 1958. "Zur lydischen Chronologie." *Historia* 7:1–47.

Kalligas, P. 1969. "ΤΟ ΕΝ ΚΕΡΚΥΡΑ ΙΕΡΟΝ ΤΗΣ ΑΚΡΑΙΑΣ ΗΡΑΣ." *Archaiologikon Deltion* 24.A:51–58.

Karst, J., ed. 1911. *Die Chronik. Eusebius Werke.* Vol. 5. Leipzig.

Kirk, G. S., ed. and tr. 1970. *The Bacchae of Euripides.* Englewood Cliffs, N.J.

Kleingünther, A. 1933. ΠΡΩΤΟΣ ΕΥΡΕΤΗΣ: *Untersuchungen zur Geschichte einer Fragestellung.* Leipzig, Philologus Supplementband 26.

Kock, T., ed. 1880–1888. *Comicorum Atticorum Fragmenta.* Leipzig.

Koller, H. 1972. "Epos." *Glotta* 50:16–24.

Kontoleon, N. M. 1963. "Archilochus und Paros." *Archiloque,* Fondation Hardt 10 (Geneva):39–73.

Kranz, W. 1924. "Das Verhältnis des Schöpfers zu seinem Werk in der althellenischen Literatur." *Neue Jahrbücher für Paedagogik* 27:64–86.

Kroll, J. 1936. *Theognis-Interpretationen.* Leipzig.

Labarbe, J. 1972. "Les premières démocraties de la Grèce antique." *Bulletin de la Classe des Lettres de l'Académie Royale de Belgique* 58:223–254.

Lanata, G. 1963. *Poetica pre-Platonica.* Florence.

Lang, M. 1962. "Kylonian Conspiracy." *Classical Philology* 64:243–249.

Leaf, W., ed. 1886–1888. *The Iliad of Homer.* 2 vols. London.

Legon, R. P. 1981. *Megara: The Political History of a Greek City-State to 336 B.C.* Ithaca.

Leutsch, E. L. von, and Schneidewin, F. G., eds. 1839–1851. *Corpus Paroemiographorum Graecorum.* Göttingen.

Lévi, S. 1898. *La doctrine du sacrifice dans les Brāhmaṇas.* Paris.

Levine, D. B. 1984. "Counterfeit Man." In *Classical Texts and Their Traditions: Studies in Honor of C. R. Trahman,* edited by D. F. Bright and E. S. Ramage, 125–137. Chico, Calif.

Liddell, H. G., Scott, R., and Stuart Jones, H., eds. 1940. *Greek-English Lexicon.* 9th ed. Oxford.

Lloyd-Jones, H. 1971. *The Justice of Zeus.* Berkeley and Los Angeles.

Lobel, E., and Page, D., eds. 1955. *Poetarum Lesbiorum Fragmenta.* Oxford.

Lord, A. B. 1960. *The Singer of Tales.* Cambridge, Mass.

LP. *See* Lobel and Page 1955.

LSCG Suppl. See Sokolowski 1962.

LSJ. *See* Liddell, Scott, and Stuart Jones 1940.

Macan, W. R. 1895. *Herodotus: The Fourth, Fifth, and Sixth Books.* London.

McKay, K. J. 1959. "Studies in *Aithon.*" *Mnemosyne* 12:198–203.

————. 1961. "Studies in *Aithon* II." *Mnemosyne* 14:16–22.

Maehler, H. 1963. *Die Auffassung des Dichterberufs im frühen Griechentum bis zur Zeit Pindars. Hypomnemata* 3. Göttingen.

Martin, R. P. 1981. *Healing, Sacrifice, and Battle: Amēchania and Related Concepts in Early Greek Poetry.* Innsbruck.

Martina, A., ed. 1968. *Solon: Testimonia veterum.* Rome.

Marzullo, B. 1958. *Studi di poesia eolica*. Florence.

Mayo, M. E. 1973. "Honors to Archilochus: The Parian Archilocheion." Ph.D. diss., Rutgers University.

Meiggs, R., and Lewis, D. M., eds. 1969. *A Selection of Greek Historical Inscriptions to the End of the Fifth Century B.C.* Oxford.

Meiggs-Lewis. See Meiggs and Lewis 1969.

Menéndez Pidal, R. 1960. *La chanson de Roland et la tradition épique des Francs*. 2d ed. Paris.

Merkelbach, R., and West, M. L., eds. 1967. *Fragmenta Hesiodea*. Oxford.

Meyer, E. 1954. *Pausanias, Beschreibung Griechenlands*. Zurich.

Michelini, A. 1978. "ΥΒΡΙΣ and Plants." *Harvard Studies in Classical Philology* 82:35–44.

Muller, A. 1981. "Megarika III–VII." *Bulletin de Correspondance Hellénique* 105:203–225.

Müller, K., and Müller, T., eds. 1841–1872. *Fragmenta Historicorum Graecorum*. 5 vols. Paris.

Murray, R. D. 1965. "Theognis 341–50." *Transactions of the American Philological Association* 96:277–281.

MW. See Merkelbach and West 1967.

Myres, J. L., and Gray, D., eds. 1958. *Homer and His Critics*. London.

Mylonas, G. E. 1961. *Eleusis*. Princeton.

Nagler, M. 1977. "Dread Goddess Endowed with Speech." *Archeological News* 6:77–85.

Nagy, G. 1973. "Phaethon, Sappho's Phaon, and the White Rock of Leukas." *Harvard Studies in Classical Philology* 77:137–177.

———. 1974. *Comparative Studies in Greek and Indic Meter*. Cambridge, Mass.

———. 1974b. "Six Studies of Sacral Vocabulary Relating to the Fireplace." *Harvard Studies in Classical Philology* 78:71–106.

———. 1979. *The Best of the Achaeans: Concepts of the Hero in Archaic Greek Poetry*. Baltimore.

———. 1979b. "On the Origins of the Greek Hexameter." In *Festschrift for Oswald Szemerényi*, edited by B. Brogyanyi (Amsterdam Studies in the Theory and History of Linguistic Science IV, Current Issues in Linguistic Theory, vol. 11), 611–631.

———. 1980. "Patroklos, Concepts of Afterlife, and the Indic Triple Fire." *Arethusa* 13:161–195.

———. 1982. "Hesiod." In *Ancient Writers: Greece and Rome*, edited by T. J. Luce, 43–73. New York.

———. 1982b. "Theognis of Megara: The Poet as Seer, Pilot, and Revenant." *Arethusa* 15:109–128.

———. 1983. "Poet and Tyrant: Theognidea 39–52, 1081–1082b." *Classical Antiquity* 2:82–91. The last two articles are earlier versions of parts of the larger work represented by Ch. 2 in this volume.

———. 1983b. "Sēma and Noēsis: Some Illustrations." *Arethusa* 16:35–55.

Nilsson, M. P. 1938. "The New Inscription of the Salaminioi." *American Journal of Philology* 59:385–393.

Nock, A. D. 1928. "Notes on Ruler-Cult I–IV." *Journal of Hellenic Studies* 48:21–43 = *Essays on Religion and the Ancient World*, edited by Z. Stewart, 134–157. Cambridge, Mass. 1972.

North, H. 1966. *Sophrosyne: Self-Knowledge and Self-Restraint in Greek Literature*. Ithaca.

Ognenova, L. 1960. "Les fouilles de Mésambria." *Bulletin de Correspondance Hellénique* 84:221–232.

Okin, L. A. 1974. "Studies on Duris of Samos." Ph.D. diss., University of California, Los Angeles.

————. 1980. "A Hellenistic Historian Looks at Mythology: Duris of Samos and the Mythical Tradition." In *Panhellenica: Essays in Ancient History and Historiography in Honor of Truesdell S. Brown*, edited by S. M. Burstein and L. A. Okin, 97–118. Lawrence, Kans.

Oost, S. I. 1973. "The Megara of Theagenes and Theognis." *Classical Philology* 68:188–196.

Page, D. L. 1936. "The Elegiacs in Euripides' *Andromache*." In *Greek Poetry and Life: Essays Presented to Gilbert Murray on His Seventieth Birthday*, edited by C. Bailey et al., 206–230. Oxford.

————. 1955. *Sappho and Alcaeus: An Introduction to the Study of Ancient Lesbian Poetry*. Oxford.

————, ed. 1962. *Poetae melici Graeci*. Oxford.

Palmer, L. R. 1963. *The Interpretation of Mycenaean Greek Texts*. Oxford.

Parke, H. W., and Wormell, D. E. W. 1949. "Notes on Delphic Oracles." *Classical Quarterly* 43:138–140.

————. 1956. *The Delphic Oracle*. Oxford.

Parry, M. 1971. *The Making of Homeric Verse: The Collected Papers of Milman Parry*, edited by A. Parry. Oxford.

Pedersen, H. 1949. *Lykisch und Hittitisch*. 2d ed. Danske videnskabernes selskab, Copenhagen. Historisk-filologiske meddelelsen, bd. 30. nr. 4.

Pedley, J. G. 1968. *Sardis in the Age of Croesus*. Norman, Okla.

Peek, W. 1966. "Ein milesisches Polyandrion." *Wiener Studien* 79:218–230.

————, ed. 1955. *Griechische Vers-Inschriften*. Berlin.

Peretti, A. 1953. *Teognide nella tradizione gnomologica. Studi Classici e Orientali* IV. Pisa.

Petersen, E. 1917. "Ein auf die Eroberung von Salamis bezügliches Vasenbild. Mit einer Beilage." *Jahrbuch des Deutschen Archäologischen Instituts* 32:137–145.

Pfeiffer, R., ed. 1949–1953. *Callimachus*. 2 vols. Oxford.

Piccirilli, L. 1973. "Su alcune alleanze fra *poleis*." *Annali della Scuola Normale Superiore di Pisa*. 3d ser. 3:717–730.

————. 1974. "Susarione e la revendicazione megarese dell'origine della commedia greca." *Annali della Scuola Normale Superiore di Pisa*. 3d ser. 4:1289–1299.

————. 1975. ΜΕΓΑΡΙΚΑ: *Testimonianze e Frammenti*. Pisa.

Pickard-Cambridge, A. 1962. *Dithyramb, Tragedy and Comedy*. 2d ed., revised by T. B. L. Webster. Oxford.

Podlecki, A. J. 1968. "Simonides: 480." *Historia* 17:257–275.

Powell, J. E. 1938. *A Lexicon to Herodotus.* Cambridge.

Powell, J. U. 1925. *Collectanea Alexandrina.* Oxford.

Prakken, D. W. 1941. "A Note on the Megarian Historian Dieuchidas." *American Journal of Philology* 62:348–351.

———. 1943–1944. "On the Date of Hereas, the Megarian Historian." *Classical World* 37:122–123.

Preller, L., ed. 1838. *Polemonis Periegetae Fragmenta.* Leipzig.

Prier, R. A. 1976. "Some Thoughts on the Archaic Use of *Metron.*" *Classical World* 70:164–169.

Rabe, H. 1908. "Aus Rhetoren-Handschriften." *Rheinisches Museum für Philologie* 63:127–151.

Radt, S., ed. 1977. *Tragicorum Graecorum Fragmenta* 4: *Sophocles.* Göttingen.

Redfield, J. M. 1975. *Nature and Culture in the Iliad: The Tragedy of Hector.* Chicago.

Renehan, R. 1975. *Greek Lexicographical Notes* I. *Hypomnemata* 45. Göttingen.

Richardson, N. J., ed. 1974. *The Homeric Hymn to Demeter.* Oxford.

Robert, L. 1938–. *Bulletin Epigraphique. Revue des Etudes Grecques* 49 (1938)–.

Roebuck, C. 1959. *Ionian Trade and Colonization.* New York.

———. 1972. "Some Aspects of Urbanization in Corinth." *Hesperia* 41:96–127.

Roehl, H., ed. 1882. *Inscriptiones Antiquissimae praeter Atticas in Attica Repertas.* Berlin.

Rose, V., ed. 1886. *Aristotelis Qui Ferebantur Librorum Fragmenta.* Leipzig.

Rösler, W. 1980. *Dichter und Gruppe: Eine Untersuchung zu den Bedingungen und zur historischen Funktion früher griechischer Lyrik am Beispiel Alkaios.* Munich.

Ross, W. D., ed. 1915. *The Works of Aristotle,* vol. 9. Oxford.

Rossi, L. E. 1971. "I generi letterari e le loro leggi scritte e non scritte nelle letterature classiche." *Bulletin of the Institute of Classical Studies* 18:69–94.

Sacks, R. 1978. "ΥΠΟ ΚΕΥΘΕΣΙ ΓΑΙΗΣ: Two Studies of the Art of the Phrase in Homer." Ph.D. diss., Harvard University.

Saïd, S. 1979. "Les crimes des prétendants, la maison d'Ulysse et les festins de l'Odyssée." *Etudes de Littérature Ancienne* (Ecole Normale Supérieure) 9–49. Paris.

Ste. Croix, G. E. M. de. 1972. *The Origins of the Peloponnesian War.* Ithaca.

Sakellariou, M. B., and Faraklas, N. 1971. *Corinthia-Cleonaea.* Athens.

———. 1972. ΜΕΓΑΡΙΣ, ΑΙΓΟΣΘΕΝΑ, ΕΡΕΝΕΙΑ. Athens.

Salmon, J. 1972. "The Heraeum at Perachora and the Early History of Corinth and Megara." *British School at Athens, Annual* 67:159–204.

Sandys, J. E. 1912. *Aristotle's Constitution of Athens.* 2d ed. London.

Sealey, R. 1976. *A History of the Greek City States ca. 700–338 B.C.* Berkeley and Los Angeles.

SEG = *Supplementum Epigraphicum Graecum.* Leiden. 1923–.

Seidensticker, B. 1978. "Archilochus and Odysseus." *Greek Roman and Byzantine Studies* 19:5–22.

Shackleton Bailey, D. R., ed. 1965–1970. *Cicero's Letters to Atticus.* 7 vols. Cambridge.

SIG. See Dittenberger 1915–1924.

Silk, M. S. 1974. *Interaction in Poetic Imagery with Special Reference to Early Greek Poetry*. Cambridge.

Sinos, D. 1980. *Achilles, Patroklos, and the Meaning of* ΦΙΛΟΣ. Innsbruck.

Slatkin, L. M. 1979. "Thetis, Achilles, and the Iliad." Ph.D. diss., Harvard University.

SM. *See* Snell and Maehler 1971.

Snell, B. 1924. "Die Ausdrücke für den Begriff des Wissens in der vor-platonischen Philosophie." *Philologische Untersuchungen* 29. Berlin.

————. 1964. *Tragicorum Graecorum Fragmenta*. Hildesheim.

Snell, B., and Maehler, H., eds. 1971. *Bacchylides*. Leipzig.

————, eds. 1975. *Pindarus: Fragmenta*. Leipzig.

Snodgrass, A. M. 1971. *The Dark Age of Greece: An Archaeological Survey of the Eleventh to the Eighth Centuries*. Edinburgh.

Sokolowski, F., ed. 1962. *Lois sacrées des cités grecques, Supplément*. Paris.

Solmsen, F. 1909. *Beiträge zur griechischen Wortforschung*. Strassburg.

Sperdutti, A. 1950. "The Divine Nature of Poetry in Antiquity." *Transactions of the American Philological Association* 81:209–240.

Sulzberger, M. 1926. "ONOMA ΕΠΩΝΥΜΟΝ: Les noms propres chez Homère." *Revue des Etudes Grecques* 39:381–447.

Sumner, W. G. 1906. *Folkways*. Boston.

————. 1963. *Social Darwinism: Selected Essays*. Englewood Cliffs, N.J.

Sutton, D. F. 1980. *The Greek Satyr Play*. Meisenheim am Glan.

Svenbro, J. 1976. "La parole et le marbre: Aux origines de la poétique grecque." Doctoral diss., Lund.

————. 1982. "A Mégara Hyblaea: Le corps géomètre." *Annales: Economies, Sociétés, Civilisations* 37:953–964.

Szegedy-Maszák, A. 1978. "Legends of the Greek Lawgivers." *Greek Roman and Byzantine Studies* 19:199–209.

Tarkow, T. 1977. "Theognis 237–254: A Reexamination." *Quaderni Urbinati di Cultura Classica* 26:99–114.

Tigerstedt, E. N. 1965–1978. *The Legend of Sparta in Classical Antiquity* I–III. Stockholm.

Tod, M. N. 1933. *A Selection of Greek Historical Inscriptions*. 2 vols. Oxford.

Treu, M. 1955. *Von Homer zur Lyrik*. Zetemata 12. Munich.

Ure, P. N. 1922. *The Origin of Tyranny*. Cambridge.

V. *See* Voigt 1971.

Valesio, P. 1960. "Un termine della poetica antica: *poiein*: analisi semantica." *Quaderni dell'Istituto di Glottologia* (Università degli Studi di Bologna) 5:97–111.

Vallet, G., and Villard, F. 1952. "Dates de fondation de Mégara Hyblaea et de Syracuse." *Bulletin de Correspondance Hellénique* 76:289–346.

———— 1958. "La date de fondation de Sélinonte: Les données archéologiques." *Bulletin de Correspondance Hellénique* 82:16–26.

Verdelis, N. M. 1956. "Der Diolkos am Isthmus von Korinth." *Mitteilungen des Deutschen Archäologischen Instituts, Athenische Abteilung* 71:51–59.

Vermeule, E. D. T. 1979. *Aspects of Death in Early Greek Art and Poetry*. Berkeley and Los Angeles.

Vernant, J.-P. 1974. *Mythe et pensée chez les Grecs: Etudes de psychologie historique*, I, II. 2d ed. Paris.

———. 1974b. *Mythe et société en Grèce ancienne*. Paris.

Vetta, M., ed. 1980. *Theognis: Elegiarum Liber Secundus*. Rome.

Voigt, E.-M., ed. 1971. *Sappho et Alcaeus: Fragmenta*. Amsterdam.

W. *See* West 1971/1972.

Wade-Gery, H. T. 1943. "The Spartan Rhetra in Plutarch *Lycurgus* VI. A. Plutarch's Text." *Classical Quarterly* 37:62–72.

———. 1944. "The Spartan Rhetra in Plutarch *Lycurgus* VI. B. The EY-NOMIA of Tyrtaios." *Classical Quarterly* 38:1–9.

———. 1946. "The Sixth-Century Attic Decree about Salamis." *Classical Quarterly* 40:101–104.

Wallace, M. B. 1970. "Notes on Early Greek Grave Epigrams." *Phoenix* 24:95–105.

Warner, R., tr. 1954. *Thucydides: The Peloponnesian War*. Harmondsworth.

Watkins, C. 1972. "An Indo-European Word for 'Dream'." In *Studies for Einar Haugen*, edited by E. S. Firchow, K. Grimstad, N. Hasselmo, and W. O'Neil, 554–561. The Hague.

———. 1979–1980. "*Is tre fír flathemon*: Marginalia to *Audacht Morainn*." *Eriu* 30:181–198.

Wehrli, F., ed. 1953. *Die Schule des Aristoteles*. Vol. 7. *Herakleides Pontikos*. Basel.

———, ed. 1957. *Die Schule des Aristoteles*. Vol. 9. *Phainias von Eresos; Chamaileon; Praxiphanes*. Basel.

———, ed. 1974. *Die Schule des Aristoteles*. Suppl. Bd. 1: *Hermippos der Kallimacheer*. Basel.

Weil, R. 1960. *Aristote et l'histoire: Essai sur la "Politique."* Paris.

Wendel, C. T. E., ed. 1914. *Scholia in Theocritum Vetera*. Leipzig.

West, M. L. 1974. *Studies in Greek Elegy and Iambus*. Berlin.

———, ed. 1966. *Hesiod: Theogony*. Oxford.

———, ed. 1971/1972. *Iambi et Elegi Graeci* I/II. Oxford.

———, ed. 1978. *Hesiod: Works and Days*. Oxford.

Whallon, W. 1969. *Formula, Character, and Context: Studies in Homeric, Old English, and Old Testament Poetry*. Washington, D.C.

Wickert, K. 1961. "Der peloponnesische Bund von seiner Entstehung bis zum Ende des archidamischen Krieges." Diss., Erlangen-Nürnberg.

Wilamowitz-Moellendorff, U. von. 1875. "Die megarische Komödie." *Hermes* 9:319–341.

———. 1884. *Homerische Untersuchungen. Philologische Untersuchungen* 7. Berlin.

———. 1937. "Besprechung von Urkunden dramatischer Aufführungen in Athen mit einem Beitrage von Georg Kaibel herausgegeben von Adolf Wilhelm, Wien, 1906." *Kleine Schriften*, vol. 5, pt. 1, 376–401. Berlin = *Göttingische Gelehrte Anzeigen* 1906:611–634.

Will, E. 1950. "De l'aspect éthique des origines grecques de la monnaie." *Revue Historique* 212:209–231.

———. 1955. *Korinthiaka*. Paris.

———. 1955b. "Réflexions et hypothèses sur origines du monnayage." *Revue Numismatique* 17:5–23.

Wiseman, J. 1978. *The Land of the Ancient Corinthians.* Göteborg.

Woodbury, L. 1952. "The Seal of Theognis." In *Studies in Honor of Gilbert Norwood*, edited by M. White, 20–41. Toronto.

Young, D. 1967. "Never Blotted a Line? Formula and Premeditation in Homer and Hesiod." *Arion* 6:279–324.

———, ed. 1961. *Theognis.* Leipzig.

Zwettler, M. 1978. *The Oral Tradition of Classical Arabic Poetry: Its Character and Implications.* Columbus, Ohio.

General Index

Please note that most Greek words in boldface are glossed in the Glossary. The few that are not are glossed in this index.

Index of Sources

Several features of the Index of Sources should be noted. This index occasionally lists cross-references to the General Index, where passages are cited in passing to illustrate a stylistic, literary, or historical observation. Other similar groups of citations are referred to merely by page number. The reader is directed to the Bibliography for full bibliographical data. The presence of "n" after a page number signifies the appearance of the source cited solely within the notes to that page. Bold numbers are used for two purposes: (1) to signify book numbers in ancient authors such as Herodotus; (2) to denote pages on which a passage is translated, not simply cited. Finally, collections of inscriptions appear under their abbreviated titles: for a full title, see the Bibliography.

Aelian: *Varia Historia* **7**.*19:* 281, 300; **13**.*23:* 32, 78; *fr. 86:* 155
Aeneas Tacticus: **4**.*8–11:* 282–83, 285
Aeschylus: *Agamemnon 1476–1477:* 72; *Choephoroi 157–158:* 73; *324–326:* 73; *403:* 74; *562:* 262; *577–578:* 74; *924, 1054:* 72; *Eumenides 132, 246, 264–266, 511–512:* 72; *Persians 570:* 284; *586:* 150n
Alcaeus: *fr. 38A1–8:* 74; *72.11–13:* 56n, 77n; *129:* 81n; *129.13:* 55n; *130:* 81n; *208 V = 326 LP:* 24n; *348.1:* 56n
Alcman: *fr. 27:* 87n
Andron (*FGH* 10): *F 14:* 278
Androtion (*FGH* 324): *F 30:* 119
Apollodorus (*FGH* 244): *F 27:* 290
"Apollodorus": *2.5.4:* 51
Apollonius of Rhodes: *Argonautica* **2**.*655–656:* 59n
Apollonius of Rhodes, Scholia: **1**.*211–215:* 115; **4**.*1212:* 293
Apostolius (see also *CPG*): *16.87:* 103n
Archilochus: *fr. 3:* 286; *5, 101, 114, 133:* 122; *105:* 181; *174, 185:* 105; *201:* 23n
Aristophanes: *Acharnians 11:* 125; *140:* 125; *614:* 289; *729–835:* 157;

774: 278; see also **sumposion** and p.194; *Clouds 46–48:* 289; *Ecclesiazusae 723:* 142; *1073:* 140; *Frogs 186:* 77; *Knights 417–420:* 136; *431:* 181n; *Lysistrata 1149–1156:* 142; *Peace 741–749, 961–965:* 133n; see also p.195 on **spondai**; *Plutus 797–799:* 133; *Thesmophoriazusae 170:* 125; *Wasps 54–63:* 133; *1121–1264, 1299–1334:* 157
Aristophanes, Scholia *Acharnians 774:* 278; *Clouds 46a:* 289; *48b:* 289; *800:* 289; *Frogs 439:* 263; *Lysistrata 58:* 278n; *645:* 63n; *1039:* 132n; *Wasps 57b: 1223:* 278
Aristotle: *Constitution of the Athenians 5.2–3:* 43, 60n; *7.2, 11.1:* 31; *11.2–12.1:* 43; *15.2:* 289; *17.2:* 282; *19.4:* 297; *De generatione animalium 725b35:* 61n; *Historia animalium 528a10:* 78; *Nicomachean Ethics 1116a:* 15n; *1123a20–24:* 141–42; *1144a24–31:* 36, **168–69**; *1167b6–7:* 162; *Poetics 1448a29–b3:* 36, 114, 118–19, 132, 134, 137, 141, 177n, 298; *Politics 1265b12–16:* 151; *1271b20–27:* 152; *1274a29:* 152; *1274a32–b5:* 151; *1280b13–15:* 297; *1290b14:* 52n; *1300a15–20:*

The Johns Hopkins University Press

Theognis of Megara

This book was designed by Chris L. Smith and composed in London text and display type by Logoi Systems with computer programs developed by Ibycus Systems. It was printed on Sebago Eggshell Cream Offset paper and bound in Holliston's Roxite A and Payko by BookCrafters, Inc.